THE ROAD TO ANARCHY

Sussex Studies in Spanish History

General Editor: Nigel Townson, Universidad Complutense, Madrid
Consultant Editor: José Álvarez-Junco, Universidad Complutense, Madrid
Advisory Editors: Pamela Radcliff, University of California, San Diego
Tim Rees, University of Exeter

José Álvarez-Junco, *The Emergence of Mass Politics in Spain: Populist Demagoguery and Republican Culture, 1890–1910.*
Pablo Bornstein, *Reclaiming al-Andalus: Orientalist Scholarship and Spanish Nationalism, 1875–1919.*
Tom Buchanan, *The Impact on the Spanish Civil War on Britain: War, Loss and Memory.*
Miguel Ángel Ruiz Carnicer (ed.), *From Franco to Freedom: The Roots of the Transition to Democracy in Spain, 1962–1982.*
Andrew Dowling, *Catalonia since the Spanish Civil War: Reconstructing the Nation.**
Ferran Gallego and Francisco Morente (eds), *The Last Survivor: Cultural and Social Projects Underlying Spanish Fascism, 1931–1975.*
Hugo García, *The Truth about Spain!: Mobilizing British Public Opinion, 1936–1939.*
Irene González González, *Spanish Education in Morocco, 1912–1956: Cultural Interactions in a Colonial Context.*
Aitana Guia, *The Muslim Struggle for Civil Rights in Spain: Promoting Democracy through Migrant Engagement, 1985–2010.*
Ángel Herrerín, *The Road to Anarchy: The CNT under the Spanish Second Republic (1931–1936).*
Patricia Hertel, *The Crescent Remembered: Islam and Nationalism on the Iberian Peninsula.*
Silvina Schammah Gesser, *Madrid's Forgotten Avant-Garde: Between Essentialism and Modernity.*
David Messenger, *L'Espagne Républicaine: French Policy and Spanish Republicanism in Liberated France.*
Javier Moreno-Luzón, *Modernizing the Nation: Spain during the Reign of Alfonso XIII, 1902–1931.*
Inbal Ofer, *Señoritas in Blue: The Making of a Female Political Elite in Franco's Spain.*
Stanley G. Payne, *Alcalá Zamora and the Failure of the Spanish Republic, 1931–1936.*

Raanan Rein and Joan Maria Thomàs (eds), *Spain 1936: Year Zero.*

Mario Ojeda Revah, *Mexico and the Spanish Civil War: Domestic Politics and the Republican Cause.*

Elizabeth Roberts, *"Freedom, Faction, Fame and Blood": British Soldiers of Conscience in Greece, Spain and Finland.*

Julius Ruiz, *'Paracuellos': The Elimination of the 'Fifth Column' in Republican Madrid during the Spanish Civil War.*

Guy Setton, *Spanish–Israeli Relations, 1956–1992: Ghosts of the Past and Contemporary Challenges in the Middle East.*

Manuel Álvarez Tardío, *José María Gil-Robles: Leader of the Catholic Right during the Spanish Second Republic.*

Manuel Álvarez Tardío and Fernando del Rey Reguillo (eds.), *The Spanish Second Republic Revisited.*

Nigel Townson, *The Crisis of Democracy in Spain: Centrist Politics under the Second Republic, 1931–1936.*

Nigel Townson (ed.), *Is Spain Different?: A Comparative Look at the 19th and 20th Centuries.*

* Published in association with the Cañada Blanch Centre for Contemporary Spanish Studies and the Catalan Observatory, London School of Economics.

A full list of titles in the series is available on the Press website.

To my father, Ángel, my grandfather, Eduardo Herrerín,
and my father-in-law, Nicasio Torres, manual workers
who suffered under Franco's dictatorship.

Contents

2 4 6 8 10 9 7 5 3 1

First published in hardcover 2020, reprinted in paperback 2021 in Great Britain by
SUSSEX ACADEMIC PRESS
PO Box 139, Eastbourne BN24 9BP

Distributed in North America by
SUSSEX ACADEMIC PRESS
Independent Publishers Group
814 N. Franklin Street, Chicago, IL 60610

British Library Cataloguing in Publication Data
A CIP catalogue record for this book is available from the British Library.

Library of Congress Cataloging-in-Publication Data
To be applied for.

Hardcover ISBN 978-1-78976-031-6
Paperback ISBN 978-1-78976-147-4

FSC www.fsc.org MIX Paper | Supporting responsible forestry FSC® C013604

Typeset & designed by Sussex Academic Press, Brighton & Eastbourne.
Printed and bound by CPI Group (UK) Ltd, Croydon, CR0 4YY

THE ROAD TO ANARCHY

The CNT under the Spanish Second Republic (1931–1936)

ÁNGEL HERRERÍN

SUSSEX
ACADEMIC
PRESS
Brighton • Chicago • Toronto

General Series Editor's Preface

NIGEL TOWNSON

The debate over the anarcho-syndicalist *Confederación Nacional del Trabajo* (CNT) (National Confederation of Labour) during the democratic years of the Second Republic (1931-1936) has been focused above all on the question as to whether it was a social, genuinely apolitical movement or whether it was in fact – despite its rejection of political parties, parliamentarianism and the state – just another form of politics. Ángel Herrerín's *The Road to Anarchy* endeavours to answer that question by subjecting the struggles which raged within the ranks of anarcho-syndicalism to forensic scrutiny not only at the national level, but also at the regional, provincial and even local levels. He explores, too, other facets of the CNT which have received scant attention from historians so far, but which are crucial to understanding the appeal of anarcho-syndicalism in the 1930s and the failure of the governments of the Second Republic to incorporate it within the democratic framework of the regime. The result is a compelling, multi-layered interpretation which revisits the Republic by means of a wealth of new research.

Damnification of the anarcho-syndicalist movement from the outset of the Republic was, *The Road to Anarchy* contends, an egregious error by the republican-socialist governments of 1931-1933. In reality, the moderates or syndicalists were prepared to work within the democratic bounds of the nascent regime, regarding the pursuit of revolution as "inopportune". Such a modus vivendi was a distinct possibility during the early months of the Republic, as the syndicalists still controlled the movement, but by the spring of 1932 the radicals or anarchists had seized control of the CNT. This lost opportunity would have far-reaching consequences for the history of the democratic Republic. The radicalisation of the movement not only meant that a substantial part of the working class was alienated from the regime, but also that the political climate was further polarised. On the other hand, Herrerín insists, the degree to which the CNT contributed to the destabilisation of the Republic should not be overdrawn, as the movement's two principal insurrections failed miserably, while during 1934 and 1935 it was consumed above all by the campaign to rebuild and relaunch itself following the devastating setback of the uprising of December 1933.

The Road to Anarchy corrects the historical record in relation to two uprisings which have hitherto been universally attributed to the CNT. The author convincingly demonstrates that the miners' revolt of January 1932 in Fígols in

Catalonia was not organised by the CNT, but by local, unaffiliated workers. He also shows that the anarcho-syndicalist uprising of January 1933, famous for the massacre in the Andalusian *pueblo* of Casas Viejas, was not orchestrated by the CNT, but by the extremist FAI (*Federación Anarquista Ibérica*/Iberian Anarchist Federation) alone. Additionally, the wide-ranging research that underpins *The Road to Anarchy* sheds new light on issues that have received little or no attention from historians. Herrerín highlights, for example, the profound inequity of the legal system under the Republic. The number of 'governmental prisoners', that is, people incarcerated without charge, ran into the hundreds in the case of the CNT, but this issue has been virtually ignored by scholars. In the same vein, just one Civil Guard was put on trial for the cold-blooded murder of twelve people in Casas Viejas, while twenty-six locals were prosecuted for the deaths of three policemen. The author also lays bare the Civil Guard's crass lack of preparedness for crowd control. In dispersing unarmed protestors in Arnedo (La Rioja) in January 1932, for instance, the Civil Guard killed eleven people and wounded nineteen. Still, not a single Civil Guard was put on trial for the shootings.

In sum, Ángel Herrerín's *The Road to Anarchy* offers a rigorous, richly-researched reassessment of the role of the anarcho-syndicalist movement in Spain under the Second Republic that furnishes myriad new insights, and in particular provides an arresting answer to the debate over the nature of the CNT between 1931 and 1936.

NIGEL TOWNSON
General Editor, Sussex Studies in Spanish History

List of Figures

“We do not reject utopia, hopefully there will always be a dose of utopianism in the human soul, but let us not confine it within the framework of a closed, definitive, perfect system.”

Abad de Santillán

Introduction

The study of the Second Spanish Republic has become one of the main focal points for historians in recent decades. As in the case of other important periods, like the Civil War or Francoism, historiography has taken a major qualitative leap in terms of both knowledge and analysis. There have been monograph works on this period, at both a national and local level, and also on the subject of parties and unions across the political spectrum, with the purpose of clarifying the political, social and economic keys to the evolution of Spain's first democratic experience.

In this respect, works on the activity of the *Confederación Nacional del Trabajo* (National Confederation of Labour, CNT) during this period represent a significant part of this research. The libertarian militants were the first to attempt, with their virtues and defects, to explain the role played by the confederal union in the Republic. One recalls in particular the work by José Peirats (1971) who, without abandoning his militant stance, addressed the study of not only of the Republican period, but also of the Civil War. A special contribution was made by César Martínez Lorenzo (1969 and 2006) – son of former CNT secretary general Horacio Martínez Prieto – who considered not only the Republican era, but the general history of the libertarian movement.

With regard to historians, and in a brief review that is anything but exhaustive, one recalls, in the first place, the work by John Brademas (1973). His research analyses the CNT's conduct during each and every phase of the Republic, in spite of the fact that his sources were limited, to a large extent, by the earliness of his work. Other research on a local scale has made fundamental contributions to knowledge of this subject: one need only mention the excellent works by Eulalia Vega (1987) and Ángeles Barrio (1988), concentrating on the Levante and Asturias, respectively. In a similar vein, the various works by Javier Paniagua (1982, 2008) have provided considerable information about the libertarian world in general. There have been excellent interpretations of this period, such as those by Antonio Elorza (1973 and 2013) and Julián Casanova (1997), but which, unlike Brademas's work, did not offer deep or detailed analysis of the entire Republican cycle. To all this should be added the interesting contribution by Anna Monjo (2003), vis-à-vis the confederal reality in the 1930s; and the more recent one by Josep Termes (2011), who produced, following his earlier contributions in relation to the workers' movement in Catalonia, a general work on anarchism which summarises the CNT's activity during those years.

In much of this research, but also that which addresses other organisations during this period and that of the Republican regime in general, a series of questions reappear which constitute the key points that explain the CNT's evolution during the Second Republic. For instance: its opposition to the new regime, demonstrated by the significant degree of labour conflict that existed from the very beginning, and which was one of the most pressing concerns facing the Republic; the internal struggle, with the consequent schism; the three *cenetista* insurrections that invariably feature in all the publications on this period; the inconsistent application of the abstentionist principal with which it tackled the different elections; the change of direction taken at the congress in Zaragoza in 1936; and its presence in the major mobilisation, seen by some as revolutionary, during the final months of the Republic.

It is my belief that all these issues require further analysis in the light of new sources and contributions, all the more so if one bears in mind that much of the research referred to above was published decades ago. Consequently, this work seeks to take up the fundamental idea of carrying out an in-depth study of the evolution of the CNT in the national context throughout the Republican period, with two main objectives. On the one hand, analysis of anarcho-syndicalist union's activity in relation to the Second Republic. Although the standard interpretation is the strong opposition exercised by the CNT against the Republican regime, practically from the moment of its constitution, the fact is that this approach requires, in my opinion, an exhaustive study that transcends generalisation provides in-depth exploration of each of the periods of the existence of both the Republic and the confederal union. On the other, thorough research into the internal life of the CNT, from ideology to practice, including its organic structure, decision-making, the power struggle, the importance of the individual, and the weight of history, all of these basic elements in order to understand the conduct of any organisation. With regard to these two basic questions, this research will address other issues that had a decisive influence upon both the republican regime and the actions of the CNT itself, such as the political and social evolution of parties and unions, social-labour legislation, labour conflict, violence and problems of public order. Without forgetting the international context, with the economic crisis and the advance of fascism in Europa, at the expense of democratic regimes.

In order to achieve these objectives, I conducted exhaustive research in national and international archives and documentation centres. I began with documents issued by the libertarian organisations themselves, in both the Salvador Seguí Foundation Archive in Madrid, and the International Institute of Social History in Amsterdam. Incorporated into to the latter, a few years ago, was the documentation belonging to leading confederal militants, like Ramón Álvarez, alias *Ramonín,* and Horacio Martínez Prieto, which I have had the opportunity to consult. The correspondence between militants, reflections upon confederal activity and comments regarding the organisation and colleagues contribute particular value and interest to these archives.

I was able, after no little effort, to consult the Civil Guard Historical Studies Archive, specifically, barracks records and personal files, which offer very

General Series Editor's Preface

NIGEL TOWNSON

The debate over the anarcho-syndicalist *Confederación Nacional del Trabajo* (CNT) (National Confederation of Labour) during the democratic years of the Second Republic (1931-1936) has been focused above all on the question as to whether it was a social, genuinely apolitical movement or whether it was in fact – despite its rejection of political parties, parliamentarianism and the state – just another form of politics. Ángel Herrerín's *The Road to Anarchy* endeavours to answer that question by subjecting the struggles which raged within the ranks of anarcho-syndicalism to forensic scrutiny not only at the national level, but also at the regional, provincial and even local levels. He explores, too, other facets of the CNT which have received scant attention from historians so far, but which are crucial to understanding the appeal of anarcho-syndicalism in the 1930s and the failure of the governments of the Second Republic to incorporate it within the democratic framework of the regime. The result is a compelling, multi-layered interpretation which revisits the Republic by means of a wealth of new research.

Damnification of the anarcho-syndicalist movement from the outset of the Republic was, *The Road to Anarchy* contends, an egregious error by the republican-socialist governments of 1931-1933. In reality, the moderates or syndicalists were prepared to work within the democratic bounds of the nascent regime, regarding the pursuit of revolution as "inopportune". Such a modus vivendi was a distinct possibility during the early months of the Republic, as the syndicalists still controlled the movement, but by the spring of 1932 the radicals or anarchists had seized control of the CNT. This lost opportunity would have far-reaching consequences for the history of the democratic Republic. The radicalisation of the movement not only meant that a substantial part of the working class was alienated from the regime, but also that the political climate was further polarised. On the other hand, Herrerín insists, the degree to which the CNT contributed to the destabilisation of the Republic should not be overdrawn, as the movement's two principal insurrections failed miserably, while during 1934 and 1935 it was consumed above all by the campaign to rebuild and relaunch itself following the devastating setback of the uprising of December 1933.

The Road to Anarchy corrects the historical record in relation to two uprisings which have hitherto been universally attributed to the CNT. The author convincingly demonstrates that the miners' revolt of January 1932 in Fígols in

Catalonia was not organised by the CNT, but by local, unaffiliated workers. He also shows that the anarcho-syndicalist uprising of January 1933, famous for the massacre in the Andalusian *pueblo* of Casas Viejas, was not orchestrated by the CNT, but by the extremist FAI (*Federación Anarquista Ibérica*/Iberian Anarchist Federation) alone. Additionally, the wide-ranging research that underpins *The Road to Anarchy* sheds new light on issues that have received little or no attention from historians. Herrerín highlights, for example, the profound inequity of the legal system under the Republic. The number of 'governmental prisoners', that is, people incarcerated without charge, ran into the hundreds in the case of the CNT, but this issue has been virtually ignored by scholars. In the same vein, just one Civil Guard was put on trial for the cold-blooded murder of twelve people in Casas Viejas, while twenty-six locals were prosecuted for the deaths of three policemen. The author also lays bare the Civil Guard's crass lack of preparedness for crowd control. In dispersing unarmed protestors in Arnedo (La Rioja) in January 1932, for instance, the Civil Guard killed eleven people and wounded nineteen. Still, not a single Civil Guard was put on trial for the shootings.

In sum, Ángel Herrerín's *The Road to Anarchy* offers a rigorous, richly-researched reassessment of the role of the anarcho-syndicalist movement in Spain under the Second Republic that furnishes myriad new insights, and in particular provides an arresting answer to the debate over the nature of the CNT between 1931 and 1936.

NIGEL TOWNSON
General Editor, Sussex Studies in Spanish History

interesting visions with regard to public order. In a similar vein, I worked with various military archives, such as the General Military Archive in Segovia, in Ávila, and the Archive of the Institute of Military History and Culture in Madrid, with documents related to military actions in uprisings and insurrections, but also in relation to social unrest, political activity and the corresponding personal files of military personnel. I also consulted various other Spanish sources: the Historical Memory Documentation Centre in Salamanca, which contains letters from *cenetistas*, minutes from confederal meetings and highly interesting police reports; the National Historical Archive, with the important series corresponding to the Ministry of Interior, familiar and oft-used but interesting and necessary for any study of this nature; and the archives of the Congress of Deputies, where the records of parliamentary sessions are to be found. In addition, I explored French archives, like the Diplomatic Archives of France, a source of valuable information from the embassy and consular centres in Spain, and the Police Prefecture Archive in Paris, which houses the personal files of anarchist militants and reports on the activity of Spanish exiles in France. Added to all these public archives were the personal archives of Eduardo de Guzmán and José Peiró, which their families kindly allowed me to consult.

As well as national and international archives, I also consulted a considerable number of newspapers and journals published by different organisations and ideologies, with particular focus, inevitably, on the anarchist and anarcho-syndicalist press, indispensable in any research into libertarian organisations.

As I have commented in earlier publications, any historical research is based upon the previous work of many other historians – among others, those referred to above and in the bibliography – to whom I should like to express recognition and gratitude for their contributions, without which I could never have written this book. My special thanks to Clara E. Lida, firstly, for her friendship, but also for her interest, advice, and invariably constructive criticism in relation to my research. Similarly, I should like to make particular mention of Professor José Mª Marín, reader and implacable critic of my work, to whom I shall be eternally grateful. My thanks to other friends and colleagues too, like Juan Avilés and the other professors in the Contemporary History Department of the UNED, and to those who have offered to read these pages and have shared with me their valuable opinions and suggestions: Eduardo Juárez, Jorge de Hoyos and Nigel Townson.

I would like to acknowledge the assistance provided by the staff of all the archives I visited, since without their collaboration, no research would have been possible. A special mention to my friend Enrique Gallego and his colleagues Mar González and Jesús Puente of the General Military Archive of Segovia, to my friend Kees Rodenburg, of the International Institute of Social History in Amsterdam, and to Carlos Ramos, of the Salvador Seguí Foundation, who not only offered his assistance, but shared with me his interesting reflections on the libertarian movement.

I am grateful to the institutions that have collaborated in financing this book's translation into English, to the Real Sitio de San Ildefonso Centre of Historical Research (CIGCE), in Segovia (Spain), and to the Rectorate, with Ricardo Mairal in the lead, Geography and History Faculty and Contemporary History Department of the Universidad Nacional de Educación a Distancia (UNED). In addition, I should like to thank translator Mark Hounsell for his commitment and professionalism.

Finally, my thanks to Sussex Academic Press, all their staff and, in particular, to Anthony Grahame and Nigel Townson for their work, dedication and interest in the publication of this book.

1

Anarchists and Anarcho-syndicalists in the Early Days of the Republic (April 1931–June 1931)

The Desired Republic

The Second Republic was proclaimed on 14 April 1931. It was the consequence of the major economic and social transformation that Spain had undergone during the early decades of the 20th century: industrialisation, emigration from rural areas to the city, urban growth; but also the political crisis that, after the fall of Primo de Rivera's dictatorship (1923–1930), materialised in the unpopularity of a monarchy that was perceived as an obstacle to the modernisation of the country. A Republic desired by large unempowered sections of the population, who presented it as a solution to the social injustice they experienced and saw it more as a revolution than a change of political regime. This perception was reinforced not only by the propaganda deployed by republican and socialist groups during the election campaign, but also by the massive presence of people in the streets.[1]

The sympathies and hopes aroused by the Republic among the working classes had a long history, with a significant moment occurring during the constitution of the 1st International in Spain, in the final decades of the 19th century. Leaders belonging to republican groups, like Rafael Farga Pellicer and Tomás González Morago, created the first internationalist groups in Spain, although there was a rapid shift of their ideological approaches towards anarchist positions. An evolution that was related, on the one hand, to the dynamic of the sections of the International and, principally, to contacts with those who represented the most radical position within the organisation, the Bakuninists (followers of the Russian revolutionary Mijail Bakunin); but, on the other hand, and perhaps more importantly, to the unfolding of events in Spain, which generated distrust of political activity and facilitated criticism by the most radical elements.[2] It is sufficient to note the evolution of the First Republic (1873) – with the frustrated reforms announced by the Federals, plotting by the most powerful classes against the new regime, and the political activity of the supporters of the monarchy – to which was added heavy repression of the Cantonalist movement (advocates of radical federalism based on independent cantons) in places like Sanlúcar de Barrameda or Alcoy, where the protagonists were the internationalists.[3] These actions reaffirmed the anarchists in their ideology of negation of the state, antipoliticism and direct action – understood as opposition to any kind of mediation by the authorities in political, social or labour issues – and facilitated criticism of any regime, including a democratic republic.[4] In spite of everything, anarchists and republicans continued to share important elements of their political cultures, such as anticlericalism, federalism, rationalist teaching and insurrectionism.[5]

In spite of the anarchist hostility to any regime, a vast majority of workers continued to place their hopes in the establishment of a republic as a facilitator of social justice. A situation that was made very evident on 14 April 1931, when thousands of people took to the streets of Spain to celebrate the advent of the Second Republic. Among them, a sizeable number of members of the CNT (*Confederación Nacional del Trabajo* or National Confederation of Labour), an anarcho-syndicalist organisation with anarchist elements, founded in 1911. In 1931, the main CNT committees and the confederal press were run by anarcho-syndicalists, like Ángel Pestaña and Juan Peiró. The former, who bore a certain resemblance to Don Quijote, on account of both his slim physique and his ascetic and puritanical lifestyle – he neither smoked nor drank coffee – and ideals, which saw him defend to the bitter end, at all times, that in which he believed. The latter, of heavier build, ideologically upright and molded, though moderate and practical when pursuing his ideal, was not only simple and modest in his union activity, but also courageous in speech and implacable in pursuit of his final goal. The ideological touchstone of the anarcho-syndicalists lay in the revolutionary syndicalism of French origin.

In the neighbouring country, the CGT (*Confédération Général du Travail*) held its first congress in Limoges, in 1895. In the anarchist press, the word "union" appeared – in reference to the new organisation as the "unions of France"[6] – and revolutionary unionism was born, before evolving and definitively establishing itself at the Amiens Congress, held in October 1906. Its ideological foundations were reflected in the famous Charter of Amiens, which marked the separation between union and political action, ultimately sought the emancipation of workers, and aspired to control of production and management of society through the unions, which would eventually involve supplanting the state. The general strike was the tool by means of which to attain this end. If all the workers downed tools at the same time, the revolution would be achieved, with the corresponding collapse of the capitalist system and the workers gaining control of society. But revolutionary unionism had not given up on improving the living conditions of workers, whether through direct negotiation – in other words, between employees and employers, without intermediaries – or through strikes with a specific objective, such as a pay rise or reduction in working hours. In essence, revolutionary unionism assigned the union a double function: reformist and revolutionary.[7]

However, the anarcho-syndicalists were not alone in the CNT. They shared militancy with different anarchist groups who identified in the union the indispensable force with which to implement the social revolution. Their entry into the unions extended, mainly, until the early 20th century, when the predominance of individualist anarchism gave way in light of the new syndicalist winds blowing in from France. In any case, unionism was not the goal, but the means with which to achieve revolution. To this end, they maintained their structures of small groups, acted within the union organisation and dealt uncompromisingly with any reformist deviations. For them, the union had to be anti-political – opposed to political action, to participating in the parliamentary game – but could not be apolitical or devoid of political definition. Consequently, the union had to be anarchist.[8]

The fact is that both, anarcho-syndicalists and anarchists, have always been present, though under different names, in the unions and revolutionary movements that have existed in Spain since the workers' organisations created in the days of the 1st International. As occurred with the first of these, the FRE (*Federación Regional Española* or Spanish Regional Federation), where collectivists and Bakuninists formed a majority that, at the 1870 constitutional congress, led the organisation towards anti-political and anti-state positions, ultimately, in accordance with principles related to anarchism.[9]

The Restoration years (1875–1923) saw the formation and consolidation of workers' organisations, such as the founding of the UGT (*Unión General de Trabajadores* or General Workers' Union), predominantly socialist, constituted in 1888, and of the aforementioned CNT, in 1911. These were times of major protests and strikes with the primary objective of improving the social and labour conditions of the working classes. A period of collaboration between both unions, as in the December 1916 strike, but also of discrepancies marked by different ways of understanding the workers' movement: the UGT more reformist, linked to the Socialist Party and seeking, principally, to bring about a change of regime; the CNT eminently revolutionary, not subordinate to any political power and intent on social revolution. All the same, the CNT also experienced, during this period, internal confrontation between groups: some that defended what was essentially union activity, others that advocated violence within the context of the workers' struggle.[10]

Primo de Rivera's dictatorship exercised firm control over the CNT, while repression against the anarchists was particular bloody, forcing into exile such representative figures as Buenaventura Durruti, Francisco Ascaso and Gregorio Jover. The CNT militants – anarchists and anarcho-syndicalists – who remained in Spain engaged in a fierce debate over whether to go underground, which was what the former tended to favour, or maintain the union's legality, as the latter preferred. Moreover, the anarchists, in their struggle against what they considered "neutral unionism" – without political definition – tended to unify and organise their forces via the formation, in 1927, of the FAI (*Federación Anarquista Ibérica* or Iberian Anarchist Federation).

The new organisation was born with the aim of avoiding any doctrinal deviation within the CNT. The FAI adopted the approach of the Spaniards Diego Abad de Santillán – pseudonym of Baudilio Sinesio García Fernández – and Emilio López Arango, both resident in Argentina, known as the "*trabazón*" (organic link at every level between the anarchist organisation and the union). This new situation triggered increased tension in the confederal ranks, even among the anarcho-syndicalists: while Pestaña, along with militants like Juan López, complained about the anarchists' interference in the union, demanding greater independence, Peiró accepted the anarchist intervention, seeing it as defence of the CNT's principles. The three-way confrontation was further complicated by the increasingly critical situation in which the CNT found itself, largely caused by the refusal to participate in joint committees imposed by the dictatorship for labour negotiations. The CNT's survival involved, according to Pestaña, acceptance of that legality, while Peiró opposed it on the grounds that it was contrary to direct action, a principle adopted by the confederal union at its 1919 congress. The end of the dictatorship solved the problems facing the union organisation, although, at the same time, it failed to settle the differences revealed during this period.[11]

The CNT, Dazzled by the Light of the Republic

Anarchists and anarcho-syndicalists demonstrated a certain unity of action during the electoral period prior to the advent of the Second Republic. The main publications by both groups showed their opposition to participation in the elections. The anarchist weekly *Tierra y Libertad* placed the accent upon the release of prisoners and denounced elections that should be "prevented at all costs" or, in the worst-case scenario, "the results of which should be rejected".[12] While *Solidaridad Obrera*, the CNT mouthpiece, criticised the republicans and the socialists for indulging in sleight of hand, as democracy was no more than a failure with regards to "proletarian grievances"; so the workers could never protect their "aspirations of equality (...) behind monarchies, nor behind republics". Moreover, these were "elections rigged by the Monarchy" which could not "make any favourable contribution to the triumph of the Republic".[13]

But the CNT newspaper was wrong, because the republican candidacies did win in the principal cities of Spain. The electoral victory was followed by hours of uncertainty. Doubts vis-à-vis the attitude of both the King, Alfonso XIII, and some generals. Although for the CNT, the key to the establishment of the new regime lay not in the actions of the King and the generals but in the exceptional social mobilisation, which they called "the people in the streets".[14] A circumstance that helped to moderate the anarchists' position with regard to the recently constituted Republic. To the extent that they greeted the new regime "with a gesture of cordiality" and were prepared "to defend the life of the fledgling Republic" to prevent the possibility of a reaction "seeking a return to the old regime". A defence that stemmed partly from the exhilaration of the people who roamed "the streets drunk with enthusiasm", but which did not prevent them from evidencing their mistrust and even predicting that this same Republic would adopt, in time, "an openly conservative stance vis-à-vis the interests of the eternally oppressed". Though they acknowledged, in a memorable sentence, that if "the republican regime that has come upon us" is bad, "worse still was the monarchic regime swept away by the people".[15]

The CNT's *Solidaridad Obrera* was more optimistic, and regarded the advent of the Republic as "the first step towards the conquest of the citizens' rights despicably trampled upon after the Great War by global plutocracy". The CNT defended the "rights secured against possible reactionary attacks" and, more significantly, considered it absurd that:

> Inopportunely and systematically the new regime is hounded in the name of revolutionary principles (…) It would be a ridiculous contradiction if we anarchists and trade unionists, who for over seven years have been advocating a change in situation to attain a minimum of freedoms that, in part, we are beginning to enjoy (…) committed a regrettable tactical error and jeopardised what we have just achieved, which might not be much, but has cost us great sacrifice.[16]

Consequently, the Republic facilitated an important framework of rights and freedoms that had to be exploited in order to organise and educate the masses and raise their awareness with the aim of bringing about the social revolution. Nobody could imagine that "as if by magic the masses have become empowered (…) in twenty-four hours, that today they are capable of conquering what yesterday they were unable to understand".[17]

Juan Peiró provided, years later, a fairly accurate analysis of those turbulent days. He acknowledged that the CNT did not campaign in favour of participation in the April elections, that no article was published to encourage voting, nor did they tell "the workers to go to the polls, or not to go". Peiró acknowledged that the CNT contributed to the electoral triumph of 12 April, but in response to the anarchists' criticism that the anarcho-syndicalists were the seed of the Republic, he stated that, if this were the case, it was because the land was prepared for the latter and not for social revolution. The masses wanted to alter the political scenario in Spain, and their desires became a republican yearning. Anarchists and anarcho-syndicalists were incapable of channelling that movement along higher paths than the Republic, so the CNT stood aside and let "the people overflowing with holy enthusiasm express their will". Because attempting anything else, apart from madness, concluded Peiró, would have been a historical irresponsibility.[18]

Ultimately, the anarcho-syndicalists, who headed the main CNT committees, understood that they needed time to subvert the situation, and change conditions so that land prepared for the republican seed might have the necessary characteristics for the revolutionary seed to flourish. A scenario for which it was fundamental to exploit the freedoms and rights of the new regime, which would serve to extend, improve and structure the organisation, but also to educate and train workers.

However, the anarchists understood that the conditions in which the revolution might thrive were already present and that the situation could be redirected. All that was necessary was to encourage constant unrest that would maintain the revolutionary momentum.[19] In any case, the anarcho-syndicalists and anarchists, in spite of their differences with regard to analysis of the moment and the tactics to be employed, shared ideological principles, such as federalism, anti-statism and direct action; and objectives too, since both were revolutionary, and their goal was none other than the establishment of a libertarian communist society.

But the events of April had astonished everybody, and practically every political group was talking of revolution. When, in fact, what was happening was not revolution, but a political change that left social and political structures intact. The concept of revolution, as Julio Aróstegui has said, was "a kind of hydra with a hundred heads". So that even republican Manuel Azaña included his group among "the forces that have prepared and achieved revolution".[20] Many anarchists also identified the significant civilian mobilisation with the advent of the revolution. Although, according to their interpretation, it was a revolution that had not been steered in the right direction. What had emerged was a bourgeois, not a proletarian, republic, owing "to the lack of revolutionary preparation of the CNT, or rather of its militants". Advantage had not been taken of what was termed the "psychological moment of revolutions", in other words, that moment of indecision in which an idea, a programme or a group prevails whilst others are still hesitating. The CNT militants should have taken to the streets, occupied public buildings and spurred the people into revolutionary action, should have "stormed into the barracks, embracing the soldiers (disarming them), with cries of "Long live the children of the People!", and confederal orders to demilitarise and disband the national army", which would have initiated "social liberation".[21]

These anarchists were not the only ones to be dazzled by the radiance of the masses on the streets. The Russian communists were also blinded by the crowds that occupied the streets of Spain, and could not understand how the Communist Party had not directed them at a moment they regarded as revolutionary.[22] But the reality was much more complex than taking to the streets and leading the proletarian masses or embracing soldiers in the barracks, inciting them to rebellion. Reality suggested, in the Communist case, the irrelevance of its organisation at that time. While the CNT was far from the splendour of earlier years, a consequence of both the long dictatorship and the internal conflict that had significantly eroded the organisation during this period.

Consequently, the first and most important task facing the CNT was that of reorganisation. The regional confederations were structured while the workers flocked to the union offices. There was a notable CNT presence, as in the past, in Catalonia and Andalusia – called the Andalusia and Extremadura confederation, as it included Badajoz – and in the Levante. The Catalan confederation had, in June 1931, almost 300,000 members, and the Levante confederation over 53,000.[23] In areas like Asturias there was a medium-sized membership, with around 25,000 members in May.[24] Other confederations found it more difficult to grow, such as Galicia, the North – due to the strong socialist presence – or the Centre – which included the provinces of both Castiles and

Caceres – where the local Madrid federation, in light of the meagre confederal forces, acted as regional committee until the constitution of the latter in November 1931.[25]

This union reconstruction was completed with the education, awakening and extension of a particular culture that, also developed in parallel organisations such as athenaeums, social centres and rationalist schools, created the necessary conditions for the attainment of a libertarian society.[26]

The Importance of the Anarchist of Action

In this context, the anarchists, with the perception that they were living through an eminently revolutionary moment, directed their activity towards the confederal unions with two fundamental objectives: encourage non-conformist tension among the workers, and remove the anarcho-syndicalists from the main committees in order to take control of the organisation and launch it into revolution. Crucial to this end was the confluence of various internal and external factors. Among the former, the idiosyncrasy and history of anarchism in Spain. Among the latter, the socio-economic situation, both international and national, and the actions of the Republican-Socialist governments in questions of employment and public order.

With regard to internal factors, it is essential to understand the ascendency that the anarchists of action always enjoyed within the libertarian movement. Pestaña pointed out how "the anarchist tradition has admired and cultivated the myth of the personal assault",[27] largely because they went further than others wished, were able or dared to go. Some of the earliest examples of these actions were the attacks carried out at the end of the 19th century by anarchists in what became known as "propaganda by deed". By means of this tactic, they sought to propagate their ideas but also to defend themselves against an authoritarian state that, along with the bourgeoisie and the Catholic Church, made almost exclusive use of repression as a weapon with which to maintain social order. Although these attacks contributed nothing towards the ultimate objective of achieving social revolution, it is no less true that, for broad defenceless sectors of society, they represented acts of bravery, of rebellion and even justice against those in power. Anarchists of action like Paulino Pallás – author of an attack against General Martínez Campos – or Michelle Angiolillo – who killed Cánovas del Castillo, Prime Minister – had sacrificed their lives for an idea, which had transformed them into "martyrs". A very powerful argument that aroused admiration and solidarity in those who felt mistreated by a state that employed torture and the courts to eliminate any kind of opposition.[28]

Use of violence that was once again present in Catalonia in the first decades of the 20th century. Spanish neutrality during World War I particularly benefitted a bourgeoisie that, along with smugglers and speculators, made sizeable profits. While the less privileged classes suffered before the indifference of various governments, from food scarcities and price rises, with salaries failing to increase at the same rate. Circumstances that propitiated considerable labour unrest that was not devoid of violence on the part of both management and unions, and which resulted in personal assaults, in which the state took the side of the bourgeoisie. The brutal repression, with torture, exile and application of the "*ley de fugas*" (prisoners shot while allegedly escaping), encouraged the role of men of action, who swelled the ranks of anarchist heroism and martyrdom. Their actions served as an example for the multitude of young emigrants who travelled to Barcelona from the poorest areas of Spain in search of work, and who, due to their lack of qualifications, struggled to find work – genuine "unemployment fodder" – or who, at best, had the worst jobs in mines, workshops and industry. Here the action groups did their recruiting.[29]

After Primo de Rivera's dictatorship, anarchists of action, like Durruti, Ascaso or Juan García Oliver, returned from exile or came out of prison with the aura of freedom fighters, arousing the admiration of many confederal militants. Durruti, a stout individual with an indomitable character, whose popularity among the workers owed as much to his history as a man of action as to the proletarian culture he made plain at political meetings, reflected in an impetuous, sincere and emotional discourse that stirred the masses. Francisco Ascaso, Durruti's constant companion, who along with his brothers Joaquín and Domingo was the example of a conduct as diverse as it was difficult to define, in which there was room for revolutionary action, but also bank robberies and organic leadership. García Oliver, wiry and bald of pate, was authoritarian in manner, a rousing speaker and obsessed with forming an organisation capable of directing the revolutionary uprising.

These anarchists, heirs of the great "martyrs" of the previous century, used their ascendancy in union assemblies, meetings and newspapers with a twofold objective: on the one hand, to maintain revolutionary momentum via the proliferation of protests, strikes and uprisings to create, as García Oliver observed, "the habit of revolutionary actions". Although, on this occasion, they shied away from individual attacks and promoted collective action against the structures of the capitalist system in order to overcome "fear of the forces of repression, the army, the Guardia Civil, the police". Ultimately, what García Oliver called "revolutionary gymnastics", the practice of which would develop the workers' rebellious temperament;[30] and on the other hand, encourage the most virulent criticism not only of the republican state, as chiefly responsible for social injustice and repression, but also of the anarcho-syndicalists who dominated the confederal committees. The objective was none other than to assume control of the organisation.

As regards external factors, the national and international socio-economic situation was marked by the crisis of 1929. A crisis that, though very present, had less of an impact in Spain than in industrially more developed neighbouring countries. To the economic contraction was added the restrictive public investment policies of the republican governments and the misgivings, on occasions outright opposition, of capitalist media, both national and international, vis-à-vis the new regime. Thus, for example, the British financial world expressed its concern from the beginnings of the Republic. The conduct of the provisional government and fear of a significant communist presence in the new parliament were at the heart of its unease.[31] Meanwhile, the Spanish capitalists opted for caution in investment and the flight of capital. Between April and July 1931, the banks lost over 900 million pesetas, in other words, 15% of their total deposits, and by September of that year the figure had risen to 1,300 million pesetas, taking the loss of funds to 20%.[32]

These circumstances contributed, inevitably, to an increase in unemployment, with a deterioration in labour relations and an ensuing repression. Indeed, the actions of the Republican-Socialist government vis-à-vis both labour issues and public order were arguments employed by the anarchists in their struggle for control of the CNT. In the area of labour relations, Minister of Labour and UGT leader, Francisco Largo Caballero, implemented policies consistent with the principles and actions of the socialist union and, therefore, incompatible with confederal ideas. A situation that heightened the confrontation between the two main union organisations in their dispute over control of the workers' movement. An old confrontation most recently witnessed during Primo de Rivera's dictatorship.

The socialists did not support any kind of action against the General's coup, and went from neutrality to collaboration with the dictatorship. Largo Caballero participated as spokesman on the Work Council and also on the Council of State, a consultative body that assisted the Military Board. The UGT also collaborated in the corporative organisation created by the Ministry of Labour. The model was based on the Italian fascist system, though with certain differences. The basis of the new organisation were the "*comités paritarios*" (joint committees), where workers and employers discussed their differences under the presidency of a representative of the state. The UGT conditioned its participation in these committees upon being the only union present. Thus, it not only avoided its possible illegalisation, but consolidated its organisation and increased its membership. By contrast, the CNT, advocate of direct action, did not participate in the negotiations in which the state had mediated. A circumstance that led to repression and the dismantling of its structures.[33]

With the advent of the Republic, Largo Caballero was appointed Minister of Labour. One of his first decisions was to approve a decree, dated May 7, 1931, which introduced mixed juries, the republican version of the previous joint committees of the dictatorship. In these, the state administration played a significant role in negotiations between workers and employers, with the primary objective of preventing labour conflicts leading to strikes or lockouts. Mixed juries were formed of representatives of management and of the workers, chosen by the corresponding professional associations. Their president and vice-president were selected by both parties and ratified by the ministry provided there was agreement; in the absence of agreement, the ministry appointed them directly from a list of three appointed by each group. The jury intervened in all labour issues, such as wages, regulations, contracts, etc. In the event of lack of agreement, the president had the casting vote.[34] Therefore, these appointments were a crucial element in the resolution of labour lawsuits, and their political orientation fundamental in tipping the balance one way or another. The new Socialist mayors and councillors in rural areas occupied the presidencies of many of these mixed juries, which influenced not only the improvement of working conditions, but also the application of new legislation. Their influence was also important, among other questions, in awarding public works contracts, supporting peasant strikes called to guarantee rights, or obliging landowners to dispense with machinery and recruit labourers through the labour exchange. In this context, there was no shortage of bosses who accused these mayors of a lack of neutrality in exercising their responsibilities at the head of the juries; but neither did they heed the warnings issued by socialists like Fernando de los Ríos, Julián Besteiro or Indalecio Prieto aimed at moderating their actions. In any case, the mixed juries took time to become operational owing to the prior elaboration of the electoral roll, so the joint committees continued to function throughout 1931.[35]

If the CNT had defended direct action in such adverse times as Primo de Rivera's dictatorship, now, in republican times, with their rights and freedoms, they were not going to abandon so precious a commodity. Consequently, the CNT began its union activity in the Republic with the intention of imposing its principles upon the legislation introduced by the Ministry of Labour. This was made clear by the telegram sent by the Governor of La Coruña to the Minister of the Interior, informing him that the dock unloaders, members of the CNT, did not accept the "joint committees", and threatened to go on strike if management did not agree to a pay rise.[36] Whilst workers in the chemical industry, already on strike, refused to "reach an agreement with the joint committees". The CNT press accused the ministry of wanting to place the Confederation in a "blind alley", and worse still, present it, on account of the considerable labour conflict, "as a source of disruption".[37]

Labour Conflict

At this juncture, it is important to make a series of observations that will help us to explore the reasons for this conflict and the responsibility of each of the actors. Because the labour problems that beset the young Republic, practically from the moment of its constitution, were, to a large extent, inherited from the previous period. Employers had taken advantage of the dictatorship's control over the unions to impose their conditions in the workplace. Therefore, in the wake of General Primo de Rivera's resignation, and before the advent of the Republic, there was an increase in the number of strikes, from 96 in 1929, to 402 in 1930 and 734 in 1931; while the number of strikers increased fivefold during these last two years compared with the year before.[38] Strikes that had a double objective: on the one hand, force employers to recognise the union; on the other, improve work and pay conditions. Grievances that involved the recovery of rights secured in the past, but which the dictatorship had annulled, such as the ban on overtime, pay rises, the statutory eight-hour working day, or seven hours for mineworkers in Asturias, which had been secured in 1919 and lost during the dictatorship.

The legalisation of the CNT, in April 1930, facilitated confederal presence in conflicts, where there was defence of union action independently of the joint committees.[39] In this conflict, as in the one that accompanied the advent of the Republic, the participation of the workers was fundamental. The confederal press observed how in the years of the dictatorship "workers had been treated in the most shameful and despicable fashion"; as a result of which many union sections hastened to present labour rules in order to obtain economic improvements, when "the reorganisation of our union groups" had barely begun.[40]

The workers understood that, with the fall of the monarchy, the new period would see their prior situation redressed. For its part, the new Republican-Socialist government thought that, as a result, the Republic would enjoy the social peace it required. Accordingly, in May 1931 the *Caja Nacional contra el Paro Forzoso* (National Fund against Layoffs) was set up, of an advisory nature, and a decree was passed relating to compulsory health insurance. In June, the law on accidents at work was applied to farmers; while in July, the maximum working day of eight hours was accepted, even for miners. In September, the Cooperatives Law was passed, and for the following year projects were prepared sickness, old-age, invalidity and maternity insurance.

But the implementation of all these laws was highly problematic, sometimes owing to lack of funding, since the economic situation rendered their adoption impossible. Thus, for example, the National Fund against Unemployment barely had resources, as it received only 0.5% of the state budget.[41] On other occasions because, as Marta Bizcarrondo has pointed out, in order for this legislation to be applied, state intervention was required, via the creation of provincial work delegations and the intervention of inspectors who would substitute civil governors in matters of social policy, as the Ministry of Labour intended. However, Parliament did not permit certain changes and, moreover, the intervention of the provincial work delegation was restricted and dependent on the civil governor.[42] Azaña described the confrontation, in this respect, between Miguel Maura, Interior Minister, and Largo Caballero, when the latter complained that the governors exceeded their remit in the drafting of labour contracts and imposed them without respecting labour legislation. To which Maura replied that the absence of labour representatives in many zones led to non-compliance with labour legislation, so governors could not "simply sit back and wait until mutinies broke out, suppressing them with gunfire". Both agreed that the governors were not responsible for these questions, but the economic problems involved in forming the provincial work delegations contributed to the lack of solutions. A further influence, according to Maura, was the pressure exerted by the banking sector, commerce, industry, owners and the military upon social legislation they regarded as mistaken.[43]

The living conditions of workers and, particularly, of day labourers in the south, were so miserable that they were unlikely to be improved by measures that might function in more advanced countries, but which were clearly insufficient for Spain at the time. Because, as Mercedes Cabrera has noted, there were no nationalisations in mining or in banking, not even in railways, despite Indalecio Prieto's initial intentions. The closest was the draft law on "workers' control" – involving workers in the management of the company – which was attacked by pressure groups and employers' organisations, resulting in its paralysis in the parliamentary committee.[44] All of this in a context in which a large proportion of workers associated the Republic with the attainment of social justice and the emancipation of the working class, issues far removed from the reformist objectives of the new Republican-Socialist government.

The civil governors sent notifications to the Ministry of the Interior, highlighting the difficult situation in which thousands of workers found themselves. The Governor of Algeciras observed, on April 27, that a group of unemployed people had walked through the streets begging in shops and houses. In Jerez de la Frontera, in June, there were "large processions (of) hungry workers" and that the authorities found it impossible to "attend to (their) legitimate demands, not just for work, but (for) alms in order to live". To this situation was added the conduct of employers. The Governor of Cadiz repeated his misgivings regarding the attitude of many bosses who were preparing to sack workers in the short term". The governor of Jerez de la Frontera reported that the Compañía Fierro refused to respect the approved labour agreements, which had led to the calling of a partial strike that threatened to become general.[45]

In this context, it is easy to understand how from the outset the social pressure upon the young Republic was exceptional. A pressure for which the CNT was deemed chiefly responsible, when it was the workers themselves who flocked to the unions and urged the leadership cadres to strive to improve their working conditions. Furthermore, the committees and the confederal press issued calls for calm. The urge to make up for lost time and redress as soon as possible the "abuse and harassment" suffered by the workers during the dictatorship, was described by the Confederation as "suicidal haste". Because there was considerable impatience, and before establishing a strong organisation there was a desire to "express demands that are bound to provoke conflicts that apart from breaking up the organisations affected, must hinder the progress of the organisation in general". There were unions that did not even have statutes or the necessary means to function and had already "drafted and adopted rules to present them to employers". In Barcelona, there were union councils that were "constantly besieged by new union members", who already carried in their pockets the labour rules they wanted to present to the management. The latter insisted that "this nonsense" should not prosper, and that it was necessary for councils, union members and committees to maintain the balance, "not letting themselves be dragged down the slope that would rapidly lead us to failure". The workers had every right to voice their grievances, but the organisation could not "improvise a solution for each case and less so for this lightning procedure". If their demands were to be met, it was fundamental "to get organised first, and grow in strength afterwards". Basically, it was necessary to "contain impatience" at a moment of reorganisation that would culminate in the CNT National Congress and the AIT (*Asociación Internacional del Trabajo* or International Work Association) World Congress, where it was possible to "address with greater efficiency" that which they aspired to achieve.[46]

Impatience that was materialised in the labour rules, and which was determined, as in the pre-republican era, by two fundamental questions: recognition of the union and the need to improve the economic-labour situation, which were known as moral and material improvements. Regarding the former, on the one hand, was the recognition of union delegates in the workplace; and, on the other, the union's right to intervene in the recruitment of new workers, via the so-called "*bolsas de trabajo*" (labour exchanges). A basic question not only for the growth of the union, but also for its survival, as during a period of economic crisis and high unemployment, its recognition as "placement agency" was key to the arrival of new members.

Thus, in labour rules, moral improvements took pride of place. Like those presented by the *Sindicato Único de Trabajadores* (Single Workers' Union) of Prat de Llobregat, which on the first point called for recognition of the union and, subsequently, forced management to employ workers via its labour exchange.[47] The *Sindicato de Luz y Fuerza* (Light and Energy Union) in Catalonia achieved, after days of strikes, recognition of factory committees and delegates, as well as the right to intervene in work issues.[48] Moral improvements that were even given priority over other grievances. Thus, for instance, police reports, obtained in Telefónica strike assemblies, indicated that those involved affirmed that "even if the Company offers more benefits than those requested by the Confederation, it must first recognise the personality of the union".[49]

There were other questions that revealed the social justice aspect that the Republic represented for many workers. The *Sindicato Fabril y Textil* (Manufacturing and Textile Union) of Tarrasa called a general strike because, though in the past some "exploiters and tyrants "had been endured", now "the working class, in possession of freedom", demanded"the right to welfare and social justice". Thus, moral and material improvements were proposed, as in the work of women: "almost double that of men and paid half"[50]. But also the readmission of those sacked while on strike since over a decade ago. Thus, for example, the Telefónica CNT union included among its demands the readmission of those sacked during the 1917 strike;[51] the Light and Energy Union in Catalonia had achieved the readmission of those sacked over labour issues in 1919; while the *Sindicato Único de Mineros* (Single Miners' Union) of Asturias demanded the return of all those sacked since September 13, 1923, the date of General Primo de Rivera's coup.[52]

In respect of economic and work improvements, many of these had their origin, specifically, in salaries, work conditions and lost rights that were once again claimed. The bakers of Barcelona presented rules in which they proposed the elimination of night work, via a legal provision, transformed into an international law, to begin the working day at 5 a.m. Day work that already existed in 1919, but which employers, taking advantage of "the reign of terror and then the dictatorship", had abolished; the Gastronomic Union *Sindicato Gastronómico* (Gastronomic Union) raised the need to address the legal enforcement of the eight-hour day; the Asturian Miners' Union requested, among other things, retirement at the age of fifty, a day's wage of 5 pesetas and the abolition of piecework.[53]

In short, one could say that, during the first months of the Republic, the working masses took the offensive and sought to improve their situation thanks to the union freedom offered by the new regime. Whilst capitalism went on the defensive. The French Ambassador in Spain noted how consuls all over Spain were sending him "alarming reports vis-à-vis the spirit (state of mind) of the workers" in labour grievances. To this situation was added, according to the ambassador, the fear on the part of both the UGT and the government, that the workers, disappointed "by the mediocre benefits" afforded by the Republic, would turn "to extremist organisations". Circumstances that obliged the authorities to support the unions in social conflicts and exert pressure upon industrialists to yield to workers' grievances.

But it was not possible to consolidate this favourable situation in relation to workers' interests, due, among other reasons, to the confrontation between the two main union organisations, UGT and CNT. It should not be forgotten that these were times of economic crisis and that the unions were recruitment centres, which involved the struggle between both unions for the control of work. The same French Ambassador reflected this conflict when he observed that the Minister of Labour, Largo Caballero, was "violently hostile to the CNT", while the newspaper *El Socialista* accused the Confederation of being "an organisation of gunmen".[54]

Public Order and Repression

But the confrontation not only reflected the union struggle; it involved many other questions, such as public order policy. The first important event, in this respect, was the celebration of the First of May, which triggered the first serious battle between anarchists and police in Barcelona. The First of May had been declared a national holiday by the government in the days following the proclamation of the Republic, but the confederal press placed the accent, as had been the case since it was first celebrated in 1890, on the essentially political character that the anarchists attributed to the day;[55] because in the workers' calendar there continued to be "three hundred and sixty-five days of capitalist exploitation, legalised robbery, harassment, forced labour, poverty, humiliation and opprobrium". So, unlike the socialists, who saw this as a largely recreational commemoration, for the anarchists the First of May should be a day of struggle.[56]

García Oliver recalled, years later, how in Barcelona the First of May 1931 was a genuine day of struggle. The CNT had organised a meeting in the Palacio de Bellas Artes, while the anarchist groups, linked to the FAI, assembled at the Arco del Triunfo, barely two hundred metres away. The anarchists displayed large red and black flags with the initials CNT-FAI and the slogan: "First of May. International fiesta of revolutionary gymnastics". Speakers at the meeting included Luzbel Ruiz, Arturo Parera and García Oliver, who declared that he could count from the podium "no fewer than one hundred comrades who, with their pistol between trousers and belly, were merely awaiting the opportunity to throw themselves, in their own fashion, into the sport of 'revolutionary gymnastics' ".[57] An atmosphere that, apparently, lent itself more to violent confrontation than to a day of union grievances.

Meanwhile, the demonstration organised by the CNT left the Palacio de Bellas Artes and headed for the Plaza de la República, where the headquarters of the Generalidad was located, to submit, as was traditional, the conclusions of the meeting to the authorities. The rally was celebratory and multitudinous – around 150,000 people, according to *Tierra y Libertad*. In the van, "the red and black flags of the syndicalist organisation, the black flag of the FAI, some republican colours and countless banners expressing the will of the people".[58] Once in the Plaza, according to García Oliver, the anarchists controlled the different corners granting access to the square.[59] A delegation moved forward to hand in the document detailing the agreements that had been adopted, when one of the *Mozos de escuadra* (Catalan police) assaulted one of the flags being carried by the commissioners, at which point an anonymous shot, answered by other, led to a pitched battle, gunfight included, which lasted about 45 minutes, resulting in the death of a metal worker and a security guard.[60]

The First of May became one of García Oliver's favourite "gymnastic circuits", where unrest, through violence, sought to undermine the credit of the new regime and develop the muscle necessary for the revolution. Incidents that surprised many workers, who saw how the events of Barcelona occupied the headlines, and relegated to a secondary position the demands approved at the confederal meeting, such as the dissolution of the Civil Guard, more work to offset the crisis or a reduction in rental costs.[61] Demands that evidenced latent problems in society and were omnipresent in the events that dominated the ensuing weeks.

That same month of May, on the 10th to be precise, the *Círculo Monárquico Independiente* (Independent Monarchic Circle) was founded in Madrid, with Torcuato Luca de Tena, editor of the pro-monarchy newspaper *ABC*, one of its chief promoters. A consequence of this act, as we shall see later, was the burning of convents that, beginning in the capital, spread throughout Spain. The presence of the Catholic Church at the birth of the Republic was important. In 1930, there were some 109,000 clergy members in Spain, between secular and regular. The proportion of Spaniards directly serving the Church was, approximately, one per 493 inhabitants, a figure that, in the Catholic world, was only surpassed by Italy. Maintenance of the Church depended, in the first place, on the state, in accordance with the concordat signed in 1851, but also on donations by believers and income from its considerable estate. The Church possessed around 12,000 rural land holdings and approximately 8,000 urban buildings that, along with other properties, had a declared value of about 244 million pesetas. Moreover, there was a sizeable number of properties that were not recorded in property registers and eluded state control. Added to this significant economic power was the Church's presence in many of the towns and villages of Spain, where an army of priests exercised considerable influence over the lives of citizens. The Catholic Church was distrustful of, and often openly opposed to, the new regime. Monseñor Segura, Archbishop of Toledo and Cardinal Primate, published a pastoral, at the beginning of May, in which he extolled the monarchy and the dethroned king, and called upon Catholics to prepare for future elections to parliament so as to make a stand against those intent "on destroying religion".[62]

So when the provisional government attempted to regulate, also in May, the presence of the Catholic Church in barracks and schools via the suppression of military honours to the Most Holy, of obligatory mass in prisons and barracks or their belonging to the Council of Public Instruction, it comes as no surprise that in the Catholic world this was experienced as an attack on the clergy. Although these measures were logical in a democratic society and far from exceptional in other Western countries. Indeed, Jean Herbette, French Ambassador in Spain, always maintained that the actions of the Republican-Socialist government, in its attempt to separate Church and State, had been no more stringent than those undertaken in France, a lay country par excellence.[63]

However, the past, with its history of privileges and customs, operated to the detriment of legislation that, in most democratic countries, while no less emphatic, had been addressed earlier and over a longer period. Moreover, it should not be forgotten that the republicans largely blamed the Church for Spain's ancestral backwardness compared with neighbouring countries. A feature of their political culture was a conspicuous anticlericalism they shared with other left-wing forces, mainly, the anarchists. While the Spanish people had demonstrated time and time again, throughout history, its rejection of a Church closer to power than to the poor, with significant outbursts of anti-clerical violence.[64] A circumstance that was very present in the new republican Spain, not only due to the ecclesiastical hierarchy's opposition to the new regime, but because of the actions of priests in the towns and villages of Spain. In this respect, there was no shortage of telegrams sent to the Ministry of Interior reporting clerical activity against the Republic; as in Denia (Alicante), where the local parish priest was carrying out an unsettling campaign against the new regime, leading to requests for "his expulsion in order to prevent (the) people from retaliating"; or in Rafal, in the same province, where the priest was politically active in the "Catholic unions of the dictatorship" and from the pulpit provoked "conflict between peaceful neighbours with the imminent danger of bloody clashes", so the request was for his replacement by another priest "more versed in spiritual affairs than in the politics of action".[65]

In this context, the inauguration in Madrid of the *Círculo Monárquico Independiente* gave rise to an anticlerical movement. The assembled monarchists, in a building on the central Street of Alcalá, decided to play the Marcha Real (Spanish national anthem), which prompted the indignation of those who began to mill around and attempted to enter the building, before setting off for the *ABC* offices. The newspaper's monarchist sympathies, along with its call a few days earlier to supporters of the King to assemble in the said Circle, and the leading role in the new formation of its editor, Luca de Tena, made it a target for anger. The newspaper offices were protected by eight civil guards and an army corporal, at the editor's expense. In the clash between the demonstrators and the guards two people died and several were wounded. The local CNT federation in Madrid organised the funeral for both victims, as one of them, Martín Ulloa, belonged to the builders' union, while the other, a boy, Edito Alonso, was the son of another confederal member.[66]

The shooting dead of these two people by the Civil Guard was the event that triggered the subsequent burning of religious buildings. Azaña told in his memoirs how, on the night of 10 May, thousands of people gathered in the Puerta del Sol of Madrid to protest over what had happened at the *ABC* offices. Miguel Maura, Minister of Interior, wanted to "send out the Civil Guard and teach them a lesson", but was prevented from doing so by Indalecio Prieto, Fernando de los Ríos and Azaña himself, who had to "physically hold him back to stop him leaving his office and giving the orders". That same night, a delegation from the Madrid Athenaeum handed Azaña a document requesting Maura's dismissal, the dissolution of the Civil Guard and the expulsion of the monks.[67] The night passed without further incidents of note, but the next day events developed rapidly.

The CNT and the Communist Party called a general strike for the 11th of the month, while the socialists abstained from the call. That day, some groups directed their anger at churches and convents, which they set fire to while many citizens looked on passively. Initially, the government attempted to address the situation via the use of the forces of public order, but on the 12th it declared a state of war in Madrid, extending the measure two days later to the provinces of Alicante, Malaga, Seville, Cadiz, Murcia, Cordoba and Badajoz.[68] The Ministry of Interior sent telegrams to civil governors indicating the need to tighten "vigilance to avoid the repercussion of events in Madrid posting soldiers in banks, convents, churches and public buildings", and called for any "attempt (at) disruption (of) public order (to be) energetically suppressed".[69] The state of war was maintained until May 21, except in Andalusia where it was prolonged as a consequence of the confrontation between the army and the confederals. There, the Captain General of Seville, Miguel Cabanellas, had issued orders to the military governors indicating that it was essential to "rid Andalusia of disruptive and foreign elements that criminally attack the Motherland", so he recommended the arrest of "all suspects".[70]

In the libertarian world, *Solidaridad Obrera* highlighted the people's yearning for justice and the supposed collusion between the conservative elements of the government and monarchists and reactionaries of the old regime. The editorial specifically mentioned Niceto Alcalá Zamora, Miguel Maura and Alejandro Lerroux, asking them to resign so their positions might be occupied by young people from the Athenaeum of Madrid, "much more intelligent and republican than these last-minute converts". Meanwhile, *El Luchador* – an anarchist newspaper owned by the Urales family, in other words, Federico Urales (pseudonym of Juan Montseny), his wife, Soledad Gustavo (pseudonym of Teresa Mañe), their daughter, Federica Montseny, and her partner, Germinal Esgleas – condemned the reactionary attitude of the Church, "mainstay of injustice, ally of the tyrant, poisoner of human consciousness", and described the situation as "the defence of freedom", while it demanded the dissolution and disarmament of the Civil Guard, maintenance of which would be the men of the Republic's gravest error.[71]

After the events of May, the government and the Church maintained their positions. The Vatican refused to grant the *placet* to the new Spanish Ambassador, Luis de Zulueta, while the government decreed the estrangement of Cardinal Segura. The Vicar General of the dioceses of Vitoria was also expelled, after the seizure of a series of letters from Segura issuing instructions for the sale to strawmen of Church property and the placement of profits abroad. Both sought exile in France, where they continued their crusade against the Republic.[72]

With regard to the other underlying problem – the Civil Guard (also known, since 1929, as *la Benemérita*) – the government tried to address problems of public order with the formation of the Guardia de Asalto (Assault Guard) which, more in line with the times, carried truncheons and handguns, rather than sabres and rifles. Its main mission was to break up demonstrations without bloodshed. Ángel Galarza, Director General of Security, also proposed, in agreement with the government, the creation of a civilian guard, composed of members of the government coalition parties.[73] Azaña noted, in his diary, how Diego Martínez Barrio, Minister of Communications, presented it to the government as a means of "controlling the anarcho-syndicalists". Although its creation was initially opposed by Maura's unwillingness to arm the masses, Azaña argued that 500 socialists and republicans was not a mass, and that in other countries this idea had worked. So its proposed creation prevailed.[74]

Despite all these initiatives, in essence the government maintained the organisation and discipline of the Civil Guard. It retained its military character by reporting to the Ministry of Defence, and its officers were former soldiers. The problem was that, as Gabriel Cardona has observed, the Civil Guard and the army were employed by the Republic, in the absence of an efficient civil police force, for situations of disruption of public order. This circumstance gave rise to another far more worrying consequence: any problem resulting from the clash between these forces and citizens would be settled in the military courts.[75]

In this respect, Manuel Ballbé has underlined the fact that although the advent of the Republic brought the derogation of the 1906 Law on Jurisdictions, which placed under military jurisdiction certain crimes of (mainly printed) expression, a circular order was passed, dated April 20, 1931, maintaining military jurisdiction over cases brought against people charged with attacks, contempt, defamation and slander against the military authorities and the Army. Jurisdiction that included crimes committed by civilians. This order was completed with the 11 May decree, which established the sphere of military jurisdiction, and declared that, since the administration of public order maintained a militarised structure, cases related to this matter fell within this jurisdiction.

Furthermore, the government created the Court of Military Justice in the Supreme Court (sixth chamber), which was assigned the competences of the

Supreme Council of War and Navy, now abolished. In this new court, there were two civilian and four military magistrates. As it had to resolve conflicts between civil and military jurisdiction, it is not surprising that its rulings mostly favoured military jurisdiction in cases of insults or attacks directed by civilians against members, for example, of the Civil Guard. Basically, concludes Ballbé, this judicial organisation maintained, in essence, the Law of Jurisdictions, now repealed, as it retained the competence of councils of war against civilians who criticised the armed forces. At the same time, it facilitated the lack of responsibility of members of the military police forces in many of the cases of public disorder, "as it was both judge and defendant in the trial and there was no control of the excesses (committed) by the police in their interventions".[76]

All this legislation did little to help the *Benemérita* adapt to the new reality, since, anchored to the social and political past, it clashed with the rights and freedoms of the new democratic regime. A reality that was more evident in rural areas than in big cities any demonstration, protest or strike that took place in a small village or town was too often interpreted, in spite of its possible legality, as an attack on public order. It was not unusual for a landowner to request the presence of the Civil Guard, to whom he offered board and lodging, when harvest time arrived or given the possibility of a demonstration or a strike.[77] In these circumstances, it could be said that the Civil Guard was "closer" to the power of the great landowners than to the Ministry of Interior. The UGT leader Enrique de Santiago himself noted that the struggle was harder "in towns and villages, where the *cacique*, close friends with the Civil Guard sergeant, is lord and master of the freedom and lives of the citizens".[78]

One of the most dramatic early examples of the problems of public order occurred on 27 May 1931 during a demonstration by the sailors of Pasajes who were on their way to San Sebastian. Here the fishermen had been on strike throughout the month of May. The Single Union of San Sebastian agreed to call a 48-hour general strike in protest against the arrest of several of their representatives. According to *Solidaridad Obrera*, around 5,000 workers left Pasajes en route to the Gipuzcoan capital to demand the release of those under arrest. At the head of the demonstration "were over two hundred women". When they reached the neighbourhood of Ategorrieta, about forty civil guards blocked their way, urging them to disband. After issuing a warning they "fired at will against the demonstrators", leaving eight dead and over fifty wounded.[79]

The Commander of the Civil Guard in San Sebastian wrote a report at the request of the civil governor, in which he stated that on 27 May, at approximately 9 o'clock, 29 infantrymen and 9 cavalrymen left the barracks, under the command of Captain Primitivo Ezcurra and Lieutenant Calixto González, in order to prevent the entry into the capital of an unauthorised demonstration. In the demonstration, according to his information, were approximately 3,000 people, who had overrun the army forces deployed on the road, and were continuing their progress towards the city. The captain advised the governor of the situation, and the latter "repeated the order to prevent at all costs the demonstration's entry into the city". So the captain ordered the demonstrators to stop, but they continued to advance. At the same time, according to his version, various gunshots were heard from the demonstration, so he ordered his men to open fire, "firing ten or twelve shots that produced several casualties among the demonstrators", who were taken "by some of them to the nearest hospitals", while the majority fled. The commander indicated that his forces had acted "*with utmost prudence and with the maximum sense of humanity*"; and that the cavalry had not been employed, on account of their limited numbers and the difficulty in manoeuvring in that spot "where the road is hemmed in between walls and fences". The local commander ended by stating that "there was not a single volley, only occasional shots, because if there had been, not three volleys but just one, there would have been many more casualties".

For his part, the governor acknowledged "the desperate situation" in which "the sailors of Pasajes, all Galician", found themselves, uprooted from their families, and that "the month-long strike (...) had rendered their situation tragic". Before continuing by adding that the demonstration made its way towards San Sebastian "in a threatening manner" in order to join those already on strike in the city and provoke considerable unrest. The governor, according to his version, ordered the Civil Guard to stop the demonstration "when the city was already under the mob's control (...) and the army and security forces powerless (...) to maintain order". Which was when he ordered Captain Ezcurra "to prevent, *with maximum discretion,* but employing all the energy that were necessary, entry into the city of the *mobs that intended to attack it* adding it to those already under its control". The governor thanked the forces deployed there for recovering "order in the city, seriously threatened by those bent on looting, which was prevented by the *discrete and efficient* intervention of the aforementioned Civil Guard officer". By way of conclusion, he declared that all social elements had recognised "that this Civil Guard commander, through his loyalty and *the tact* with which he fulfilled the painful duty required of him, saved San Sebastian and Spain from a tragedy the consequences of which cannot be foreseen".[80]

The fact is that a reading of both documents raises important questions. In the first place, it should be noted that Civil Guard reports on any incident invariably referred to shots, attacks and insults originating from demonstrators, strikers or those attending a meeting. There is not one single report that acknowledges an initial excessive action on the part of the guards. This circumstance alone arouses a degree of suspicion. Secondly, imagining that a demonstration of 3,000 or 5,000 people, some armed, according to the report, could be stopped by ten or twelve shots, with not a single volley of fire, when the governor described the demonstration as a mob intending to attack the city, while he had a force of 29 infantrymen and eight cavalrymen with which to stop them, is, to say the least, surprising. The Minister of the Interior himself, Miguel Maura, admitted, in his memoirs, that it was "a true miracle that the volley of fire did not cause more victims in such a confined area and given the power of the weapons used"; adding that another force, like the Assault Guard, "would probably, without needing to fire a shot, have broken up the demonstration using their truncheons and, at most, their short-range pistols".[81] Which, ultimately calls into question both the violence implicit in the word "mob· and the appropriateness of using a force like the Civil Guard, with their Mausers, to solve problems of public order.

Ultimately, one wonders what the local commander understood by "prudence" and "sense of humanity", or the civil governor when he used terms like "discretion" and "tact" in an action that had killed eight people and wounded over fifty. It seems more to be a case of excess and maladjustment to the new reality, which is patent in many other reports issued by Civil Guard detachments. For example, the one sent by the captain of the Jaen Headquarters with regard to the crowd of workers that attacked the Civil Guard in the village of Villanueva del Arzobispo, obliging them to employ their weapons. The result was "one civilian killed and three wounded", while one civil guard was injured "in the face by a stone".[82]

In spite of everything, the CNT committee leaders maintained, in general, a critical but moderate attitude towards events. The CNT national committee itself, headed by Ángel Pestaña, published a note strongly condemning what had happened in San Sebastian, Seville and other parts of Spain, and criticised the way in which the government was tackling social conflict. But it also aimed its criticism at the confederal unions and committees because they were calling for mobilisation and protests, bypassing confederal laws. Each section could draft its agreements, but could not negotiate these directly with management, since first they had to be "approved by a general union assembly, the assembly itself determining the optimum moment for their presentation". The entire situation was a misinterpretation of the concept of autonomy enjoyed by each section, which some identified with doing "whatever they want". The national committee also issued a call to the organisation not to be influenced "by those who screamed and shouted most at assemblies and meetings".[83] Even *El Luchador* called for moderation, and observed that if one compared what the Republic offered with what the anarchists desired, this was little, but if compared with what the dictatorship provided, "it is quite a lot". It understood that the workers wanted to recover lost rights, but what had to be avoided was "demanding these only because there was now a Republic", or shouting at assemblies, "which provoke states of agitation".[84]

In this context of social conflict, repression and internal unrest, the CNT prepared for its extraordinary congress, the first since La Comedia in 1919. But a few days earlier, the FAI held its own meeting.

The FAI Conference

Throughout the history of the libertarian movement, from the 1st International until exile during the civil war,[85] the anarchists had made a habit of holding meetings in advance of those convened by the union organisation in order that their delegates might adopt a unified position and, in this way, influence union agreements. Moreover, the anarchists, members of the

Bakuninist Alliance, exploited their significant presence in the Spanish Regional Federation, in the 19th century, to shape the evolution of the organisation. Anarchist Anselmo Lorenzo noted how *Alianza* members influenced the regional federation's meetings and conferences, by means of a type of what in the days of the Republic was known as a "*trabazón*" (organic link at every level between the anarchist organisation and the union), as "most delegates from regions where there were already sections of the latter (FRE) were also pro-*Alianza*".[86] An attitude they maintained over time. Juan López complained that during the CNT federal committee plenary session, held on 13 April 1931, in other words, one day before the proclamation of the Republic, there were delegates who spoke in the name of anarchism, more than on behalf of the union.[87]

Anarchists that, although they maintained their typical organisation of affinity groups, based on the low number of activists united by camaraderie and ideological proximity, tended to assemble in the FAI. This was the case of one of the better-known groups, *Los Solidarios* (from 1933 onwards, *Nosotros*), formed by such prominent anarchists as Buenaventura Durruti, Francisco Ascaso, Juan García Oliver, Gregorio Jover, Ricardo Sanz and Aurelio Fernández. Members who played an important role in the mobilisation and integration of the anarchists around the FAI, although, as a group, they did not form part of the organisation until late 1933 or early 1934. The same thing happened with the Urales family that, despite its influence in anarchist circles, did not belong to the FAI; Federica Montseny herself did not even belong to an affinity group until 1934.[88] In other words, the anarchists constituted an extraordinarily heterogeneous world made up of people particularly proud of their individuality. But their revolutionary ambitions fostered unity within the FAI, with the aim of preventing supposed ideological deviations, influencing and even orientating the confederal union so as to immediately introduce the social revolution.[89] Hence the fact that the organisation had a parallel structure to that of the CNT, with local federations of groups, county and regional federations and, at the top, the peninsular committee, not national like the CNT's, since the FAI, as its name suggested, was Iberian, so it included the Portuguese federation.

At the beginning of 1931, Juan Manuel Molina, *Juanel*, was secretary of the peninsular committee, having replaced José Elizalde who, as we shall see, was removed from this post. At that time, the FAI's presence was minimum and the handful of anarchist groups operated without connection.[90] In April, the situation was not much better. The peninsular committee itself admitted that there had only been "a slight intensification in the activity of our groups". So it requested of members a special effort to make themselves heard:

> In every production centre, where people work, in the neighbourhood, in the village, in the county (…) where there are no Athenaeums or cultural centres we must create them; where they exist, join them, and workers' organisations too, in order to propagate our ideology a direct them towards our anarchist objectives, in constant contact with the FAI.[91]

The calls to enter the anarchist organisation were constant. *Juanel* himself urged the anarchists to channel their efforts and aspiration by joining the organisation, unless they wished to "go down in History as no more than passionate utopians dreaming of a brilliant myth".[92] At the same time, "propaganda excursions" were introduced to travel all over Spain. In parallel with this activity, the anarchists voiced strong criticism of those who controlled the CNT, and warned of a proliferation therein of "collaborationist and republicanising tendencies and traces" which sought to eliminate the anarchist influx.[93]

Implicit within this criticism was an element of interest in reconstructing the movement's recent history through a discourse that would justify its actions. A discourse as simple as it was unreal. They acknowledged that they too had failed to respect the principles, like the Confederation, but, according to their interpretation, they had done so only "to make it easier for the CNT leaders to return to the straight path". They made this "sacrifice" "generously and sympathetically in spite of being exposed to criticism by the majority of anarchists". Although fortunately their attitude had been met with understanding, the only criticism being that they "had not been more energetic". If that "political lobbying" had not been permitted, they would have achieved, in April, "a sure and easy victory". But the CNT leaders had prevented it, and now the objective was clear, "anarchism's direct intervention in union organisations (...) orientation, leadership; every Union Executive Board should for a long time now have been directly influenced by the FAI, controlled by the militant anarchist groups".[94] As had occurred in the 19th-century FRE. However, that intervention was not taken into account, as Anselmo Lorenzo had pointed out, it was not the most appropriate: "How much more beneficial it would have been if, instead of snatching agreements and solutions by surprise, the *Alianza* had proposed a project of education and training, directed towards obtaining agreements and solutions as the sum of conscious wills!".[95]

But the anarchists were mobilising and convened an FAI conference for 8 June, two days before the CNT congress. This was an initiative of the Urales family, via *El Luchador*, and was reflected and disseminated by other anarchist newspapers, like *Acción Social Obrera*, *Tierra y Libertad*, and *El Libertario*. The call to the conference indicated that in it should participate "delegates with anarchist ideas who will attend the Confederation congress". Because that, and nothing else, was the primary objective of the meeting, manifest a joint position to influence and control the CNT.[96] So, the agenda, apart from the corresponding report by the peninsular committee and the organisation of propaganda excursions, included a section on the FAI's relationship with the CNT, "its problems and trajectory", and the procedures of anarchist unity so their actions would have an impact wherever they participated as "workers, speakers and writers".[97]

The conference was attended by 130 delegates representing 240 groups and 27 affiliates. The secretariat of the Peninsular Committee informed that it had taken charge of the organisation at the beginning of the year, replacing its predecessor, at the helm of the FAI since October 1930. The committee briefly reviewed the forces at its disposal, and noted both the insufficient presence of the organisation throughout the peninsula, and the lack of structuring. The regional federations of Aragon, Rioja and Navarra represented 17 groups; Andalusia, 47; the number in the Levante was unknown; it was difficult to become established in Madrid because it was a city that was "not very industrial or labour-oriented and the centre of all political parties"; Catalonia, a cornerstone of the movement, had libertarian centres and athenaeums, but the number of groups was not specified; while in Portugal the clandestine nature of the situation rendered a stable organisation impossible.

The conference voted to begin the propaganda excursions on the first Sunday of August, "attending to farm labours", which were by then drawing to a close. Speakers were to take with them books and pamphlets. Meanwhile, the anarchist newspapers would open subscriptions for their financing. The propaganda commission was formed by José Alberola, Tomás Cano Ruiz, Daniel Alcaide, Arturo Parera, Juan García Oliver, Progreso Fernández, Vicente Ballester, and Antonia Maymon and, as alternates, Domingo Germinal and José Xena.

One of the highlights was the creation of a commission that would analyse the political deviations of the members of the previous peninsular committee, specifically, José Elizalde, Hernández and Manuel Sirvent. The commission accused them of carrying out activities that exceeded their authority and of collaborating with politicians. These committee members were the ones who, according to the anarchist press, had sacrificed themselves "to make it easier for the CNT leaders to return to the straight path". Now, the anarchist representatives prohibited them, for a time, from "occupying positions in the organisation". But not content with this, they advised delegates attending the confederal congress to "attempt to have the latter adopt the same measure, vis-à-vis similar deviations that had been perceived in some committee members". A recommendation that, as we shall see, sought to pave the way towards control of the union organisation via the expulsion from their posts of the most prominent anarcho-syndicalists.

The FAI wanted to retain the role of CNT guardian and watchdog. A self-appointed role that the vast majority of workers, union members, had not requested, but which the *Específica* – as the FAI was known – was determined to play. Consequently, the conference delivered an opinion in which it stated unequivocally that:

> The position of the FAI members within the CNT will be that of influencing from the unions, so that the CNT always acts in accordance with its apolitical, anti-authoritarian and federalist principles (...) the FAI will always oppose from the unions any deviation within the CNT, preventing the formation of any schisms and exercising through its conduct and coherency a decisive moral influence.[98]

In short, the FAI "recommended that all anarchist workers should participate in the Confederation and not refuse, henceforth, any of the positions that the workers in their respective unions might assign them . . .".[99] The first attempt to seize confederal power came at the imminent CNT congress.

Second (II) Extraordinary CNT Congress

Wednesday 10 June 1931 saw the opening of the CNT Extraordinary Congress in the Teatro Conservatorio of Madrid – today María Guerrero, which at that time housed the Conservatorio de Música y Declamación, hence its name. It was attended by 440 delegates, representing 602,986 workers; numbers that are always imprecise when one is speaking of confederal meetings.[100] In fact, a delegate in the fifth session, held on the afternoon of the 12th, requested the number of representatives and of those represented, to which it was impossible to respond because nobody had bothered to "note them down" and because many had "arrived after the constitution of the congress".[101]

Pestaña, secretary general of the national committee, opened the congress, welcoming the participants. This committee had been formed in June 1930, following the legalisation of the CNT in April. Alongside Pestaña on the committee were, among others, Francisco Arín and Progreso Alfarache, who was secretary general at the time of its legalisation.[102] After Pestaña's welcome address, Rudolf Rocker, representing the AIT, delivered a speech in which he declared that the proletariat across the world was observing the congress, so it was important for the CNT to maintain its libertarian spirit. A principle he put above that of unionism when he attacked democracies, since, according to his interpretation, instead of destroying "the old capitalist paraphernalia, they sustain it. They propose improvements, and these improvements, accepted by the workers, side track them".[103]

Words that stoked an atmosphere, already rowdy, impregnated with a mood of confrontation between the two main persuasions, anarchists and anarcho-syndicalists. The battle would be fought, basically, on three fronts: the national committee's report, the National Industry Federations, and the CNT's position with regard to the Constituent Cortes. Although, as we shall see, the battle was general and continuous. The first clash was over the voting system. It was not the first time, but neither would it be the last, that this was the subject of fierce debate. This was no trivial matter, as on this decision depended, to a large degree, the agreements that the congress might adopt. In principle there were two options, on the one hand, the anarcho-syndicalists, led by Peiró, advocated voting according to number of people represented; the anarchists, on the other hand, represented by García Oliver, argued in favour of votes according to number of delegates. The former objected to this system, as there were representations with several delegates. For his part, Oliver wondered how one could be sure that the number of people represented was real, although he went further and asked, in a vein that raised doubts about not only confederal democracy but any kind of democracy, to what extent numbers could influence reason. Both sides had to adjust their proposals, the anarcho-syndicalists proposed the proportional vote, in relation to the number of members, and the anarchists one vote per union. The proportional system won by 291,395 votes to 177,879, with 18,791 abstentions.[104]

Such an important issue could not be separated from other questions that were floating in the atmosphere, such as political participation or the presence of communists in the organisation. The congress pointed out the incompatibility between public office and representation on the CNT, which led to the vote cast by several delegates being contested. Among others, Joaquín Pijoán and Hilario Arlandis, representatives of the Graphic Arts Union of Barcelona, who asked for the floor. There was a major scandal which culminated in the expulsion of "Arlandis, Pijoán and the communists". This would not be the last clash with the communists attending the congress. In the middle of one of the sessions, propaganda leaflets began to fall from the top floor, in defence of the confederation the communists were seeking to create, so several delegates left the hall in their pursuit and "catching up with the disruptors gave them a real beating".[105]

Francisco Arín presented the report on the work of the national committee, one of the burning issues at the congress. The fundamental question was the committee's activity in conspiring with politicians against Primo de Rivera's dictatorship. Arín pointed out that a national plenary session, in the wake of December 1930, agreed to support the political movement, but with revolutionary procedures of direct action. He admitted that he had attended meetings with left-wing parties in Catalonia, telling them that they would collaborate in a revolutionary movement, but would not participate in a provisional republican government, as they proposed. Arín observed that the FAI had exerted pressure on him to establish these contacts. Words that gave rise to considerable protest and "several scuffles".

Yet, ultimately, neither group could emerge "spotless" from this debate, however much they protested, shouted and accused one another of making contact with politicians, because both had done so. Anarchist Santiago Bilbao, from the Barcelona Construction Union, attempted to dissociate Sirvent and Elizalde from these contacts; while Germinal Esgleas condemned the lack of nobility evinced by syndicalist José Villaverde in attacking the FAI, and saying that the latter strove to contact politicians, and now could not defend itself as it had no delegate at the congress. A surprising intervention not only given the agreements reached at the conference held by the FAI barely two days earlier, but because, as *El Luchador*, where Esgleas himself wrote, observed, at one stage of the voting "the congress delegates, who had also been delegates, moreover, of the anarchist conference" met to negotiate an agreement, as we shall see below.[106]

It was, as on so many occasions, Juan Peiró who made the difference, with a courageous speech. He said that "since 1923 there has been no national committee that had not had relations with political elements"; in 1924, when the regional committee of Catalonia was in Mataró and the national committee in Zaragoza, Peiró and Arnó met Francesc Maciá (Catalan leader) the former committee to discuss prisoners and freedom, the latter the CNT's attitude towards a federal republic. He recalled a plenary session in 1928, in which all the regional committees "agreed to establish an intelligence service with political and military elements" provided that it was the committees that acted first in the revolutionary movement. Peiró also addressed the Pact of San Sebastian, of August 1930, indicating that the CNT and the UGT were invited to undertake a revolutionary movement in the streets. After the national committee had net with politicians, a plenary session was held in which all the delegations, except the Levante, expressed their approval of the contacts, so henceforth the relationship was maintained. Vis-à-vis the pressure exerted by the FAI to be in contact with politicians, he said, with a display of irony, that "we thought it was the FAI", but as the FAI "overruled and imposed sanctions upon them (i.e. the ousted former committee formed by Elizalde, Hernández and Sirvent), *we have to believe* that it was not the FAI". Finally, he argued that if there was deviation it was "due to the need to break down an obstacle that once blocked everyone's path, but has now been removed, I am pleased and happy at the mere sight of the release of my imprisoned comrades".[107]

The delegates asked repeatedly about the CNT's supposed agreement with the *Esquerra Republicana de Catalunya* leader, Luis Companys, to avoid any labour conflict during the next three months. Both Arín and Pestaña, from the national committee, and Jaime Magriñá, Francisco Isgleas and Salvador, members at the time of the regional committee of Catalonia, rejected this agreement. Pestaña censured the atmosphere fomented in libertarian media by this question, as since he had "left prison there have been three attempts on his life". So he urged the continuation of the debate to "dispel all the calumny and defamation", and also because he did not want "carry a gun all the time".[108]

The confrontation over the issue of relations with politicians with the objective of overthrowing the monarchy had reached such a point that "the congress delegates that had also been delegates at the anarchist conference assembled in search of a solution to the conflict". The FAI members presented a proposal prohibiting any CNT committee from having any relationship with politicians and relieving the national committee of its duties on account of previous contacts. In other words, they wished to repeat the agreement adopted at the FAI conference and dismiss the confederal leaders. The objective was clear: oust the anarcho-syndicalists from the leadership in order to assume control of the CNT. But they were a minority at the congress and, consequently, the proposal was rejected. So the Catalan delegation changed its approach and suggested that the national moved to another regional committee, which implicitly involved the removal of the current leadership. This motion was approved by the congress, so the national committee, interpreting this as a condemnation of its activity, handed in its resignation. Pestaña highlighted the contradictory nature of the proposal adopted, as the transfer of the highest confederal body represented "the punishment that the congress itself has rejected". With the resignation of the national committee, the FAI lowered the tension and "things (seemed) to return to normal".[109] But the last word had yet to be written, as was seen during the final sessions of the congress.

The next controversial point was the formation of the FNI (*Federaciones Nacionales de Industria* or National Federations of Industry), which involved a significant change in the organisation of the CNT. The last reorganisation had occurred at the La Comedia Congress, held in Madrid in December, 1919. This congress gave the green light to the formation of the SU (*Sindicato Único* or Single Union) – already approved by the Catalan regional committee at the Sans Congress, in July of the previous year – which grouped together all the workers from the same industrial sector. For example, the builders', carpenters', fitters', etc. unions together formed the *Sindicato Único de la Construcción* (Single Construction Union). The formation of the SU heralded the appearance of an organisation that was more in tune with industrial society. A fundamental question when addressing the union struggle, since the demands of a particular trade union became those of the SU, which increased the power of the workers when a strike was called in a particular industrial sector. However, the SU's sphere of activity was local, largely due to the embryonic nature of the industries. The La Comedia congress understood that it should not go any further and opposed the formation of the FNI, which would group together single unions from the same sector at a national level, an initiative defended by the Asturian Eleuterio Quintanilla.[110]

Now, Peiró returned to the FNI. They were necessary in two respects: as an indispensable element in workers' demands and as fundamental component of the libertarian society of the future. In relation to the former, the FNI represented the CNT's adaptation to the industrial and economic concentration effected by capitalism. In view of this situation, the confederal structure had to be complemented with these federations and, when the time came, with an International Industry Federation too. But Peiró looked beyond the union struggle and attributed to the FNI a revolutionary nature. The moment of insurgency, with the workers seizing control of factories and workshops, would be followed by the constructive phase of the revolution in which, within the tenets of revolutionary syndicalism, the FNI would have a fundamental part to play in the economic and social organisation of the new society.

The anarchists were opposed to these federations on different grounds: because they considered them to be Marxist and, therefore, contrary to the principles of the CNT; branding them useless, as Spain was a more agricultural than industrial country and they did not understand why principles should be abandoned for the sake of the evolution of capitalism; due to the singularity of Spain, as García Oliver argued, for whom the FNI were a German product that appeared to have "come out of a barrel of beer"; and because they led to "disintegration" and killed the masses that "were always at their disposal to be launched against the state"; and because, as José Alberola said, they precluded "the freedom of the union within the locality" and created bureaucratism. Ultimately, for all these reasons, because all that was sought was immediate improvement and the final objective of the revolution was forgotten.

During the debate, Peiró answered all these questions. With regard to the possible formation of a public administration whose salaries would be paid by members' contributions, he uttered a phrase – and one imagines him raising both arms and showing his workman's hands to all those present – saying that he "makes bulbs and, after making bulbs, writes pronouncements". He also said that they had to shed the stigma of Marxism, and that the reality the concentration of capital, to which the workers had to respond. He cited the example of some industries in Madrid and Barcelona, which baulked at accepting labour rules until these were adopted all over Spain, and wondered therefore: which body is supposed to resolve these cases? Finally, given the criticism regarding the circumstantial objective of the FNI, Peiró pointed out that the CNT's ultimate goal was anarchism, while the federations were the means. Because if the state were to be destroyed it was necessary to create an industrial organisation that would replace it.

The fundamental problem was that the anarchists were afraid of losing their influence where they could wield most power, at the grassroots of the confederal organisation, in the unions. They saw the FNI as the organ that was going to monitor, discipline, and break up, as García Oliver had said, those masses that, supposedly, they had "always at the ready to be launched against the state". In fact, Horacio Martínez Prieto, who later became secretary general of the national committee, declared that all these allusions the anarchists made to bureaucratisation and reformism were no more than "dialectical tricks" with which they sought to subvert power in the CNT.[111] The debate surrounding the FNI took place over various sessions and occurred in the middle of a major row. In spite of everything, the congress approved their formation by 302,343 votes in favour to 90,671 against, with 10,957 abstentions.[112]

A confrontation that was also present in the eighth point on the agenda, pertaining to the CNT's position vis-à-vis the convening of parliament. José Villaverde was responsible for drafting the motion. The Galician delegate explained that it did not advocate going to parliament, or anything of the kind, but merely suggested that the CNT accept the reality of the situation and put forward some minimum demands. The organisation opposed the Cortes, as it did any oppressive power, was still at war with the state and its mission was to educate the people so they would join the Confederation and participate in the social revolution. But along the way, according to Villaverde, it had a duty to propose a series of minimum advances in relation to teaching, unemployment, individual freedom, rights of assembly and to strike, etc.

During the debate, Germinal Esgleas and Francisco Isgleas voiced their opposition to the pronouncement, both because the organisation should maintain, in accordance with its principles, constant opposition to politics, and because the motion indirectly established a collaborationist criterion. Villaverde dismissed both criticisms and indicated that this was a realistic position. In his reasoning he asked: how many of the unions present here today are outside the law? Before answering: none. He then asked: who makes the law? And answered: the state. Villaverde evidenced the contradictions that had always formed a part of the organisation, which sometimes confused tactics with objectives. For one thing was the objective of abolishing the state and quite another acting as if it did not exist. The organisation was growing quickly, but still lacked the necessary strength to impose its type of society.

Finally, the anarchists suffered another defeat when the congress approved the motion. Although with the addition of an amendment that ratified the principles adopted in 1919, though, in fact, no-one had questioned them. In other words, the CNT would continue with its tactics of direct action, pushing the people in a revolutionary direction towards libertarian communism irrespective of what parliament might legislate, so it was bestowed with "the organisation of its revolutionary values and an eminently anti-electoral mission". All the same, 30 delegations, most of them in Catalonia, declared their opposition to the agreement adopted.[113]

Other items on the agenda did not lead to such bitter confrontation, though they dealt with important issues. Like the item that addressed "the agricultural question and the organisation of farmworkers ". In relation to the second part of the statement, the congress agreed that the agricultural unions within the CNT should bring together day labourers, sharecroppers and farm workers, organised into respective sections but united in solidarity against capital. With regard to the agricultural question, the motion, after criticising the tepidness of the reform being prepared by the government, recommended a radical change in land ownership. Specifically, confiscation of livestock, farm implements, machinery and expropriation without condemnation of large estates, hunting grounds, ploughable lands and holdings of over 50 hectares, which would be handed over to the agricultural unions for their exploitation. In other words, it was contrary to the redistribution of land among peasants, as this kind of reform perpetuated the capitalist system. The congress recognised, at the same time, the importance of proposing necessary improvements via protests that should be preparatory "for the decisive battle". The motion was passed.[114]

The congress also declared in favour of the minimum salary, against the tax on salaries and advocated the reduction of the working day, while it presented its plan to put an end to forced unemployment. The motion on the minimum salary considered the need to establish the latter so as to offer a solution to the hundreds of thousands of workers who earned, on average, approximately three pesetas, and, in any case, to apply it without distinction to men and women. With respect to the tax on salaries, it was considered to be "immoral and arbitrary", so was rejected. But not only this tax, also those levied on tenants, and by institutions and town councils, which people were urged not to pay. The eight-hour working day should be reduced to seven or even six, even if this meant the bankruptcy of the bourgeoisie, as this could lead to the hour of the proletariat. The argument was based, on the one hand, on technical improvements, which increased production and allowed for increased output with fewer hours of work; and, on the other, because it was regarded as an instrument against unemployment, a measure that had even been supported by "reformist organisations in North America, the most reactionary in the world". Even the American Federation of Labour had proposed the five-hour working day and the five-day week to provide employment for millions of workers.

Indeed, with regard to forced unemployment, the motion declared that this was a consequence of the economic crisis, caused, in the first place, by the rationalisation of technology, which had increased production, in some cases reduced labour by 50% and, at the same time, removed consumers from the system. The consequence was that there were 17 million unemployed in the world. While in Spain the unemployment figure was, according to the motion, 300,000. If we bear in mind that the active population numbered around 4 million people, the unemployment rate stood at, approximately, 7.5%. Not a very high figure, but one that took on a dramatic dimension when one realizes that, given the lack of resources available to the recently created national unemployment fund, the families affected were condemned to destitution. Faced by this situation, the motion proposed a series of measures such as introducing the six-hour day without a salary reduction, the elimination of overtime and forced movement of capital to increase investment in industry and agriculture, and obliged state and management to recruit the unemployed with union supervision. Although the motion was passed, the CNT returned to this serious problem on several occasions during the ensuing months and years. Thus, at the national plenary session in December 1931, the national committee acknowledged that it was unrealistic to demand a six-hour day, so the objective should be a 44-hour working week. Another question worthy of mention is the plenary session's opposition to unemployment benefit, in the belief that this would only create "a legion of parasites" who would live at the expense of those who worked and because state intervention was unacceptable, so, ultimately, it was capital that should defray the cost.[115]

The combination of all these measures portrayed a CNT immersed in a sea of contradictions and struggling between union activity, its principles and the revolutionary goal. But, above all, one should remember that the CNT was a union. Because, as Villaverde said, "there are many thousands of workers in the CNT and many thousands are not anarchists".[116] It would be as mistaken to think that the CNT members were all anarchists, as it would be to think they were all anarcho-syndicalists, when both groups constituted a minority. Most members were workers whose primary objective was to improve their working and economic conditions, beyond ideologies and revolutionary objectives. As Gayo Díez noted, "in the unions, there are many people who are not anarcho-syndicalists, and only a minority can call ourselves men of ideas".[117] In other words, militants would have to be differentiated from mere members, who joined the Confederation drawn by its prestige or that of its militants, because they believed that they would bring about those improvements quickly or, simply, because they constituted a majority in the workplace.[118] Along with this huge majority was the minority formed by the syndicalist and anarchist militancy, with its leaders (however much their existence was denied). The former maintained the ultimate objective of revolution, but without forgetting the need for the union struggle in order to obtain economic and labour benefits, which included the training and education of workers with a view to the future; the latter understood the union, fundamentally, as the organisation requires in order to achieve revolution. Any circumstantial improvements only served to "distract" workers from their goal, so union action was subordinated to principles.

A good example of the priorities of both groups was evidenced during the congress. For instance, the Asturian delegation proposed, no sooner had voting started, the appointment of a commission to go to the Ministry of Labour and support the miners in their demands for a seven-hour day and a pay rise. However, the regional secretariat Catalonia, ignoring the Asturian grievances, enquired about the invitation issued to the FAI by the congress. Which led the Asturian protesters to understand that the priority was addressing union matters. The confrontation resulted in mayhem, with "the delegates from different regions" shouting at each other "as if it were a Chamber of Deputies".[119] In a similar vein, during the fourth session, the question was asked whether a representative had been sent to the postal workers' congress, and answered in the affirmative. Well, a delegate suggested that, as in that congress there was a government delegation, the CNT should withdraw.[120] In other words, the intention was to put anti-political and anti-state principles before the basic work of any union. Principles that they also wanted to put before union apoliticism, understood as the union's lack of political definition, but also that of its members.[121] A question that was present in the admission of workers of a communist ideology, and in which the congress revealed the division between those who opposed and those who supported the notion that all workers could enter the CNT except "militant politicians or candidates for state office".[122]

On another front, the congress accepted changes to be applied in future confederal elections with a view to avoiding the problems that had arisen in this one, but which continued to be a breeding ground for significant confrontations in the future. For example, the national committee proposed that in voting in any plenary session, congress or national, regional or local meeting, the proportional system should be applied according to the following criteria: from 1 to 500 members, 1 vote; from 1 to 1,000, 2 votes; from 1 to 3,000, 3 votes; from 1 to 25,000, 7 votes; 25,000 plus, 8 votes. The proposal was accepted by the congress and referred to the unions for definitive approval.[123]

Another point worthy of mention: the national committee, with Pestaña as secretary general, remained at the head of the organisation after the congress. As will be recalled, the committee submitted its resignation when a proposal was adopted forcing it to leave the Catalan regional committee. However, the situation changed at the last moment, giving rise to a bitter controversy. Months later, Federico Urales described what had happened: "at the last minute, when all the delegates were anxious for that endless election to end and just when it was time to discuss where the National Committee would be based, a delegate, we do not know who, well-intentioned or not, said that the committee should continue to reside in Barcelona". A circumstance which those "relevant figures" took advantage of to feel endorsed, withdraw their resignation and continue in their posts.[124]

The congress ended on June 17, 1931 at four in the morning. But after seven days, this was only a pause in long struggle between anarchists and anarcho-syndicalists for control of the CNT. It had been the first serious, but premature, attempt to oust Pestaña, Peiró, Villaverde, and López from the confederal leadership. Their victory had been clear. They won all the votes, both on the major issues of the congress, from the national committee report to the National Industry Federations, as well as the CNT's position vis-à-vis parliament, economic demands or the proportional system of voting. Furthermore, at the very end of the congress they managed to retain control of the national committee. Peiró had even been appointed, at the regional conference of unions of Catalonia, held days before the congress, editor of *Solidaridad Obrera*. His election left no doubt as to the syndicalist predominance, since while Peiró obtained 46 votes, the first anarchist candidate, Felipe Alaiz, received only three.[125] Ultimately, the anarchists were grouped around the FAI, and did not have enough strength, nor were conditions favourable, for an assault on federal power. Conditions born of the working masses' disenchantment with the Republic, given the frustration of their economic and labour aspirations, but also of the repression stemming from social conflict.

The anarchists' impotence, realising that they were a minority and that they were losing one vote after another, resulted in the conference being excessively rowdy, with "chaotic sessions", characterised "by numerous incidents, intolerance of the opinions of others (...) and even violent language".[126] Little did it matter that the congress ratified the CNT's principles, tactics and goals, in other words, antipoliticism, direct action and libertarian communism, since its objective was to remove the anarcho-syndicalists from power, a goal that was not achieved. In any case, the anarchists knew that, in spite of their failure, they could revoke the agreements adopted. The key lay in knowledge of confederal practice and taking control of the main committees, to use them as a platform from which to prevent the development of the agreements adopted. Though reference has always been made to the internal direct democracy of the CNT and to the fact that the confederal committees has no power of decision, the truth is that both questions definitely need to be qualified. In fact, control of the committees permitted a very broad scope of action which even meant that agreements reached in congresses, and which could only be revised by other congresses, were not implemented.

Although I shall address these questions later, it is sufficient to indicate, for the moment, what occurred with the FNI and the new organic structure approved by the congress. The FNI, with very few exceptions, were not constituted, and the new organisation, consequently, was not established. The basis of this new structure was formed by factory and workshop committees, then came the professional sections, which were grouped together via branches in the industry unions, and which, in turn, constituted, on a national scale, the FNI. Each with its respective committee. Permanent representation of each FNI would be entrusted to a federal committee, and to the CNT in its assemblies and congresses. This union structure left the local and regional organisations practically devoid of content, the idea being to assign them other objectives, such as propaganda, schools for militants, population censuses, etc.[127]

However, as this structure did not actually materialise, its predecessor was maintained, on what was essentially a geographical basis. A circumstance that benefitted those whose strength resided in the sections and unions, as it was easier for them to project their influence in a local or regional sphere, than in a FNI. So, in the structures that endured, to the factory and workshop committees, the union sections and the single unions, one should add the neighbourhood committees, which kept the working masses grouped together in the big cities; above would be the local federation, which would unite the unions from one locality; the district federation, those from a "county", mainly in rural areas; the regional committee, which would assemble members of the local and district federations, and would be formed by members of the local federation of the city where it resided, to the tune of one delegate for each union in the locality; and the national committee, appointed, similarly, by the local federation where it was located, by decision of a national congress, with one delegate per union. The CNT could hold the following meetings: the local and district plenary session, formed by delegates from the local federation and the district federation, respectively; the regional plenary session, with the delegates from each local and district federation in the region; the regional congress, consisting of the delegates from each union in the region; the national plenary session (of regionals) formed by delegates from each regional committee; and the national congress, with delegates from each union in the country.

To complete the CNT organisation, it was necessary to add the prisoners' aid and confederal defence committees. Prisoners always formed a particularly respected group in libertarian organisations, not for nothing did their revolutionary struggle and long periods in hiding meant that many of their militants spent time in prison. So both the FAI conference and the CNT congress decided that prisoners should be integrated within both organisations.[128] The prisoners' aid committees took care of prisoners and their families while they were deprived of their freedom. With regard to the committees (also known as cadres) of confederal defence, they constituted a paramilitary organisation, a kind of shock force, formed in the main by anarchists. These defence committees were the successors of the action committees created in the confederal plenary session of 1928, formed by the CNT and the FAI. José Villaverde recalled, years later, that the defence cadres were created in a plenary sessions of regional committees held in Madrid in the same month of April 1931, shortly after the proclamation of the Republic. The Galician syndicalist, a member of the group that created these committees, indicated that their objective was twofold, on the one hand, "ensure the moral integrity of the Confederation", preventing the distortion of libertarian principles, and, on the other, form an "advance party of the revolution". But their birth was not free of controversy. For while the anarchists ("extremists" in Villaverde's words) sought to include among their characteristics the *trabazón*, most of the delegates present at the plenary session categorically refused, and agreed that the cadres would be composed of fellow members of the organisation who had earned the greatest trust from the committees – "no *trabazón*". In fact, that April plenary session agreed that preparation for the revolution should be carried out "only by the CNT", without prejudice to the FAI "preparing on its own account", with a relationship between both organisations, but "without mediatisation or *trabazón*". Ultimately, the defence committees would not have autonomy, but would be dependent on the responsible federal committees, in other words, they could not act "without the responsible committees giving, providing the entire organisation was in agreement, the corresponding authorisation".[129]

However, these agreements, like many others of those adopted in congress, were a cause of conflict in the future, and sometimes of reinterpretation. But these debates were not exclusive to the CNT, within the AIT the situation was very similar.

The International Workers' Association Congress

The AIT met from June 16–20, 1931 in Madrid, in other words, its sessions began just as the confederal conclave was drawing to a close. The delegations in attendance represented countries from Europe and America[130]. The official CNT representation was formed by Avelino González Entrialgo and Eusebio Carbó. Also present were Ángel Pestaña and Progreso Alfarache, from the CNT national committee, along with several regional CNT delegates, who attended in an informative capacity.

This new version of the AIT was founded in Berlin, in 1922, by the more libertarian unions that were not prepared to accept any kind of submission to the International Communist. The CNT had agreed, provisionally, to support the latter at the La Comedia Congress of 1919. But the information provided by Pestaña and Frenchman Gastón Leval on their return from the land of the soviets led the organisation to decide, at the Zaragoza conference of 1922, to withdraw its adhesion and formalise its membership of the AIT.[131]

Augustin Souchy, secretary of the AIT, reported on the state of the organisation, with the setback represented by the dissolution of the FORA (Argentine Regional Workers' Association), by the dictatorship of José Félix Uriburu, and the hope that accompanied the resurgence of the CNT. Indeed, the Confederation was the most important organisation among those present, as, compared with the more than 600,000 members represented at its last congress, the other delegations painted a very bleak picture: the Swedish SAC had 30,000 members, a long way from the 600,000 boasted by the reformist unions in their country; the Portuguese delegate claimed to represent, in spite of Salazar's dictatorship, some 15.000 members; the Dutch representative admitted that the socialists formed the majority in his country, though he pointed to the existence of a large antimilitarist movement; the delegates from Poland and Bulgaria admitted to the non-existence of unions, so requested the recognition of anarchist groups. Other delegations referred to the membership in their countries before the establishment of dictatorships, like the FORA, which had around 120,000 members, the Cuban organisation, with 2,500 and Uruguay's, with 3,500. In other words, when this congress was held, the IWA had fewer than 700,000 members, over 85% of whom belonged to the CNT.

Well, in spite of enjoying a situation that was the envy of the other delegations, the CNT representatives insisted on raising the same issues that had provoked a heated confrontation at the recently ended confederal congress, such as purported relations with politicians and petitions submitted to parliament. The confrontation between anarchists and anarcho-syndicalists was reproduced in the international organisation despite the efforts of a despairing Souchy, who asked participants not to speak of the past and issued repeated requests to address the agenda and end "those debates now". For their part, the CNT delegates, Avelino González Entrialgo and Eusebio Carbó, defended the CNT's actions and referred to the agreements adopted at the last congress. But the reproaches continued. The Argentine Martí insisted, again and again, on the relationship with politicians and with parliament. While Alexander Shapiro, from France, asked Martí, how the FORA which, in its own words, controlled the revolutionary movement "has collapsed so quickly"; going on to enquire if it were because instead of being a workers' movement of an anarchist inclination, it was an anarchist movement supported by the working classes. Meanwhile, Ángel Pestaña asked him, not without irony, whether the FORA was not now allying with the forces it had previously fought against in order to destroy Uriburu's dictatorship.

Thus the AIT congress turned into a replica of the CNT version. The confrontation between anarchists and anarcho-syndicalists was present during most of the debates, with particular focus on the organic structure that would empower the libertarian society of the future and assist in the formation of industrial federations. The French delegation of the General Confederation of Revolutionary Labour (CGTSR), led by the syndicalists Pierre Besnard and Lucien Huart, who were joined by the Spanish delegation, engaged in a bitter argument with Abad de Santillán, representative of the sections of South American countries belonging to the ACAT (*Asociación Continental Americana de Trabajadores* or Continental American Workers' Association) The origins of the confrontation were essentially ideological, but also partly practical depending on whether countries were industrialised or agricultural. Huart explained that the French confederation's programme – in tune with what the CNT had approved – maintained as ultimate objective the suppression of the state. While Besnard argued that the factory and workshop councils should be instruments for preparation of the unions in the factory, and referred to the industrial unions as fundamental elements both in the struggle against capital, and in the libertarian society of the future. In short, according to Antonio Elorza, Bernard advocated, contrary to the anarchist or destructive current, the constructive solution of anarcho-syndicalism, in similar fashion to Peiró and Pestaña, within the ideological foundations of revolutionary syndicalism. The union as central instrument of economic transformation with a threefold objective: defence of proletarian interests against capitalism, preparation of the economic cadres of the new social order and completion, after the initial insurrection, of the transformation that would facilitate the establishment of libertarian communism. The latter understood as a period of transition – in the image of the dictatorship of the proletariat in Marxism – and the final phase of which would be, following the successful transformation of man, anarchy. In this construction, the municipality, federatively structured, would be the political complement to the economic system built upon the union and the industrial federations. Unlike this approach, Abad de Santillán drew on fundamentally anarchist positions, to defend ruralism and improvisation. For the anarchists, Besnard's programme continued to be the syndicalist adaptation of what had occurred in Russia, since "it does not matter whether the state calls itself political or economic",[132] or, more adapted to the case in point, syndicalist.

The debate widened with the pronouncement on "the international class war", presented by Souchy, which raised the temperature at the congress. The report repeated the same arguments employed at the confederal congress vis-à-vis the need to articulate a response to the concentration of capital. The tactic should be "direct action on an international scale", for which it was fundamental to create the *Federaciones Internacionales de Industria* (FII or International Federations of Industry) The AIT could not accept the agreements with leaders proposed by the International Labour Organisation (ILO), because this was a procedure that remained within the "capitalist social order". Improvements for the working class should be the consequence of direct action or of "the revolutionary thrust of the proletariat". In essence, the international federations of industry should not only fight against capitalism, but prepare to produce, regulate and distribute materials all over the world.[133]

This approach triggered the same bitter debate generated by the national federations at the confederal congress. Abad de Santillán highlighted the fact that that in the AIT there were two underlying tendencies: the industrial and the agricultural, represented by the European and the American countries, respectively, each with its own issues. Santillán advocated an eminently rural revolution, as "industrialisation is not necessary, because we have lived without it for centuries". Besnard and Huart supported the endorsement of the federations of industry, including that of the agricultural workers.[134] The discussion culminated in a one-way street the only exit from which was division. But Souchy prevented this with a proposal that postponed voting on the report until a referendum were held in the member organisations, in other words, turning the page without an agreement in order to avoid a rift.

On another note, the congress accepted a pronouncement which argued that democracy eternalised capitalism, although it acknowledged that, compared with despotism or dictatorship, it offered the working class a series of rights and freedoms that facilitated the development of its organisations. The AIT also approved the reduction of the working day to six hours as a measure that would help to provide work for millions of unemployed people; it expressed its opposition to war, and urged the international proletariat to oppose the latter via direct action, general strikes and desertion from military service; it took a stand against "all nationalist theories and aspirations" because they distracted workers "from their true goals of freedom"; and, finally, voiced its opposition to the Church's cultural domination of society.[135]

Basically, the AIT congress constituted the second part of the confrontation between anarchists and anarcho-syndicalists within a movement that, in the international sphere, was very much in the minority. The resolutions adopted contributed nothing new to the movement; they expressed, to a large extent, the desire for a fairer world, without indicating which path to take, or proposing strategies as a means of attaining this new world. The only way, as was continually repeated, was direct action which, like a "friar's balsam", did everything: improve the life of the workers, conduct the workers' struggle on an international scale, against imperialism, war, etc.

The anarcho-syndicalists had emerged victorious from the CNT and AIT congresses. They succeeded in passing a number of resolutions that, without renouncing revolution, took advantage of the opportunities offered by democratic regimes to improve the living conditions of workers and peasants. The anarchists, meanwhile, who had been soundly defeated, understood that the time had come for a 360º revolutionary mobilisation of the working masses. Consequently, their activity in Spain should be focused on exploiting the social disenchantment that they hoped would bring about the advent of the Republic among the most underprivileged, as proved to be the case.

2

The Struggle for Power: From Syndicalism to Insurrection (July 1931–April 1932)

Strikes, Too Many Strikes!

The workers' increasing urge to recover lost ground, by presenting employers with their demands for improvements in economic and labour conditions, and the thorn in the anarchists' flesh represented by the negative result in the June congresses combined in an explosive mix that resulted in a growing number of grievances in confederal unions.

The FAI's calls to the anarchists to swell its ranks were constant, and coincided with the request to join the CNT and take control of its committees. Meanwhile, at the anarchist conference, prior to the confederal congress, the "Urales family" had defended the fact that the workers' unions did not admit any worker who did not depend on a bourgeois salary. However, the majority approved the affiliation of all those who lived from their work, in spite of which, they maintained that they would never join the CNT. Nevertheless, *El Luchador*, at the end of July, pointed out that many things had happened in barely a month, which led to a rectification, so Federica Montseny and his father, Federico Urales, had joined the CNT's *Sindicato de Obreros Intelectuales* (Intellectual Workers' Union) in Barcelona. The justification was that there was much "to do within the Confederation, particularly awareness". The problem was that more than creating awareness among workers, the objective was to penetrate the organisation in order to address the struggle for its control from within and follow a path that would disregard its trade union goals. From this moment onwards, the Urales family became a "Ghost Federation" that, if as such, did not exist, with the influence of its newspaper and occasional help from anarchist comrades, functioned as if it were real.[1] Within the family, Federica, near-sighted, but outspoken and sharp of pen – which earned her the nickname "the lioness" – employed a discourse directed more at the hearts than the heads of the vulnerable.

The anarchists knew how to exploit the workers' needs and encourage their mobilisation by means of union activity of an idiosyncratic nature. The CNT unions began by presenting labour rules to the corresponding employers. The fundamental tactic was direct action, understood as negotiation between workers and bosses without any kind of intervention by intermediaries unrelated to the main interested parties. If the conversations did not have the desired result, a path was taken that was repeated in many of the conflicts. The route comprised basic elements of anarcho-syndicalism, like striking, which was characterised by the continuous presence of workers in the street, the formation of a strike committee – which replaced the representation of the union councils – and discussion in assembly of progress in negotiations and possible agreements. Characteristics that differentiated them from the strikes called by the UGT, whose organic committees conducted the negotiations and reported to the *Casa del Pueblo*, where the workers met.[2] Furthermore, there was another question worthy of mention: the confederal unions did not have strike funds. The Catalonia CNT, at the Sans Congress, held in Barcelona in 1918, agreed to their suppression, a measure that was ratified at the La Comedia Confederal Congress the following year. Their absence was justified by the little money available to workers, although the basic reason was to increase revolutionary tension among the workers, because going on strike required a high degree of class-consciousness the cornerstone of which was solidarity.[3]

During the protests, it was possible to resort to other means of pressure, such as boycott, of both the end product of the factory on strike and of other articles necessary for production thereof; but also sabotage against premises or facilities to prevent the distribution of products. Another fundamental question was class solidarity between workers from different branches of production, since the slightest conflict in a factory, which triggered a partial strike, could result in the paralysation of a city or the calling of a general strike.

Thus, for example, the *Asociación Sindical de Albañiles* (Masons' Union) of Jerez de la Frontera protested against the Fierro Company, for refusing to comply with labour rules. As a consequence, a partial strike was declared which the Governor of Cádiz feared might develop into a general strike.[4] The *Sindicato de Obreros Tabaqueros* (Union of Tobacco Workers) declared a strike and a boycott against businesses owned by Manuel Reyes after the unfair dismissal of 11 colleagues and the refusal to respect the shifts established in the industry. People were encouraged to buy *Granulados* and *Virginia fuerte* brands of cigarettes made by the same union's collective, as "a duty of solidarity".[5] The workers in the port of Seville announced a "sit-down strike", refusing to remove the goods of a company on strike, making necessary the intervention of the "security and assault forces" for their removal.[6] The solidarity between workers from different branches was evident in conflicts like the Seville pit sawyers strike. The management declared a lockout against the pit sawyers, but the latter were not alone, as they were supported by the oil mill workers and metal decorators. The oil warehouses rejected any work that came from the employers involved in the dispute, while the metal decorators refused to seal the tins of oil inside those owners' wooden containers, so they could not move their goods. Meanwhile, the pit sawyers that worked in other companies contributed five pesetas a day from their wages to help the strikers.[7]All these forms of pressure based on strikes, solidarity, boycott and sabotage were very present in the multitude of conflicts that took place during the first months of the Republic.

The condemnation of the excessive number of strikes came from various sources. Republican newspapers, like *La Voz*, ran with dramatic headlines: "Strikes. Too many strikes", pointing out the problems that the CNT unions were causing the Republic.[8] *El Socialista* maintained a similar stance, though it noted that the CNT's objective was not the Republic, or even the bourgeoisie, it was simply the UGT and the PSOE, neither of which were forgiven the significant rise in their influence among the working classes.[9] In any case, it was too simple to lay all the blame for the conflict upon the CNT, when the causes of so much protest were far more complex and numerous.

The socialists repeatedly asked, in the same vein as the republican newspaper, why the CNT called so many strikes and why it had not encouraged conflict during the dictatorship.[10] The answer from the CNT ranks was always the same: "during the dictatorship, wages fell and the cost of living rose", so it was only natural that now "with more freedom, the workers should seek to recover what they then lost, without thinking of creating problems for the Republic". So they returned the question, and wondered whether it would not be normal now to raise salaries and lower food prices, unless for the workers there were no difference between monarchy and republic.[11] There were strikes because there were "pitiful wages" and because only this means of defence made employers see reason, "nobody coughs or goes on strike just for the hell of it".[12]

There is little or no doubt that wages were extremely low or that workers, in general, lived in poverty. Reports written by the French Ambassador to Spain, Jean Herbette, a sharp and well-informed observer, indicated that the high level of conflict was due to the extreme poverty in which were "submerged a multitude of workers", but also to the fact that republicans and socialists has failed to keep the promises they had made before the April 12 elections, regarding such sensitive issues as social security and measures against unemployment. A circumstance that had "contributed to the success of the (CNT) syndicalist propaganda and the proliferation of strikes".[13] Even in the socialist ranks there was admission that the high level of conflict was related to the difficult situation in which workers found themselves. Luis Araquistáin, deputy secretary for labour, said that the strikes were in part confrontation with the UGT, but were also a consequence of "the inadequacy of salaries, which were among the lowest in Europe, compared with the cost of living, which is one of the highest in the world".[14] "Hunger salaries", and much more so in the case of women, who, according to the *Sindicato de Artes Gráficas* (Graphic Arts Union), were paid "a paltry wage of three pesetas a day".[15] Which did not prevent Araquistáin himself from advocating the need for a law, which his department was preparing, against abusive recourse to strikes.[16]

In short, as I have already said, the workers raised the so-called moral and economic issues, fundamental in any negotiation and grounds for conflict. But they were not alone. Marta Bizcarrondo has noted that may of the strikes, as early as 1931, were in support of "compliance with social legislation".[17] A circumstance that involved both employers and the republican authorities. The socialists themselves condemned both situations. On the one hand, the provincial council of workers' societies of the UGT and the PSOE reported that in the province of Seville there were almost 50,000 farmers unemployed as result of the landowners' refusal to work the land, flouting the provisions set out in labour legislation[18]; while the bakers of La Coruña called for a strike "because of the bosses' refusal to respect the agreement".[19] On the other hand, a labour delegate, at the PSOE extraordinary congress, insisted that the republican authorities had to enforce the law, given the neglect evidenced by some mayors in the observance of agricultural laws.[20]

Added to these reasons behind the conflict were one or two more, like the problems arising from the crisis and the government's economic policies, not to mention the labour legislation passed by the Ministry of Labour. The crisis was more apparent where the situation was always complicated, like in the south. Azaña admitted that "the compulsory unemployment in Andalusia is extremely serious". All the mayors of the province of Jaen had travelled to Madrid to ask for money, and did not dare to return without some kind of solution. Azaña acknowledged "the need to spend two million a day, for three months, to prevent people from starving and avoid a popular uprising"; while the Minister of Communications, Martínez Barrio, envisaged the "danger of Andalusia going up in flames". The government prepared some "palliative measures", such as investment in public works, despite the fact that its economic guidelines advocated a budgetary adjustment, which meant reducing expenditure. Ultimately, Azaña feared that this sizeable investment would be no "more than a meagre handout", and that the money was being spent "uselessly".[21]

Meanwhile, labour legislation was always criticised by the CNT, but also by employers, who considered it to be partisan. Largo Caballero did not forget the fact that he was UGT secretary, and took advantage of his position and power in the ministry to favour the interests of the socialist trade union. The CNT was especially critical of the joint committees and mixed juries, since, as well as representing a direct attack on its principle of direct action, they provided a significant advantage to the UGT. It should not be forgotten that the socialists, apart from legislating, appointed the presidents of these committees from the ministry, if there were no consensus; positions that, as will be recalled, enjoyed decision-making power, of arbitration and conciliation.[22] Thus, the confederal press was filled with accusations of "social fascists" or "social traitors".[23] While *El Socialista* replaced direct action with "direct violence", declaring that "one syndicalist, one gun; two syndicalists, two guns".[24] The conflict between the UGT and the CNT was, according to Azaña, "one of the liveliest and most serious issues" with which the Republic had to deal.[25]

In spite of everything, Peiró noted that the CNT had not opposed all the republican legislation, but had accepted the laws on associations, public meetings and strikes. But what it could not be expected to do was tolerate a law that favoured "the slightest intention to restrict trade union freedom", because that was something the UGT would never accept. In any case, Peiró was very much a realist, and understood that compliance or not with the decisions of the joint committees and mixed juries depended more on the workers' needs than on confederal ideological stances, and recalled that there had been "a plethora of lawsuits and strikes resolved via the intervention of third parties". This constituted what he called "a fatal law that is morally drafted by a circumstantial determinism superior to all written laws: out of need and convenience".[26] A reality that was very present, and which the CNT attempted to redirect.

Thus, for example, the regional plenum of trade unions of Catalonia recognised the resolution of conflicts via third-party intervention, thereby defying the principles of direct action. The plenum passed a resolution that, in its half-heartedness, evidenced the complexity of the situation, admitting that any union that did not respect these principles could be overruled by the organisation".[27] In the same sense, the regional committee of Andalusia pointed to the participation of confederal unions in commissions created in local municipalities for the distribution of work. Their formation, it alleged, had been "biased and haphazard", favouring the UGT, a circumstance added to the regularly denounced participation of public authorities in labour matters. But the fatal law of need and convenience, as Peiró said, meant that "many CNT trade unions" were "participating in these commissions".[28]

Violence and Repression

The fact was that the resolution of these conflicts required an assortment of measures amongst which one could not rule out the use of violence as a means of breaking the "iron fist" of the owners. From July 1931 onwards, news items began to appear about the explosion of firecrackers during strikes in Catalonia,[29] while the Civil Guard was deployed at power stations in Huesca "to prevent sabotage".[30] This was not the first time that elements of the CNT had used violence in their pursuit of economic or labour improvements. The men of action, in the so-called age of "*pistolerismo*" (employers' use of hired guns to kill "troublesome" union leaders), around the 1920s, carried out actions of this nature which, as Pestaña acknowledged, prompted pay rises that management had refused to offer during negotiations. Anyway, anarcho-syndicalists like Salvador Seguí, Juan Peiró or Pestaña himself, opposed these actions, which they regarded as highly detrimental to the organisation, and advocated union practice without any violence.[31]

The anarchists of action took part, in parallel to that work-related violence, in actions that were closer to common crime than to the revolutionary struggle. Assaults, setting off firecrackers or acts of sabotage during a strike were mixed with robberies in companies or banks – "revolutionary expropriation" they called it – which not only benefitted the robber in question, but also, on more than one occasion, the CNT or its junior committees. The press noted the fact that every time a social issue was addressed in the courts, it coincided with a robbery, in other words, that the legal costs were paid with the proceeds of the robberies. For instance, when lawyers went to supervise the release of the members of the prisoners' aid committee arrested in the Tarrasa case, which coincided with the robbery at the Casa Juncosa, the commissioner of police told them "this time you will collect, the organisation has carried out a robbery to pay you".[32] Actions that were always difficult to prove, as in the case of Francisco Ascaso, who was arrested in Barcelona for armed bank robbery. The CNT militants protested on the grounds that the arrest was arbitrary, since Ascaso's colleagues maintained that he was engaged in a propaganda tour of the province of Gerona on the day of the crime.[33] On other occasions, the evidence submitted by the defence was even more surprising. Durruti was released on June 18 1931, as it proved impossible to charge him with the robbery at the Banco de Bilbao in Oviedo. The anarchist declared, after leaving prison, that he was innocent because "on the day of the robbery, he was in Paris preparing an assassination attempt on the former King of Spain".[34]

These "militants of action" were an example for many unqualified young migrants who journeyed to the big cities, like Barcelona or Bilbao, and who, irrevocably, were condemned to unemployment or to the hardest, most precarious and poorly paid jobs. It was they who filled the ranks of the anarchist groups and performed violent actions, the leading figures in strikes and the clashes on the street against the forces of law and order. Struggles in which, as Ramón J. Sender wrote in *Siete domingos 2*, "the unemployed are the vanguard".[35] Young members of the construction union, for example, where their radicalism dominated confederal meetings. Affiliated to anarchism, according to Horacio Martínez Prieto, "more on account of their inability to adapt to the regime than as a consequence of reflection and choice", and whose conduct culminated, on more than one occasion, in common robbery.[36]

In any case, the anarchists of action, who were their references, understood that it was not the time for individual actions, as in previous years, but for collective protests, hence their quest to take control of the union organisation. Durruti himself opposed the "measles of robberies", though he admitted that his group had

> engaged in that form of struggle in the past; but today, we consider that those times have been left behind, with the continuing progress of the CNT and the FAI. Over a million workers affiliated to the CNT, awaiting the right moment to perform 'the great collective expropriation' require of us, militants of that movement, behaviour suited to the needs of the struggle. Today there is no room for individualist actions, because only collective ones count, mass actions. Which is why what has been overtaken by the march of history cannot be maintained, because it is a counter-productive and outdated struggle.[37]

Some in Catalonia referred to these radicalised young people in pejorative fashion as Murcians, Andalusians or Extremadurans, and took advantage of their "foreignness" to differentiate between them and the "real Catalans", in factories and industry, more moderate, who sought to assert their trade union experience over the disproportionate impulsiveness of the former. These young radicals were identified, in a blatantly xenophobic manner, according to their place of origin, instead of relating their behaviour to lack of training and the need to occupy jobs that were poorly paid and, therefore, were over-exploited. Because the difference between radicals and moderates, violent and pacific, was not a question of provenance but something far more complex, in which ideology played a part, but also, in particular, life circumstances.

Francisco Isgleas, member of the local federation of Barcelona, wanted to speak in Catalan during a meeting, to prevent the so-called Catalan press from saying that the "revolutionary elements" were foreign and that it was they who were leading and implementing the revolution, to show that those who were fighting thus were "also Catalans, but not Catalans of the Statute, but Catalans of Freedom".[38] In similar vein, Federica Montseny was fiercely critical of the Catalan nationalists that numbed "the caring and welcoming instinct of the Catalan people"; of those who differentiated between "local anarchism, 'de casa nostra', and foreign anarchism, that of the Andalusians and Murcians". Those who drew a distinction between "good old platonic, amateur, harmless and romantic anarchism", and that "of today, anarchism of rebellion, of blood, of extermination, proletarian and malodorous. Murcian, Andalusian, Levantine anarchism, of emigration and rudimentary ambition. The anarchism that had brought the '*forasters*' (those from other parts of Spain) to Catalonia, cursed and reprehensible like the Jews of Germany and the '*étrangers de merde*' – Catalans included – in gentle France". Catalan MPs in the regional government who did not dare to "eject from Catalonia all the '*forasters*' that have come to work, 'to steal the bread from the mouths of the Catalans'". Catalan nationalists who also served the "the interests of those who, needing to detach and divide the proletariat, undertake in Castile, in the Basque Country, in Galicia, nationalist activities that were also anti-Catalan and reactionary". Because what they sought, ultimately, was "to isolate the workers, to leave them alone and unprotected by that union that brings strength against predatory capitalism, the butcher state, equally butcherly and predatory in Catalonia and Castile, Italy and France, Germany and Russia, all over the world".[39]

The debate in the CNT was not over provenance. Work-related violence was disapproved of, whoever was responsible, by a considerable number of anarcho-syndicalists who distanced themselves again, as in the past, from the anarchists of action. Peiró, editor of *Solidaridad Obrera*, entitled an editorial "Bombs, no!", in response to the information published by *La Tribuna* about a device that had exploded in the Paseo de Gracia de Barcelona, which was attributed to the striking Telefónica (Spanish national telephone company) workers. Peiró indicated that these actions had nothing to do with the CNT or the unions, as they retained their working-class dignity through the only acceptable means: the strike.[40]

Indeed, the Telefónica strike, which began in early July 1931, is an example of the protests and tactics employed by the CNT in more than one conflict, but also of the complicated balancing act that faced the Republic. Indalecio Prieto, Treasury Minister, had promised, prior to the advent of the new regime, that he would revoke the agreement, supposedly fraudulent, signed by the dictatorship of Primo de Rivera with the American company ITT, and return the ownership of Telefónica to the Spanish state. But the provisional government felt that it was not the moment to enter into conflict with other countries over foreign companies operating in Spain. It is worth recalling that Western democracies had received the Republic with scepticism, or even opposition. The Bolshevik revolution was fresh in their memories, and they were afraid that Spain might become a new Russia. In fact, their ambassadors met with Spanish ministers to discuss their companies' investments in the country. Azaña himself recalled in his memoirs how the Belgian Ambassador asked him for "protection for the Solvay factories in Suira". So the government sought to win foreign confidence by guaranteeing the security of foreign assets and acting with a firm hand in the case of strikes and demonstrations.[41] The Minister of the Interior himself, Miguel Maura,, was delighted, according to Azaña, because he was going "to shell to bits an empty old house" – Casa Cornelio, meeting place for Seville's communists – which, he argued, would have a "favourable influence upon the value of the Peseta". Azaña, with his usual irony, said he applauded Maura's idea, but the latter insisted that "as soon as people know that the Republic bombards its adversaries, the impact abroad will be very positive indeed". So, Maura bombarded Casa Cornelio, "a warehouse filled with ham, cold meats and canned food warehouse", and, as Azaña said, "is perfectly happy". All of this struck the president as ridiculous but, when Maura advised him of his intentions, he commented: "I shrug my shoulders and we speak of other matters".[42]

Apart from Prieto's broken promises and the American ownership of Telefónica, the company's workers, the vast majority members of the National Telephone Union, created in 1918 and affiliated to the CNT – around 6,200 out of 7,000 workers – presented labour rules in which they requested, among other things, recognition of the union, the readmission of those sacked during the strike of 1917, pay rises and sickness and maternity benefits. In the company, as well as this union, was the *Organización Telefónica Obrera*, of the UGT, and two others classified as yellow. The CNT went on strike while the other organisations opted not to. The company took advantage of this fragmentation to negotiate with the other unions, excluding the Confederation. From that moment onwards, there was a series of confrontations between those who continued working and the strikers, along with boycotts and sabotage. The subsequent repression resulted in a death in Seville and numerous arrests all over Spain. There were repeated demonstrations of solidarity, and other unions contributed "a day's wages", to help the workers and so that the "strikers' children did not go hungry".[43] But the multitude of fronts open during the protests – government, the Company, other unions, the workers themselves – were too many for the CNT, which eventually lost the strike.

The Republican-Socialist government was very worried, needless to say, about the strikes that were spreading across Spain. Azaña recalled in his diary how the government wanted to "find an urgent and tough remedy" for the situation. Two ministers stood out in this respect, Miguel Maura and Largo

Caballero. Although, according to Azaña, the latter was the more radical of the two. While the Minister of the Interior proposed legislating "to combat employers and workers" who infringed social laws, the Minister of Labour aimed to go further, and include the presentation of a decree "regarding the illegality of strikes". What all the members of the government agreed upon was that "the time has come to adopt a combative and energetic policy against the Confederation". Maura, who was in charge of implementing these initiatives, believed that with a new law it would be possible to "close most (or all) of the syndicalist centres".[44] The ensuing months saw the adoption of the law of the Defence of the Republic, which anarchism christened the "Maura–Largo law", and which they considered to be a law against the CNT.[45]

The Republic opted for the path of confrontation with the CNT, when consolidation of the new regime required a pact. Because if the socialists wanted to change things in Spain, it was necessary to reach agreements with the union that represented practically half of the workers" movement. Aspiring to social change with the opposition not only of employers, but also the other great organisation of masses, was practically impossible. However, the Republican-Socialist government passed labour legislation that the CNT found very difficult to accept, which was to the benefit of the UGT, but to the detriment of the consolidation of the new regime and the attainment of improvements in working conditions. Agreement would have been possible bearing in mind that, during the first months of the Republic, the confederal leadership was in the hands of anarcho-syndicalists like Peiró or Pestaña, who were prepared to exploit the possibilities of the democratic regime. But not only was labour legislation adopted that was divisive, for in addition the repression exercised by the government facilitated the FAI discourse aimed at stirring up the workers in its double strategy: insurrection against the Republic and discredit of the anarcho-syndicalists to oust them from the confederal leadership.

In fact, while the Telefónica strike was in its early days and the council of ministers was addressing the problem of the strikes and the subsequent repressive laws, Azaña noted in his diary, on the same day that he described the shelling of the Casa Cornelio, the "strange death of four gunmen in Seville, who were being taken to prison", to conclude by saying that this had "the appearance of an application of the law of flight". Azaña described as "gunmen" those who, in subsequent pages, appeared as syndicalists, in other words, members of the CNT. The following morning, a captain of the Civil Guard was murdered.[46]

The situation in the Andalusian capital was extremely unstable. The CNT unions had called an indefinite general strike in the province, starting on June 21, with the aim of prompting the dismissal of the governor and the imprisonment of the policeman who had killed a worker during some protests in defence of work-related grievances. In the ensuing clashes with the Civil Guard, two more workers died and around 30 were wounded.[47] In Seville, a very aggressive group of employers had established themselves,[48] which, combined with the presence of authorities with links to the wealthy classes and the increasing influence of the anarchists within the confederal union, made the Andalusian city a hotspot of violence and conflict. In fact, the Regional Government had handed over control to General Leopoldo Ruiz Trillo, who declared a state of war throughout the province of Seville, with the accompanying declaration of the illegality of the CNT.[49] Martínez Barrio himself, Minister of Communication, attributed to the governor "the crime of having thrown himself into the arms of the aristocrats and masters of Seville, just like the general, and to these masters' suggestions (attributed) the nonsense of the bombardment (of Casa Cornelio), in order to ridicule the Republic".[50]

Parliament formed a Commission, headed by MP Antonio Jaen, which travelled to Seville to investigate the death of the four syndicalists in the Parque María Luisa of Seville, in supposed application of the law of flight. Meanwhile, Azaña noted in his diary the investigations undertaken by his minister, the Sevillian Martínez Barrio, and developed them with those of Luis Fernández Clérigo, member of the parliamentary commission. In short, the security forces had arrested dozens of syndicalists who were being transferred by truck to another prison. At night the transfers were suspended, and resumed the following morning, at the unearthly hour of 4 a.m. A circumstance that was the source of considerable alarm among the prisoners. The four syndicalists arrested were in a van being followed by two cars. In the convoy were members of the civic guard and the Civil Guard, under the command of Captain Criado, whose nickname was "*criadillas*" (testicles). When they reached the Plaza de España, the van suffered a puncture or, as Martínez Barrio said, they said there had been a puncture. At that moment, instead of being transferred to the other cars, the prisoners were made to continue on foot without handcuffs. After twenty steps or so, gunshots rang out somewhere behind the prisoners, who, already very nervous, started to run, at which point the escort opened fire, and, according to Fernández Clérigo, they were "riddled with bullets".[51]

The socialists cleared the government of any responsibility, which was attributed to "monarchist sympathisers unconnected to the authorities". They also claimed that the parliamentary commission created in order to clarify events had discovered allegedly responsible parties, and urged the public prosecutor to take action,[52] However, as Ballbé has indicated, nothing happened beyond the dismissal of the governor, Sr. Bastos. There was no trial in relation to these incidents, as neither the public prosecutor, Ángel Galarza, nor any other ordinary court of justice undertook any actions.[53]

All these actions had a significant impact upon the CNT. *Solidaridad Obrera* pointed to Maura and Largo Caballero as primarily responsible for "the Seville massacre".[54] While *El Luchador* took advantage of this incident to harass the CNT national committee. Federica Montseny criticised the alleged inactivity of the confederal leadership, and lamented the absence "of someone with the drive and energy of Bakunin", to "respond to dictatorship with revolution".[55] This attack on the confederal leaders and the call to revolution was not an isolated incident. At the meeting of the Construction Union of Barcelona, attended by around 2,000 people, according to a police report, several members claimed that the national committee "had an understanding with the politicians" and had agreed to the adoption of the Statute of Catalonia, and condemned "Pestaña's actions in Seville" and concluded by demanding the immediate implementation of the revolution.[56] Meanwhile, anarchists José Alberola and Progreso Fernández, members of the propaganda commission of the FAI, declared in a meeting that the CNT had suffered "a deviation" that was evidenced by "the events of Seville". They demanded, without further ado, the expulsion of the anarcho-syndicalists from the committees.[57]

The fact is that the month of August was fundamental in the FAI offensive. At the regional plenum of trade unions of Catalonia, various delegations criticised the national committee for its alleged indifference in the face of the repression suffered and its lack of action when "the people await the revolution". Criticism that was extended to Juan Peiró, in his role as editor of *Solidaridad Obrera*. The industrial delegates from Barcelona – García Oliver, Durruti and Prades – proposed the inclusion in the agenda of the "alignment of *Solidaridad*". This was no insignificant matter because, bearing in mind that the delegates were, in theory, mere transmitters of decisions taken by the components of each union, the inclusion of a new point to be discussed in the plenum involved a significant modification in decision-making. The Catalan organisation faced a decision that was not in the hands of the union members, but depended on the personal opinion of the delegates, which meant there was no guarantee that the decision adopted represented the majority in the organisation.

But the industrial delegates insisted on its inclusion, while they accused Peiró of having "betrayed CNT principles and agreements", and even held him partly responsible for the events in Andalusia. Peiró's reaction forced his accusers to rectify to a certain extent, although they continued to demand a change in the newspaper's editorial line. A line that also revealed the division that existed, since while Sebastián Clará and Agustín Gibanel expressed their alignment with Peiró, Cano Ruiz requested that the paper exercise a more "libertarian spirit". The plenum postponed any decision in this respect, most probably due to the lack of discussion thereof within the unions. Which did not prevent the anarchists from once again criticizing the national and regional committees of Catalonia, requesting the resignation of both. The plenum rejected the proposal "by acclamation". There followed as new vote on the national committee's management, with 36 votes in favour of the committee, six against and 40 abstentions. Most of the latter were due to the lack of prior agreement in the unions.[58] The plenum had shown that the anarcho-syndicalists continued to be a majority in Catalonia, albeit an increasingly unstable one; and that the anarchist opposition was stubborn and prepared to go to any lengths in order to attain its objectives.

In this confrontation, it should not be forgotten that the national committee resided in Barcelona, and that the political situation in Catalonia, with the adoption of the statute, was an endless source of awkward situations for the anarcho-syndicalist leaders. Relations between *Esquerra Republicana de Catalunya* and the CNT were excellent. The majority of CNT workers had voted for *Esquerra*, while the latter was close to the anarcho-syndicalist union, which it regarded as fundamental for the maintenance of order in Catalonia.[59] Moreover, its leader, Francesc Macià, enjoyed a good reputation in libertarian media, both with anarchists like Federico Urales, and anarcho-syndicalists like Juan López, who had no hesitation in describing him as "an honourable man who inspires our respect".[60] So declarations like Macià's, in *El Diluvio*, in which he said that the CNT had not declared a general strike, after the events of Seville, "in order not to prejudice the Statute of Catalonia", and his defence of the Confederation against disruptive elements, in clear allusion to the FAI, upset and played into the hands of the latter. But it was not only a question of declarations. Relations between anarcho-syndicalist leaders and Catalan political leaders were sometimes so close that they aroused all kinds of suspicion. At the trade union plenum, at the beginning of August, Cano Ruiz criticised a dinner between Clará and Companys, at which the former was offered public office. Clará acknowledged that the meeting had taken place but denied "the existence of the position in the civil government".[61] It would not be the last time that an anarcho-syndicalist with responsibilities in the CNT was accused of "selling himself" in exchange for a position in the administration. Accusations that were never proven but which, in the context of personal encounters and clear political interest, appeared to have some substance and weakened the position of those who controlled the confederal committees.

Anarchists and anarcho-syndicalists were aware of the importance of the press in order to interpret this reality. Hence the former's criticism of Peiró and the editorial staff of the *Solidaridad Obrera* for attempting to take control of the newspaper; and the reaction of the latter who, in Gibanel's words, noted that "it was not in the newspapers, but in plenums and congresses where workers' collective policies should be established".[62] But these plenums and congresses had been, to date, places of defeat for the anarchists. So it was necessary to address the struggle in confederal terms, in other words, in the trade union. Where the justifiable grievances met with the "comprehension" of the more radical elements, whose interventions, amidst an intense atmosphere, were hard to answer. It came as no surprise, therefore, that protests were approved independently of the most basic rules on confederal action. At the August regional plenum of unions of Cataluña, described above, the farmers of Amposta criticised the excessive number of strikes called by the unions without consulting the committees. In fact, the number of strikes in Cataluña during 1931 shot up to 391, while the following year it decreased to 245.[63]

The national committee itself observed, in one of its circulars, that "the unions provoke excessive conflicts, giving rise to the fact that many of these, lacking vital moral and material support, are lost". The committee was of the opinion that the situation was related to abuse of "trade union autonomy". Autonomy that was viewed as positive, provided the Confederation itself was not put at risk, as was happening. So it proposed that when a union negotiated labour rules with employers, it should previously present them before the local federation or, failing this, before the local single union; organisms that would indicate the correct moment to present these bases. While the local, county or regional federations would be responsible for authorising or disallowing, when applicable, the conflict. Any union that acted independently of the decisions taken by these federations and called a strike, could do so, but would not by right enjoy the support of the other unions, although they could volunteer their support if they chose to.[64]

Ultimately, the national committee wanted to put an end to the actions of many unions, which provoked conflicts that were eventually lost due to lack of preparation. The consequences were very negative for both the workers, whose expectations were frustrated, and for the Confederation, as the accompanying repression led to the arrest of militants and the destructuring of the organisation. A reality that concealed the underlying internal problem, which was none other than the fact that the unions had become the scenario of confrontation between the dominant movements within the CNT.

Treintismo

In this context of power struggle within the CNT, thirty confederal militants published a manifesto, on 30 August 1931, with which they sought to put an end to anarchist activities in the unions and clarify a position they had been defending since prior to the advent of the Republic. Pestaña had already published a manifesto a year earlier – in August 1930 – in the name of a group of syndicalists defending the actions of the masses organised by means of a constructive, coherent, ordered syndicalism, as opposed to a destructive anarchism, situated outside social coexistence, which cursed and criticised injustice, but, as a result of its actions, could "find itself reduced to being a doctrine for misfits".[65] A group of CNT militants met at the headquarters of the Transport Union and agreed to publish a document that would address the actions of the CNT in current circumstances. After several meetings, the definitive document declared that Spain was immersed in an "intense revolutionary tendency". A reality that was not unrelated to the economic crisis provoked by the bourgeoisie and materialised in the impoverishment of the country. Meanwhile, the government proceeded in a manner that was "excessively legalist", with a leniency that was only disregarded in the repression of the workers. In these circumstances, the only possible solution, in their opinion, was revolution. Although the fundamental question was how to proceed. Until now, revolutions had been undertaken by "brave minorities" that propelled "the people against the constituted powers", and who entrusted victory to the courage of a few individuals, supported by the masses on the streets. But thinking that it was possible to "defeat a colossus", like the state, without any preparation, simply by taking to the street, was "to waste time, forget history and ignore human psychology itself". This idea, they continued, was "the daughter of the purest demagogy". Against this approach "simplistic, classical, rather Hollywoodesque", another emerged that did not entrust the revolution to the audacity of minorities, but wanted it to be "an overwhelming movement of the people en masse". So rather than the "chaotic and incoherent concept", which basically involved "mutiny, revolt", their revolutionary project was "ordered, forward looking and coherent". The signatories reaffirmed their revolutionary position, but via "a revolution born of a profound sense of the people", not of just a few. Because the CNT was a revolutionary organisation, and did not follow "the cult of violence for the sake of violence, revolution for revolution's sake". Ultimately, the Confederation should follow its own path, and decide for itself "how, when and under what circumstances to act". The document concluded by stating that this stance would be maintained "always and everywhere, even if maintaining it we are steamrolled by the contrary opinion".[66] Prescient words that revealed the uncertainty that was beginning to take hold of those in control of the organisation's committees.

The document contributed nothing new to the basic position defended by the anarcho-syndicalists in recent times, in other words, the independence of the CNT in order to decide its future and achieve the revolution when the workers were sufficiently prepared. But the adjectives used to discredit the actions of the anarchists, like demagogic, simplistic, Hollywoodesque, affected their principal leaders. Durruti made some declarations to the French newspaper Le *Temps* stating that he felt particularly targeted by the *Treintista* manifesto, while he accused the signatories of wanting to eradicate extremist militants from the organisation.[67] He also published an article in *La Nau* in which he described the document as a personal attack on García Oliver and himself. The manifesto, he claimed, confirmed the two positions that had existed in the CNT for some time and which, at that moment, were especially evident. But far from responding to the essence of the manifesto, in other words, its approach to the revolution, he returned to the discourse repeatedly heard from the ranks of the FAI, with government repression, specifically, of workers in Seville, and to the apoliticism of the anarchists in contrast to the *treintistas'* collusion with politicians. With particular reference to Pestaña and Peiró, whom he accused of having "made moral commitments that hindered their libertarian activities".[68]

The anarcho-syndicalists could not have chosen a worse moment to publish the document: on the one hand, on that same day, 30 August, there were "bloody incidents" in Zaragoza during the Telefónica strike;[69] on the other, the *presos gubernativos* (those imprisoned without trial) in the Modelo prison in Barcelona announced a hunger strike and the shutdown spread across the city. In relation to the Telefónica strike, the police action included arrests and searches that, by all accounts, were not legal. On the night of August 30, according to the police chief inspector's report, the civil governor ordered the arrest of the leading strikers in order that they might be replaced by technicians sent from Madrid. The inspector requested the order in writing and the corresponding legal warrants in order to proceed with the arrests. The governor and the court prosecutor replied that these were not necessary, as there was not yet a constitution that guaranteed the individual rights of citizens and that "with the riotous elements operating outside the law, it was not the time to mess around with legal scruples". With this guarantee, and encouraged by the Governor's urging, the inspector organised the arrest of "20 or 22 of those named in the list in question", as well as other CNT leaders. The police chief acknowledged that, lest his loyalty be questioned, he had to "act if not with severity, at least with energy".

The next day, there was a violent clash between the strikers and the Civil Guard, when the latter was protecting the strike-breakers from Madrid who were repairing the damage caused by the acts of sabotage during the strike. In response, the CNT called a general strike in Zaragoza. On Tuesday, the first of September, telephone lines were destroyed, barricades set up and there was a gunfight with the security forces. The governor decided to close down the confederal unions, while the police entered their premises looking for "weapons or documentary evidence of preparation of the revolutionary movement". During the searches, according to the inspector himself, locked cupboards and drawers were forced open. When the governor allowed the offices to re-open a few days later, the CNT reported the damage. Although the inspector enquired as to whether the damage could have been caused by the unions themselves in order to accuse the police, he admitted that he could not deny that out of "love for the city of Zaragoza" and as a "good patriot" he had acted "excitedly and caused some damage".[70]

More serious though was the situation in Barcelona resulting from the strike called by the prisoners in the Modelo. The imprisonment of civilians, whether on political or social grounds, was interpreted in the libertarian world as yet another iniquity of the system. The injustice was regarded as even more flagrant if these prisoners were *gubernativos*, in other words, people who had been arrested and imprisoned without being accused of any crime, to be released days or even months later without trial. The disruption – not only moral, but in particular economic – for those arrested and their families was enormous, as not working meant being left without money. In a society that did not provide help for the unemployed or subsidies for people with economic problems, this situation meant poverty for entire families. The CNT had hundreds of *presos gubernativos* in Spain, workers that had taken part in strikes, rallies or demonstrations and who had been imprisoned without being involved in any trial. The confederal organisation had a pro-prisoners committee that attended to those under arrest, legally and economically, via the economic contribution of part of the subscription paid by unionised workers; in addition, collections were made at meetings and assemblies to help prisoners and their families. Another way of helping those under arrest was the pressure exerted by the Confederation, through protests, rallies and complaints aimed at securing their release.

In the Modelo prison in Barcelona there were, at that time, 53 social prisoners, arrested, "most of them *gubernativos*". On Sunday 31 August, a hunger strike began in protest at their situation and demanding the presence of judges to inform them of ongoing legal proceedings, if there were any.[71] What began as a hunger strike became, with the support of the other prisoners, a mutiny. The surveillance centre was bombarded with "stools, pitchers, bottles, bricks (...) Doors were ripped out and piled up (...) Everything began to burn". The libertarian press laid the blamed on the civil governor, Anguera de Sojo, owing to his intransigent response to the prisoners' requests and the mistreatment to which they were subjected. The riot police entered the prison and suppressed the mutiny. The CNT called a general strike in support of the prisoners, which led to armed confrontation with the security forces. The clashes were particularly violent in the Construction Union, in Calle Mercaders, where there was a heavy exchange of fire. Although the most serious incident occurred at the entrance to the police station, where three workers were shot dead by the agents who were guarding them, an episode that suggested another application of the law of flight. According to *Solidaridad Obrera*, the prisoners had been searched twice, so it was impossible for them to have been armed. But the guards shot them in the belief, according to the confederal newspaper, that they had come from Calle Mercaders, in other words, from the Construction Union, when in fact they had been arrested in Calle Tapinerías, so everything pointed to an act of vengeance. The result of the repression was, according to the workers' press, 15 strikers killed and 6 seriously wounded, while around 300 were arrested.[72]

There was another facet to all this repression that evidences the lack of political intelligence in its application. Antonio Elorza has reproduced the conversations between the Civil Governor, Anguera de Sojo, and the Minister of Interior, Miguel Maura, during the strike. While the local federation of trade unions of Barcelona wanted to negotiate a return to work with the Governor, the latter refused to speak with them. Macià attempted to mediate in the conflict, but Anguera, in conversation with Maura, indicated that he would only consult the army general, the Civil Guard general and the head of police. In the end, Anguera suspended *Solidaridad Obrera* and maintained the repression.[73]

It should not be forgotten that *Solidaridad* was in the hands of the anarcho-syndicalists, with Peiró the editor and a sizeable number of *treintistas* on the staff, whose support of cohabitation with the new regime could serve the interests of both the Republic and the Confederation. So the newspaper's stance should have led the authorities to reconsider with regard to the degree and direction of the repression. Because *Solidaridad Obrera* published the declarations of the head of police, Menéndez, who claimed that the guards had not shot the prisoners in the back. The paper acknowledged that it could not confirm the application of the law of flight. But in addition to this act of equanimity, it also stood up for the police chief, saying that

> we have known Señor Menéndez since before he was head of police, as we were acquainted with him when he was just a soldier conspiring against the Monarchy; and because we know him and because we are incapable of tainting a proven truth, we have no reservations about declaring that the Barcelona head of police is incapable of authorising the infamy that is represented by the application of the law of flight.[74]

Which was not an impediment to demanding that the inspector provide a report on the incident since, he claimed, he had not been present at the time, and everything pointed to the application of that sinister law. The fact is that it took a lot of courage to sign an editorial of this nature at a time when several colleagues had fallen and many others were under arrest. Indeed, the editorial team found themselves between a rock and a hard place, "on the one hand, the threat of suspension (...) on the other, the unspeakable assumption that we are playing into the enemy's hands".[75]

Pressure that the leadership could not withstand. Juan Peiró and the members of the editorial team – Sebastián Clará, Ricardo Fornells, Agustín Gibanel and Ramón Magre – tendered their resignation on 22 September, while Felipe Alaiz and Cano Ruiz of the FAI remained in their posts. The crisis was resolved at the regional union plenum held from 11 October onwards, where Alaiz was appointed editor of *Solidaridad*, with a new editorial team of FAI sympathisers, with Cano Ruiz, Liberto Callejas, Eröfilo Labrador, Eusebio C. Carbó, Germinal Esgleas, José Alberola and Evelio G. Fontaura.[76] The *treintistas*, meanwhile, brought out, in November of that year, *Cultura Libertaria*, under the leadership of Agustín Gibanel. The new weekly was the mouthpiece for his ideas, but also the place for criticism of FAI activity.

The FAI obtained its first significant victory, *Solidaridad Obrera*, a crucial element in its strategy of removing the anarcho-syndicalists from confederal power. This new situation impacted upon the editorial line, with a considerable increase in ideological orthodoxy and the revolutionary atmosphere. The French ambassador, Herbette, noted how the confederal newspaper had become an anarchist daily that launched attacks "against everyone and everything", which had seen its circulation fall by around 7,000 copies since Peiró's departure.[77] However, the new editorial team boasted that the bourgeoisie newspapers did not copy its articles; evidence, it appeared, of the alleged collusion between anarcho-syndicalists and political power.[78]

Caught in the Crossfire

The government sought to shield the new regime by means of the adoption, on October 21, of the law of Defence of the Republic. The latter, in essence, specified, in its first article, those acts that were considered to be aggression against the Republic: resistance against and disobedience of laws, violence against people or things, justification of the monarchic regime, illegal possession of weapons... Of these, two were particularly controversial: the diffusion of news that could "upset the peace or public order", without specifying whether the news be true or false; and "strikes not declared with 8 days' notice (and) those declared for reasons unrelated to conditions of arbitration on reconciliation", a direct reference to those called by the CNT. In fact, someone as reputable as Santiago Alba, minister under Alfonso XIII, criticised the law for being "infinitely harder, more closed, more restrictive" than Canalejas's draft law on strikes, which "gave rise to enormous and very painful complications".[79]

The second article made it possible for the government to detain, banish from their hometown or fine the authors of these acts. While the third article enabled the Ministry of Governance to suspend meetings or demonstrations when "the circumstances surrounding their calling suggested that their materialisation might disturb the peace"; and to shut down centres or associations that "are considered to incite" acts of resistance or disobedience. Arbitrary questions that were not subject to judicial proceedings. It also made it easier for the authorities to intervene and investigate organisations' accounts, which alerted the confederal unions to the possibility of their lists of members being used by the police during acts of repression.

In general, the law represented the suspension of individual guarantees, which could freely be decided by the government. In fact, it was not easy to accommodate it within the constitution, so it was necessary to include a Transitional Provision to render it compatible with the latter, to maintain its validity during the life of parliament at the time, if it was not revoked previously. Indeed, its suppression occurred as a consequence of the promulgation of the law on Public Order, in August 1933. In any case, the law of the Defence of the Republic was adopted in parliament with barely any opposition.[80]

We should ask ourselves whether, in truth, the Republic was in such danger during those first months of its life that it was necessary to create a law of this nature. Because the main source of concern for the government were the strikes, and in this respect, these protests, though numerous, did not represent a great threat; moreover, they could be regarded as logical in a society that, having recently emerged from a dictatorship, was finally enjoying the democratic rights and freedoms for so long denied it. Neither does it seem the case that the actions undertaken by those nostalgic for the old regime were, for the moment, so insignificant. In the autumn of 1931, the main source of instability may have been the movements of the military in its barracks, if we heed Azaña's comments in his diary. Among other reasons, because only the military had the weapons and organisation required in order to subvert public order. But these were movements to which the republican leader attached little importance. The fact is that the new law was applied, in the main, to suspend newspapers, shut down political and union premises and carry out a substantial number of imprisonments without trial, and deportations, with a particular focus on radicals of any orientation. This is apparent from the telegrams from the Ministry of Governance to the civil governors, requesting information about the "most extremist and dangerous individuals in that province" in order to apply to them the law of the Defence of the Republic, without reference to any crime whatsoever being committed.[81]

Many compared the new law with Antonio Maura's anti-terrorist legislation, at the beginning of the century – specifically, the 1908 draft law of the Repression of Terrorism – opposed by the socialists. There was definite similarity. The 1908 law sought to punish the publication of deliberately fake or unofficial news, suppress newspapers and meeting places and force people suspected of participating in propaganda or terrorist plans, despite having done nothing that justified the involvement of the courts, to reside outside the country. The law met with enormous opposition, from liberals to anarchists, including republicans, Catalan nationalists and socialists. Its adoption was seen as a direct attack on freedom of expression, and the government was accused of assuming competences that belonged to other powers of the state. Socialist leader Pablo Iglesias believed that its implementation could be exploited to dismantle workers' organisations. Which was why he declared that its application meant the expulsion of the socialists from legality, and threatened to turn to terrorism. The project's coup de grace was delivered by the Madrid Committee for Defence of the Press, which was supported by 160 newspapers from all over Spain. This pressure rendered impossible the adoption of the project.[82]

However, in 1931, *El Socialista* ignored the law's impact upon the press, the mobilisation of workers and farmers or the strikes fomented by the CNT, to place the accent on its application against the extreme right and underplay its exceptional nature by describing it as "a simple provision of minor policing".[83] However, some telegrams between the Ministry of Governance and the civil governors of the provinces led to the possibility of a very different application. At the prospect of the lifting of the suspension of the press prior to the application of the law, Santiago Casares Quiroga – who in mid-October had replaced Miguel Maura at the head of the Ministry of Governance – did not conceal from the Governor of Barcelona the fact that "it would be counter-productive to suspend *Solidaridad Obrera* at the same time as the reappearance of the right-wing newspapers".[84] The Civil Governor of Cádiz requested the minister's permission to threaten farm labourers with the application of the law on the defence of the Republic if they refused to work the lands, as there were sufficient cases to make "serious conflict possible", a request that Casares denied. The Civil Governor of Vitoria wanted to apply it in view of the Single Metallurgy Union's refusal to accept the authority's mediation in a labour conflict, or when the Construction Union called a strike in the same locality, as he regarded this as illegal, and although "so far it is developing peacefully", he asked for authorisation to shut down the unions.[85] In other words, the application of the law depended, largely, on the people occupying positions of authority. In fact, the socialists feared that a future government led by Alejandro Lerroux, leader of Radical Party, could use it against them.[86]

For the time being, the repression was hitting the CNT hard. The national committee sent a letter to Azaña protesting at the arbitrary actions and injustice that, in its opinion, were committed by the authorities against the confederal union. The committee referred, mainly, to the civil governors of Andalusia and Catalonia, where repression had reached "inconceivable extremes". He was reminded of the events of the Parque María Luisa in Seville and the police headquarters in Barcelona, the closure of unions in both provinces and the continuous suspension of rallies, actions that, in practice, left "the Confederation outside the law".[87]

In these circumstances, the number of libertarian prisoners increased steadily. The special sensitivity about them, and the considerable presence of anarchists within their ranks, made them a key factor in internal struggles. At its plenum, the FAI raised the need to be represented in the pro-prisoner committees for two main reasons: the first, because there could be comrades in prison who did not belong to the CNT, in which case they were abandoned; and the second, because the syndicalists did not help anyone who was detained "committing an assault, expropriation or any other similar revolutionary act", that they considered to be violent.[88] However, beyond these significant considerations, the FAI's presence on these committees constituted an important asset for the anarchists in CNT decision-making, as they wanted the national pro-prisoners committee to be present at the confederal plenums. The anarcho-syndicalists, still forming a majority in the organisation, were not prepared to leave such an asset in the hands of the FAI. So the CNT national plenum, held just after the FAI's, in other words, in mid-December, denied, on the one hand, the possibility of this committee being represented by elements of the FAI; and, on the other hand, agreed to limit their presence in plenums to when the question of prisoners was specifically addressed.

The repression was obviously a concern for the entire organisation, but even the way of addressing it was a source of controversy. The simple dispatch of a letter, referred to earlier, protesting at state repression, had represented the strongest expression of criticism by the Catalan union. The situation was repeated during the plenum in the middle of December, with acceptance of the constitution of a commission, formed by Villaverde, Mendiola and Pestaña, to meet the Minister of Interior to denounce the arbitrary actions committed. Criticism of the Catalan delegation soon followed, as the visit to the authorities was interpreted as an abandonment of principles. Meanwhile, the anarchist press referred to these commissions as "committee of mourners".[89] The rest of the regional delegations declared that there was no deviation from the principles of direct action, since "with regard to the arbitrary actions of the authorities it is necessary to address the latter, just as requests of an economic nature should be addressed to the bourgeoisie".[90]

All these issues combined to demonstrate, once again, how the anarcho-syndicalists continued to constitute a majority at a national level in mid-December, and that the main opposition came from Catalonia. In this respect, it is important to recall that the composition of the national committee corresponded, according to federative regulations, to the militancy of its place of residence. Thus the main confederal committee, given that it was in Barcelona, could fall into the hands of those who did not represent a majority within the organisation at a national level, but who played an increasingly important role in the Catalan committees.

Although the CNT always emphasised the lack of decision-making power of the confederal committees, the fact is that control of the representative organs involved taking and implementing a number of decisions. *El Luchador* admitted that "in the committees, the secretary is the key, because he possesses the official seal and is most directly in contact with the unions"[91]. Hence the importance of taking control of these committees, since from this vantage point it was easier to establish guidelines for the mass membership. Consequently, the regional plenums of the FAI held in Catalonia and the Levante, in December, highlighted this question. The Catalan groups aimed to influence the workers via meetings and "and accept all the positions offered to them in the union assemblies". For their part, the Levante groups identified the need to take over "the positions without any coercion and create once again the true anarchist CNT"; an initiative which they did not regard as difficult, as the moderate CNT members had fallen into disrepute. Both groups believed that the tactic to be employed was the one they had been using for months, namely, intensify promotion of the revolution, through propaganda, "particularly in union assemblies" and show workers the conduct of "individuals who had strayed". For example, the Levante pro-culture group declared that "having activated (...) the propaganda, it has succeeded in rendering the Union administration clearly anarchist".[92]

Real infighting in which propaganda appeared, as was denounced by José Villaverde, "in supposedly supportive newspapers and on the part of elements who boast that they carry the confederal membership card in their pockets and constantly criticise the organisation's committees and the comrades that form these committees". He referred to the "Urales family", whom the regional delegations of Asturias and Galicia, at the December plenum, did not hesitate to identify as "disruptive".[93] The organisation was aware that anarchist pressure could lead to a change in control of the main confederal committee, as had already occurred with the *Solidaridad Obrera* editorial team. So the delegations from Aragon, the Levante and Asturias requested of the plenum that this committee should change its place of residence, in other words, leave Catalonia, and thus escape probable control by the FAI. Because, as Isaac Olmos, secretary of the regional committee of the North, recalled, the organisation was not only in Catalonia.[94] However, he agreed that this change would be debated at the following congress.[95]

They were postponing a fundamental decision for the future of the organisation at a time when, even for the AIT, the conflict between the FAI and the *treintistas* severely threatened the integrity of the CNT. The International sent Augustin Souchy to mediate between them at the end of December. Both groups recognised that it was necessary to prepare for the revolution and send the workers a clear message of unity. Eusebio Carbó was responsible for drafting the manifesto. But Pestaña expressed his doubts vis-á-vis the document, because even if he set an "example of loyalty to what had been agreed upon", he was distrustful of the other group's attitude.[96] However, the anarcho-syndicalists neither knew how to tackle the anarchist campaign, nor possessed a joint strategy to defend their positions in the organisation. They completely relied upon their union strength and the conviction that the workers would not leave the Confederation in the hands of people who put insurrection before the struggle to improve working conditions. But time and circumstances did not favour him.

Protests and Repression at the Start of the Year

Public order deteriorated considerably in the months of December and January. The unaddressed needs of workers and farmhands, along with non-compliance with negotiated labour conditions, heightened the conflict. Industrial strikes and protests in the agricultural sector that ended in bloodshed. In the village of Bujalance (Córdoba), the Civil Guard opened fire on farm labourers who were protesting about their working conditions, causing one death. In Almodóvar (Cordoba), the actions of the Civil Guard in the clash between farmhands and non-local strike-breakers, "introduced by the Almodovar bourgeoisie", resulted in the death of one striker and several wounded.[97] In la Almarcha (Cuenca), the striking farm workers clashed with the Civil Guard to demand that only unionised labourers should work, leading to one dead and three wounded.[98]

Though the bloodiest incidents in the month of December took place in the province of Badajoz. The *Federación Nacional de Trabajadores de la Tierra,* or FNTT (National Federation of Land Workers), attached to the UGT, called a 48-hour general strike in protest at the actions of the Civil Governor, Manuel Álvarez Ugena, and the colonel in command of the Civil Guard, in view of their blatantly despotic policies. In the town of Feria, the clash between the security forces and the workers left one labourer dead and two civil guards wounded.[99] But it was in Castilblanco where events had a national impact. The local town council was still controlled by monarchists converted into republicans by the application of article 29 of the decree law that regulated the municipal elections of April 12, 1931, according to which elections were not to be held where there was only one candidacy. The farm workers had been protesting for months, demanding work, while the funds sent by the government were siphoned off by the municipal corporation. Specifically, there was talk of money sent from the ministry to resurface local roads and provide work for the unemployed. The council gave the funds to a company that, according to the workers, had not spent them honestly, so they directed their complaints to the Civil Governor of Badajoz and the Mayor of Castilblanco, "who turned a deaf ear". In the demonstration organised on 31 December, the mayor ordered the Civil Guard to break it up, although it was taking place peacefully. Following some pushing and shoving, insults and protests, the guards opened fire on the demonstrators, killing one of them. The furious farmworkers attacked the guards with stones and knives, slaughtering four agents.[100]

These events had an enormous impact. The conservative press focused on the farm workers' vicious attack on the civil guards, virtually ignoring the death of the labourer. In fact, when you read the news in these papers, you wonder whether that first death actually existed, though it was as real as the other four. The message repeated was that the origins of the rural protests and the brutality of the killings lay in the revolutionary propaganda that left-wing groups spread amongst the uneducated locals. They did not consider the possibility that the strikes and uprisings were the consequence of the situation of extreme poverty in which the farmworkers lived, or that the workers' furious reaction, as well as to the death of their colleague, stemmed from the injustice and repression suffered over decades. Local newspapers, like *La Voz de Extremadura,* blamed Manuel Muiño, Socialist MP, for having stirred up the farmworkers in rallies and meetings. The latter, for his part, claimed that responsibility lay primarily with the secretaries of the town council and of the courthouse, leading *caciques* (local political bosses) in the area and connected to the well-heeled of the town.

But he also blamed the civil governors, who instead of sending delegates to find out what was happening in the towns and villages sent the forces of law and order, with the aggravating circumstance that "in the Civil Guard posts" of these small towns, "*los caciques*" gave the orders. According to Muiño, around 50 men and 6 women were arrested and mistreated and beaten, and left for 36 hours in the town square, unprotected against the elements, without food, water or blankets. Until the arrival of the military judge, nobody was permitted to go near the square – called, to make matters worse, "of the Constitution" – well, no-one except the *caciques* who, sitting opposite the town hall, contemplated the members "of the la Casa del Pueblo tied up with their hands in the air and trembling with cold".[101]

Similar situations had already been repeatedly denounced by different sectors of society, libertarian spheres in particular. *Solidaridad Obrera* insisted that the same thing had happened in Castilblanco as had previously occurred in other towns in Spain, the difference being

> that, instead of four workers being killed, as happens so deplorably often, four civil guards had died. Otherwise, everything has taken place in the same fashion. The people have taken to the streets to protest; the Civil Guard has tried to prevent this, firing into the crowd, as usual, and the crowd, instead of running in fear, has reacted against the aggressors and punished them on the spot. That is all.[102]

For their part, the socialists appeared to awaken from a dream to a sharp reality check. The initial sensation was one of incredulity, since *El Socialista* questioned, at first, that the events had originally been caused by the general strike called by the UGT, owing to the "sensible and peaceful spirit that reigns among the proletariat",[103] differentiating it, without saying as much, from that other syndicalism represented by the CNT. Before acknowledging, the following day, that the Republic had not changed the customs and practices of rural politics, and that "many members of the Civil Guard" were quicker to obey "a suggestion made by the *cacique* than an order issued by a socialist mayor". It concluded by indicating the need for the government, in which socialist comrades served, to work to free the Civil Guard from that nefarious influence.[104]

Meanwhile, General Sanjurjo, head of the Civil Guard, declared that the country was the victim of a generalised uprising, and that "the big landowners live in terror".[105] His discourse, as unreal as it was extremist and xenophobic, laid the blame on farmworkers and socialists, and in particular Margarita Nelken, PSOE MP for Badajoz. Regarding the former, he said that in the area there was "a Riffean element". In other words, he identified the labourers with the "savage Moors", and what had befallen the civil guards with the terrible mutilations suffered by the Spanish troops during the Moroccan war.[106] The socialists he accused of provoking the workers, focusing his criticism on Nelken, who was Jewish, and regretting the fact that she had been admitted into Parliament, given that she was "foreign and a member of a race very skilled in organising espionage".[107] A discourse that tied in with that of Onésimo Redondo, leader of the JONS *(Juntas de Ofensiva Nacional Sindicalistas* or Committees of Nationalist Syndicalist Offensive), a far-right organisation, for whom the Socialist MP was a "protegé", to which he added two other "disqualifications": "foreign (and) woman".[108]

Azaña said, in the parliamentary session that addressed these events, that they could only be "attributed to barbarism, ignorance, lack of sensibility", and that the government was satisfied with the Civil Guard's conduct.[109] Although in his memoirs, he referred to the requests that this force be disbanded, "or at least reformed". The president knew that the working classes hated the *Benemérita* and was perfectly aware of the problem he faced:

> the Civil Guard has always been hard, and worse still, irresponsible (…) it has served the old political system and its *caciques* long and well (...) In small towns, the post commander was a little king. And personal harassment is endless. All this sows the seeds of hatred. As does the unjustified use of force, because those persecuted do not stop to think if this persecution is justifiable. Like every instrument of force and repression, it is not popular among the unfortunate. However, since the advent of the Republic, the situation of the Civil Guard in towns is more serious, because many mayors and councillors used to be victims and regular targets of the Civil Guard, which does not enjoy the best of relations with the new authorities; the new authorities in the towns also contribute in part to destroying harmony.

With regard to Sanjurjo, Azaña felt that his reaction to the events had been unfortunate. Added to his criticism of the socialists were "inopportune" declarations and insults against the government, which demanded "Sanjurjo's removal". But such a measure under current circumstances represented a supposed loss of "authority" which the Republic could ill afford, so it was advisable to wait for the situation to calm down.[110]

Yet rather than calm down, the situation deteriorated. After the events of Castilblanco, the Civil Guard toughened its stance. In Zalamea de la Serena (Badajoz), the clash between farmworkers and guards left two of the former dead and three wounded. In Épila (Zaragoza), the neighbours assembled in the square to request that available jobs at the local sugar factory be given to residents, the *Benemérita* wanted to disperse them and fired into the crowd, leaving two dead and several wounded. In Jeresa (Valencia), the town council attempted to mediate in the assignment of jobs by presenting a list to employers, who removed eleven names and imposed a right of veto vis-à-vis giving work to the others. As a result of which a strike was called. The Civil Guard commander decided that the protest was of a "revolutionary nature", so sought to intervene, while the mayor requested calm and assured him that the people would disperse. But "when he was going to speak to the demonstrators, the Civil Guard carried out a sabre charge". The people continued protesting and "when they threw some stones the response was to open fire". The result was two workers dead and a dozen wounded. In Calzada de

Calatrava (Ciudad Real), striking farmworkers headed to the estates to ensure that other colleagues joined the strike, and the ensuing clash with the Civil Guard left one labourer dead and two wounded.[111] In Santa Marta de Nagasca (Caceres), the forces of law and order opened fire on the workers who were threatening to enter an estate, leaving four of them wounded.[112] But the worst was still to come.

In Arnedo (Logroño), the Civil Guard opened fire on a crowd gathered in the town square, killing eleven and wounding thirty. According to Carlos Gil,[113] among the dead were five women and a child; one of them, Micaela Pérez, 26 years old, was buried in the same coffin as her only son. Of the wounded, 11 were women and 3 children, including Pilar Pérez, aged 24, who received a shot in the side that also wounded her one-year-old son, who she was carrying, and Gerardo Hernández, aged five, whose left leg had to be amputated. But apart from this brief yet shocking summary, it is worth focusing on the events of Arnedo, because among the causes and consequences of what happened there are to be found, to a large degree, many of the ills that, deriving from social problems and those of public order, were afflicting much of Spain.

The history of Arnedo is an oft-repeated history. As early as 1905, workers at the town's shoe factory tried to form a workers' association. But the owner, Faustino Muro, would not employ the promotors of the idea, so they abandoned the project. Ten years later, the situation repeated itself. The workers registered a new society and the owner fired those who joined it. At the time, the president of the local social reform board was the mayor, and Faustino Muro happened to be the mayor of Arnedo.

During the time of the Republic, the conflict dated from March 1931, when a commission of workers from Muro's factory denounced, before the civil governor, the sacking of a colleague on political grounds. The owner himself admitted to the authorities that he had given certain indications to the workers in favour of the candidacy of the monarchists in the April municipal elections, which they went on to win. However, the republicans triumphed in the parliamentary elections in June, which facilitated the formation of the *Sociedad de Profesionales y Oficios Varios* (Society of Various Professionals and Trades), linked to the UGT.

In August 1931, the new union denounced the fact that the owner refused to readmit those who had been sacked, despite the agreement that had been reached in this respect, and was, however, employing farmworkers, provided they did not belong to the workers' association. Furthermore, in his factory there were minors working on the machines and the working day was not respected. The workers lodged an appeal before the joint committee of industries of the sector, which found in their favour. But Faustino Muro challenged the resolution on formal grounds. In October, the Civil Governor, fed up with this "intransigent attitude", urged him to comply with the decision within 72 hours, "warning him that if he persisted in his intransigence and disrespect towards the working class", he would be obliged "to impose the maximum possible sanctions". But the ruling was not complied with, and the Governor issued a detention order against Faustino Muro, which could not be implemented either because, officially, the factory owner was actually his son, Felipe, who was arrested and taken to prison, where he spent a night. Time passed and the situation remained unchanged. The Society of Various Trades sent a document stating that this strike was the consequence of negligent handling of "unresolved conflicts, especially the one involving the industrialist shoe manufacturer Felipe Muro". The union again cited the problems with the working day, child labour and the difficulties experienced by socialist workers when looking for work.[114]

The year 1932 began with the conflict that had started in March of the previous year still unresolved. The workers called a general strike for 5 January. That very day, the Ministry of Labour ratified the joint committee's resolution. Meanwhile, the owners of different factories and businesses, assembled in the town hall, agreed to employ those who had been sacked. When the news broke, people began marching peacefully towards the square in in order to celebrate. Awaiting them there was the Civil Guard, with Lieutenant Juan Corcuera, chief of the Arnedo headquarters, who had requested reinforcements during the strike to "guarantee freedom to work". Tragedy struck in the square.

According to Logroño Civil Guard records, on 5 January "a major demonstration" gathered in the square in front of the Town Hall. The report indicated that "apparently, there was an attempt to disarm one of the guards, who fell to the ground, and, simultaneously, a shot rang out". The demonstrators, instead of breaking up, bulldozed their way forward, and "the Commander ordered the guards to open fire", as a result of which they "succeeded in dispersing the rioters", leaving "an unconfirmed number of victims, estimated at around 11 dead and 30 wounded".[115] As in all the Benemérita reports, the guards had done nothing more than repel an aggression.

However, other versions are very different. According to the socialist Sabrás, the guards wanted to clear the square so the owners could leave the Town Hall, and began to dish out blows. One of the guards hit a woman, slipped and fell to the ground. Then the other guards, 25 in total, thinking that he had been attacked, opened fire. The prosecution and defence reports coincided in saying that the guards wanted to disperse the groups, moving their guns in front of them from side to side, though, they said, without issuing blows. One of the guards struck a woman in the head, at which point her father and her uncle knocked the guard to the ground, and the shooting began. In any case, there was some doubt as to whether the first shot had been fired by the demonstrators or the Civil Guard.[116]

The government was practically overwhelmed. Azaña noted in his diary that what had happened was attributed to the impotence of the authorities and the fact that the guards were afraid after what had occurred in Castilblanco, though he went on to say "But there twenty-eight of them!", so he did not rule out a lesson" or vengeance.[117] However, in the parliamentary session of 6 January, the President ignored what had really mattered, that is, the root causes of the incident, to focus on the tragic consequences. The government had to know, said Azaña, what had occurred in Arnedo,

> dispensing with the whole background to the strike (…) that is no longer the specific case, the political case, the Government's case: with or without a strike, whether the strike is justified or not, whether this or that is the will of the working masses, what interests the government, in the case of this lawsuit, is why and how the Arnedo tragedy occurred; whether the aggression, if it took place, was justified, whether or not the Civil Guard carried out its duty (…) and when we know this (…) whoever has committed a crime or erred shall suffer the consequences. There is nothing more to be said in this respect.[118]

Azaña's words surprisingly ignore the lack of respect shown by employers for labour legislation and resolutions issued by competent bodies, the underlying cause of many of the conflicts all over Spain. Although, as we shall see, it would not be the last time that the Prime Minister neglected the root of the problem, or the need to reform the Civil Guard. Socialist MP Margarita Nelken believed that the latter had fulfilled its duties "in its day, tackling the bandits of Sierra Morena, but its conduct above and beyond the civilian authorities continues to be, in countless localities, a constant and intolerable provocation".[119] But Azaña was loathe to promote any changes in the *Benemérita* because, he said, if people interpreted this as the government "punishing them, they would turn against them, in bloody fashion".[120] Although he may also have feared that the armed force itself would interpret as a punishment any kind of reform, and he preferred not to inconvenience the Civil Guard and keep them, supposedly, on the side of the Republic. Or perhaps he was more afraid of those who were protesting, albeit they were the artifices of the advent of the new regime, on account of their allegedly revolutionary inclination.

For the moment, the Ministry of Governance, Casares Quiroga, appointed a delegation led by the Civil Governor of Vizcaya, José Calviño, to shed light on what had occurred. However, as Carlos Gil notes, the report did not reach Parliament, in spite of the repeated requests to this effect issued by MPs between January and March of that year. The Minister did not submit it to Parliament because, according to his version, he sent it directly to the Ministry of War to be included in the summary, without even keeping a copy. Well, Calviño's report indicated that it was a proven fact that the demonstration had taken place pacifically and without incident until Lieutenant Corcuera ordered its dispersal. Then the Civil Guard proceeded to empty the square with their rifle butts and, in one of the scuffles, a guard fell to the ground, and then shots were fired. Calviño was not sure whether any shots had been fired by civilians. Though a councillor and the secretary of the town council, expert witnesses given their position in the square, declared that they were sure that the first shots had not been fired by the demonstrators. Meanwhile, the Civil Guard provided no information regarding the alleged author of the gunfire, and no weapons were found in possession of the victims. In his final considerations, the author of the report stated that the Civil Guard should not have broken up the demonstration, since it was peaceful, that there was no collective aggression against the Civil Guard, nor warnings issued, and if there had been an aggression it would have been by an individual, so the crowd should not have been fired upon. Calviño attributed the incident to an excess of zeal, in fear that the demonstrators might be armed, with the recent memory of Castilblanco.[121]

After these events, General Sanjurjo's position at the head of the Civil Guard was unsustainable. Although Azaña continued to treat the General in a manner that would have been the envy of the victims of Arnedo; he had avoided, until now, his removal so as not to "upset him, as everyone would see this" as a punishment and "he would feel offended".[122] Azaña's sensitivity resulted, possibly, from Sanjurjo's actions in April 1931, upon the proclamation of the Republic, when the General placed the Civil Guard under the command of the provisional government. Support that was crucial in the light of the weakness of the new government and the extreme political instability related to the change of regime.[123] But the relationship was rendered unsustainable by the Civil Guard's recent actions and Sanjurjo's verbal clashes with the Socialists. So Azaña had no choice but to remove him. Although, as an expression of deference, he assigned him command of the *Carabineros*, another armed force. The dismissal came as a major blow to Sanjurjo, no doubt convinced that her had acted correctly, and once again he voiced harsh criticism of Azaña's partners in government, declaring that there were "many socialist town councils participated in by the worst kind of people. 'Undesirables' who promoted disorder, intimidated owners, caused damage to property and inevitably clashed with the Civil Guard. The Socialists, (he said), should not be in the Government, because their presence encourages those who favour excess".[124] All of this in the wake of events in which 11 civilians had been killed and 30 wounded.

However, the Socialist presence in the government was evaluated very differently by Azaña himself, and also by members of the diplomatic corps of such important countries as France and Germany. Herbette had a very positive opinion vis-à-vis the presence of the Socialists in the republican government, not only in terms of their constructive contribution, but also on account of their qualities of moderation, something necessary in order to channel the workers' aspirations along reformist rather than revolutionary paths.[125] In similar vein, the German Ambassador, Conde de Welczeck, argued that the socialist presence helped to "impose upon the working masses . . . , indispensable patience and sacrifice". The ambassador compared Spain's situation with that of Germany after the First World War, when the Socialist Ebert became president of the country, and was a significant moderating influence upon the workers' masses in the early years of the Weimar Republic. Therefore, despite the warnings, the situation was not so serious while Azaña was at the head of the government and the Socialists were participating.[126]

But the tardiness of reforms, the government's inhibition the face of the refusal on the part of the former *caciques* and some employers to accept the new political situation, labour legislation and even the agreements reached with the workers themselves, undermined the popular support that the government had enjoyed since the change of regime. And in addition to all this, the repression exercised by the Civil Guard, which made disproportional use of force and turned any legal demonstration into a problem of public order.

Circumstances repeatedly condemned in the anarchist press, and which were beginning to appear, increasingly often, in socialist papers too, for example:

> we have yet to see the imprisonment of any of those thieving owners that are happily ignoring the recently approved labour rules (...) we have yet to see behind bars any of those murderous landowners who, rather than giving work to day labourers, prefer to leave the land uncultivated; we have yet to see the confiscation of even one of the palaces belonging to those hundreds of aristocrats that have fled abroad with their millions (...) But the hungry workers, criminally ejected from the land, the workshop or the factory (...) Oh yes, they need a good beating! More Civil Guards, no; more justice. That is what's needed in the towns and villages of Spain.[127]

But justice did not appear to be the new regime's forte either. Largely because, as I have already said, in some respects it was the heir to the past. This was the case with the assignation of military tribunals for proceedings against civilians for aggression, contempt or insult against military authorities, which made them judge and plaintiff. This is apparent in the two main incidents described above, in Castilblanco and in Arnedo. In the former around a hundred neighbours were arrested. The war council was held in Badajoz, in mid-July, 1933. The prosecutor requested for the murder of four civil guards: eight death penalties, six life sentences and other lesser sentences. However, no-one was tried for the killing of the worker. The farmworkers' defence insisted that the Civil Guard committed an illegal aggression against a legal and peaceful demonstration, and had even broken the law by not issuing a warning. In spite of everything, the court sentenced six of the defendants to death and the rest to prison terms. Alcalá Zamora exercised the right of pardon and reduced the death penalty to 30 years in prison. All those involved were released in February 1936, following the electoral triumph of the Popular Front.[128]

In the case of the events of Arnedo, the legal process was slower, in spite of the two incidents coinciding in time. The sentence, in this case, was issued at the end of January 1934, in other words, six months later than that of Castilblanco. It should be noted that the verdict emerged following the victory of the conservative parties in the elections of November, 1933. The sentence, applicable to the only defendant, Lieutenant Corcuera, indicated that given the lack of "necessary and absolute certainty with regard to the way of developing the accusation", it was "mandatory to acquit the accused in the absence of sufficient evidence to consider him guilty of the actions in question". The prosecutor did not appeal against the verdict, so the sentence was final. Meanwhile, the fundamental causes of the conflict persisted, in spite of the deaths, with much ducking and diving on the part of employers in Arnedo. At the end of January, 1932, Muro still had not re-employed the sacked workers, as obliged to by the joint committee resolution. And the Casa del Pueblo remained closed, as ordered by the Mayor, José Mª Fernández Velilla, in collusion with local bosses. The latter, in turn, refused to respect the agreement to offer jobs to the workers, as had been stipulated in court, and moreover, as "things have changed a lot since the 5th", and production had fallen, instead of employing workers, almost certainly, they would have to make them redundant. In mid-February, Muro agreed to give victims and workers 11,673 pesetas, a sum established by the mixed jury. An agreement that did not materialise until two months later.[129]

In relation to the Civil Guard post in Arnedo, so as to avoid conflict with the victims" families, "it was moved (...) with all the agents" to another town. Although in February 1934, in other words, after the conservative electoral victory, it returned to Arnedo. But not only the post, for it appears that the same guards who were involved in the incidents also returned. This one infers from the Civil Guard records, which state that, in March, 1936, after the February elections, "due to political pressure, exercised by the Mayor and elements of the popular front, all those who occupied the Post were transferred, and in April, it was reorganised with new personnel".[130]

The anarchists were fiercely critical of the Socialist-Republican government on account of all these incidents, but they also took advantage of circumstances to censure those who formed a majority on the union organisation committees, with special mention for Pestaña. Although they acknowledged that there was a considerable amount of conflict, "there would have been more were the Confederation led by true revolutionaries", if "there had not been a pusillanimous or astute hand putting out fires".[131] Fires like the one that was about to break out in Alto Llobregat.

The Movement of January 1932: A CNT Uprising?

Historiography of the CNT during the republican period has always highlighted the confrontation between anarcho-syndicalists and anarchists, culminating with the former being replaced by the latter at the head of the principal committees during the months following the first of the three uprisings – January 1932, and January and December of 1933 – which, allegedly, were perpetrated by the CNT. I say allegedly because it is somewhat strange that the first movement occurred while those in control of confederal policy were the anarcho-syndicalists who, as I have mentioned, advocated union work rather than anarchist insurrection.

A reasonable doubt that makes it necessary to analyse the historiographical assertion, repeated over and over again not only literature on the CNT but also in that which addresses the Second Republic, that the CNT led three uprisings during the days of the Republic. In other words, it is a question of examining the extent to which the alleged uprising of 1932 was, in fact, planned, organised and led by the Confederation, in such a way that it can be considered, as has been the case until now, a CNT insurrection. Otherwise, it would be necessary to turn our attention to the most significant consequence of this uprising, in other words, analyse the resources exploited by the anarchists to assume control of the organisation.

On 18 January 1932, the miners of Alto Llobregat called a strike that turned into an insurrectional uprising. Days before, the *Sindicato de Arte Textil y Manufacturas* (Textile Art and Manufacturing Union) of Alto Llobregat came out on strike in the town of Berga because of management's non-compliance with the negotiated labour rules. The miners of Figols believed that other factories in the area had supported the walkout, so, as the entire mining basin was "a domain of the "most despotic "capitalism", they decided, to prevent inevitable repression, to disarm the "*somatén*" (an armed organisation formed by "people of order"). The movement spread to other towns in the area like Cardona, Suria and Sallent. Most of the miners were emigrants from poorer parts of Spain: Andalusia, Extremadura and Murcia. They lived in colonies that they had built themselves, in unhygienic conditions, without drinking water, located near the mines, but apart from the towns. Thus the mining company exercised close control over the lives of these workers, with the company owning, for example, the commissary and the tavern in the colony. The marginalisation extended to the workplace, where the immense majority of those who worked down in the mines were emigrants, while the Catalans occupied other positions in the company, in offices and workshops, for example.[132]

The proclamation of the Republic led these emigrants to believe, along with the other workers in Spain, that the development of freedoms and rights inherent to the new democratic regime would mean the end of the *caciquil* system and its abusive practices. However, the situation in the mines barely changed, and the owners continued to act as in previous decades, in possession not only of taverns and the commissary, but even, as one of the miners said, the Civil Guard.[133] The reasons behind the uprising were specifically related to the owners' intransigence and lack of respect for republican legislation. In particular, they did not respect the right to meeting and association, "with rallies and public meetings systematically banned"[134], added to which were the tough working conditions in the mines and the lack of hygiene in general. The anarchists also condemned an attempt by the owners to re-establish the nine-hour working day and the intention not to respect negotiated labour rules, in the words of the Catalan president, Francesc Macià, "of agreements that were not complied with".[135]

The textile strike in Alto Llobregat increased the atmosphere of protest that prevailed throughout Spain and materialised in other areas in accordance with specific problems. In Figols, workers took advantage of the situation to protest about their poor living conditions, without any leadership or preparation on the part of the CNT. In fact, on 19 January the first news reached Barcelona about the miners' uprising in this locality. In other words, the regional committee of Catalonia learnt of what was happening after the action had already begun. Emilio Mira, committee secretary, had to travel to the area to find out what was going on. Upon his arrival in Figols, he contacted the revolutionary committee, who informed him "that (they had) taken up arms". When asked by the secretary what they hoped to achieve, the insurrectionists replied, quite simply, that they wanted to start a revolution. Mira was part of the moderate sector of the organisation, so, "fearing that his report might be regarded as biased, he decided to take back with him one of his comrades from Figols". So it was that he was accompanied by the person at the head of the movement, Manuel Prieto. The latter presented a manifesto to the organisation in Barcelona, in which it was stated that "Figols had risen up in the belief that a dictatorship was going to be established in Spain".[136]

A consideration that clearly had its origins in the news arriving about the bloody repression that was taking place in different parts of Spain. The national committee itself explained that both they and the leaders of the Catalan regional committee sent circulars to the entire organisation to inform people about the "major repression all over Spain", in which they emphasised the "revolutionary nature" of the moment.[137] In fact, in the days prior to the uprising, the anarchist weekly *Tierra y Libertad* highlighted, as well as the "wave of blood" that was crossing our nation, two other main ideas: that a dictatorship was hatching in Spain and that the revolution was under way. The newspaper called upon workers and peasants to "Establish anarchic communism!"[138] Against this backdrop, the reaction of the Figols miners was hardly surprising.

On the night of the 22nd, county, local and the Barcelona federation agreed to call a revolutionary general strike for the next day, and asked the national committee to apply this to the whole of Spain, so delegates were sent to all the regional committees to spread the word. At the same time, a revolutionary committee was created "with absolute authority" to take the necessary decisions and report "back to the national committee". The decision was important because, as was thought at the time, the action taken by the Barcelona federation would set the tone for the rest of the organisation, in other words, Catalonia was waiting to see what Barcelona did and Spain was watching Catalonia. However, Mira was not so sure, the problem was that "there was a lack of enthusiasm or the organisation was not prepared" for an insurrectionary endeavour of this calibre. Moreover, the Catalan secretary cited another rather more prosaic question: the day scheduled for the declaration of the strike was Saturday, 23 January, payday, which he feared might dampen the workers' supposed revolutionary ardour.

In fact, at that day's meeting, the delegate from the Barcelona federation expressed some doubt and suggested that "the Barcelona organisation may not be able to respond to the agreement reached". To which the national committee replied that this should have been taken into account before and not when the entire organisation was already committed. It was also announced that "no county federation" had fulfilled its pledge to take action. Furthermore, the news from the area of the uprising indicated that the movement had "slowed down considerably" as soldiers and civil guards had entered the towns and put an end to the insurrection, except in the San Cornelio neighbourhood in Figols. Anyway, they agreed to wait because six o'clock was "the scheduled time for acts of great violence".

But, to "everyone's surprise", it turned out that "the revolutionary actions promised the previous day were not undertaken, and that the trams, buses, underground trains and the Sarriá railway" were operating normally, "signalling the end of the strike", while in the region "absolutely nothing had happened". Contemplating this situation, the delegates turned to the national committee, which declared that it had "not attempted anything on account of a complete lack of means", while it sought to elude its responsibility for the disorientation created by "the local and the regional committees not having published even a sheet, a manifesto, nothing". As a result, the national committee, in the absence of a response, decided to withdraw the strike order that it had issued for the whole of Spain.

Gregorio Jover, delegate from the Timber Union of Barcelona and member of the national committee, opposed this decision. Jover placed all the blame on the secretary-generals of the regional and national committees, Mira and Pestaña, respectively. As far as he was concerned, the triumph or failure of the movement had depended on something as simple as the launch of a manifesto, to which the committees had made a commitment, but one which they had not fulfilled. In any case, Jover acknowledged that "Although in material terms Spain was perhaps not completely ready, morally it was and the revolution could have taken place . . . " The problem would not have arisen, he said, "if the Regional Committee had not sabotaged it", before concluding that consciously or unconsciously, "the movement has been betrayed".[139]

While all these meetings were taking place in Barcelona, and the CNT organisation oscillated between confusion and the need to show its solidarity with the rebels, the Figols uprising spread to towns like Cardona, Sallent, Suria, Balsareny and Gavá. Mines and factories were left empty, shops closed, the "*somatén*" was disarmed and the Civil Guard took refuge in its barracks. At the same time, town halls were occupied and the red and black flag raised. The government sent in the army and the mutiny was soon quelled. By 25 January, order had been re-established.[140]

Once the turmoil was over, and the movement crushed, the anarchist press stressed its significance. Federica Montseny wrote, in his usual style, that the uprising of the towns of Alto Llobregat would go down "in history as the first serious attempt at social revolution in Spain, after the Jerez rehearsal of 1892".[141] A surprising comparison bearing in mind that this "first serious attempt at revolution" had consisted in the occupation of the town by around 200 men who wandered its streets before abandoning the locality half an hour later, leaving three people dead, specifically, a shop assistant, a councillor's brother and a soldier.[142]

Meanwhile, Eduardo de Guzmán, a journalist with connections to the CNT, pointed to the "victory in a town, for the first time in Spain's history, of libertarian communism". Before providing an epic account of the miners' actions, and of how the enemies of the movement, "bourgeoisie, director (of the mine), priest, judge, technical staff, etc.", were free, but disarmed. The miners appointed a revolutionary committee that was responsible for organising production and consumption, while money was abolished and replaced by vouchers issued by this committee. There were elections to form a commune, while the miners returned to their work in the mines. Included in the article were the religious references so entrenched in anarchist discourse. In this case in allusion to Manuel Prieto, leader of the movement, who was not "an extraordinarily intelligent man, or a philosopher of the revolution. But he was a worker illuminated by a great internal faith. The stuff of apostles. Like Peter, the fisherman from Galilee, who spread Jesus' rebellious ideas across the world. Like Bakunin, constantly battling against injustice and calumny".[143] The description of the events in the anarchist press paid particular attention to the absence of violence. Anarchy had been a "reality for a week", and "nowhere has there been robbery, murder or rape" which, according to its detractors, were "the essence of anarchism". Ultimately, what had occurred in this corner of Catalonia was proof that "our ideal can become reality".[144]

But what happened in Alto Llobregat would do more than demonstrate the viability of the anarchist project. Appropriate use of what had happened, with special focus on the actions of the CNT regional and national secretaries, Mira and Pestaña, acted as a hobbyhorse for the power struggle within the Confederation. Throughout this process, the Republican government played, without seeking to do so, a fundamental role.

Companys approached Azaña in the corridors of parliament, shortly after the start of the movement in the Catalan region, hoping to resolve the problem via negotiation. Specifically, he proposed that one of the members of his party, MP José Grau, familiar with the problems in the area, should go there and negotiate with the miners. Grau had already mediated successfully, in May 1931, in the strike planned by the miners when the owners refused to accept the labour rules presented.[145] But Azaña was not prepared to allow a negotiated end to the conflict. Undoubtedly, he needed to give a demonstration of authority at a time when social protests appeared to be overwhelming the government. So the Prime Minister declined the offer of help and reiterated that "the only people that would go to the zone of the uprising were the soldiers".[146] Moreover, in the parliamentary session of 21 January, Azaña reported that he had issued orders to the general of the 4th Division in Barcelona to send to the conflict the forces necessary "to crush it immediately (...) so this riot is put down in a matter of hours". A period of time that, given the need to assert his authority, must have struck him as excessive, as he then referred again to the orders given to the general, but this time to indicate that he had allocated no "more than fifteen minutes between the troops' arrival at the venue of the incidents and the termination of the latter". Words received by MPs with applause and cries of "Long live the Republic!"

Though Azaña went much further in his parliamentary intervention, attributing to the miners' movement no less than the status of an international conspiracy designed to overthrow the Republic, "prepared inside and outside Spain", by far-left elements interspersed with "a breath, something more than complaisance (...) on the part of the far right". To conclude by saying that

> this has nothing to do (...) with specific labour conflicts. No. There were agreements between owners and workers. I am not sure it concerns me right now whether they are respected or not. Negotiated labour rules never give anybody the right to occupy factories, attack town halls, take control of telephone

exchanges or assault the forces of law and order. For that there are never grounds.[147]

Words that, as we recall, were not new, and must have had a considerable impact upon the workers that had pinned their hopes of social justice on the new regime, but now saw how the Prime Minister was neglecting to ensure that the rich and powerful obeyed the law.

The government clearly had the right to repress any kind of uprising against the Republic, but it is no less true that it also had an obligation to ensure that employers obeyed the law. However, many systematically violated not only republican decrees and laws, but also the labour rules agreed upon in the mixed juries. In this respect, the Catalan MP Grau, in the parliamentary session of February 10, declared that the companies in the area had a long history of labour-related infringements, abuses that had "led as a consequence to a regrettable state of unrest in that basin".[148] In fact, after the strike of May 1931, there were further conflicts in August. The workers of Cardona, Suria, Figols and Berga suffered the arbitrary actions of owners who sacked those "marked" elements that formed commissions and trade union boards, while they sought "amendment of rules that had already been accepted and signed by both parties".[149]

Violations that were, to a large extent, the cause of protests and strikes all over Spain, combined, on too many occasions, with the disproportionate action of the forces of law and order. Although, in this case, the response was less violent, because, as Casares Quiroga himself acknowledged, the rebels did not offer resistance and "surrendered at once"; but also, according to Ballbé, thanks to the restrained attitude of General Batet, in charge of the forces posted in the vicinity.[150] Anyway, as Cristina Borderías and Mercedes Vilanova have noted, the repressive after-effects were felt for a long time in the area, with an increase in the owners' power, which reinforced the *caciquil* structures that had led to the uprising, and to sacking, with the government's support, of those workers that taken part in the movement. *Solidaridad Obrera* observed that the most "rebellious" were imprisoned, while the companies implemented "a barbaric and inhuman selection process among the miners", with a hundred sackings, and entire families forced to return to their places of origin.[151]

The situation was further complicated by the arrest of over a hundred people who boarded the steamship *Buenos Aires* to be deported to the Spanish colonies in Africa. Among those detained were not only the miners involved in the uprising, but also anarchist militants who had not participated in the movement but were on the police files and very well-known. Like those arrested in the bar "*La Tranquilidad*", a CNT meeting point, Buenaventura Durruti, the brothers Francisco and Domingo Ascaso, Cano Ruiz and Bruno Lladó, among others, and even militants that were in prison during the days of the uprising.[152] Basically, it appears that the government, applying the law on Defence of the Republic, took advantage of the situation to get rid of those regarded as a threat to the regime. The S.S. *Buenos Aires* sailed out of Barcelona on 10 February 1932, with 105 prisoners, picked up 112 more in Valencia and another two in Cadiz. In other words, a total of 118 people were deported, of whom between 8 and 10 were communists, and none of whom had been tried in court.[153] Incidentally, among the passengers there was no sign of those extreme right-wing conspirators the Prime Minister had referred to in his speech, and repeated by *El Socialista* in its headline: "Communists and syndicalists, in collusion with extreme right elements, seek to overthrow the Republic".[154]

The libertarian media directed their criticism, as was to be expected, at the government, but also at the anarcho-syndicalists. In the wake of the uprising, the confederal organisation did not open any serious debate to examine what had occurred in Alto Llobregat, to ascertain responsibility, or to identify errors committed so that future movements, should they arise, would not result in disaster. The anarchist reactions took the form more of furious condemnation of confederal leaders than analysis of the facts and the search for solutions, with the sole objective of occupying the key positions in the organisation.

At the head of this campaign was the "Ghost Federation", with Federica Montseny in charge. A long-standing campaign, which had already been criticised, one recalls, in the national plenum of the CNT in mid-December 1931. I say campaign because this is how Federica herself described it when in late January 1932 she acknowledged that "*El Luchador* will continue its campaign until the Confederation Committees, and above all their secretaries, are the true representatives of the Confederation".[155] A campaign that culminated in the article entitled "*Yo acuso*" – in imitation of Emilio Zola's condemnation of the injustice of the Dreyfus case in France. Federica blamed the *treintistas* for the failure of the revolution and, therefore, held them responsible for the deportations. Because when throughout Spain people were only waiting for a signal to launch the revolution, in reference to the manifesto that did not materialise, when the CNT identified the "possibility of realising its aspirations, they betrayed the movement once again". Although her most incendiary criticism was aimed at the organisation's leaders, Emilio Mira and Ángel Pestaña. With regard to the former, she wondered "what favour, what sinecure, what special position, he has been promised" for his "admirable work of fire-fighting (…) for his attitude in opposition to any supportive strike and for everything he did to prevent the strike, agreed upon in principle and implemented on Saturday in Barcelona, from spreading throughout Catalonia", before answering that "this is worth a monthly salary of at least 500 pesetas". As for Pestaña, "what provincial council, ministry or civil government has he been promised" for having sabotaged the movement, for delaying the strike, "for not launching the manifesto as he had pledged" and leading to "people, disorientated, indecisive, returning to work", to conclude by saying "Oh, that's worth over a thousand pesetas a month". She accused them of being "direct or indirect informers", of acting "as saboteurs of every agreement; betraying every movement", of having "filling the country's prisons with comrades", of having "divided and sterilized the organisation". Ending with the primary objective of this diatribe, which was none other than bringing about their exit from the confederal committees.

So she accused all the workers, all the comrades in Barcelona, of having allowed Pestaña "to still be in possession of the CNT's resources", of having enabled Mira, "a contemptible individual (…) to appropriate the secretariat". Both were responsible for "the 125 men that are being deported, almost a thousand in the prisons of Spain, those who have fallen in so many sabotaged movements, shamefully betrayed".[156]

The anarcho-syndicalists attempted to halt the anarchist offensive via their allies in the press, while they negotiated with the Republican government. Peiró highlighted the failure of the movement, "the fatal and collective irresponsibility (of) the maniacs of the revolution", who had spread "pain and poverty throughout countless proletarian households (and) the blow dealt to the CNT and to the reputation of the seriousness of libertarian ideas". While, in response to Federica, he said "when an anarchist accuses, they prove; and whoever accuses and does not prove is not an anarchist", but a "scoundrel and an agent provocateur".[157] For his part, Pestaña appealed to Azaña himself for clemency for the deportees. The Prime Minister, according to his own version, barely allowed the CNT delegation to speak, while he held them responsible for the consequences of their actions. Pestaña struck him as a broken man, and he understood that his position was "difficult among the revolutionaries". So he noted in his diary that he would be "relieved to have escaped the control of the *pistoleros*".[158]

Azaña was mistaken. One cannot but be surprised by his ignorance of what was happening within the confederal union and the lack of political vision that prevented him from seeing that exclusively repressive, and badly directed policies, could play a decisive part in the leadership of the union changing hands and being assumed by those who advocated insurrection, with the corresponding instability for the republican regime. A circumstance perceived by other observers. *El Socialista* reported, in August 1931, that the anarchists were taking control of the unions and that their work was destructive.[159] While Herbette noted the differences between Pestaña and the anarchists, between *Solidaridad Obrera* when Peiró was at the helm and when it was directed by Alaiz, who had turned it into a newspaper very much orientated towards extremist ideas. With this new editorial staff, according to the French ambassador, the CNT had lost influence, as was evidenced by the paper's circulation and the number of members, but continued to advocate violence.[160]

By 1931, there was already a sizeable anarchist presence on the main committees, as Eulalia Vega has pointed out, with Gregorio Jover, Ricardo Sanz and Juan García Oliver on Pestaña's national committee. While, at the beginning of January 1932, Francisco Ascaso, Canela, Patricio Navarro and Porquet formed part of Mira's regional committee, and anarchist Segundo Martínez was the secretary of the Barcelona local federation.[161] On top of which was the notable anarchist representation, via the *trabazón*, in the pro-prisoner organisations and the defence committees.

Meanwhile, the campaign continued and was bearing fruit. There were also attacks by a "sacred" collective within the CNT, namely the prisoners. The CNT inmates in Barcelona prison, led by García Oliver, unanimously agreed to subscribe to the "*El Luchador* campaign of renovation and cooperate with it". This was the result of the meetings in prison in which Oliver provided his version of Pestaña's activity at the head of the national committee in calling the general strike on February 15, the objective of which was to prevent the deportations on the S.S. *Buenos Aires.* According to García Oliver, Pestaña had acted independently when he had the committee seal in his possession and did not consult the other members when he sent a circular postponing the calling of the strike until the deployment of a propaganda campaign, as had been requested, according to Pestaña, by most of the regional committees. He was also accused of having distorted the information received from the latter, since, according to him, of the five that replied, four were in favour of the strike and one against; so he was accused of answering without knowing the opinions of the others, among which were the two most important committees, Andalusia and Catalonia. In short, Pestaña had deceived the organisation and with his attitude made it impossible to stop the deportations, as the circular called off the strike and postponed it until after the propaganda campaign, in other words, "without the circular, the departure of the deportees would never have taken place". The conclusion was that Pestaña was a traitor who was responsible for the deportations. So 197 prisoners in the Modelo jail signed a document, on 10 March 1932, requesting the expulsion of the CNT secretary general, with an interesting footnote: if what Oliver said were true, but the latter's if it were a lie.[162]

The seriousness of the allegations, the category of the accusers and the radicalised atmosphere of conflict provided no opportunity for calm analysis, far less for differentiation between truths, half-truths or lies. But the campaign continued and the anarchists put aside their differences, clear as they were between individuals like Jover, Durruti, García Oliver, and the Urales family. In fact, García Oliver commented, years later, that "the Urales family was always a very disruptive influence for the Organisation (...) one of the factors, doubtless never acknowledged, that originally produced most elements of discordance".[163] Federico Urales himself wrote an article at the beginning of March, 1932, that was quite on a par with his daughter's "Yo Acuso". The basic reasoning behind his attacks were two of the most contemptible questions for a "good anarchist": "political activity", synonymous with betrayal, and trade union bureaucratisation. For Urales, the CNT was immersed in a struggle "between the more or less hard-working politicians that aspire to live from the union organisation and the true workers". Among the former, the *treintistas* who sought to erase from the CNT statutes no less than its economic principles, libertarian communism, and direct action, and expel "the 'extremist' elements". Before returning to the main objective and criticising the fact that, "in defiance of all dignity", Pestaña was still the secretary general.[164]

But this bitter campaign was not going to end, as one can easily imagine, as the patriarch of the Montseny "predicted", that is, with the expulsion of the "extremists". A few days later, Pestaña abandoned his post as CNT secretary general, and was replaced by the FAI's Manuel Rivas, a close collaborator of García Oliver; while Ricardo Sanz, member of Los *Solidarios* (*Nosotros* in

1933), along with Durruti, Ascaso and Oliver, occupied the vice-secretariat. This was a crucial victory, after Peiró's replacement as editor of *Solidaridad Obrera*, on the path towards control of the Confederation. A victory in a campaign in which the CNT leaders had been subjected to fierce attacks, without the organisation having carried out a serious analysis of what had occurred. Incomprehensibly, they had to wait for Pestaña to abandon the secretariat before the CNT could assemble and analyse exactly what had happened in Figols and how the confederal leaders had acted during those tumultuous days.

The Enigma of Figols

The CNT held a national plenum of regional committees in Madrid from 13 to 16 April 1932. The report compiled by the new national committee, represented at the plenum by Manuel Rivas, Marcos Alcón and José Ramos, indicated that the most important topic at the meeting was what had taken place at Figols. Among the documentation submitted was a declaration to the effect that only at a meeting held in Barcelona from 5–7 March, attended by a delegate from Figols and another from the pro-prisoners committee, "was it possible partially to decipher the enigma".

The events described earlier were reviewed, via the minutes taken at the time, with particular focus on the actions of the national committee and its communications with the regional committee. According to the documents, the committee performed an analysis of the situation all over Spain in order to decide which path to take. Nothing could be expected of Barcelona and Cataluña, as their own local and county committees admitted. Galicia had ended the movement, which had nothing to do with the events of Figols, since there the strike was "directed against maternity insurance", which made it impossible to consider a new conflict. In the North, the CNT had little representation so would be smothered by the socialists and the government. The centre advised that it could not "do much", but could try. Andalusia said that several members had been arrested, which would be detrimental to the movement's unity. Which left Aragón and the Levante, but, as they were alone, any protest might lead to their being crushed. Therefore, the national committee proposed that the call for a general strike be withdrawn "to avoid a real catastrophe". A proposal that was accepted by all those present, except Gregorio Jover, as I have mentioned, who insisted on continuing with the movement "waiting for the actions of those on the streets to drag in the rest". An approach repeated over and over again by those who put their evolutionary longings before the real circumstances at the time. In the end, the national committee suspended the movement and informed the regional committees of the new agreement. After the minutes had been read, and following a long discussion, the plenum expressed its approval of the confederal committee's response to the events of Figols, leaving the way open for future congresses to reconsider the question.[165]

Ultimately, the strike of January 1932 cannot really be described as a CNT uprising. Because the CNT neither led, planned nor organised it. Because the movement did not involve any kind of call at a national level, not even a communication issued by the county to the Catalan regional committee informing of action that was being prepared. In fact, the first news item that appeared in *Solidaridad Obrera*, on 20 January, said that the Figols miners' strike could be due to "the heartless exploitation to which those workers are subjected", before recognising that "we do not know, at the time of writing these lines, whether some local or specific incident may have triggered events in Figols". The following day, the newspaper commented that, according to information received, "slavery (was) the main reason behind what had happened". In both cases, the news occupied a minor place in the paper.[166] For its part, the CNT did not call the general strike until the night of the 22nd, before calling it off on the 24th, given the lack of support. One cannot even refer to the FAI as the organiser of the uprising. Despite the fact that early in January, anarchist militants like Vicente Pérez "Combina", Arturo Parera and Durruti mounted a campaign of agitation in the area.[167] Actions that formed a part of, since the early days of the Republic, what were known as "propaganda outings", in which the federation of anarchist groups selected speakers to address rallies in different parts of Spain.[168] But one thing was for anarchists to address meetings and insist on the need for revolution, and quite another to interpret those interventions as part of the organisation or leadership of the insurrection. In fact, the FAI's peninsular committee itself acknowledged that it "never received news of those comrades' intentions", in reference to the miners of Figols.[169]

Added to all this confusion was the appointment of Manuel Prieto as leader of the movement. An individual unfamiliar, according to records, with what was happening in his hometown, and who had not been involved with the organisation for some time. Not to mention the information provided by Bruno Lladó, one of the anarchists deported in the S.S. *Buenos Aires*, who claimed that those arrested in the towns of Llobregat were more "individual victims of betrayal and identification by republican *caciquismo*" than revolutionaries, as "most are unfamiliar with the anarchist ideal". Although, at least, the absence of ideology was being corrected by means of "conferences and giving them books", to the extent that "most of them, today, are supporters at least".[170] So, rather than a CNT insurrection, this was a local movement, like those cyclical uprisings that took place in the Andalusian countryside, involving workers who, just like those Andalusian day labourers, found themselves in a situation of poverty and social injustice. In fact, Horacio Martínez Prieto noted that the uprising "was restricted to Figols and a few small Catalan localities, without any significant impact beyond Catalonia".[171]

Moreover, what historiography has repeatedly referred to as a CNT insurrection, was not interpreted thus by the CNT at the time. This is apparent from the minutes of the major congress held by the organisation in May 1936 in Zaragoza. In the section on revolutionary actions performed during the Republic there is no mention of the Alto Llobregat movement. It is entitled:

"Review of activities: Movements in January, December and October", in reference to the movements of 1933 and 1934. In fact, the delegates analysed these movements, without mentioning that of 1932, like that of the Barcelona Manufacturing and Textile Union, headed by García Oliver, who said: "the CNT has made two attempts at revolution: 8 January and 8 December", the dates of the start of the 1933 insurrections.[172]

The 15 February Strike

But let us return to the national plenum of April 1932, for following approval of Pestaña's national committee's reaction to the events of Figols, the former secretary general faced another major obstacle before he recovered, if that were possible, his respectability. Specifically, his conduct during the 24-hour strike, called for15 February, in response to the deportations on the S.S. *Buenos Aires*. The reason why, one recalls, the prisoners in the Modelo in Barcelona, led by García Oliver, had called for Pestaña's resignation, holding him virtually responsible for these deportations.

The plenum recognised that the handling of the strike began before the departure of the deportees on 10 February. Specifically, the national committee issued a statement, on 31 January, stating that the deportations constituted a direct attack against the CNT, indicating the need to do something, and referring to the intention of some regional committees to call an indefinite general strike. The entire organisation was consulted with regard to its disposition: the Levante warned that its situation, after the last strike, was "a bit delicate", though it insisted that this did not mean it would not support the strike, but that if there were "other means of making the protest effective, they should be employed"; Galicia would initiate criticism of the government decision and hoped to organise an act of public solidarity with the deportees , though "if this were impossible, a manifesto would be printed"; Asturias would protest to the government, as well as staging acts of protest. But with regard to the strike, would support it "if possible", but without prejudice to the organisation which "is constantly required to waste energy that is so important to us"; the Centre, meanwhile, replied that, if the other regional committees decided to join the protest, it would support it, but went on to say that, "in accordance with our possibilities". Although it proposed meeting with the government first and conducting a campaign with rallies, telegrams and visits to authorities in order to generate a strike atmosphere. The remaining regional committees, namely, the North, the Balearics and the two strongest, Catalonia and Andalusia, did not even answer. So, given the ambiguity of these answers, the committee sent a circular on February 8 saying that it would organise a protest campaign to foster a mood of public opinion that would make the government back down and, if necessary, prepare "higher profile actions".

But at the meeting held on 9 February, the delegates from the Construction, Chemical Products and Manufacturing and Textile Unions, including García Oliver, expressed their disapproval of the national committee's interpretation, since, as they saw it, there were several regional committees that wanted to conduct a general strike throughout Spain, so it was agreed to amend the previous day's circular. Thus, on 11 February, telegrams were sent to the regional committees, asking each to state its position in relation to the movement. Seville answered "Mum worse. We are prepared for operation. Respond"; Palma de Mallorca declared that "given special situation we cannot indicate attitude", but said it would do the most it could; Coruña gave the national committee a vote of confidence, but warned that the strike should be for a "limited time"; while the Centre advocated a 48-hour general strike. On the 12th, the decision was taken to call a 24-hour general strike, which, according to the organisation, "enjoyed huge support, in spite of the biased efforts of the bourgeois, cave-dwelling press". According to the French consulates in Spain, the situation was normal in Madrid, Alicante, La Coruña and Bilbao, while in Barcelona the strike had failed and in Valencia, thanks to the pre-emptive arrests, order was "guaranteed in the long term". There was greater support in Andalusia, with stoppages in Jerez and Seville, and a general strike in Malaga that had paralysed the city.[173]

But beyond the result of the strike, what interests us here is to ascertain whether Pestaña, as secretary general of the CNT at the time, had acted as a traitor, as García Oliver had claimed while in prison in Barcelona. The plenum of April 1932, which reviewed the national committee's actions, highlighted "the lack of organic dynamism" inferred from a reading of the minutes, while it stressed that the regional federations had answered with "such laconism, lack of clarity and ambiguity that they are the cause, no longer of varied and capricious interventions, but of it always being the national committee that carries the stigma of not fulfilling its duty and not responding to the organisation's mandate". Consequently, the plenum agreed that the national committee had "quite rightly" consulted the entire organisation regarding what to do and, in view of the regional committees' answers, taken a reasonable decision, reflected in the 8 February circular, which responded "genuinely to the rather ambiguous mandate provided by the regional committees that replied". So the following day's agreement was not justified, "as contrary to how the minutes of that meeting record that various regional committees support a general strike across Spain, this is not reflected in the documentation". The verdict also meant that the national committee, "thanks to its adept coordination (...) succeeded in ensuring that the general strike had the desired effect". Therefore, the commission requested that the plenum accept "without any reservation whatsoever, the national committee's handling of this strike movement".[174]

Ultimately, the organisation in the form of the national plenum voiced its approval of the actions of the committee presided over by Pestaña both during the January 1932 movement, and in the calling of the 15 February general strike. A resolution that questioned the harsh criticism directed at the secretary. The rectification was late, for the damage was already done. Although it should really be said that this resolution did not matter much, since one of the objectives of the campaign had been achieved, namely, the removal of the anarcho-syndicalists from key positions in the confederal leadership. What is more, one might even say that this resolution was necessary for the new national committee presided over by Manuel Rivas, since some of its members had also sat on the previous committee.

What is important now is to analyse what the CNT did to delimit responsibilities and analyse the cascade of serious accusations and insults proffered by prominent anarchists against the anarcho-syndicalist leaders whose conduct had been approved by the organisation

But Mira was Missing

The CNT made an initial attempt to establish responsibilities at the same national plenum that analysed the actions of Pestaña's committee. However, in spite of the fact that the organisation had summoned the *El Luchador* editorial staff, they did not show up. Anyway, the plenum passed a resolution expressing "its strongest protest against the actions of Urales", which were "regarded as schismatic and filled with hatred and personal ambition", concluding with a request for the end of "tendentious and personalist campaigns". Ultimately it can only be described as strange that the organisation, now, was expressing its indignation, when the new national committee was the consequence, to a large extent, of that "tendentious and personalist" campaign. As strange too was the fact that the same plenum spoke of punishing "whoever accuses without proof" and, however, left in the hands of the Catalan regional committee, main anarchist focus and centre of the confrontation, possible responsibilities.[175]

For their part, the "Urales" justified their absence from the plenum with "the trap that some leaders had set them in Madrid", since in the committees they had "enemies as a result of our campaigns against political deviations". Enemies who were none other than "the worker politicians" who sought their expulsion. So they did not hesitate to question the internal democracy of the Confederation by observing that "the CNT representation is in the unions and not in the committees". An affirmation that was no coincidence if we bear in mind the federal system that regulated relations in the CNT, where fines and expulsions of members depended on each union, and not on the organisation as a whole.[176]

The "Urales" once again employed their favourite tactic, which was none other than presenting themselves as victims when really they were the aggressors. Because the campaign promoted by the anarchists and developed, in particular, by *El Luchador* would not end with the expulsion of the famous family, but with that of those who, like the *treintistas*, had a different vision to theirs, or, put another way, a primarily syndicalist vision of the CNT. This objective was shared by a broad majority of anarchists, whether in the FAI or not, which Federica called "a sacred union between all libertarians, all the apolitical, all of those of us who are within principles (...) against reformism and that pure syndicalism"; in other words, against "los Pestaña, los Peiró, los Clará, los Gibanel (...) los Torres, los Sánchez, los Pla, los Villaverdes", traitors who had collaborated with the repression of the deported anarchists and who were advised that in order to defend the Republic they should occupy the "vacant posts in the Civil Guard or the Assault Guard".[177] But of all of these, one was a particular target for the anger of the Urales, especially Federica, and this was none other than Emilio Mira, the secretary general of the Catalan regional committee, largely because, following Pestaña's resignation, this was the bastion to be conquered. Despite the fact that at the beginning of April, in other words, a month after Pestaña's departure, *El Luchador* published an article, entitled "History and Liquidation of a Campaign", announcing the end of its work against the moderate leaders.[178]

The regional committee of Catalonia had already held a meeting with the "Urales", on 28 February, in the *El Luchador* newsroom, to resolve the confrontation with Mira, with the family having vetoed the latter's presence. A strange circumstance if we bear in mind that Mira was still, on that date, secretary of the regional committee. Sebastián Flor, member of the regional committee, read out the entire battery of insinuations that Federica had included in her now famous "*Yo acuso*". Following discussion, the regional committee recorded the minutes of the meeting, noting that

> Federica Montseny declares, with regard to the specific data taken from her article, that she is not in possession of objective proof of what she claims, but that it was common knowledge that Mira was capable of these things, and that it was no secret for those who know him that he can do what has been said. She is absolutely convinced of his lack of scruples, and that what has been published reflects his personal morality.[179]

So the regional committee published a note in *Solidaridad Obrera*, dated 7 March, to the effect that the meeting "clarified nothing insofar as, we reiterate, the accuser based her arguments on a personal conviction that, she said, she will maintain if necessary before the Catalan organisation". In conclusion, the committee indicated that the action of one of its members "cannot be at the mercy of the suppositions of anybody, and even less so when these leave an atmosphere of doubt". The note ended by ratifying, with one member, Arnau, voting against, the committee's confidence in Mira.

For her part, Federica offered a different interpretation of the meeting. For her the committee that she was confronting was not "the regional committee of Catalonia, but a committee that was an enemy of the Urales family", in short, "a *treintista* committee". As for the list of questions that she was asked, she had no hesitation in describing it as "loaded". Although her response, as she acknowledged, was that "no government instrument leaves evidence of its pacts. It is signs, words, acts, the history of the individual, which provide it". Basically, she had no proof, only suspicions and personal appraisals that supported her position. The "Urales" demanded the withdrawal of the note published in *Solidaridad*, and said that they could not agree to the Mira issue ending in this manner, leaving them "so unfairly prejudiced in the eyes of their comrades". So they urged the committee to rectify the situation, and were even prepared to help, provided they knew how to "tackle the causes of evil and take drastic action".[180]

The regional plenum of Catalonia, held in Sabadell, at the end of April 1932, was the perfect scenario in which to "take drastic action". What first needs to be noted is the sharp fall in membership of the Catalan CNT, since if at the plenum held in early August, 1931, at the Radical Republican Athenaeum, 321,394 members were represented – though evidence points to a real membership of around 400,000 – now, eight months later, there were 223,732 members.[181] In other words, if we take the figures for members with representation, membership had decreased by around 30%, while if we employ the figure for real membership the reduction was about 44%. Quantities that evidenced the crisis, resulting to a large extent from the internal struggle in which the CNT's most charismatic committee was immersed.

In fact, the plenum revealed the bitter confrontation that existed between anarchists and anarcho-syndicalists. Tthe Catalan anarchists wanted to "correct the mistakes" made by the CNT national plenum that had approved the actions of Pestaña's committee during the Figols incident and the subsequent general strike. The regional plenum proposed a motion that, via consultation of the same documentation to which the national plenum had access, considered "that comrade Pestaña exceeded his authority as secretary general of the National Committee", as, given the importance of the circular of the 8th, he should have convened the committee, but did not do so. While the anarcho-syndicalists pointed to the contradiction implicit in this resolution when the national `plenum had exonerated him.

Against this background, the sessions were unusually lively, and the chairman found himself continually calling for "calm and serenity". The culminating point was the direct clash between García Oliver and Pestaña. The former accused Pestaña of taking action on his own, without consulting the rest of the national committee, although he recognised that his criticism also served to "offer elements of proof to Federica Montseny for her article 'Yo acuso' ". A truly surprising declaration that shows, on the one hand, the imperious need to back up certain accusations that were lacking any proof; and, on the other, the "sacred union" of the anarchists, above and beyond their differences – which between Federica and Oliver were evident – against the common *treintista* "enemy".

Meanwhile, the former secretary defended his actions on the grounds of the necessary haste to prevent the deportations, and "the chaotic way" in which the committee functioned. An argument corroborated by such disparate unions as the Construction Union Barcelona or the Glassmakers of Badalona: the former indicated that there was no daily meeting, "but a daily exchange of impressions", the latter that as a rule they met on Tuesdays and Thursdays. Confusion that continued when there was an attempt to find out whether committee members had to meet every day. In this respect, Francisco Arín, of the Barcelona Transport Union, pointed out that, in other times, they also agreed to meet on a daily basis, but "almost always the majority did not turn up. There were two or three that had to reach agreements and put them into practice". Furthermore, when asked if the circular of the 10th was drafted at a committee meeting, members' answers were contradictory. Faced with such confusion, the plenum resolved that a national congress should decide, in other words, true "pie in the sky".[182]

The plenum's response to the other major confrontation that stirred up passions at the assembly, between Federica and Mira, was not much better. The plenum had to deliberate on the regional committee's intervention in the Figols movement and with regard to Federica's serious accusations against its secretary. Questions that the national plenum had also tried to analyse, but the "Urales'" refusal to attend, as we recall, prevented this. Now, in Catalonia, conditions were more favourable, and they decoded to attend the regional congress in spite of the fact that, according to them, they had not been invited.[183] But the plenum agreed, before it began, not to address this important question, "alleging dangers and compromises for the organisation that might derive from the discussion". In the light of this resolution, Mira, who had already presented his irrevocable resignation, protested and described this fear as unfounded, since the uprising had concluded some time ago. However, what had not ended were the accusations of "treason and police collaboration that had to be paid for" in economic terms, allegations that undermined his morale. Federica, meanwhile, considered this debate "inopportune", as it should have been postponed until discussion, in secret, of events in Figols. The *treintista* sectors argued that "when the accusation has been public, public too should be the verdict that condemns or acquits". Meanwhile, the delegations with an anarchist majority requested a postponement of the debate, interpreting that both Mira's dignity "and that of comrade Montseny have been safeguarded". In short, the plenum opted to defer discussion of this question.[184]

Federica, from her vantage point at *El Luchador,* described the agreement as "a measure of discretion and humanity", reached after a battle with certain delegations that were determined that the debate should unfold "before the eyes and ears of the governor's delegate and four individuals from the Social Brigade". In contrast with the delegates seeking to attribute responsibility, continued Federica, were the comrades from Figols, who revealed their dignity "in the face of the inhuman and offensive attitude of a sector of the Plenum that insinuated that my attitude (...) was born of a lack of concrete evidence". Thankfully, she said, "manhood and common sense prevailed".[185]

The plenum still had to address two more thorny issues: the situation of *Solidaridad Obrera,* and the appointment of the new secretary of the regional committee. Regarding the confederal newspaper, one should first allude to the economic difficulties it was experiencing, because of the reduced circulation. According to the paper's director, in order to cover costs they need to sell 30,000 copies, but at the moment were only managing 26,000. Long gone were the numbers upon the advent of the Republic, when the newspaper had an average circulation of 31,900 copies in April, and 39,000 the following month;[186] in other words, a fall of one third. The main reason for the decline was, they said, government repression with continuous censorship and confiscation of copies. Although it is true that the authorities' actions considerably influenced its diffusion – in fact, the newspaper had reappeared, following a five-week ban, on 2 March – the paper's new direction, after Alaiz took over as editor, with an intransigent editorial line, which paid particular attention to internal polemic that were of little interest to the workers, reduced its presence on the streets.

The newspaper also had leadership problems. Felipe Alaiz had presented his resignation on account of some militants in the organisation having written articles in the paper and not assumed responsibility for their content, as a result of which, as editor of the newspaper, he found himself in prison. The regional committee, still controlled by Mira, decided to reorganise the editorial team, with José Robusté, as acting chief editor, Ramón Segarra, Erofilo Labrador, Manuel Medina and Benigno Bejarano, editors, as well as appointing Ramón J. Sender as Madrid correspondent, maintaining Gil Bei's collaboration.[187] Now, in April 1932, the former editor had presented a report that was highly critical of the new team. Present in this debate too, Federica accused the editorial staff, critical of Alaiz, "of a lack of consideration and manhood". Federica was in favour of the censorship applied by Alaiz, as with him "there would be no deviations, traps or trampolines", which would have purged *Solidaridad* of political messages. The change in the newspaper's management had not found favour with *El Luchador*, which soon began to accuse it of being as a mouthpiece of the *treintistas*, and had little time for Sender either, who was described as opposed to the CNT because he called "the anarchists of the FAI fanatics".[188] The plenum confirmed its trust in the new editorial team and agreed "to grant the editorial team absolute freedom and autonomy (…) and not to hinder in any way its work as a provider of information", provided, of course, the opinions expressed reflected CNT principles.[189]

Finally, the plenum voted on the appointment of the new secretary general, which went the way of Alejandro Gilabert, who obtained 111 votes, compare with 74 for Juan Manent, Peiró's right-hand man. The appointment was not without controversy, as the *treintistas* delegations complained about the voting system, arguing that it should only include members up to date with their payment of the confederal stamp, as had been decided at the previous meeting held in Lerida. As a result, the local Sabadell federation abandoned the plenum. The following months saw the expulsion from the CNT of these unions, with their 15,000–20,000 members.[190] The regional plenum of Catalonia opened the way for the witch-hunt that was performed in the CNT.

Responsibilities and Expulsions

The press had been the key channel for anarchist propaganda in the quest for power, while the unions constituted the launch pad and played a fundamental role in in the purging of *treintista* elements, owing to the CNT's organic regulations. Thus, for example, when the Galician delegate asked, during the national plenum, about Catalonia's actions against the Urales on account of their campaign in *El Luchador*, the response was that the Catalan regional committee could not assume responsibilities to which it was not entitled, since the fines, if applicable, corresponded exclusively to the Union of Intellectual Workers, to which the "Urales" belonged.[191] But there was no need, as only the anarcho-syndicalists were expelled: the Barcelona Construction Union dismissed Juan López; the Food Union, Ricardo Fornells and the Metallurgy Union, Ángel Pestaña, among many others. Cases deserving of special attention.

In the case of the former, proceedings were opened when he wrote an article in the *treintista* weekly *Cultura Libertaria*, entitled "A revolutionary institution". López returned to Federica's "*Yo acuso*" and pointed to the organisation's silence during the attacks against Pestaña and Mira. At the same time, he accused the "revolutionary" faction of "perfectly counter-revolutionary and anti-workers behaviour", while he described its members as fanatics and accused them of disrupting union assemblies.[192] So the national committee published a circular indicating that López had provided no proof of his accusations in the article, and, in accordance with the resolution adopted at the 1931 congress, which agreed to sanction those who accused without proof, urged the Barcelona organisation to intervene. Though if the latter did not, the committee itself offered to do so "in energetic fashion against those who slander sand do not provide proof".[193] The Construction Union demanded the presence of Juan López on various occasions, but when he failed to appear he was expelled in 1932.[194]

In Fornells' case, the single union of the Barcelona Food branch held an extraordinary assembly on November 16, 1932. Among those present was Durruti who, according to the minutes, played the part of "accuser". He described as "insidious" the contents of a letter written by Fornells in which he said "the watchword is the expulsion from the unions of the signatories of the '*treintista*' manifesto and columnists of *Cultura Libertaria*", as well as referring to some colleagues as bank robbers. Durruti demanded that Fornells clarify his comments, and warned that, otherwise, he would invoke what had been agreed at the organisation's last national congress, namely, "whoever accuses without providing evidence will be expelled"; while le accused the *treintistas* of having "submitted the organisation to the will of the Catalan Left".

The minutes reflect a "flattened" Fornells, who barely responded to Durruti's intervention. Although in his defence, he explained that his words were a reaction to the attacks launched by his comrade Agustina, who said "that all the signatories of the manifesto were protégés". Vis-à-vis the allusion to robbers, he referred to the *Solidaridad Obrera* of 1922 and 1923, which said "the organisation opposed these robberies and the pro-prisoner Committee refused to aid some individuals in the belief that they had participated in the latter". Finally, Fornells pointed to some irregularities in the current assembly, such as the presence of individuals from outside the branch, without mentioning names, though everything suggests that he was referring to Durruti, who belonged to the Manufacturing and Textile Union.

Another of those present, a certain Marco, dared to ask Durruti and Agustina to justify their accusations. To which the former replied that he was prepared to do so where necessary, and, by way of challenge, suggested that, as the belonged to the same union, Marco propose an assembly there to discuss this question. No reply to this is recorded in the minutes, although Marco had already shown considerable courage in requesting explanations from Durruti at a union assembly. For her part, Agustina said, in her defence, that she only referred to one of the *treintistas*, without going into more detail. These "explanations", which maintained the accusations with providing proof, satisfied Durruti and Agustina but not Fornells. So their expulsion was proposed on account of not clarifying their accusations, and "when the assembly was asked the question (…) a unanimous yes was the response".[195]

Finally, the Metallurgy Union published a document detailing the grounds for Pestaña's expulsion. The text began with what, in truth, formed the basis for the accusations, which was the *Treintista* Manifesto, regarded as a "negation of principles". But Pestaña, the document went on to say, "not only did not rectify" the situation, but through his writings and addresses "continues to add to the confusion" and, more importantly, discredits all those occupying posts, calling them "irresponsible and cowardly", without ever offering proof. Pestaña had also published articles in the bourgeois press in relation to the Statute of Catalonia and advising workers "not to employ violence to the detriment of the new Statute of autonomy", which was regarded as going against the CNT's apoliticism, voicing opinions contrary to the organisation's postulates, from an "openly reformist" position. In short, he was asked to rectify, but did not. To the contrary, Pestaña made a show of his support for the Sabadell unions, expelled from the organisation, and branded as traitors the committee members "without providing evidence". Conduct that justified his expulsion.

A controversial expulsion in itself, given both the substance of the person, and the insistence on providing proof of his accusations when he had been at the centre of a campaign that had not excelled in terms of supporting very serious allegations. But also because it occurred in a manner that questioned his "legality". Specifically, the voting with regard to is expulsion did not take place in a plenum of the Metallurgy Union, but votes were cast in each of the sections before the result was communicated to the branch, without any option of rectifying the agreement already reached. Although the organisation declared that this method was logical in such a large union, some members did dispute the resolution. This circumstance seems to suggest that the smaller the organisation's sphere of decision, the greater the anarchists' influence. The presence of individuals like García Oliver, Ascaso or Durruti, as we have seen in the case of Fornells, to name the best-known anarchists, must have imposed considerable "respect". Ultimately, the sections of the Metallurgy Union approved Pestaña's expulsion, an agreement that was presented before the general assembly of the branch on 4 December 1932, and ratified.[196]

Although all these decisions taken in the unions appear to be democratic, this is somewhat misleading. It is true that the measures were taken in assemblies, but it should not be forgotten that the campaign promoted by the anarchists was based on accusations that were never substantiated, lies or half-lies that were used to discredit those whom they sought to remove from the confederal leadership. A strategy in which it seemed that anything was acceptable, from insults to personal attacks, including accusations of corruption, treason or dishonesty without any evidence beyond the personal opinion of the accuser. Union assemblies in which radicalisation was very present and in which swimming against that current could lead to being branded a *treintista* or, much the same, a "bureaucratised politician". The federal structure also influenced the result of the internal confrontation. The autonomy of the grass roots union when calling strikes, independently of the rest of the organisation, was denounced as a malpractice of the federal system that governed the CNT. Autonomy that became pre-eminence when addressing the responsibility of militants involved in the internal struggle. Decisions that should have been taken by the organisation as a whole, because they mainly concerned the latter, were taken in a grass roots union where the mere presence of prestigious militants imposed a line of action that could not easily be challenged.

At the end of the day, what happened in the CNT was the pure and simple expression of a power struggle, as occurred in any political party or in the parliament of any country, however much the word "politician" was employed, in libertarian circles, as the ultimate insult. The culmination of the campaign not only elevated the anarchists to the confederal leadership, but also changed the very essence of the organisation. The CNT abandoned the path of union struggle to follow, now unmistakeably, the path of insurrection.

3

To the Barricades! (May 1932–December 1933)

Fresh Anarchist Winds

The new national committee of the CNT had begun its journey, as we have seen, in March 1932. Along with the secretary general, Manuel Rivas, from the Construction Union, was, in the post of deputy secretary, another important FAI member and one of *Los Solidarios*, Ricardo Sanz, from the Merchants' Union; Ricardo Peña, treasurer, from Transport; Emilio Molins, accountant, member of the Leather Union. The remaining committee members were, Eugenio Benedicto, of the Barbers' Union; Oscar Gonbau, Chemicals; Francisco Señer, Metallurgy; José Ramos, Railways; José Cuevas, Manufacturing and Textile; Emilio Cuadras, Entertainment; Miguel Terrén, Telephones; Julio Campos, Public Services and Marcos Alcón, Glassmakers. All were members of the Barcelona local trade unions.[1]

A composition that was not free of controversy, since, as F. Wilkens, secretary of the Centre regional committee, noted, the national committee exhibited "merely local characteristics", and did not respond to the organisation's federalist tenets. Wilkens proposed two fundamental reforms for the constitution and activity of the highest confederal organ. On the one hand, that the committee should cease to be an "office of simple processing and public relations", in order immediately to set the organisation in motion whenever necessary, in other words, have "a flexibility" which it lacked. On the other hand, and in complementary fashion to the latter, that the committee should be formed by direct delegates from the regional committees and not by those from the local unions. Because the highest confederal organ should represent the entire organisation and be thoroughly familiar with its situation so as to transmit the necessary instructions as quickly as possible. Only thus was sit possible to avoid "the lamentable spectacle" of a committee telephoning or sending telegrams to the regional committees to ask how it should act.[2]

These questions were the subject of discussion at the first national plenum held by the organisation with the new national committee, in April 1932. It was clear to all that the confrontation in Catalonia between anarchists and anarcho-syndicalists had resulted in radical change, and that the local Barcelona unions had played a fundamental role, tipping the balance in favour of the former. So the Catalan regional committee, understandably, was opposed to any change, and pointed out that the plenum was not authorised to adopt such resolutions, so the discussion should be deferred until a later congress. An argument that, on the basis of confederal rules, was supported by the plenum.[3]

The national committee, led by Rivas, showed that times had changed at the CNT. Thus, in one of its first notes, dated March 24, it sent messages for those inside and outside the organisation. Externally, it established its position against everything and everybody, which meant the isolation of the Confederation: "nobody should approach us if they are not from our media, we will not listen to anybody". Internally, with the warning that any comrade who, "rightly or wrongly", publically asked questions that might harm the organisation could be disqualified from holding any office, and, if they reoffended, would be "definitively expelled from the CNT".[4]

New times that were also appreciable in the change of strategy in the confederal struggle. The June congress adopted, as will be recalled, the reduction of the working day to limit lockouts, although the real solution was revolution. Now another step was taken, and partial or general battles were said to serve only "to satisfy an immediate economic need". The time had come to transcend these occasional battles and contribute with every means available to the expeditious preparation of resources for the "implantation of libertarian communism". In short, the union struggle was postponed in the interests of insurrection.[5]

The April 8 Law

This new strategy coincided in time with the government's adoption of the Law on Professional Associations of April 8, 1932, which completed the May 1931 decree on the setting up of the mixed juries. The functioning of the associations was strictly regulated, from their inscription in the company registry to the obligatory presentation of membership and accounts books. The Provincial Labour Delegation would conduct strict control of members and in particular of executive boards. The labour delegates could fine and even suspend the legal activity of associations, with the approval of the Ministry, although under legal control, alone in its authority to suspend them.[6] The Law insisted on conduct in accordance with the approaches and characteristics of the UGT, with the corresponding benefits. Thus, its promulgation fostered, even further, the rivalry with the CNT. Azaña himself again referred to this confrontation in his diary, and to how the socialists were determined to retain control in social questions, or, more accurately, to "guarantee via the ministerial bodies a defence against their terrible enemies, the CNT syndicalists".[7]

The confederal media emphasised, once again, how the new law represented an attack on the principle of direct action. This was nothing new. It had been the case with the joint committees and, later, with the mixed juries. But the recently adopted law posed two new problems: its potential use for repression and the possible illegalisation of the organisation. Regarding the former, the CNT feared that the lists of members and, particularly, of the executive boards could end up in the hands of the police, which would facilitate the arrest of leading militants with the ensuing disruption for the organisation. Secondly, the national committee itself thought that the CNT's legal life was under threat, with a more than likely return to clandestinity; in fact, the Ministry of the Interior sent a circular to civil governors demanding of all entities "immediate and precise compliance with its provisions", and, otherwise, "suspension of their activities and closure of their premises".[8] In any case, the application of the law was not so strict, and it did not come into force, according to the CNT, "with the rigour that the government and the socialists had hoped for".[9]

The national committee's viewpoint was shared, inevitably, by the new editorial team of *Solidaridad Obrera*, led once again by Felipe Alaiz, albeit symbolically, as he was still in prison. Liberto Callejas occupied the post of interim director, while Arturo Parera, José Bonet, Juan Manuel Molina alias *Juanel* and Evelino G. Fontaura were the editors.[10] Well, *Solidaridad Obrera*, in line with the national committee, put a new spin on the objectives of the April 8 Law, and warned that it was an attack not only on direct action, but on something much more important, "the apoliticism of the CNT". The intention was none other than to introduce the organisation into "trade union politics . . . , to curtail its revolutionary virility and turn it into a shapeless organism, duplicitous and inefficient like the UGT". So the confederal leadership even considered clandestinity rather than acceptance of the law, with the support of *Solidaridad*, for whom clandestinity was "purity", the stronghold where "the flames of the struggle" were rekindled.[11]

In any case, although the regional committees were opposed to the law, it was not easy for the organisation to articulate a general response, and all the more so when the dilemma seemed to be legality or clandestinity. But also because the workers were always seeking, as Peiró had observed – with his theory of need and convenience – the best way of achieving their goals, beyond maximalist positions. Thus, the Railway Federation had qualms about not obeying the law, as it would mean the disappearance of its organisation, while the regional federation of Andalusia asked the national committee if it was necessary to respect confederal agreements or, given the situation, change tactics to avoid closure.[12]

Meanwhile, Largo Caballero exerted pressure on the government, denouncing the administration of some governors who recognised the CNT unions, although they were not legally constituted.[13] A circumstance that further complicated confederal life, and facilitated the omnipresence of the UGT in numerous negotiations, with the resultant increase in membership, which had been growing in exponential fashion since the beginning of the Republic. The *UGT Bulletin* reported that between April and June of 1931 there was an average of 2,000 new members every day, which meant 180,000 in the first three months of the new regime. In October 1931, there were over 600,000 members, and by the start of the following year, around a million. A significant element of the UGT's growth came from the *Federación Nacional de*

Trabajadores de la Tierra (National Federation of Land Workers or FNTT), affiliated to the UGT, which had expanded from 36,000 members in June 1931 to around 400,000 one year later, in other words, about 40% of the total membership.[14]

Conflict in the Countryside

In spite of the socialist union's impressive growth in rural areas, farmworkers continued to live in extreme conditions, especially in Andalucía and Extremadura. Telegrams sent to the Ministry of Governance from Andalusia, in the spring of 1932, reported that in towns like Ronda there were 900 workers unemployed, or in Fuengirola 1,000, while in Jubrique they were expecting "probable riots because of hunger". News that was mixed with thefts of olives from farms in Antequera or the actions of groups of unemployed workers in Granada who forced shops to give them food.[15]

In this context, the provincial plenum of CNT in Seville drafted some labour laws to be presented to employers on 5 May. As no response was forthcoming, a strike was called for the 19th. However, two days earlier, in the town of Montellano, two bombs exploded in the house of Ildefonso Jiménez Arenillas, president of the local CNT unions, leaving his mother dead and seven other family members injured. The next day, the Civil Guard discovered a significant quantity of explosives in Morón.[16] This situation caused considerable confusion within the organisation, as no sooner had the strike been called than telegrams were sent suspending it. So "in this atmosphere of doubt and hesitation" the movement erupted. The union of farmworkers, in their headlong flight, requested help from the regional committee in the form of a general strike. As usually happened in these cases, the unions declared in favour of the strike, but, as also tended to be the case, the regional stoppage did not have the hoped-for impact, because "many organisations that had pledged to go on strike, when the time came, failed to meet their obligations".[17] One thing was the drive of militants and leaders and quite another the mood of a sizeable proportion of members.

The repression of the movement meant the closure of the unions in the city and province of Seville, and the arrest of hundreds of comrades. Of these, 186 were tried, in October 1933, for sedition and possession of explosives. The public prosecutor requested, in total, over 2,000 years' imprisonment.[18] In spite of the failures, the harsh repression and internal confrontation, the Andalusian organisation called a new strike for June 1 and 2 in protest against the labour laws issued by the government as a solution to the conflict that had led to the previous month's strike. The new repression meant that the number of those arrested, according to confederal sources, climbed to a total of 600.[19]

But if the CNT protested against the laws imposed by the government, employers simply ignored them and the UGT called for them to be observed. The socialist union denounced the use of machines for all harvesting activities, which left specialised workers without work, as well as the refusal to employ of unionised workers, or respect negotiated salaries. All this despite "a magnificent harvest".[20] Employers' non-compliance was a constant factor in a multitude of conflicts, to the extent that, according to Ministry of Labour data, 83% of infringements of labour legislation in 1932 were attributed to management.[21] In Carcabuey (Córdoba), bosses "systematically refused to give work to fathers because they were union members". The president of the tenant farmers on agricultural landholdings in Andalusia noted that they were "prosecuted by the owners (…) leading to their ruin", so he requested government protection against "this persecution and cruelty". However, the authorities sought the provisional remedy of repression, normally of the weakest, to tackle a problem that involved respect for the law and negotiated labour rules. The Civil Governor of Cordoba reported that in the town of Villa del Río there were numerous unemployed workers, so in anticipation of excesses he ordered "the closure of the workers' centre and the arrest of the leading agitators to avoid a day of mourning", though he acknowledged that the situation of the workers was "truly desperate". This did not preclude him from ordering the deployment of the Civil Guard to prevent "as had occurred during previous strikes (…) attacks on owners' businesses and homes".[22]

The UGT saw how the reactionary stance of employers anchored in a past of arbitrariness jeopardised its attempts at reform. Frustration that was reflected in the XVII UGT congress held at the end of 1932, with references to how the caciques persecuted "workers in ruthless fashion" and refused to employ "socialist comrades", situations that became increasingly frequent during the legislature.[23] Azaña himself observed how difficult it was to implement the decrees on forced ploughing and on the revision of smallholding rental rates in Andalucía.[24]

In these circumstances, the pressure executed by both the workers themselves, increasing angry at how difficult it was proving to achieve long-awaited improvements, and by the CNT, which repeatedly denounced the socialist restraint and the republican repression, led the UGT militants to begin to undertake actions incompatible with the principles of their union. Thus, in Cartagena, both unions, whose approaches were "normally different", met in the Casa del Pueblo, and called a general strike to resolve the unemployment problem, which surprised the French Consul and demonstrated "the gravity of the situation".[25] An atypical circumstance, certainly, in the middle of 1932, but which, with the advent of the Republic, was losing its element of eccentricity. In fact, at the end of that year, the UGT executive committee published a manifesto voicing its opposition to the increase in labour conflict: "enough sympathetic strikes, enough sentimental strikes; enough strikes against the employment crisis". Protests it regarded as "utter folly" because, to a large degree, they were beyond its control.[26]

But the CNT pressed on. Between the strike in mid-May and the one early in June, it called another protest, for May 29. Firstly, in defence of the *Buenos Aires* deportees, but also because of everything in general: state interference in economic conflicts; the *presos gubernativos*; the absence of freedom to hold meetings and demonstrations; and the closure of newspapers and unions.[27] The protests spread right across the country: in Barcelona, there were demonstrations and clashes with the assault troops, leaving 17 injured; in Bilbao, five telephone poles were brought down with dynamite; in Alcañiz (Teruel), CNT leaders were arrested; in Cádiz and Jaen there was major unrest that was "energetically repressed"; and in Archidona (Malaga) two demonstrators were shot dead by the Civil Guard. Other places, like Segovia, Ceuta and Murcia, were calm.[28]

Protests that did not resolve any of the problems as a consequence of which they were organised, but which placed the organisation in an increasingly weak position. The national committee issued a circular, in the month of July, acknowledging that there were "more unions closed down than when the congress was postponed (in other words, in April) and that their number had increased as a result of the events of May 29". The more powerful regional committees suffered the greatest repression, so Andalusia found itself in a critical situation with "the bulk of the organisation forced underground". A similar scenario to that of Catalonia, where Barcelona's unions continued to be illegal; and the Levante, with some county committees and trades unions shut down.[29] But the evolution of events would not improve the situation in the coming months, even years, which meant that the anticipated confederal congress was not held until May 1936.

All these circumstances – economic crisis, unemployment, disenchantment with the Republic, internal confrontation, lack of results in strikes and mobilisations – led to disillusion among the workers, evidenced by, among other factors, the reduction in CNT membership. Although membership statistics should always be treated with caution, there was certainly steady growth following the proclamation of the Republic, with over 600,000 members, at the time of the June 1931 congress, until the confederal apogee, in autumn of the same year, with estimates of between 800,000 and one million members. This trend was also apparent in such important regional committees as Catalonia and the Levante. In the former, there were around 195,000 members in May 1931, while by the regional plenum in August there were almost 400,000, nearly double; with regard to the latter, if at the confederal congress of June 1931 it had 53,768 members, by the following January this number had risen to around 100.000, almost twice as many. In other words, membership of both regional committees had increased by around 100%.

However, the trend changed in 1932. At the Catalan regional plenum, held in April, the delegates represented 223,732 members, a figure that when compared with those represented at the August plenum of the previous year, 321,394 (though membership stood at around 400.000), represents a decrease of almost 100.000, in other words, about 30%. Meanwhile, in the Levante, the regional congress held in the summer of 1932 reflected a total of 70,295 members, compared with 100.000 in January, almost 30,000 members fewer, which represented, as in Catalonia, a 30% reduction.[30]

This situation was aggravated by the major unemployment problem that affected, in particular, Andalucía, where of the 325,000 members registered in

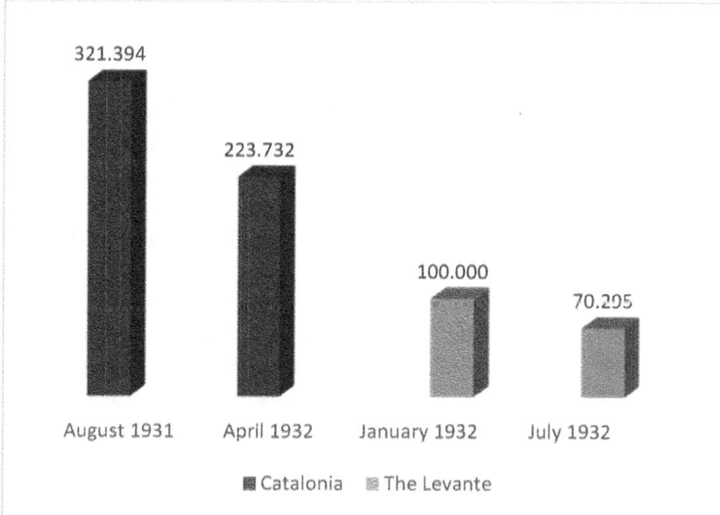

Figure 1 Membership in Catalonia and The Levante.

April 1932, 65% were out of work, with the corresponding impact upon confederal membership fees.[31] Figures, all of them, that affected confederal activity in the press, committees, prisoners, and propaganda. The weekly membership fee was, in the early days of the Republic, 0.25 pesetas for men and 0.15 for women and apprentices, added to which was payment of the confederal stamp, which was one peseta per month, and funded the activities of the national and the regional committees. Of this stamp, two cents were employed, in Catalonia, to maintain *Solidaridad Obrera*.[32] In short, reduced membership and the inability of the unemployed to pay their fees significantly undermined confederal activity.

Although an incident that endangered the Republic served to improve the situation of the CNT and also that of the deportees: General Sanjurjo's coup d'état.

Sanjurjo's Coup, the CNT and the Deportees

On August 10, 1932, General Sanjurjo initiated a coup d'état against the Republic. This was the most serious attempt since the proclamation of the new regime, but not the only one. A simple reading of the diaries of Azaña, Minister of War at the time, reveals all the activity in the army barracks. The August coup involved, according to Cardona and Ballbé, from members of the military, like Orgaz, Goded, Varela and Cabanellas – dismissed as director of the Civil Guard because of his "lukewarm response" to the coup, and later discovered to have been involved – to aristocrats, like the Count of Vallellano, as well as bankers, Oriol, Subiría and Urquijo, and politicians, Fuentes Pila, Onésimo Redondo and "maybe Lerroux".[33]

Sanjurjo himself was in Seville and, given the lack of support in the rest of Spain, he decided to flee to Portugal. En route, he was aided by the Civil Guard, according to the Huelva command records. The Villalba del Alcor station received a detention order that "was not obeyed by the commanding officer, Sergeant Don Matías Sánchez Guerra, although he had conversed with the General, when the latter passed him on the road". According to the document,

> everything was ready at this command post, with the mission of entrusting to its agents the safe passage of His Excellency General Sanjurjo to Portugal, who, from Seville, in the Company of General García de Herranz, Lieutenant Colonel Esteban Infantes and suitably escorted by an officer and several agents entered our province, arriving at the outskirts of the capital.[34]

But at the Isla Chica inn, where the convoy paused, Sanjurjo was recognised by a security guard, who had served in Africa under his command, and who was accompanied by several police officers, who arrested him and transferred him to the civil government.

The CNT national committee was in session at the time of the coup. The highest confederal organ considered taking to the streets, but in defence of the organisation and "of our own lives", not to save the Republic. The Confederation faced the dilemma that its "hostility towards the dictatorship that was seeking to impose itself would favour the designs of government elements, irreconcilable enemies of the working classes". A predicament that continued until the publication rebel general's proclamation, at which point the decision was taken to act firmly to quash the uprising. So the CNT took to the streets, "not to defend the Republic, evil stepmother of the people", but to prevent a dictatorship, though not before confirming that it lacked sufficient fighting tools to achieve the revolution. In any case, the advantage for the Andalusian regional committee consisted in the opening of some unions.[35]

The French ambassador, Jean Herbette, acknowledged that the action of the popular masses in places where the authorities were unable to control the rebels, as in the case of Seville, was decisive. But his reflection went further, as it was commonplace to see regime that depended on the energy of a small elite, but an adverse political system unable to establish itself because the masses responded to an attempted counter-revolutionary coup with a strike or a mutiny was unusual. Herbette illustrated his argument with the historical reminder that nothing similar had happened "neither in Italy nor in Germany, when the Brüning and the Braun governments fell". Herbette's conclusion, undoubtedly the cause of considerable concern, was that in Spain there existed "grounds for social revolution", but also "temperaments capable of giving free reign to this revolution".[36]

Sanjurjo was sentenced to death, and subsequently pardoned and imprisoned. The government, according to Cardona, "though aware of the wide support for the movement, acted with caution and restricted itself to punishing those whose involvement was most evident".[37] As a result, it applied the Law on the Defence of the Republic and deported 142 conspirators, civilian and military, to Villa Cisneros.[38] These incidents rekindled the demonstrations in favour of the CNT deportees on the S.S. *Buenos Aires.* The Ministry of Governance received a host of telegrams requesting not only the return of the deportees, but also the release of political prisoners and the opening of unions, "since the Republic has been benevolent with the Monarchic general and less so with the only true defenders of the Regime".[39]

The deported CNT members had been on quite a voyage since they left Barcelona on 10 February, 1932. The steamship, after calling in at Valencia and Cádiz to pick up more prisoners, stopped off in Dakar and headed for Guinea. But the pressure exerted by Spanish residents forced it back to Dakar, after which it set sail for the colony of Río de Oro and, later on, for Villa Cisneros, where it arrived on 27 March. However, the governor of the city, Captain Ramón Regueral Jové, refused to guard Durruti, as his father had been murdered in the 1920s by anarchist militants, so the ship made for Las Palmas. Meanwhile, several deportees had been taken ill, and before they docked, 24-year-old Antonio Soler Falcó died. Married, and a CNT member, he was from Sallent and worked in the Cardona mines, where he had taken part in the January strike. In Las Palmas, 30 prisoners were released and another 19 were hospitalised, and the steamship set sail once again without a specific destination. Passengers were dropped off during the voyage, with Durruti, Ascaso and Prieto, among others, disembarking in Fuerteventura, where they stayed until September. The ship then returned to Río de Oro and later to Villa Cisneros, where it left most of the deportees.[40]

Conditions on board do not appear to have been ideal. According to Bruno Lladó, one of the exiles, they were all put in the hold without a minimum of hygiene, or medical attention, which resulted in stomach infections and Soler death.[41] Their accomodation in Villa Cisneros also gave cause for complaint. The MP Ramón Franco, the general's brother, visited them and reported that their situation "could not be more depressing. Clothes in shreds, barefoot, some covering their nakedness with a blanket, badly shaven or bearded, they revealed the degree to which they had been abandoned by the republican state". Indeed, Franco supported, along with MPs Barriobero, Sediles and Soriano, who belonged to the radical minority, known as *jabalíes* (wild boars), a parliamentary motion requesting the suspension of the deportation or, at least, a fixed duration thereof. The Minister of the Interior, Casares Quiroga, ignored Franco's report and refused to set a date for their return because the Republic could be in danger. He mentioned the names of Durruti and Ascaso, "leaders of the *pistolerismo*", whose presence in Barcelona could provoke a "resurgence of crimes". Parliament opposed the motion by 119 votes to 39. Not before hearing MP Guerra del Río, of the Radical Republican Party, criticise the government for maintaining the Law of Defence of the Republic and, addressing the government benches, ask them:

> Do you really think the Republic is so eternally linked to yourselves that when you fall the Republic must necessarily fall too? (Major rumours) (…) that those who put the Republic at risk will find as soon as possible, not the exceptional arbitrariness, justified during the moments of danger when it was voted (…) but a law of a general nature, applicable to all.[42]

But those who had endangered the Republic were, in fact, a sizeable number of military personnel and civilians who were also deported to Villa Cisneros, which made it necessary for the CNT members to return. The new deportees were transported in the *Spain no. 5*, and escorted by the gunboat *Canalejas*. They appear to have been treated very differently from their predecessors. The gunboat commander "even offered the rebels a cocktail", while Captain Ruderal "stood to attention before one of the insurgents, the oldest in the group, the infantry Colonel Ricardo Serrador Santos and gave him news of the city". Though within conservative ranks there was talk of mistreatment and inhospitable conditions, it seems that they enjoyed walks, fished and bathed at the beach. Even the governor "with that spirit of fraternity that governs military life, sacrificed his family privacy to invite to his table his most prominent comrades in arms".[43] Questions that were denounced by the confederals, pointing out that the passengers on the *Spain no. 5* had enjoyed a "pleasure trip, humble and respectful salutes", as opposed to the "brutality and cruelty" dealt out to the occupants of the *Buenos Aires*.[44] Casares Quiroga himself admitted, in a parliamentary session, that the government had

> sent these deportees in better conditions – I regret to say – than those who went in the 'Buenos Aires' (…) (who) were placed in the orlop, where the bunks had not been set up in such good conditions as in the 'Spain no. 5' (…) so they have fared better, not much better, but certainly better, than the previous deportees, in conditions that I will not describe as exceptional, but which have not given rise to one single complaint.[45]

Although they were not alone in enjoying special treatment since, as Azaña acknowledged, the leader of the rebellion, Sanjurjo, was detained in el Dueso, where "the director and administrator of the prison are on his side, and let him do as he wishes".[46]

Ultimately, the CNT's reaction to Sanjurjo's coup had improved the organisation's status in Andalucía and prompted the return of the deportees. But the uprising had also made it easier for the government to adopt reforms that had been held up in Parliament, practically, since the beginning of the legislature, such as the law on land reform and the autonomy of Catalonia. Issues with regard to which the CNT also had its own vision.

Land Reform and the Autonomy of Catalonia

Land ownership in Spain was not homogeneous: there were around 12,000 large landowners, over 60,000 owners of lands of a certain dimension and a million and a half small and medium-sized landowners. Meanwhile, share-croppers and tenant farmers numbered half a million, and there were two million farm labourers, distributed, mainly across the south of Spain, where landowners possessed 42% of agricultural wealth. Large landowners who belonged, above all, to the bourgeoisie, since the nobility owned only 6% of the land.

The provisional government began the land reform with a series of decrees in the spring of 1931, which became laws in September, and sought to alleviate the poverty in which the most vulnerable lived. It is worth highlighting the Decree on Municipalities, which made it obligatory to offer work to local people rather than outsiders, with a view to improving day labourers' wages and preventing discrimination on political grounds; the *Decreto de Prórroga de los Arrendamientos* (Decree on Renewal of Leases), known as the eviction decree, which made it illegal to expel from the land tenants who earned less than 1,500 pesetas a year; the *Decreto de Laboreo Forzoso* (Decree on Forced Labour), which obliged owners to continue cultivating the land in order to avoid a probable boycott of the new regime, made visible by the famous: "Didn't you want a Republic? Well eat the Republic"; the *Decreto de Autorización de Arrendamientos Colectivos* (Decree on Authorisation of Collective Tenancies), which enabled peasant unions to occupy abandoned farms, with priority over individuals, which combatted sub-letting; and the *Decreto de Jurados Mixtos* (Decree on Mixed Juries), which we have already seen, and the introduction of work accident insurance and the eight-hour working day for workers, previously from dawn till dusk, which meant a pay rise for hours worked. The primary objectives of the reform were to reduce unemployment, improve working conditions and, at a later stage, redistribute the land, based on the criteria embodied by the republican left, in other words, defence of the smallholder and private ownership. Approaches that were imposed on the socializing of the PSOE

These decrees were extremely difficult to implement. Some more than others, due to the resistance displayed by the peasants themselves. As was the case with the Decree on Municipalities, since, though it is true that it attempted to prevent abusive hiring practices on the part of employers, it often prevented day labourers from nearby towns, also affected by unemployment, from working. On other occasions, more typically, given large landowners' reluctance to respect republican laws, as we have seen throughout this work. The fact is that, in August 1932, the situation in rural Spain continued to be of extreme poverty, with large areas of unfarmed land and thousands of labourers going hungry, which caused, in repeated fashion, the occupation of farms, theft of animals, olives and acorns to eat.

Sanjurjo's frustrated coup hastened the necessary land reform. The law, passed in parliament on 9 September, expropriated, without compensation, the estates of Spanish ex-grandees, who were accused of having supported the military coup. It also provided for expropriation, in this case with compensation, of seigniorial jurisdictions, uncultivated or poorly cultivated lands, lands leased for 12 years or located near small villages, the owner of which had a certain level of income, as well as irrigable land. The main objective was the distribution of these lands among the peasants. The law would be applied, first and foremost, where there were large landowners, in other words, Andalusia, Extremadura and Castile. For its implementation the Instituto *de Reforma Agraria* (Institute of Land Reform or IRA) was set up, which did not receive sufficient investment for so important an endeavour, and the *Banco Nacional de Crédito Agrícola* (National Agricultural Credit Bank), which met with the resistance of private banking, which had close ties with landowners. In these conditions, the results were very modest, as by the end of 1933, with a new cycle following the elections, land had been shared out among barely 7,000 peasants.[47]

The CNT did not care for the land reform promoted by the Republican-Socialist government: in the first place, because of its half-heartedness, but also because of its ideological approach. It was in favour of expropriation, of course, although without compensation and of any property larger than 50 hectares, including the confiscation of livestock, farming implements and machinery. But, above all, it was opposed to the distribution of land among the peasants, insofar as would create new small landowners, with the consequent reinforcement of capitalism and reduction of the workers' revolutionary ambitions. For the CNT the expression "the land for those who work it" was a bourgeois concept, because the land should belong not to individuals but to the community as a whole. Accordingly, it made a case for the town taking control of expropriated lands before handing them over to the unions to be farmed collectively, with the possibility of forming production and consumption cooperatives, but controlled and orientated in a libertarian sense as a prelude to the necessary social reform. In any case, it supported existing small landholders, via the reduction of taxes, and tenants, settlers and sharecroppers with a ban on evictions. Though the definitive solution, as in many other areas, was none other than social revolution.[48] The fact is that, apart from the CNT's criticism, the reform proved disappointing, due to both limited economic resources and bureaucratic slowness when it came to redistributing the land, and the authorities' reluctance to confront landowners who did not respect the law.

With regard to Catalan autonomy, the tension between the Catalan nationalist parties and the provisional government was evident from the word go. Three ministers had to travel to Barcelona to redirect the proclamation of the Catalan republic towards an autonomous government, the *Generalidad de Cataluña*, headed by Francesc Macià, the leader of *Esquerra Republicana*. A commission, appointed by the *Generalidad*, drafted the so-called Statute of Nuria. A majority of Catalans endorsed it in a referendum, early in August 1931, with 595,205 votes in favour, 3,286 against, from an electoral roll of 792,524 voters.[49] There were some amendments to the statute during its adoption in the Spanish parliament, which was not completed until 1932, after the attempted coup.

The CNT maintained an ambiguous stance in relation to the *Generalidad* during the early days of the Republic. On the one hand, its internationalism prevented it from supporting the existence of "a Catalan state, within a Spanish state", because it signified "barrier, unity, nationalism, which is the arch enemy of peace and freedom for municipalities and above all individuals".[50] On the other hand, however, the anarcho-syndicalists, who occupied the leadership cadres of the CNT, maintained a good relationship with the Catalan republican parties, especially with *Esquerra*, with a view to consolidating and extending the organisation in what was historically Spain's libertarian region par excellence. So they supported the statute in the referendum on autonomy and encouraged people to vote for the party of Macià and Companys.[51] A relationship that the Catalan nationalists also endeavoured to protect because, as Azaña said, "electorally they depended very much on the votes of the syndicalists".[52] The Prime Minister was quite right, given that, as we have seen, the CNT had, at the time of the regional plenum of Catalonia held at the beginning of August 1931, almost 400,000 members. Bearing in mind that there were 792,594 people on the voters' register for the referendum on the statute, which was held that same month, it was logical to conclude that CNT support was fundamental.

The anarchists, meanwhile, always denounced this relationship, and even used it, as we have seen, to discredit the anarcho-syndicalists. Thus, by September 1932, with the national committee controlled by the FAI, criticism of the Catalan government, mainly because of repression, but also due to ideological internationalism, assumed a special nature. *Tierra y Libertad* asked who was controlling Catalonia's destiny, and answered "not the *Generalidad*, but the Police Headquarters". While *El Luchador*, in its editorial on the statute, observed that the problem of nationalities could not be addressed by the anarchists "given the universality of our ideas" and because "the worship of the motherland is as pernicious and futile as the worship of God". The statute, continued the anarchist newspaper, would be no guarantee of freedom, justice or equality, because it ignored the main problem, which was none other than the economic inequality between men; "we, Catalans by accident, anarchists by conviction, above and beyond all nationalisms, all conventional homelands, all political boundaries, feel a brotherhood with men". The statute, like the constitution, represented for the anarchists "a limitation on freedom. And the state its firmest denial". Ultimately, freedom was only to be found in Anarchy.[53]

The CNT's response to the *Sanjurjada* had alleviated, in a way, its confrontation with the state, despite its continued opposition to the reforms promoted by the government and adopted in parliament. But the internal struggle had become its major weakness.

Towards Division

The regional plenum of Cataluña, held in April 1932, had concluded with the withdrawal of the Sabadell local federation, for the most part *treintista*. There were basically two problems to be addressed, both of which were interrelated: the FAI's interference in the CNT, and the failure to comply with agreements adopted in regional plenums and confederal congresses, relating to voting on the basis of proportional representation. The previous plenum, held in Lérida, has decided that voting would take place in accordance with the confederal stamps acquired monthly by the unions. In other words, the only votes counted would be those cast by members who were up to date with their payments, and not the total number of members each union claimed to have. This agreement followed denouncements that, at the time of voting, "ridiculous numbers of members" were claimed. The transport delegate spoke ironically of the situation, and noted that in the Catalan federation there were many members, "but only to vote; when it's time to pay there are very few of us".

The Sabadell unions met at various assemblies immediately after the April regional plenum. Peiró proposed, at the Manufacturing and Textile Union assembly, that the confederal stamp should not be acquired during the validity of the agreements adopted at the recently held plenum. A motion that was approved and supported by the rest of the unions. Added to this decision was the criticism of the Intellectuals' Union, led by Federica Montseny, on account of its attitude at the last plenum, and of *Solidaridad Obrera*, with particular focus on its director, Felipe Alaiz, and one of his editors, Arturo Parera, who were accused of conducting a smear campaign. The Sabadelll unions also condemned the continual mobilisations promoted by the CNT, because, they said, they did not want "to be the plaything of any anti-union manoeuvres". Their objective, they claimed, was none other than to "free the CNT of tyranny and dependence upon political parties and sects, even if some called themselves revolutionaries and others anarchists".[54]

So, from May onwards, the Sabadell unions paid the stamp to the local federation, but the latter retained the contributions without giving the corresponding part to the rest of the organisation. Henceforth, *treintistas* and *faístas* (FAI sympathisers) became involved in an all-out struggle. The latter maintained regular correspondence with the regional committee, providing regular information regarding the activity of the fractious unions. Alejandro Gilabert, regional secretary, advised them,

> in order to counteract the mood of those who seek to divert the Confederation from its revolutionary and anarchist tactics, you militants that are closer to the latter should organise yourselves into a group or union cadre and seek always to undertake common action that is popular with the masses, so they elect you to occupy the representative positions in the organisation and you will be able to put the critics on the right track.[55]

In other words, what he proposed was nothing new. It was a case of militants meeting prior to the assemblies in order to adopt a stance that was "popular with the masses" and facilitate the occupation of posts so as to control the organisation.

An exchange of letters that also took place between the national and regional committees and the Sabadell local federation, in which the former asked for rectification, and the latter replied that it was merely acting as instructed by the unions. Letters with curious closings: while Rivas, as national secretary, ended with a "without further ado, I wish you health and Anarchy", and Gilabert, from the regional committee, with "once again yours and Libertarian Communism's", J. Virgili, secretary of the local committee, closed "with syndicalist greetings, which are more interesting".[56]

As each party remained steadfast in its position, the regional plenum of Catalonia, held at the end of September, expelled the Sabadell local federation for refusing to pay the confederal stamp. The regional committee published a note in *Solidaridad Obrera* in which it argued that the expulsion of the Sabadell unions was a measure of "union sanitation", contrary to its reformist proposals, while it accused them of using "infamy and deceit to maintain their executive positions".[57] Which is quite extraordinary given what Gilabert himself was proposing to the anarchists.

The Catalan regional federation attempted to form a General Union in this locality to cater for almost 3,000 supporters that, it claimed, were not in the local union.[58] But the fact was that membership of this union was residual, as over 20,000 members remained in the Sabadell union. To this collective expulsion was added the individual expulsion of *treintistas* during the ensuing months. Among others, Agustín Gibanel, Juan López, Ricardo Fornells, Bartolomé Viñas, Ángel Pestaña and Bautista Marco, which left the Catalan regional federation, by the end of 1932, practically in the hands of the FAI.[59]

Confrontation also took place in other regional committees, mainly where there was a sizeable *treintista* presence, such as the Levante and Huelva. In the former, unlike what happened in Catalonia, the most powerful unions were *treintistas*. Unions that refused to pay, like Sabadell, the confederal stamp. In this case, on account of lack of clarity in their accounts, unsubstantiated accusations against militants and the imposition of the *trabazón* in the prisoners' aid and defence committees.[60] With regard to Huelva, Juan López's actions in this province were decisive. At the national plenum, in August 1932, the Andalusian representative had already complained about the problems in this province because, he said, unions were being organised "by political elements". In clear allusion to López, who, it will be recalled, had been expelled from the CNT the previous month. The plenum agreed that measures would be taken to prevent those separated from the organisation from no acting in the regional federations.[61] But they could do nothing to stop the *treintista* leader from directing dissidence that placed Huelva outside the Andalusian organisation.

Juan López's determination to challenge the *faístas* was not shared by many of his fellow *treintistas*. He himself complained, in a letter to Pestaña, about the group's lack of action, about the absence of expansion in areas where it would be feasible to take control. He contrasted this attitude with that of the FAI, which deployed considerable activity, "not even against the state do they employ so much saliva and paper". López advocated structuring a national organisation that would confront the FAI, and criticised the prevailing doubts. The Sabadell federation was the foothold that would help to extend the new organisation. To which should be added the creation of a federation of groups and athenaeums that would in principle make it possible to coordinate actions.[62] In fact, in the second half of 1932, the Libertarian Athenaeum was founded in Barcelona, with Fornells as president, while in Valencia the Libertarian Syndicalist Athenaeum and the Federation of Syndicalist Athenaeums were created.[63] Pestaña received letters from unions that had been expelled or marginalised from the organisation and asked for instructions or called for action to be taken. For example, the Single Workers' Union of Palafrugell asked if they should turn the union into a libertarian cultural athenaeum, while the local federation of Single Unions of San Sebastian explained how a group of militants had stood up to the *faístas* and regained control of the federation.[64]

Juan López strove for all these actions to converge in the constitution of a national organisation that would structure the movement, which some comrades began to refer to by the name of Federación *Nacional Sindicalista Libertaria* (National Libertarian Syndicalist Federation or FNSL), the future FSL. But among the treintistas there was indecision, maybe even fear, with regard to extending their actions to the point of no return that would result in a schism within the CNT. López understood the caution and prudence, but repeated that in the end there would be "no choice but to face reality".[65]

A reality of expulsions and personal clashes that culminated in violence. Manuel Molina wrote an article in *Solidaridad Obrera* in which he accused *treintista* José Moix of taking a pleasure trip to America paid for with union funds. Moix turned up at the newspaper to demand an explanation and, when none was forthcoming, punched and knocked down his accuser, at which point the latter drew a pistol and wounded Moix. Meanwhile, the disagreements in a workers' meeting, in the Manufacturas Querol factory, between anarchists José Esparza and Francisco Fournier, and treintistas, S. Vera and Saturnino Nicolás Antolín, alias *Lino*, ended in gunfire when the latter fired several shots at the anarchists, killing Fournier and seriously injuring Esparza.[66]

Violence that fed off the insults and egocentricity of the attacks. *Tierra y Libertad* said that "Beltrán, Vera, Moix, Mira, Soler and company" had used *Lino* "as a blind instrument of their evil revenge". Syndicalist politicians like Piera, Barrera, Botella, Delaville, Magre, and Clará had "blood on their hands". While *El Luchador* spoke of "republican syndicalist fascism in Sabadell", like a new "Free Union" – created by employers in the 1920s during the days of *pistolerismo* – killing workers belonging to the CNT. An accusation that Peiró also levelled against the *faístas*, months later, when he branded them robbers, members of the Free Union and frequenters of cabarets.[67]

The confrontation between *treintistas* and *faístas*, present throughout the organisation, had taken a dramatic turn in Catalonia. With every passing day, the schism became less of a possibility and more of an immediate reality. The confederal leadership, rather than offering an inclusive response to the problem, favoured the hard line of expulsion. In these circumstances, the Asturian regional federation decided to opt for dialogue between the parties in an attempt to prevent what appeared to be inevitable. The group Libertarian Education of La Felguera, Centre "La Justicia", convened a meeting of regional federation militants early in November 1932, which was held in the Casa del Pueblo of Gijón. The aim of the meeting was to find a middle way between the *faísta* stance, of imminent revolution, and that of the *treintistas*, which postponed the revolution until the strengthening of the confederal cause. Eleuterio Quintanilla proposed as a basis of understanding the agreements on principles, tactics and goals that had been reached at previous congresses, the Comedia in 1919 and the Conservatorio in 1931, in other words, apoliticism, direct action and libertarian communism. The meeting approved the motion and appointed a commission to organise the meetings with the rival parties. Its members were José Mª Martínez, Aurelio Álvarez, Avelino González Entrialgo, Manuel Nieto, Eleuterio Quintanilla and Agapito González. The latter two were to travel to Barcelona to meet the *faístas* and *treintistas*. In any case, in order to understand the situation within the CNT, one needs to be aware that the confrontation between *treintistas* and *faístas* was also evident in the Asturian meeting, with moments of considerable tension. In fact, Avelino Menéndez expressed his fear that a divided commission might return to Gijón.[68]

Pestaña greeted the initiative with suspicion. In his view the solution was not to promote a meeting of "half a dozen more or less well-known militants" and draft a note stating that there had been nobody had been "vilified, slandered or insulted", because that would be no more than a "pudding". Pestaña regarded these initiatives as "absolutely pointless", since to be aware of what was happening in Catalonia it was necessary to spend a few months attending union meetings. It was not sufficient to go to Barcelona and meet a few militants, everything else was a mere "poultice".[69] It goes without saying that, against this backdrop, the Asturian initiative ended in abject failure.

This entire situation coincided with the electoral campaign for the elections to the Catalan parliament, on 20 November. The CNT campaigned heavily in favour of abstention. *Solidaridad Obrera* ran the headline: "Don't vote!" while the editorials insisted, time and time again, on not voting for anybody.[70] The CNT's relationship with *Esquerra*, and therefore with the *Generalidad*, had deteriorated since the anarchists' occupation of the principal positions in the organisation. The adoption of the Catalan statute in the Cortes, in September 1932, assigned to the *Generalidad* control of public order, which worsened relations that were already complicated. Anyway, in spite of the abstentionist campaign, one saw "outside the polling stations (...) a few queues of sheep", according to Federica Montseny, who handed victory to *Esquerra*, along with the *Unión Socialista de Cataluña*, with 57 seats, compared with the 17 obtained by the conservative *Lliga*[71]. Which did not prevent the confederal press from proclaiming the "abstentionist victory", because if in June 1931 the turnout had been 73%, now it had fallen to only 56%. The result, it said, "of the deportations, the tragedies of Seville and Pasajes, the martyrs of Arnedo (...) the law of 8 April".[72] Added to which was the first uprising on a national scale involving the CNT, or, more accurately perhaps, the FAI.

The January 1933 Uprising

The start of the January 1933 uprising was related to both the attempt to transform a strike into a revolutionary movement, and the coexistence of CNT and FAI members on the organisation committees.

The CNT supported the *cenetista* (pro-CNT) railways, affiliated to the *Federación Nacional de la Industria Ferroviaria* (Railway Industry National Federation or FNIF), which wanted to call a strike to improve working conditions. For its part, the railways committee was sure that the conflict would lead to "an act of force against the workers' will, as a consequence of the government's repressive action", so, in order not to be crushed, they were prepared to follow the path recommended by the national plenum, which was none other than that of insurrection.[73]

But both the strike and the revolutionary movement existed more in the yearnings of a group than in the analysis of reality. On the one hand, because the strike that had to open the way to revolution was no longer going to be called, since most of the railways were affiliated to the UGT, which advocated negotiation. On the other, because the *cenetista* railways themselves were extremely divided; indeed, 36 sub-sections announced that they were unprepared for the strike, while 35 stated that they were. Thus, without the support of the major union in the sector and with considerable internal division, the *cenetista* federation had to desist, as it acknowledged, because it did not "have the support of all the railways".[74] A circumstance that, incomprehensively, had no impact upon the revolutionary aspirations, and the insurrection was called for 8 January at 8 p.m.[75]

A call with a date and a time that was accompanied by warnings during the preceding days. The accidental detonation of an explosive device, in Calle Mallorca in Barcelona, put the police on the track of a cache of 185 bombs in the Sans district, with the subsequent arrest of *cenetista* militants in what was regarded as a bomb factory[76]. Situations like these, in which the detonation of a bomb led to the discovery of a sizeable cache, made the Ministry of the Interior aware, in the words of the Minister, Casares Quiroga, of "a terrorist movement, organised by the FAI". Azaña was prompted to write, with his proverbial irony, "As I say: the police in Spain, as well as useless, are unnecessary: when there are bombs, they explode by themselves, and when there is a conspiracy, the conspirators tell everybody". With everyone prepared and alerted, Casares telephoned the Prime minister that very same day (8 January) to inform him that the anarchist movement they were expecting would erupt that evening, so the army had been advised accordingly. So Azaña, "as he had plenty of time and it was a glorious day" went for a walk in the Alto del León, a mountain range near Madrid.[77] In short, the actions of all those involved could have inspired one of the most significant pages of Spanish surrealism.

In the CNT, with the explosion of the bomb, everything had been rushed and confusion began to reign. The call to insurrection had come not from the CNT national committee, but from the national committee of Confederal Defence. These defence committees, one recalls, formed a paramilitary organisation, by way of a strike force, composed in the main of anarchists. According to a CNT agreement, they were not autonomous, in other words, they could not act without authorisation from the appropriate confederal committees. The anarchists wanted these committees to be integrated within the organic structure of the CNT throughout Spain, but the fact is that, according to García Oliver, they only achieved this in Barcelona. A city in which *Los Solidarios* were formed by, among others, Aurelio Fernández, Gregorio Jover, Ricardo Sanz, Buenaventura Durruti, Francisco Ascaso and García Oliver himself.[78] All known as anarcho-Bolsheviks, in other words, anarchists closely aligned to the Russian revolutionaries, who sought to assume power via a show of strength led by a brave minority. More a putsch than a revolutionary popular movement. Along with these were many of the components of the *Federación Ibérica de Juventudes Libertarias* (Iberian Federation of Iberian Youth or FILJ), founded in Madrid in June 1932, whom García Oliver called "eaglets of the FAI", always ready for combat in their "street empire".[79]

The Catalan defence committee, with García Oliver at the helm, encouraged the movement, and had the support of the secretary of the national committee of the defence committees, Manuel Rivas, who, in turn, was secretary general of the CNT national committee. So when Rivas signed the document calling for protest as secretary of defence, he put only his name, in other words, without indicating the capacity in which he was signing. As a result of which many CNT members believed that it was the union organisation calling for action, and not this committee. All of which gives the impression of a calculated ambiguity directed towards conducting a policy of faits accomplis. The Catalan defence committee hoped that once they had taken to the streets, the rest of organisation would support the movement. But the CNT dissociated itself from the uprising, while the FAI endorsed it, with the resultant turmoil.

The CNT national committee issued a formal declaration, on the 10th, stating that events had been "of purely anarchist significance without any intervention whatsoever on the part of the confederal organ", though it expressed its solidarity with the movement. The newspaper *CNT*, reported that same day that "it was not our revolution"; and *Solidaridad Obrera* said, in its editorial, that it could not "accept it as a CNT action", because it was "removed from events". Meanwhile, the Catalan regional federation declared that nobody could suspect "that the CNT has participated in this movement", or had given "any instructions"; in short, that the CNT had declared the general strike. A stance that was also endorsed by the Barcelona local federation.[80]

Therefore, if the Alto Llobregat strike of January 1932 cannot be regarded, as we have seen, as an insurrection encouraged, planned and directed by the

CNT, in the case of the January 1933 protest, responsibility seems to lie very clearly with the anarchists, though support for the strike was the source of considerable confusion. Confusion that was reflected in the Zaragoza congress of 1936. The Barcelona Manufacturing and Textile Union delegate read a statement issued by the CNT national committee, denying authorship of the movement, and attributing to the latter an exclusively anarchist content. However, the Seville delegate said that in Andalusia it was the CNT and not the FAI that had proposed the action. While the Asturian Miners' representative declared that 8 January "belonged not to the CNT, but to the FAI". Even the Madrid Timber Union delegate, to crown things off, said that "it is called by the FAI, but affects the CNT".[81]

This imbroglio forced the union organisation to reconsider the composition of its committees. The national plenum, held at the end of January 1933, decreed the incompatibility of the post of secretary of the CNT national committee and that of secretary of the national defence committee, a decision that extended to the secretariats of the county, local and regional committees. The plenum also reiterated that the defence committees should limit their activity to the preparation of revolutionary movements, and could never take the decision to initiate these actions, which was a function restricted to the union organisation.[82] The disastrous evolution of the uprising resulted in the debate over the defence committees continuing for months. At the June plenum, the organisation returned to the issue to ratify the previous agreements and specify that these cadres would only enter into action at the moment of an "act of insurgency particular to the revolution". But the CNT went a step further, as a consequence of what had happened when the insurrection was linked to the railway strike, and made it very clear that the defence committees could not intervene "in mere strike movements, whatever their nature or significance, unless this has been expressly approved by the National Union Organisation".[83]

This entire situation invites reflection upon the degree to which CNT members really supported the actions of their leadership cadres. For if the anarchists employed a strategy of confusion to trigger these kinds of uprisings, it was because they knew that, although they had occupied key positions within the CNT, the vast majority of members did not support these uprisings, and were undoubtedly more concerned about working conditions and essential needs. In other words, the FAI minority had controlled the confederal committees, but their revolutionary ambitions did not connect with the mood of the membership. The *faístas* exploited circumstantial factors like unemployment, repression or disenchantment with the Republic, and had propagated the image, in misleading fashion, of anarcho-syndicalists as political traitors, just as responsible for the situation as those in the Republican government. A tactic that enabled them to attain power in the union organisation, but not to convince the confederal masses to rise up in revolution, because the latter did not share the FAI's objective. The CNT was a trade union, and its essential goal was the improvement of workers' social, economic and labour conditions. For this reason, when the FAI took to the streets, it found itself alone. Hundreds of energetic, heroic but unsupported militants, without the collaboration of the workers. As Galo Díez said, at the 1936 Zaragoza congress, "in January everybody was taken into account except the workers".[84]

Workers that needed realities – like pay rises or improved working conditions – as evidence of the collective strength represented by the union. Later would come awareness-raising and the belief in a fairer and more egalitarian society. Because, at that time, libertarian communism was, according to Ramón J. Sender, "as utopian as Paradise and the gardens of Mahoma".[85] The workers wanted, for the time being, those tangible improvements, which they had dreamed of until yesterday and which now, be it via the mediation of the state or by dint of protests and strikes, they sensed were within their grasp. But the CNT, with its move towards insurrection, was skipping that first step, and preferred to dream of the immediate imposition of a new society without laying the necessary foundations to support the future revolution.

Moreover, everything suggests that even decision-making within the FAI itself – as in the la CNT – was conditioned by the atmosphere and even by the fear of not appearing to be sufficiently revolutionary. One member of the defence committee, who belonged to the FAI, commented, at the same 1936 congress, that in the meetings prior to the uprising "there was no going back. There was continual pressure exercised by all corners of our Movement. *There was suspicion of anybody* who was not a part of that mood stirred up by revolutionary enthusiasm".[86] If a *faísta*, a member of the defence committee, felt pressure and even fear if he did not show himself to be in favour of the revolution, one can easily imagine what happened with members of the confederal assemblies.

The fact that the movement was a disaster did not prevent it from having a certain impact in Catalonia, the Levante and Andalusia. The uprising in Barcelona led to armed clashes between anarchists and the security forces. A number of anarchist militants were arrested, among them García Oliver, who denounced "the terrible beatings (they) received from the assault guards".[87] An accusation that was borne out by MP Eduardo Barriobero's intervention in the parliamentary session of 2 February, when he read out from the prison medical records, which reported that García Oliver suffered "ecchymosis in both eyes, with haemorrhaging of both sclera. Infected hematoma in the upper part of the intraparietal region. Yellowish ecchymosis on the back and forearm and right arm and both hands. Cuts on the knee and the left leg".[88]

In the Levante, the regional committee issued a call to action to the workers, but the publication of the confederal press, in which the CNT distanced itself from the protests, caused confusion and a return to work. The situation in the Levante was further complicated by the major confrontation between *faístas* and *treintistas*, since while the former controlled the regional committee, the latter were majority in the unions.[89] In any case, several town halls hoisted the red and black flag. The *modus operandi* was all too reminiscent of the uprisings of the previous century, as the revolutionaries disarmed the citizens of "order", confronted the local Civil Guard, occupied the town hall, declared libertarian communism and set fire to ownership documents in the town square. The mutineers were waiting for news that the revolution had triumphed all over

Spain, but it was the security forces that arrived and triggered a retreat in disarray followed by the accompanying repression. The Civil Guard reported conflict in various localities such as Bugarra, Benaguacil and Pedralba, with the raising of barricades, clashes with the security forces and several deaths.[90]

In Andalusia, the movement enjoyed particular support in Seville and Cádiz. In the former, there were armed clashes between guards and rebels, and attacks on companies. There were also assaults on company directors, such as that suffered by the engineer Mantecón, who was forced out of his car along with his chauffeur, before shots were fired into the engine and a firecracker was placed under the vehicle, which then exploded.[91] But where the movement had a special impact was in a small town in the province of Cádiz, called Casas Viejas, though not on account of the uprising itself, but due to the repression unleashed on 11–12 January. The uprisings in towns and villages of Andalusia or Extremadura were related, in many cases, to the situation of poverty in which peasants were immersed. In this respect, one wonders whether the insurrectional movement in these localities represented anything more to the inhabitants than getting hold of a piece of land that was necessary in order to escape hunger and survive. A struggle for life that, since time immemorial, had been met with fierce repression.

Casas Viejas

Among the reports written at the time describing the events in that Cádiz village, it is worth highlighting those written by author Ramón J. Sender and journalist Eduardo de Guzmán. They travelled to the village together, a few days after the incident, as reporters from the newspapers *La Libertad*, and *La Tierra*, respectively. Eduardo de Guzmán noted that during the preceding days there had been a peasants' strike in the provinces of Cádiz and Seville, in protest against the forced layoff affecting thousands of day labourers since the end of the harvest. One recalls that of the 619,000 unemployed in Spain in 1933, according to the Office of Recruitment and Defence against Unemployment, approximately 395,000 were agricultural day labourers. In Casas Viejas (the real name of which was Benalup), the lands belonged to landowners – the Duke of Medinaceli and the Pina and Vela families. With the exception of those who worked as foremen, guards or servants for these families, the inhabitants of the village, around 500 people, were day labourers. The majority members of the CNT, "a solid organisation, because they are united by hunger". Because hunger was here, in Sender's words, "a sallow and vindictive hunger, of a stray dog". So the Civil Guard looked "with one eye at the owners and another at the peasants", in order to exercise "a civil protectorate or a despotic dictatorship, as appropriate". There was an attempt to alleviate the absence of work with a kind of subsidy – known by the peasants as "the handout" – one peseta for bachelors and one and a half pesetas for married workers, when a kilo of bread cost 95 cents.[92] Tired of living in misery, they rose up that January in the belief that the revolution had spread throughout Spain. As had occurred in other localities, they took control of the village, after attacking the Civil Guard barracks, where they killed two guards.

According to Civil Guard records, following the capture of the barracks, "the red flag" was raised. Then, the rebels committed "the most criminal excesses, the most sickening acts. Rape, murder, previously hidden loathing. The village is a centre of lust, horror and death". But the report largely ignored what followed, with the arrival of Captain Manuel Rojas and his assault guards, since that "has little or nothing to do with the Civil Guard".[93] Just as there has been no verification of the rapes and murders described by the report, but clear evidence of the actions of Captain Rojas and the hundred or so guards under his command. When they arrived in Casas Viejas, according to Sender, most of the peasants fled into the mountains. Some took refuge in their homes, like sixty-year-old Curro Cruz, or *Seisdedos* (Sixfingers) – nicknamed thus due to his physical defect – his sons, Pedro and Paco, his son-in-law and neighbour, Francisco Lago, the latter's daughter, 18-year-old Paca Lago, *Seisdedos's* daughter-in-law, Josefa Franco, his grandchildren, Mariquilla, aged 17, and a boy of 10. Eight people in total. The guards surrounded and tried to enter the shanty house. The besieged occupants defended themselves, killing one of the guards and wounding another. The two children managed to avoid the attackers' gunfire and escape. Captain Rojas decided to burn down the humble building, instead of waiting for hunger or fatigue to lead to surrender. Paca Lago died in a hail of shots while attempting to escape the flames. Her father also attempted to get out but was shot down in the doorway of his home. The other four men and the woman were burnt alive. The guards then arrested 14 peasants, some of whom had not taken part in the uprising, took them to *Seisdedos's* yard and shot them.[94] In total, 23 people had died: two civil guards, an assault guard and 20 peasants.

However, the government made clear, before these events came to light, its determination to continue with the repression, and its dissatisfaction with the soft attitude of the security forces. According to Azaña, the Minister of the Interior, Casares Quiroga, complained that they were not acting "with sufficient energy. They allow themselves to be killed, but do not strike hard". While "Largo, Prieto and Domingo wanted immediate and energetic solutions". The President of the Republic himself, Niceto Alcalá Zamora, called Casares Quiroga to tell him "that there was evidence of a certain weakness in the authorities' repression on the streets, and the latter required stimulation". Azaña appeared to be alone in advocating moderation on the part of the security forces – "that was sound doctrine" – though he went on to say that this attitude was due "to the campaigns in Parliament and in the press against the excesses of the Civil Guard". In any case, Casares Quiroga reported that, given the turbulent situation in the province of Cádiz, he had sent "a lot of guards, with very strict orders". On the 13th, the Minister met with Azaña again, and informed him that in Casas Viejas there had been "a bloodbath, with casualties on both sides". At the cabinet meeting, held that afternoon, Casares complained about the criticism that was raining down on the government because of the repression, including that which appeared in *El Socialista*. Yet, as Azaña observed, the

Socialist ministers were not of the same opinion, since Fernando de los Ríos argued that what had happened in Casas Viejas was "absolutely necessary, given the situation in the Andalusian countryside and the anarchist history of the province of Cádiz". While Largo Caballero maintained that "while the struggle continues, repression is inevitable".[95]

Casares Quiroga pointed to the need for, come the time, "the judicial authorities not to waiver". But Justice, as on other occasions, surprised rather than waivered. There was no trial with regard to the incidents relating to the burning down of *Seisdedos's* house, with his family inside, only of the shooting of the other 14 people: "ten of them handcuffed, four unarmed and all powerless before a firing squad". None of the assault guards that participated in the execution were tried, while the first trial of Captain Rojas, the sole defendant, was suspended. The second trial was held in June 1935, and the jury sentenced Rojas to 98 years' imprisonment, which was reduced to the legal maximum of 21. However, the defence lodged an appeal before the Supreme Court, which described the murders as simple acts of homicide and reduced the sentence to 14 years, one for each of the victims. This sentence was reduced to three years in accordance with the rule of tripling the highest conviction in the event of various crimes. So Rojas was released from prison in March 1936.[96] Quite a contrast with the peasants on trial for the same incidents. Initially, 26 were tried for the murder of two guards, with the prosecutor requesting life imprisonment for six and sentences of 6–14 years for the rest. One of the accused, Antonio Cabañas, union secretary, was sentenced to six years, five of his comrades to five years and another ten to 1–3 years, while the rest were acquitted.[97]

Five captains supported Rojas during the trial, and affirmed that he received orders from Arturo Menéndez, Director General of Security, to leave "neither wounded nor prisoners". Orders of which there was no firm evidence, and which Menéndez himself denied, although he acknowledged that his instructions had been for "very energetic" action. The conservative press placed the emphasis upon, rather than the shooting of the peasants, the orders supposedly issued, and targeted Azaña. To the testimony of soldiers and guards was added the statement given by Bartolomé Barba, Army Captain, who attributed to the Prime Minister the expression "shots to the stomach". Azaña always denied this, and, although Barba was referring to possible attacks on the barracks in Madrid, it became a symbol of events in Casas Viejas.[98]

Both Manuel Rojas Feigenspan and Bartolomé Barba fought on the side of the rebels during the Civil War. The former, according to his military record, maintained his rank and pay in the wake of the events of Casas Viejas. This is evidenced by a Ministry of War document, dated September 1933, which states that he was "on forced leave" and receiving "his salary from the paymaster". On 18 July, 1936, he joined the military rebellion in Torrenueva (Granada). He was posted to the Falange militias, initially, as Motril Sector Chief, and later as Head of the Falange Militia until the capture of Antequera (Malaga). He fought in Zaragoza and Huesca and, in March 1938, was promoted to commander. Conviction by a military tribunal for the theft of a military vehicle during the war in order to travel from Seville to Zaragoza, prevented him from being promoted to honorary lieutenant colonel in 1972.[99] Bartolomé Barba, meanwhile, was one of the founders of the *Unión Militar Española* (Spanish Military Union or UME) and, from his position in the Military High Command, collaborated in the conspiracy against the Republic. Although at the moment of the military rebellion he was in a republican zone, Madrid to be precise, he managed to report to the rebel headquarters in Salamanca, on February 7, 1937. Barba was Chief of Staff of the Second Legionary Mixed Brigade, the "Black Arrows". He was on the northern front with the forces that occupied Guernica, and with the Italian Lieutenant Colonel Farina, at the capture of Laredo. Along with the latter, he was responsible for establishing the terms of the Basques' surrender on 25 August. He was also on the Jarama and Aragón fronts.[100] During the Francoist dictatorship, he was Civil Governor of Catalonia in August 1945 and May 1947.

Returning to the January 1933 uprising and the events of Casas Viejas, the fact is that the bloody and illegal repression facilitated the redirection of anarchist propaganda vis-à-vis the result of the insurrection. The libertarian movement once again deployed what I have called "propaganda through repression", a term I have already employed to refer to the anarchists' activities at the end of the 19th century. During that period, the negative impact of attacks justified by what was known as "propaganda by deed", forced them to deflect attention to the illegal and brutal repression exercised by the Restoration governments.[101] Now, at the time of the Second Republic, the CNT saw how insurrectional movements were not only failing to achieve the social revolution, but that the results were completely negative: the organisation had been dismantled, its militants killed or imprisoned, the unions closed and the libertarian press banned. While the workers had achieved no improvements courtesy of these uprisings, quite the contrary in fact. Despite the fact that for some what had occurred in Casas Viejas was "an epic", there were also those who, like Galo Díez, at the Zaragoza congress in 1936, reasoned that "epics like that do not benefit us". García Oliver himself admitted, at the same congress, that the insurrection had failed, although, at the same time, he said that the movement had completely destroyed "the left after the crime of Casas Viejas".[102] In other words, what was not achieved by means of insurrectional activity itself was "attained" via the brutal, illegal and disproportionate conduct of the security forces. As Samar, Sender's literary character would say, "our problem is that we have no aptitude for victory (…) We only know how to take advantage of our defeats".[103] So the CNT devoted itself to the publication of pamphlets describing "the heroic deeds of *Seisdedos* of Casas Viejas, as an element of agitation that would be hugely beneficial to the prisoners' cause".[104] In short, the organisation focused its protests on the repression suffered, instead of taking a self-critical look at the path being pursued. As a result, it entered a spiral in which it proposed new demonstrations and strikes in protest against repression, like the 48-hour general strike called for 9–10 May, 1933, which enjoyed limited support but led to further repression.[105]

With regard to the pulverisation of the left, in the words of García Oliver, in clear reference to the Republican-Socialist government, one could say that the government itself collaborated in the considerable price it paid as a consequence of these incidents. In the first place, because it once again spoke of international funding of the uprising by reactionary groups, "in a monarchic atmosphere, with anarcho-syndicalist thunder and lightning". Shots from below, as journalist Luis Sirval ironically noted, were always the consequence, according to the authorities, "of a sinister international plan".[106] The conspiracy theory seemed more like a government strategy to maintain a parliamentary majority in the confidence votes to which it was subjected, and thus avoid the constitution of committees of enquiry. Secondly, because of the three politicians mainly responsible for events, in other words, the Director General of Security, Arturo Menéndez, the Minister of the Interior, Casares Quiroga and the Prime Minister, Manuel Azaña, only the former abandoned his post. Casares Quiroga submitted his resignation to Azaña when the President of the Republic, Alcalá Zamora, criticised his lukewarm repression of the rebels, but he did not resign, nor was he dismissed in the wake of the events of Casas Viejas. As for Azaña, not only did he not assume due responsibility for so serious an occurrence, but his handling of the incident revealed a considerable absence of reflection on his part. Generally speaking, the Prime Minister was aware of what was happening in rural Spain. On 19 January, he noted in his diary that the invasions of estates were continuing in Cáceres and that there was "propaganda to the effect that these were attacks by communists and syndicalists. This is not true. Small farmers are starving to death, and many owners refuse to give them land and work. Will they ask us merely to repel the invasions with gunfire?"[107] While in the specific instance of Casas Viejas, neither could he seek shelter in ignorance of what had occurred when in Parliament, on 2 February, he uttered his famous words: "what has happened in Casas Viejas is no more than what had to happen". Azaña argued that in a situation of rebellion against society and the state, what had occurred "was absolutely inevitable", because if other people had occupied the positions of responsibility in the government they would have struggled to "find a procedure by means of which things might have developed (…) differently from the way in which they developed".[108]

The Prime Minister committed a serious error, at the very least, of imprudence, as it seems logical to think that he was abreast, as he often indicated in his diaries, of what was published in the Spanish press; including the articles by Ramón J. Sender that, entitled "Storm in the South", appeared in *La Libertad*. On 26 January, he described the

> heavy gunfire on the other side of the fence (…) the eight detainees died and each one was hit by at least six Mauser bullets fired from the same angle and at the same time. One by as many as eleven. Then those bodies appeared in the shanty house, one on top of the other. The house had been burnt down and they had no burns. The guards said that they had appeared alongside the family of '*Seisdedos*' and that they were inside. But…

On the 27th, Sender noted how the guards continued to search the shacks and described the final moments of those who were burnt "alive in the blaze". Sender concluded his article with the moment when the dead were taken to the cemetery, where the judge was to perform the post-mortem. When he asked why those on top were not burnt, nobody answered him.[109]

In addition, Azaña described in his diary the parliamentary session of 1 February, in which there was discussion of Casas Viejas. According to the Prime Minister, "various honourable gentlemen competed in shamelessness. The prize for brutality went to Eduardo Ortega, and for political immorality to Guerra del Río, Lerroux's lieutenant; he had already had the audacity to say in the press that in Casas Viejas eight prisoners had been shot against the wall", as he had been informed by the Mayor of Medina Sidonia. Azaña noted that the mayor was a close friend of Guerra's and under his authority had been disseminated the most virulent propaganda against the Republic.[110]

Everything suggests that Azaña did not believe what was said by certain newspapers or journalists or the criticism voiced by other MPs, considering that everything was a manipulation of the facts intended to wear him down and gain political advantage. He preferred to restrict himself to the official reports which, undoubtedly, he regarded as more truthful. But this does not appear to justify such categorical and, at the same time, hurtful declarations, not only for the victims, but also for those who had dreamed of the Republic. When Azaña said that another government could not have acted differently, he seemed to ignore the fact that he was the head of a Republican-Socialist government, and that the popular masses expected things to develop very differently from during the times of the monarchy. It is incredible that Azaña had no doubts with regard to what had really happened. It was not until 13 February that he noted in his diary, "I have bad news about Casas Viejas. I fear the worst".[111]

Although the confederal organisation blamed the authorities for the repression, there were those who regretted that "the dead, wounded and imprisoned are, in part, the victims of an error due to which they have squandered their bravery and heroism". These were the terms employed by the members of the AIT secretariat, Carbó and Shapiro, to promote an uprising without counting on the necessary resources for its success and ignoring "the participation of the working classes". But the criticism went further, targeting the defence committees, headed by García Oliver.[112] The latter not only acknowledged the failure of the movement, but recognised its scant possibilities of success.[113] It appeared that the 50 killed and 100 wounded [114] in the uprising had served only to build up some muscle within the strategy that advocated "revolutionary gymnastics". For the time being, revolutionary circles pointed to García Oliver as responsible for the failure, and nicknamed him the "cardboard Napoleon".[115] But little else, as the national plenum held in Madrid at the end of January, in order to analyse responsibility within the movement, passed a vote of no-confidence in the national committee (…) but of the railways, while the CNT national committee was absolved of blame.[116]

The *treintistas*, unsurprisingly, were quick to criticise the uprising. They published a manifesto entitled "Against everyone", in which, firstly, they regretted the casualties, then condemned the "strange power" that controlled the CNT. Their position was none other than to situate themselves "in opposition to those who seek to destroy this organisation (...) against all and opposite all".[117] The time had come to get organised.

The Libertarian Syndicalist Federation and the Opposition Trade Unions

The turbulent events of the month of January coincided with the constitution of the *Federación Sindicalista Libertaria* (Libertarian Syndicalist Federation or FSL), with Pestaña in the secretariat. Its origins were to be found, according to Elorza, in the *Unión de Militantes* (Union of Militants), formed in the 1920s, representative of the syndicalist line, with Juan López, Pestaña and Peiró at the helm. The three *cenetista* leaders represented different positions that coexisted within the *feselista* (FSL) organisation: Juan López, eminently syndicalist, Pestaña, with a track record shifting from anarchism to syndicalism and a markedly political evolution, and Peiró, anarcho-syndicalist, who emphasised the constructive nature of syndicalism and contrasted the latter with the violent and spontaneous actions of the anarchists.[118] Although Peiró, unlike the other two, defended the presence of anarchism in the CNT, "as a spiritual and ideological current, a guiding moral value". For this reason, he regarded the presence of anarchist groups in the union as necessary, though not in a controlling or directing capacity. Each specific group should be the forge in which to shape "the orientation of the proletarian masses and the champions of the fundamental transformation of society". They were to be a forum for the discussion of ethical, economic and social problems, for ideas to emerge and then be communicated to the unions. Because the union and the specific group were "two different, independent and, therefore, unmistakeable things".[119]

However, the FSL was born with a similar vision to the FAI, of control of the union organisation. Because, even if it declared that its goal was to work in favour of the union's independence, its limits were to be found in the tenets of revolutionary syndicalism, in other words, an obligatory objective was the attainment of a libertarian society, although without foregoing social, economic and work-related improvements. The new *feselista* organisation was not open to one and all, because "it is not those who want to who must enter, but those who should".[120] In fact, it defined itself as a homogeneous organisation in which revolutionary syndicalist militants were united, as in the FAI, by affinity. The union was not to be confused, in any case, with the federation, since the former was the class organisation, which admitted "all the workers irrespective of their ideas"; the latter was the ideological organisation, with room only for "militants that professed the ideas of revolutionary syndicalism". Therefore, if as workers they were organised within the union, as members of the FSL they had a duty to their groups, where they were shaped intellectually.[121] The FSL wanted to regain control of the CNT, and proposed similar actions to those of the FAI, in other words, the struggle within the union assemblies. But it was lacking coordinated tactics with clear and specific objectives that went beyond opposing the *faístas* in the unions. Its strategy was to demonstrate, with its arguments, that they were the true depositories of confederal principles, while the former represented, in reality, no more than genuine deviation.

After legalising its statutes, in February, the FSL promoted a federal internal organisation, modelled on the CNT, with local, county and regional committees and a national committee. Alongside it were the *Ateneos Sindicalistas Libertarios* (Libertarian Syndicalist Athenaeums), which would have an essentially cultural mission. Linked to them would be the *Juventudes Sindicalistas Libertarias* (Libertarian Syndicalist Youth or JSL), with the same federal structure and domiciled in the athenaeums. The parallelism even included the constitution, by the syndicalist youth organisation of Valencia, of *Comités de Defensa Sindicalistas* (Syndicalist Defence Committees or CDS). Moreover, the FSL focused on "incorporating women into social struggles" via groups, whether added onto local committees or athenaeums or acting independently.[122]

The truth is that all the libertarian organisations encouraged women to join the movement. As did prominent militants like Emiliana Morin, Durruti's partner, who asked her comrades not to simply attend meetings and applaud those speakers who praised women's grace or "maternal feelings", but to refuse "to continue being household slaves", and to demand their "place in the struggle, no longer with a fan, but with the same weapons as your male comrades". Morin quoted the example of the English women who fought for the right to vote, not to defend the latter, which she considered "derisory", but for having proven "with their courage and tenacity that they were no longer prepared to remain isolated from the political and social life of the country". The same reasoning was employed by Dolores Sierra, secretary of the *Sindicato Único de la Mujer Obrera* (Single Union of the Working Woman) in Andalusia, who urged her colleagues to organise themselves into "unions, groups and athenaeums". Like the *Agrupación Femenina de Educación Libertaria* (Female Association of Libertarian Education) which promoted the emancipation of women via the acquisition of knowledge by means of reading, conferences and talks, with the objective of forming a clear definition of anarchy and sowing the seeds of rebellion amongst women.[123] In any case, the presence of women in union assemblies and on the committees of the different organisations was always minimal, in spite of the argument that a revolution would be incomplete if women did not participate.

Meanwhile, on 14 February, in Barcelona, the FSL published the first issue of *Sindicalismo*, which replaced *Cultura Libertaria.* Juan López was the director, with prominent *treintistas* among the contributors: Pestaña, Fornells, Peiró, Torres, Robusté, Alfarache, Arín, Sebastián Flor alias *Nono.*[124] During the following months, as the schism within the CNT grew deeper, the Opposition Unions were set up and new publications appeared, like *Combate*, in Catalonia, directed by Pestaña, and *El Combate Sindicalista*, in Valencia.[125]

It was in the Levante that the most important unions were in the hands of *treintistas* such as Domingo Torres, José Borrul and F. Fenollar, who refused, as had occurred in Sabadell, to pay the confederal stamp and found themselves excluded from the CNT. However, the *faístas* controlled the *cenetista* regional committee. The rebellion, claimed the unions, had three fundamental causes: the lack of clarity in regional accounts, the unproven accusations against comrades and the *trabazón* in the prisoners' aid committees. In February 1933, the CNT sent a delegation to Valencia to attempt to resolve the conflict, formed by Marcos Alcón, of the national committee, and Eusebio Carbó and Alexander Shapiro, on behalf of the AIT. At the meeting, particular attention was drawn to the last two points. The delegates proposed that it was necessary to seek those responsible for the defamation and take action against them. With regard to the prisoners' aid committees, they acknowledged that in other regional federations like Galicia, Asturias and Baleares there was no *trabazón* with the FAI, so they would permit the Levante not to have one either. The unions declared that, if agreements were respected, they would pay the stamp. But the national committee denied the validity of the agreements.[126] It was not a time for pacts, but for impositions. Therefore, the Opposition Unions of the Levante were structured over the course of the year, and in February 1934 they held their first regional meeting, with 67 delegations representing 37 unions and 23,308 members, 16,000 of whom were from Valencia.[127]

Another important place for the opposition was Huelva. There, the local federation in the capital had already been targeted by the CNT when ,at the national plenum in August 1932, the Andalusian regional federation was authorised to take the necessary steps in order to put an end to the activity of "political elements" like Juan López. But the latter's work could not be neutralised by the regional federation, which voted to expel the Huelva local federation at the Andalusian congress held in Seville at the end of March 1933. At that time, the local federation had around 5,000 members, and in the following months it joined the Opposition Unions.[128]

In Catalonia, *Sindicalismo* published a manifesto, dated January 1933, signed by unions from Sabadell, Manresa and Mataró, demanding, somewhat optimistically, the resignation of the regional and the national committee and of the management of *Solidaridad Obrera,* and the renunciation of the *trabazón* in the prisoners' aid committees to "remove from the Confederation the strange powers" that controlled it, in clear allusion to the FAI.[129] But what occurred was quite the contrary, and the regional committee, which met in March 1933, approved the definitive expulsion of the unions from those localities. There were violent clashes, with reciprocal accusations of dictatorial conduct and killing of comrades, combined with a major controversy regarding the voting system employed for approval of the regional committee's report, which included the expulsion of the opposition. While the anarchists defended delegates' votes according to the number of members each union claimed to represent, the opposition claimed that this system was a violation of the agreements reached at the previous plenum, where it was agreed that votes would be according to the number of paid-up confederal stamps. The regional committee's supporters argued that the unemployed, who did not contribute, were also militants. While the rest recognised the previous agreements, but questioned the authenticity of the figures provided by each union. Ricardo Fornells stated that the membership reflected in the plenum proceedings, listing 208,821 members, was exaggerated, as was evidenced by the confederal stamp payments and the regular contributions to *Solidaridad Obrera*, which gave an average of 70,000 contributors.[130]

Although what Fornells claimed should be taken with a pinch of salt, since as a *treintista* he could reduce the figures of those who paid their contributions. Be that as it may, the fact is that the difference between the number of members and contributors in the entire organisation was significant. It is difficult to obtain official data, although, for example, the local San Sebastián federation said it had, in February 1933, 926 members, of whom 449 paid their contributions, in other words, fewer than 50%.[131] In any case, a difference of this magnitude was important enough to change the decisions to be taken, so the voting system was a fundamental issue. Furthermore, it should be borne in mind that their was growing criticism of the conduct of many delegates, who were accused of not respecting the agreements they brought from their respective unions, and voted on the basis of their own criteria, as we shall see later. Anyway, the plenum accepted, in the middle of a huge row, the first formula, and the regional committee report was approved by 129 unions representing 152,704 members, against 30 unions with 15,652 members.[132]

Although beyond the personal confrontations, unproven accusations or the voting system, the opposition demanded, above all, the FAI's exit from union life. However much the *faístas* denied it, the evidence was overwhelming, and was repeated over time. To everything described on the previous pages can be added the agreements reached at the meeting of the local federation of anarchist groups held in Barcelona, in February 1933, in which the peninsular committee of the FAI was asked to convene a plenum prior to the confederal congress in order that anarchist comrades present in the union could endeavour "for delegations to take to that Congress as mandated by their respective unions (...) anarchist postulates". Which combined with the call, once again, to "occupy the leading positions in the Confederation".[133] A penetrative strategy that bore fruit, since as *Solidaridad Obrera* observed, the regional plenum of Catalonia was "represented to an overwhelming degree by anarchists".[134]

The first regional plenum of the Opposition Unions of Catalonia, held on 4 June, 1933, took the definitive decision to organise the movement independently, accommodating the CNT unions that, disagreeing with the leadership, had declared their independence. This was the decision taken by the 53 delegations representing over 26,000 workers. A letter was duly sent to the regional committee instructing it to retract. An impossible request met only with silence.[135] Ultimately, membership of the Opposition Unions in the three main areas of influence was around 54,000 workers, distributed, approximately, as follows: Catalonia, 26,000, the Levante, 23,000 and Huelva, 5,000.

The schism considerably deepened the crisis affecting the Catalan regional federation. On the one hand, owing to the repression that, following the last attempt at insurrection, had resulted in the closure of many unions. On the other, given the continuous loss of members, since if in August 1931 these numbered around 400,000, by the time of the March 1933 plenum, numbers were down to only 208,821, a fall of almost 50%. To these figures were added the cost of the schism itself, around 26,000, and the expulsion of unions from the local federations of Lérida, Gerona and Tarragona, which fell into communist hands[136]

Added to these figures were those members distanced from the Confederation, who did not belong, in principle, to the Opposition Unions, and who formed *the Federación de Sindicatos Expulsados* (Federation of Unions Expelled) from the CNT. This Federation held a regional conference on 21–22 October 1933 in Barcelona, attended, according to its records, by 45 unions with approximately 30,000 members; numbers that clearly appear to be exaggerated. Its representatives began to negotiate its integration within the Opposition Unions early in November, although, the following month, Francisco Aguilar was still signing on behalf of the Federation in the constitution of the *Alianza Obrera* (Workers' Alliance) in Cataluña.[137]

Although the Catalan regional committee mainly attributed the steady loss of members to unemployment, the direct consequence of the economic crisis, one cannot ignore the internal conflict and the new confederal dynamic of abandoning the union line for an insurrectional one, or the violence that was employed, with increasing frequency, in the resolution of labour disputes.

The Benefits of Negotiation and Labour Conflict

Labour conflict during the Second Republic reached its peak in 1933. According to official records, in 1931, there were 734 strikes, in 1932, 681 and in 1933, 1.127. In other words, an increase of approximately 53% and 66%, respectively, compared with the previous two years.

While the number of strikers was, in 1931, 236,117, in 1932, 269,104, and, in 1933, 843,000, more than triple that of the previous two years. The number of days lost was 3,843,290 in 1931, 3,589,473 in 1932, and 14,440,629 in 1933, almost four times as many.[138]

The causes of this major increase are to be found, on the one hand, in increasingly organised management that strongly opposed the workers' goal of recovering rights and improving their economics and working conditions; on the other hand, in the impact of the global crisis upon the Spanish economy, with the resultant rise in unemployment. If the CNT congress of June 1931 quoted a figure of 300,000 unemployed, by June of the following year, official estimates put this figure at 446,263, and by December 1933, 618.947; in other words, more than double, just one and a half years later.[139]

In short, this was a period marked by the working masses' campaign to achieve improvements in their economic and working conditions, in addition

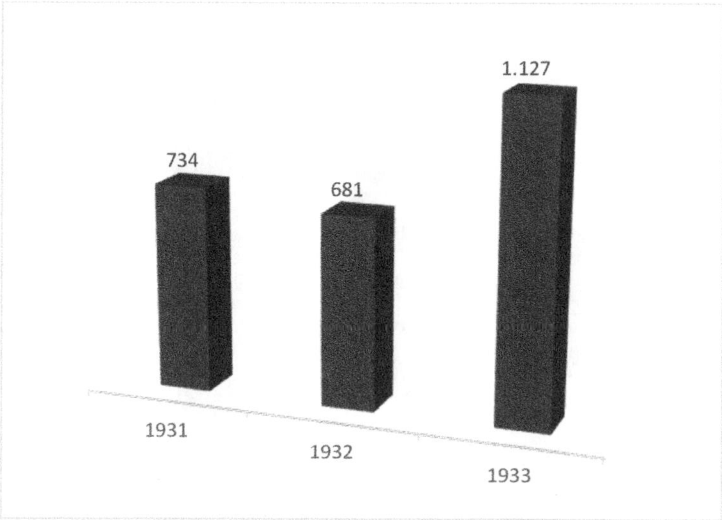

Figure 2 Number of Strikes, 1931–1933.

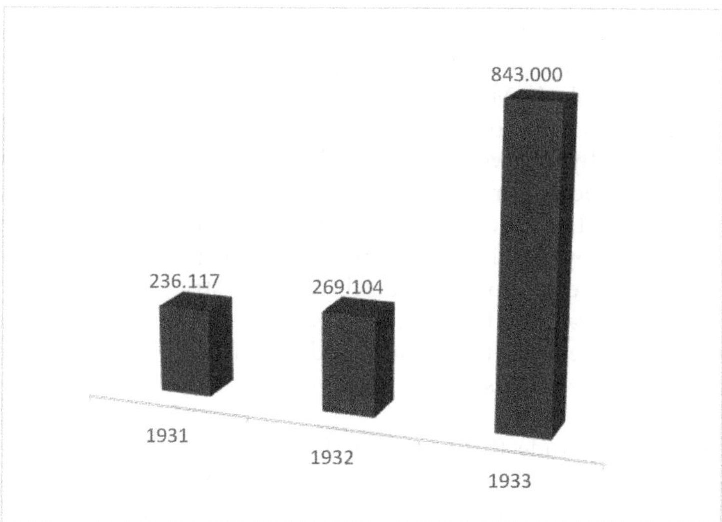

Figure 3 Number of Strikers, 1931–1933.

to the struggle to maintain their jobs. In this context, it is necessary to return to the competition between the two main unions and the internal evolution of each. The continuous protests, the repeated condemnation of repression, and the growing criticism of the government, all protagonised by the CNT,

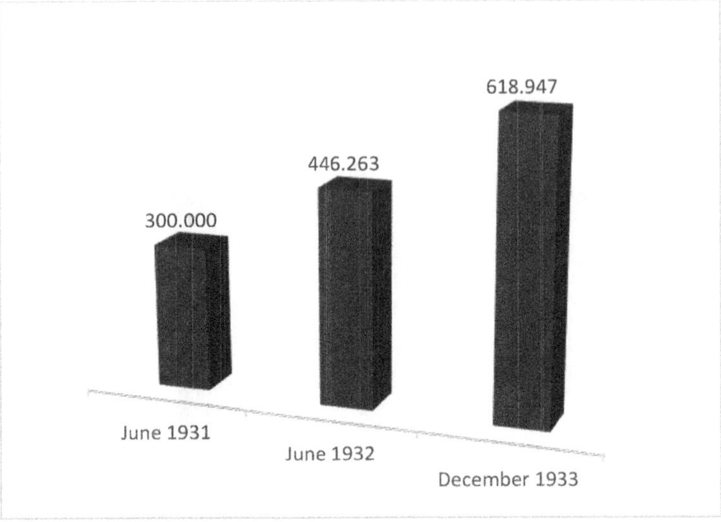

Figure 4 Number of Unemployed, 1931–1933.

were permeating the UGT militancy, which increased its presence in strikes and demonstrations. This was the case in Zaragoza during the 48-hour general strike, called by the CNT for 9–10 May 1933, which continued for several days with the presence of the UGT members.[140] As also occurred in the construction sector strike in Madrid, in October, in defence of a shorter working day and higher pay. The socialist union initially opposed the protest, but the pressure exerted by the workers themselves forced it to rectify. The CNT referred to the useless efforts made by the "the *caudillos* of the UGT" to avoid the strike, but also the importance of this conflict, as it represented "the greatest progress made by the CNT" in many years. With good reason, it took place in Madrid, "the preserve of state socialism". The strike was not free of violence, with the death of four socialist workers who did not support the protest, but it achieved, after months of dour struggle, the reduction of the working week to 44 hours and a pay rise for each worker of 4.40 pesetas per week.[141]

A change of attitude that was also shown by socialist leaders from the summer of 1933 onwards, influenced as they were by the confederal pressure that impacted upon their militancy, the economic crisis and its effect on unemployment, the weakness of the reforms introduced in the face of employers' resistance, and the advance of fascism throughout Europe. Without forgetting socialist disenchantment with judicial rulings that were hard to comprehend. Like the verdict on the events of Castilblanco which, issued in July, sentenced six defendants to death (commuted to 30 years' imprisonment) and the rest to long prison terms,with nobody standing trial for the killing of the young peasant. Azaña himself, after admitting that the sentence was "very harsh", said that its announcement had been delayed for fear of disturbances of public order, as had been requested "two or three times" by socialist Jiménez de Asúa, defence lawyer.[142] A sentence that appeared harsher still if compared with the one issued by the Supreme Court, also in July, against those responsible for the August 1932 coup. General Cavalcanti and Captain Fernández, for whom the death penalty had been requested, had seen their sentences reduced to ten and eight years respectively. The toughest sentences were for General Fernández Pérez and Colonel Cano Ortega, who received 20 years' imprisonment. The fact that army officers who had rebelled against a democratically elected government received a milder sentence than a handful of peasants from a small village in Extremadura, who amidst the tumult had killed some civil guards, was an incomprehensible fact that much of society found hard to digest. The French Ambassador, Herbette, provided the key to understanding such questionable rulings, which was none other than the difference between the nature of both courts, since it was "civil justice that has tried the seditious soldiers, while (it was) military justice that had judged the civilian rebels".[143] A truly surprising state of affairs.

So it was not surprising that, under all these circumstances, Socialist Party members and leaders expressed their doubts and reservations. UGT membership fell significantly, from approximately a million in June 1932 to 400,000 a year later.[144] In this context, Largo Caballero, during a meeting in the Pardiñas cinema in Madrid in the same month of July, said, "before the Republic I did not think it possible to undertake a socialist project in bourgeois democracy, and after 24 months in the government of the Republic, if I had any doubts, they have disappeared. Today I am convinced that undertaking a socialist project in bourgeois society is impossible". Two weeks later, at the Socialist Summer School in Torrelodones, he contemplated taking the revolutionary road, should they be ousted from government.[145]

The CNT, meanwhile, after the failure of the January protest, maintained the revolutionary momentum with demonstrations, protests and increasingly long strikes. For their part, the Opposition Unions continued with their struggle to improve conditions for workers. *El Combate Sindicalista* denounced the fact that, on more than one occasion, the unions had to fight on three fronts, against the backdrop of the law of 8 April, against the authorities, the bosses and the UGT. Thus, for instance, in Valencia, the construction union engaged in a dispute with the Hurtado y Carbonell Company, in which the UGT, "in collusion with management and the authorities", did battle with the CNT. The paper mills of the Alicante town of Alcoy achieved a significant victory after 20 days on strike: of the 27 points under negotiation, 25 were resolved favour of the workers, including recognition of the union and the factory committee, and a pay rise of between 1 and 1.50 pesetas.[146] Meanwhile, following a six-week struggle, the metallurgy sector of Valencia succeeded in reducing the working week to 44 hours. However, as occurred on more than one occasion, a few days later the agreements were violated by the management, with attempts to sack workers and close down factories unless there was a return to 48 hours and lower salaries.[147]

One of the most significant disputes was the one in the construction sector in Barcelona, which began in mid-April and lasted four months. The union presented new labour rules, including a reduction of the working day from eight to six hours, with the objective of absorbing some of the unemployment which, in construction, stood, according to confederal data, at 70%. In addition, it requested a minimum wage of 13 pesetas for an official and 11 for a labourer, a minimum legal working age of 16 and the abolition of piecework, as well as improvements in safety and hygiene.

The first obstacle was the division of the workers vis-à-vis membership of the UGT or CNT. While the former defended dialogue via mixed juries and a pay rise, the latter advocated direct action and the reduction of the working work as a solution for unemployment. Meanwhile employers were also affected, in their own way, by Peiró's "theory of need and convenience", as their primary objective was to resolve the conflict in the best possible conditions for their own interests, irrespective of the system of negotiation. For any agreements that excluded the union that controlled the majority of workers, even if legal, were difficult to apply, particularly if that union were the CNT.

Therefore, employers insisted that the government address "the duplication of action and representation between the mixed juries and the workers' associations" which opposed their existence, and argued that regulation of working conditions should "be the result of free negotiations between the interested parties, without arbitration in the form of opposition or intervention by representatives of the state". So they advocated recognition of "the efficiency and legality of the work rules and regulations agreed upon inside or outside the mixed juries". Management found it intolerable to have to accept the intervention of juries that, on more than one occasion, did not represent the workers of the sector affected by the conflict. It was not a case of management having become a supporter of direct action; far from it, it was a simple question of "need and convenience". So employers blamed everybody, according to Mercedes Cabrera, "the CNT for the extremist tactics and violence it encouraged; the socialists, for attempting to instrumentalise the mixed juries, in the service of their own partisan interests, and the authorities, for their lenient treatment of both".[148]

The construction union, in view of the lack of progress in negotiations, called a strike for 17 April. Initially, the strike enjoyed maximum support and was free of violence. The solidarity of other sectors, like the port workers of Barcelona or the miners of Cardona, Sallent or Figols, meant that the conflict spread, and led to the closure of union premises and athenaeums and the arrest of prominent militants. At the beginning of July, the dispute was deadlocked, so the union accepted mediation by the mayor of Barcelona. The latter's intervention questioned the principle of direct action, however much the strike committee insisted that for them the town council was "just one more boss", as there were workers on strike who were employed by the municipal institution. The main problem was the reduction of the working day, which management refused to accept, as well as demanding that the agreement be applicable at a national level. Which raised the spectre of the Federations of Industry since, as Peiró had said at the Conservatorio congress, they were necessary when management proposed an agreement that transcended local or regional limits. The mayor proposed, in order to unblock the situation, acceptance of the "English week" of 44 hours, in other words, working from Monday to Friday, which management did not accept.

The strike was resolved in mid-August. The confederal press insisted that there had been direct negotiation with management and that a victory had been won, although, fundamentally, it was more a mid-point between the situation prior to the conflict and the workers' demands. Specifically, the rules agreed included the 44-hour week, comprising 8-hour days Monday to Friday, and four hours on Saturday morning. Wages rose by one peseta for journeymen, while apprentices would be paid 10 per day. Piecework was abolished, hygiene and safety conditions at work were improved, and tools were to be provided by employers, a "conquest of singular importance" imposed "for the first time in Spain, and rarely seen in other countries". The agreement had the support of 1,227 workers, while 616 voted to continue the strike. The Opposition Unions criticised the resolution of the dispute as, after four months on strike, this was no more than the "crumbs" offered by management, very inferior, they claimed, to the initial demands.[149]

In any case, although not all the workers' demands were met, the fact is that the union struggle did bear fruit, and the "moral and economic" improvements were evident. Salaries for example, rose by around 20% between1931 and 1933.[150] An increase that was related to the offensive launched by the working masses during this period, but also to the fact that the Socialists were in power. Because the improvements had as much to do with the actions of the mixed juries, which followed socialist guidelines and supported the workers' demands, as with the workers' pressure led by the CNT, which through strikes and protests succeeded in resisting the "iron fist of management". In this respect, it is no coincidence that the increase in the number of strikes and strikers was constant, as we have seen, until 1933.

Violence

Work-related violence and government repression were also present in the dispute in the construction sector in Barcelona. There was even condemnation of the death of a member of the ceramics union mixed jury, which the press blamed on the strikers, while the CNT attributed it to "a vulgar brawl".[151] Those arrested, meanwhile, who claimed they had been subjected to ill-treatment, were released at the end of the dispute, and union premises that had been closed down were re-opened.

Violence and repression that were increasingly present in the union struggle. Throughout 1933, some labour-related conflicts were peppered with attacks on employers, strikebreakers or the property of companies on strike. At the beginning of the year, several bombs exploded in Elda (Alicante) during a strike in the shoe industry. One exploded on the stairway of the home of Francisco Rivas, a factory owner, another at the home of businessman

Riera, and a third at the entrance to a factory owned by Rodolfo Guariñas. A device also exploded at the home of a worker at the Pedro Rico Factory who had not supported the strike. In Almería, a bomb was found in the employers' federation building, with suspicion falling on the striking carpenters' union. In Barcelona, two firecrackers exploded on a barge during the stevedores' strike. In La Coruña, there was an explosion directed against the hauliers that were not participating in the sector strike organised by the CNT. In Huelva, a firecracker went off in José Domínguez's ice factory, an incident that the police connected with the dispute involving waiters belonging to the CNT.[152]

But it was Seville that witnessed the most violent situations. In April 1933, Pedro Caravaca, director of the *Federación Económica de Andalucía* (Economic Federation of Andalusia or FEDA) was killed. The police arrested Manuel García Rodríguez alias *Martín II*, secretary of the food division, olive-producing section, of the CNT. A bomb exploded at the home of Marcelino Bonet, president of the FEDA, causing major damage. On the same day, a firecracker exploded in the shop owned by Miguel C. Longoria, member of the same federation and olive oil exporter. The following month, another bomb exploded in the home of the president of the federation of oil producers of Alcalá de Guadaira, Pedro Gutiérrez Calderón, while in June, a local businessman, Domingo Días, was the victim of an attack. During the same month, unidentified individuals shot Germán González Céspedes and Norberto López de la Rosa in a bar in Seville; the former, a police informer, was killed, while the latter was seriously wounded. In August, José Fernández Aramburo, dock foreman, and his children José and Leandor, aged 18 and 15, were shot and seriously wounded[153]

The workers themselves were also victims of attacks. A baker belonging to the CNT was shot dead because he was working early in the morning (a circumstance opposed by the union). A doctor Ferreras, Communist Party leader and member of International Red Aid, was shot down while leaving his home.[154] Meanwhile, the anarchist groups of Barcelona agreed, in view of the repression, that when a comrade was sentenced by a court they should proceed "immediately to the execution of the prosecutor in question".[155] Azaña declared that "we live, as they say, on a volcano". In fact, for fear of an attack, he did not allow the waiters at the Hotel Nacional, CNT members, to serve the banquet where he was going to hold a meeting.[156]

Individual actions that were mixed with robberies, and which facilitated an image of the CNT removed from that of a union. Although the anarchists denied it, there was a close relationship between their organisations and the robbers. This was evidenced by the French police's report on refugees, according to which those gunmen spread "terror throughout certain provinces, in order to obtain money, which sometimes serves to benefit anarchist organisations".[157] But also, the Spanish Ministry of the Interior, which warned civil governors of the increased activity of the anarchists "committing attacks (and) robberies". The Ministry placed the emphasis on arresting those that were dangerous, with particular focus on the prisoners' aid committees, not only "due to their protection and concealment of the authors of attacks, but also their more or less direct participation in the latter".[158]

Although these actions were performed by a minority, the fact is that the profusion of news about or related to anarchist robbers encouraged this association. In Barcelona, the police located, in a premises where the Piquet Factory robbers were hiding out, 120 primed bombs, 160 sticks of dynamite, weapons and ammunition. They also found documents related to Antonio Seva, who participated in the attack on the Fundición Girona, and a plan to obtain bombs and attack official buildings and barracks.[159] In Tarragona, the security forces arrested Pedro Martí Regat, who had taken part in robberies at the Telefónica Company, the Banco Urquijo in Manresa and a branch of the Banco de Bilbao, in which a security guard died. He was also involved in a shootout in a bar in Calle Urgel, in which a police inspector lost his life. Martí was arrested at the home of anarchist De las Heras, retired from the active struggle.[160] Peiró spent time in prison for refusing to give the name of the author of an article published in *Solidaridad Obrera* when he was the director. It turns out that the individual in question was a member of the FAI, "the bank robber José Gardeñes (...) convict and self-confessed author of a robbery in Sabadell".[161]

Attacks on individuals and robberies that were all too reminiscent of past times, when guns replaced the union struggle and indiscriminate repression only served to exacerbate the situation. In these circumstances, the anarcho-syndicalists attempted to dissociate this violence from the social question as, they claimed, the working-class struggle against employers and the authorities had nothing to do with these incidents: "This is no longer a social struggle. It is a terrorist system. Violence is met with violence, and, on both sides, there are victims of the obdurate obstinacy of uncontrolled force and terror".[162] Once again, the anarcho-syndicalists were caught in a crossfire, since criticism of the violent anarchists was mistaken for support for management and the authorities, when they also condemned the violent and illegal methods employed by the latter. Employers in Seville declared a lockout, while the government closed down unions and imprisoned their representatives in a period of indiscriminate and senseless repression that did not differentiate between those who employed different tactics. Thus, the police arrested José Gómez, Emilio Angulo and José Bravo, members of the *Agrupación Sindicalista Libertaria* (Syndicalist Libertarian Association), who were subjected to ill-treatment.[163]

But the violence did not only occur on the anarchist side. The authorities had their own quota, as did other groups, parties or social classes, which employed force to achieve their objectives or prevent others from doing so. The Ministry of Governance was flooded with telegrams from all over Spain, during the municipal elections of April 1933, in which there were accusations of all kinds of violence. In Badajoz, individuals armed by local *caciques* prevented certain left-wing electoral meetings from being held. The Socialist MP Vidarte denounced interference in the distribution of electoral propaganda in Mérida by means of coercion, where the Civil Guard accompanied "*caciques* house-to-house buying votes". In Tenerife, owners of large areas of land in the Orotava Valley coerced sharecroppers and employees, threatening to evict them from the land unless they voted for the monarchic radical Catholic agricultural conglomerate. The Mayor of Huesa (Jaen) accused the Civil Guard commanding officer of threatening a Socialist leader and another "four communist rogues", whose heads, he claimed, "smelled of gunpowder". In the village of Villahermoso (Ciudad Real), a radical rally was suspended when a stone was thrown at the speaker and diverse political groups uttered serious threats at one another.[164] In short, 1930s Spain was a violent society, manifestations of which were very varied in both nature and direction. At the same time, the government promoted laws that went beyond the prosecution of offences and opted for repression that was difficult to justify.

Public Order and Vagrancy Laws

The Law on Defence of the Republic was replaced, in August 1933, by the Public Order Law. The new law provided for three degrees of exceptionality: the state of prevention, of alarm and of war. Of most significance was the fact that, in the first case, the government could take measures in the event of "disruption of public order" in those situations where, without being a crime, it constituted an infraction. In the second case, it was possible to enter residences, detain without trial, suspend meetings and associations and relocate "alleged disrupters" of order. With the third, civil authority deferred to military authority, given the impossibility of maintaining order. The "preventive" nature of the law facilitated its arbitrary application by the government, a question that was the object of particular condemnation during its passage through parliament. Added to which was its lack of precision, which meant its possible application as judged appropriate by the particular authority involved at any given moment, rather than according to the criteria of public order for which it was supposedly designed. In fact, the Socialist-Republican government mainly applied this law against reactionaries and *cenetistas* in alleged conspiracies against the Republic, while during the Conservative biennium, the period in which it was applied with most frequency, it was employed against strikes and left-wing opposition in general.[165]

During that same month, the Vagrancy Law was also passed. Like the Public Order Law, it had a "preventive" character, as it sought to take action against potential offenders before any crime were committed. Regarded as suspects, so liable to be arrested, were those who did not have "a known or legitimate source of livelihood". The law provided for their internment in work camps for a maximum of three years or on remand for between one and five years.[166] The *cenetistas* criticised its content on various grounds; on the one hand, because it came at a time when unemployment was having a devastating effect on workers, which meant that any of the thousands out of work could be arrested at will; on the other, because it affected in particular the idiosyncrasy of the doctrinal dissemination that, since its beginnings, had inspired anarchism. In other words, the "propaganda outings", in which militants, like true "apostles of ideas", travelled to farms and factories to preach their message. In fact,

Francisco Ascaso and Buenaventura Durruti were arrested during a propaganda trip around Andalusia in 1933, along with Paulino Díez, Antonio Paniza and Vicente Pérez, in application of this law.[167]

But there was also criticism of the fact that the government could use it against those militants who were most active in the unions. The governor of Seville, for instance, arrested 33 individuals with a history of *pistolerismo* and "other dangerous activities" that were not specified.[168] The confederal press reported, among others, the case of the militant in Zaragoza to whom the law was applied for spreading "anti-social propaganda".[169] Basically, the Vagrancy Law could be used to arrest offenders and maintain "public order", but could do so in arbitrary and unfair fashion. Furthermore, it did not address the underlying problems, in other words, the social injustice and poverty in which workers and peasants were immersed. The French ambassador observed that the application of the law made it possible to control those guilty of violence, but warned that if order were established in this way it would not bring an "end to regrettable and dangerous poverty". Meanwhile, *El Socialista* went further in its analysis, declaring that it was "the rich who, by maintaining over centuries a state of hunger, have created today's '*pistoleros*', or at least the reason for their existence". Which Herbette endorsed when he indicated the "anti-democratic fanaticism" of many Andalusian *señoritos* who made it very difficult to reduce social tension.[170]

The fact is that the confrontation between employers and workers gave rise to labour conflict with serious outbreaks of violence that had a particular impact on Seville society in the summer of 1933. Francisco León Ledesma, manager of the Carbonell olive oil refinery, died from the wounds received during a shooting. Nicanor Díaz Alonso, the manager of a drinks company, was shot by two members of his staff. The supervisor of the Fernández Palacio factory was also the victim of an attack when accompanied by a security guard. Timber manufacturer Víctor Ramos Catalina was killed in an attack intended, according to the governor "to scare timber sector employers and workers into continuing the strike which the Confederation called over a month and a half ago". The response to this wave of violence was none other than more repression. On 18 August, the government declared a state of prevention throughout the province of Seville. The civil governor, it seems, went further than arresting those who were using guns to resolve conflicts, for Seville's prisons had so many inmates that they were filled "well over capacity", in spite of the transfer of prisoners to Huelva.[171]

The CNT stated that the problem in Seville was "neither extremism, nor *pistolerismo*, nor *atraquismo* (bank robberies). Hunger (...) A lot of hunger!" So the struggle was addressed with reciprocal violence. The bosses employed strike-breakers, and businessmen, like Victor Ramos Catalina, fell "victim of what seemed to be social attacks, paying with his life for the despotism with which he had always treated his workers". Because according to the CNT, if the struggle saw workers fall every day, it was understandable to see the fall of "bosses too (...) the logical consequence of all combat". But the "terrorist state" that existed in Seville was not only the responsibility of the employers, but also of the authorities, as both were violently opposed to "the just grievances of the workers". Essentially, if the *cenetistas* used violence, it was as a last resort and always in response to the hired gunmen recruited, armed and paid by the FEDA, who acted "as strike-breakers in disputes" and murdered confederal militants with absolute immunity. According to the CNT, neither was it possible to speak of *atraquismo*, "because the greatest and most ignoble robberies are those which the bosses (...) commit against the workers", keeping part of their wages every day. So the problem was "the lockouts and the hunger", and while this continued there would be conflicts and violence and "workers, bosses and policemen" would fall victim. So long as the cause existed, the effects would persist.[172] Considerations that were reinforced by the accusations of torture levelled by prisoners against the security forces, as occurred during the trial of the case of the bombs that exploded during the peasants' strike of May 1932 in Seville, where 180 workers were charged. Although they were acquitted, the confederal press railed against the "judges who (...) conducted the trial in the interests of the deceitful Seville bourgeoisie".[173]

The Demotivation of Members

All these questions – unemployment, lengthy strikes, and major opposition on the part of employers, violence and repression – combined with the endless internal conflict reported on by the main newspapers on either side, *Solidaridad Obrera* and *Sindicalismo*, led many CNT members to refrain from participating in union life. The pages of the libertarian press were filled with smears, insults and information that portrayed opponents as traitors, informers and gunmen. The anarchists directed their attacks on the *treintista* leaders, while the latter spoke of the "Court of the FAI", or referred by name to *faístas*, whom they accused of being bank robbers or police informers, like Vicente Reche alias "Trillo", secretary of the regional federation of anarchist groups of Valencia, Fernando Cid, FAI delegate in the prisoners' aid committee, or Félix Pros, member of the regional committee of Catalonia.[174]

Union assemblies were increasingly poorly attended, and were too often preceded by meetings of militants whose predetermined position was subsequently adopted. But in addition, the union delegates, who attended the plenums, often voted according to their own particular criteria, either because they did not respect the agreements reached by their unions, or simply because they did not bring these to the meetings.[175] Delegates who voted in favour of strikes and protests, influenced by the revolutionary atmosphere that impregnated the meetings, or to avoid projecting a reformist image but who were unable to implement these decisions, because the organisation was not suitably prepared to do so, or because their members did not sympathise with their ideas.

As a result, it was difficult to know how much real support there was for some of the decisions taken by the national plenums. For example, the CNT called a 48-hour general strike for May 9, 1933 in defence of social prisoners. However, when the national committee contacted Andalusia, Asturias, Aragón, the Levante and the Central federation, they objected to the recently adopted agreement, while the most important local federation, Barcelona, withdrew its support. The regional federations accused the national committee of acting under the influence of the Catalan federation, and the latter's defence was to allude to the "zigzagging" of the former, because "either agreements are not reached or if they are adopted they have to be respected".[176]

The truth was that the Catalan regional federation exercised considerable influence over the national confederal committee, so there were repeated requests for the latter to be moved from Barcelona to prevent his from happening. Thus, when the national plenum in June called a referendum for members to decide on the possible relocation of the committee, the *Específica* published a circular warning that this change would also lead to the departure of other committees, such as the FAI's own peninsular committee, the prisoners' aid and the defence committees. Therefore, "in view of this serious turn of events, we have a duty to warn all our members of their responsibility and of what this agreement represents for the Revolution".[177] But since it was a referendum, without the filter of representation, members voted in favour of transferring the national committee to Zaragoza, a city that received 230 votes, compared to 153 for Madrid and 100 for Barcelona.[178] Thus, in November 1933, Joaquín Ascaso replaced Manuel Rivas as secretary general.[179]

A relocation intended to defuse the bitter internal confrontation affecting the CNT. For some regional federations, the Catalan dominance was behind the repeated organisation of protests, like the general strike of May, which did not enjoy the support, as we have seen, of most of the organisation and, consequently, had insufficient impact. To this circumstance was added, on the one hand, the lack of clear objectives, since to the original goal of protest in defence of social prisoners was added a multitude of accumulated grievances, like the law of 8 April, the closure of premises, the arrest of militants, etc., which made it difficult to know the exact reasons for protesting. But in addition, the fact that, while the organisation proposed a peaceful strike, there were always groups that sought to turn it into a revolutionary movement, which led to confusion. The CNT, meanwhile, had entered a perverse spiral, as the failure of an uprising and its subsequent repression led to new protests, which again foundered, and were met with further repression that debilitated the organisation. In fact, the governor of Barcelona declared that, in spite of the significant FAI presence, the general strike was not "possible after (the) last failure", and although he expected a campaign based on "explosives and attacks", he detected "despondency, lack of enthusiasm".[180]

The positive results of the strikes and protests were practically non-existent, while the repression decimated the organisation. In Barcelona alone, according to the governor's own information, crowded into the Celular prison, a month after the 9 May strike, were around 400 social prisoners waiting to go before the judge and another 40 at the disposal of the Ministry of the Interior. Most of the CNT leaders and the men of action were behind bars.[181] The Northern regional federation had 150 members imprisoned; Aragón, 187; and the Levante, 500, and a quarter of its unions shut down. In Andalusia and Extremadura there were 790 under arrest, and, if before the strike 71 unions were closed down, afterwards the figure was 171, including the regional committee.[182] So it was hardly surprising that the membership of so important a regional federation as Andalusia's decreased significantly: a total of 325,000 workers in 1932 fell to 242,630 in the same month of the following year, which represented a loss of 25%.[183]

Yet, in spite of everything, the representatives of the regional committees took another step along the path of insurrection and abandoned the essence of trade unionism by deciding, at the same June plenum, "to sacrifice strike movements and replace them with revolutionary action".[184] In any case, in the CNT everyone went their own way. This is apparent from the pages of the libertarian newspapers that reported on the numerous disputes over economic and labour issues in which the CNT workers were immersed. The struggles of exploited women with "miserly wages" in the Valencian manufacturing and textile industry; the miners in the basins of Alto Llobregat following the sacking of colleagues; the sit-in strikes against boycotted companies in the port of Seville.[185]

In mid-1933, Shapiro, AIT delegate, painted an internal portrait of the organisation that was, to say the least, worrying. In relation to the national committee, he said that in the meetings he had attended, some elements had no prior opinion of what was being discussed, while most spoke little and appeared to refuse to accept the moral force of reason. Uncertainty in meetings was absolute, as nobody knew how a debate would be settled until the moment of voting, which could go the opposite way of what had been argued during discussion. He also criticised something as dear to the libertarians as the press.

The internal struggles impacted negatively upon both Solidaridad *Obrera* and the *CNT*, since, according to Shapiro, they placed "a moral obligation on contributors to follow the *faísta* line". So "everything that touched upon either criticism of the FAI's activity, with regard to confederal life, or the calm and objective examination of reconstructive problems was in one way or another excluded from (its) columns".[186] The organisation recognised the journalists' inability to reflect "the palpitations of the proletariat", but also, the way in which the confrontation between *faístas* and *treintistas* was censoring and harming the newspaper. Simple discussion of the appropriateness of publishing articles that addressed confederal unity led to clashes between members of the editorial time, while differences over the paper's editorial line resulted in changes in leadership.

But the confederal press's problems went beyond criticism of its own management. According to the CNT administration, in a report dated June 1933, the newspaper's situation was fine until the authorities began its persecution, added to which was the "scant interest shown by the staff" in maintaining it. Stamps issued to raise defence funds totalled 11,989 pesetas, of which only 1,319.20 had been received. While the case of stamps issued for the confederal pro-newspaper commission was "even more woeful", since the regional federations owed in total around 50,000 pesetas. *CNT* had a circulation of approximately 27,000 copies, barely enough to cover costs. The weekly deficit was estimated to be around 3,600 pesetas. In short, the newspaper's situation was "it could be said, unsustainable".[187]

A far as *Solidaridad Obrera* was concerned, its circulation had fallen considerably, from 39,000 copies when it was launched in May 1931, to a figure two years later of 25,000.[188] The problems were similar to those of its counterpart in Madrid, in other words, economic and arising from internal conflict. Early in July 1933, the unions elected Liberto Callejas as director, but he tendered his definitive resignation. The reason was the visit he was planning to make to Madrid, unbeknownst to the regional committee, to meet José Franchi y Roca, Minister of Industry and Commerce, to prevent the repeated kidnappings of the newspaper by the authorities. Although Callejas could not attend the meeting owing to illness, he resigned because, he said, he was opposed to engaging in any kind of dialogue with politicians and authorities, an approach which, he argued, he had "to subordinate to the interests of the organisation and the newspaper". This was the absolute contradiction inhabited by many anarchists who had criticised and demanded of anarcho-syndicalists accountability for any dealings with politicians, but could not escape the reality of negotiating with the authorities if they wanted the organisation to survive. The regional committee of Catalonia expressed its sympathy with Callejas, and urged him to remain in his post provided he promised in future to seek the organisation's approval. But Callejas was adamant, and the organisation had to embark on an authentic pilgrimage in the quest to find a director.[189]

The crisis at *Solidaridad Obrera* also affected the workers at the newspaper. Two of them, Lino and Badori, were sacked. The former, according to the Catalan regional committee, for participating in a *treintista* rally, being a member of a Socialist athenaeum and attacking a colleague. But Lino denied this and protested that his expulsion was illegal, as it was decided by the committee itself, which was a violation of confederal rules since, as we have seen, he had to be expelled by the union to which belonged, in this case Graphic Arts. Badori was accused of appropriating furniture that belonged to the prisoners' aid committee. However, he claimed that his dismissal was a personal vendetta on the part of certain members of the regional committee, namely "Bilbao, Ordaz and others". The crux of the question was, as in the previous case, "thinking like a 'treintista' to lose one's job". Badori's colleagues at *Solidaridad Obrera* accused the regional committee of acting like "the most recalcitrant bourgeoisie" that sacked workers for reasons unrelated to work. In short, they denounced the fact that in the role of "boss (was) none other than the regional committee". As the union board accepted the sackings, the workers in the newspaper workshop, nine in total – from the accountant to the storeman – went on strike, and the regional committee responded by looking for replacements to fill their positions,[190] in other words, strike-breakers. A circumstance that did not go unnoticed by the anarcho-syndicalists, and *Sindicalismo* opened a section for donations in favour of the *Solidaridad Obrera* workers.[191]

Against the Advance of Fascism: Frente Único

The proclamation of the Second Republic had come at a delicate moment for democracies. Gone were the days of the democratising drive that emerged in the wake of the First World War. The right underwent a radicalisation, a shift towards authoritarianism that, to a large extent, was the consequence of fear of the expansion of the communism that was triumphing in Russia. The crash of 1929 had accentuated instability all over the world and sown doubts regarding the response of liberal democracy. In the light of the latter, the radicalised right identified in fascism the means of halting the political participation of the masses and the mobilisation of workers' organisations. Meanwhile, the left had the reference of soviet communism, and its revolutionary dreams were mixed with the struggle against fascism.

This combination, revolution and antifascism, was very present in republican Spain, particularly since Hitler's rise to power in Germany in March 1933. The attempts to form an anti-fascist *Frente Único* (Single Front) gained momentum from that moment onwards, and were led by the communists. But the anarcho-syndicalists were always suspicious of the attempts to form a common block with them. Long-standing distrust, most recently explained by the communist attempts to take control of the CNT during its reconstruction in the early days of the Republic. Though with little success, as apart from the formation of the "CNT Reconstruction Committee" in Seville and its presence in the Asturian miners' unions, the communist strategy to control the syndicalist organisation failed. This attempt was followed by the tactic of union unity, in mid-1932, with the same result. The communist efforts to constitute their own union did not bear fruit until March 1934, with the first congress of the *Confederación General del Trabajo Unitaria* (General Confederation of Unitary Work or CGTU).[192]

Now, in 1933, one of the left's concerns was the advance of fascism. On 1 April an assembly was held in Madrid in order to form the *Frente Único Antifascista* (Anti-fascist Single Front or FUA), with the presence of, among others, Dolores Ibárruri, *Pasionaria*, Luis Salina, Wenceslao Roces, Francisco Galán, César Falcón and Ramón J. Sender. At the meeting, there was criticism of the Spanish government for favouring and encouraging the far right, because, they said, "tolerance of fascism begins in the ranks of the government itself". The constitution of the front was followed by rallies and committees, all with a considerable communist presence.[193] Anarchists and anarcho-syndicalists were, inevitably, concerned about the progress of fascism in Europe, but distrustful of the communists. The anarchists accused them of wanting to impose their "imperialist dreams" since, though it was true that the fascist threat existed and presented the examples of Italy and Germany, the communists were forgetting the very first fascism, that represented by "Soviet Russia". For their part, the anarcho-syndicalists warned workers of the advance of the far right, and although the proposal for a single front initially met with reticence, they understood the need for "workers' unity against fascism", which included unions and left-wing parties.[194]

The left's fear of fascism included groups and parties that occupied the Spanish right. The conservative forces, led by Julio Gil, focused their propaganda, since the start of the Republic, on the defence of social order and Catholicism, in addition to questioning the new regime. These groups adopted, in many provinces, the term agricultural. In others, like the Basque Country and Navarra, the nationalists joined forces with traditionalists and Catholics, while in Catalonia, the *Lliga* continued to be the conservative reference. Meanwhile, *Acción Nacional* was founded at the end of April 1931, in response to the Vatican's recommendations and with the goal of defending conservative values. Its motto was none other than "God, Country, Family, Property, Work, Order". The first fascist group was the *Juntas de Ofensiva Nacional Sindicalista* (Councils of National-Syndicalist Offensive or JONS), formed in October 1931, under the leadership of Ramiro Ledesma Ramos and Onésimo Redondo. While the Spanish Falange was not constituted until October 1933, with José Antonio Primo de Rivera, Sánchez Mazas and Julio Ruiz Alda at the helm. The union between Falange and the JONS did not take place until early 1934.

Before that, *Acción Nacional* changed its name to *Acción Popular*, in April 1932, owing to the legal ban on using the term "nation" in a partisan sense. Within the party were the "accidentalists", led by José Mª Gil Robles, who put conservative values before the type of regime, and the "fundamentalists", led by Antonio Goicoechea, who regarded the monarchy as indispensable. The latter eventually joined the *Comunión Tradicionalista* or *Renovación Española* which, founded at the beginning of 1933, defended the establishment of an authoritarian monarchy. Its leader, José Calvo Sotelo, did not reject the adjective fascist, though his party was, essentially, of a clerical and traditional nature. Meanwhile, Gil Robles's followers created, in March 1933, the most important conservative party in republican Spain, the *Confederación Española de Derechas Autónomas* (Spanish Confederation of Autonomous Rights or CEDA). The new party united regional and local groups, bound together by Catholicism. Their ultimate objectives were not clearly defined, though they sought to attain power by legal means, reform the constitution and found a Catholic and corporative state. But Hitler's rise to power had dazzled the right, and led it to flirt with fascism.[195]

Gil Robles travelled to Germany, in the summer of 1933, with the Nazi party already in power. For the French ambassador, Herbette, this trip could not be considered a surprise, given that the Spanish Catholic right had always displayed clear sympathy for Germany. Relations that were tempered by the fascist regime's rise to power, but which were revived following the signing of the Vatican Concordat, in July 1933. So it came as no surprise that for *El Debate*, the CEDA's mouthpiece, Hitler's regime had "become a kind of example" for politicians or publicist that were Catholic militants. Herbette constantly insisted on the need to support Azaña so as to prevent, among other things, a possible right-wing government coming under the influence of the enemies of France. The French government was responsible, he said, for whether or not Gil Robles had undertaken "in vain his *ad limina* Hitlerian pilgrimage".[196] In other words, *ad limina* was the obligation placed on certain members of the ecclesiastical hierarchy to visit at certain times "the thresholds of the apostles", Saint Peter and Paul, namely Rome, and present themselves before the Pope to give an account of the state of their dioceses. Ultimately, this was to acknowledge the Pope's universal jurisdiction, receive his admonitions and counsels and thus bind the members of the Church more closely to its head. Herbette pointed to Hitler, in this case, as supreme leader of the movement of which the leader of the CEDA formed a part.

The fact is that the Catholic leader's "pilgrimage" raised many doubts. Gil Robles was informed of the fall of Azaña's government via telephone call from none other than the Nazi leader Goebbels, when he was in Berlin, after attending the National Socialist Congress in Nuremberg. The Nazi Propaganda Minister himself placed at his disposal, according to Gil Robles, "his well-organised services so that very same night" he could depart for Spain. A circumstance that prevented him from meeting Hitler.[197] Upon his return from Germany, he published an article in *La Gaceta Regional de Salamanca*, CEDA mouthpiece in that locality, entitled "Antidemocracy", which *ABC* reviewed. Gil Robles stated that reality was leading the way "towards a new conception of the state" and the leaders of the masses should pay attention "without closing their spirit to the fertile innovations of the times", and that young people on the right should know how to act in harmony "with the immortal principles of our Catholic tradition".[198] This seemed to be the great stumbling block: how to harmonise Catholic doctrine with fascism. A factor to which Gil Robles again referred in an interview with *El Debate*, in which he insisted on the problem of reconciling Catholicism with "the doctrine of a movement fuelled by pantheistic principles", which ended up "cancelling out the individual and deifying the state". In his declarations, he also condemned another of the trademarks of fascism, which was violence. Though with the qualification that "violence in response to aggression, when exercised in legitimate defence, is not only something that I permit and preach, but I shall be the first to practise it". There his reservations ended, for he admitted that,

> these considerations apart, in fascism there is much that is beneficial: its origin and its action, which are eminently popular; the way in which it exalts the values of the homeland; its distinctly anti-Marxist signification; its hostility to liberal and parliamentary democracy (...) a new order of things that we have a duty to retain, to harmonise with the postulates of Catholic doctrine.[199]

These were notions that considerably worried the left and increased in the build-up to the 1933 elections.

The Elections of November 1933

The fall of Azaña's government, in September 1933, had a mixed reception in the libertarian press. *Solidaridad Obrera* celebrated the end of the "government of Casas Viejas", which was responsible for 300 deaths and the imprisonment of 9,000, the laws of Defence of the Republic, Public Order, Vagrancy and 8 April, on account of which it "was especially deserving of proletarian hatred". While for *Sindicalismo*, Azaña's fall was the confirmation of a failure, the crisis of a regime that represented the advance of fascism, the return to the political stage of the "grim men of the old regime".[200]

On the horizon were new elections in which the CNT campaigned strongly in favour of abstention. The propaganda was continuous, nagging, disparaging of politics as an immoral business. Its maximalist discourse equated "Democracy" to the proclamation of "God, Country, and King". An argument that repeated the reasons not to vote, not to choose the "new executioner, the new tyrant, a new exploiter, a new sluggard", ultimately, because voting was "stupid". Large confederal rallies preceded the election. Bullrings, like those of Barcelona or Zaragoza, were filled with tens of thousands of people who came to hear Durruti or Ascaso shout out slogans in favour of abstention and march "towards libertarian communism".[201]

But behind this campaign were, as well as principles, the revolutionary yearnings so characteristic of the anarchists. At the plenum at the end of October, the representatives of the regional federations agreed to take advantage of the elections to embark on the revolution, but also manifested their fear of the advance of fascism. The CNT revealed the two sides of the same coin. On the one hand, the Aragón delegate proposed "in the event of politicians finding themselves in a minority after the elections, not to wait a moment longer and proceed to implement the revolution". While, on the other hand, the Northern federation recommended that "before fascism prevailed" the struggle should be accepted with all its consequences. In essence, the plenum agreed that in the event of "the triumph of fascist ideas, and for this and other reasons the people becoming impassioned", the CNT had "the duty to encourage this popular yearning to convert into reality its libertarian communist purpose". Therefore, if just one regional federation were to initiate an uprising "immediately, without requiring orders" the rest would support it.

A resolution that attributed an obligatory nature to what had been the basic tactic of the anarchist movement; in other words, take to the streets, irrespective of circumstances or support, in the hope that their evolutionary example would infect the masses. So, when the time came, the action of a single group could be interpreted as the uprising of a federation and prompt the entire organisation into action. Added to the implausibility of the plan was the lack of means necessary to deploy a movement of these characteristics. The regional federations themselves referred to the need to increase "the CNT's tools of combat", and even the national committee asked the representatives, attending the plenum, for "a loan to cover the cost of preparation". However, the international organisation refused, believing that he plenum had taken an extremely unfortunate decision and had failed "to interpret the true social and political situation in Spain".[202]

For their part, the anarcho-syndicalists, via the Opposition Unions, also advocated abstentions in the forthcoming elections. However, they regarded the CNT's abstentionism at any cost as a dangerous stance that could facilitate the arrival of fascism. Far from anarchist maximalism, in which all political parties and regimes were equal, they believed that the reactionary forces represented a return to the past, to "a dead Spain" that planned to revive and employ "its mortal talons". In any case, anarcho-syndicalists, like Peiró, believed that fascism had to be stopped in its tracks, and did not rule out revolution, because "between the possibility of being physically or morally killed and the possibility of risking our lives fighting for an ideal, we prefer the latter".[203]

Fascism that, for much of the left, took the form of the non-republican right-wing forces that, prior to the elections, constituted the *Unión de Derechas y Agrarios* (Union of the Right), with *cedistas*, *alfonsinos* (supporters of King Alfonso XIII), traditionalists and agrarian and Catholic independents. The main goals of its program were: revise the constitution and the legislation of the first biennium, especially in religious and social questions; repeal the agricultural reform; and grant an amnesty to political prisoners. Its main leader, Gil Robles, was highly critical of parliamentarianism and maintained an anti-democratic stance, arguing that for them democracy was not "an end, but a means by which to establish a new state. When the time came, Parliament will submit, or we shall make it disappear". Words that were overly reminiscent of what had occurred in other countries, like Italy or Germany, where authoritarian or dictatorial parties had grown within democracy, exploiting rights and freedoms in order to, once in power, do away with it. Meanwhile, left-wing republicans and socialists took part in the elections separately. Largo Caballero's "revolutionary" postulates prevailed in the PSOE, while Indalecio Prieto and Fernando de los Ríos, who hoped to repeat the pact with the republicans, were in the minority. After quite a hard campaign, the election results were as follows: the right obtained around 200 seats (of which 115 corresponded to the CEDA); the centre around 175 (with 104 won by the radicals); and the left around 100 (58 for the PSOE). 42% of the electorate voted for the right and centre parties, 24% for those on the left and 32% abstained.[204]

With regard to the factors that influenced the election results, it is worthwhile highlighting the mobilisation and coalition of the right compared with the disunity of republicans and socialists. To which should be added the powerful pro-abstention campaign conducted by the CNT, the influence of the Catholic Church and other factors, like the women's vote, which was then highlighted, but was revealed by the passage of time and further elections to be far less significant. For a qualified observer like Herbette, the attitude of the Catholic Church had been fundamental. The electoral strength of the right was inconceivable "without the Church's instructions and the zeal of the clergy", because the institution had bound together conservative forces. So the ambassador had no hesitation in affirming that "the Church has won".[205]

Vis-à-vis the significance of the CNT's abstention in the election results, there is a degree of polemic between those who regard it as decisive and those who qualify its importance.[206] Differences that arise when the voting data is studied, between those who analyse the data, in the main, in terms of provinces or constituencies in cities with diverse union membership, and those who examine the results in places where the confederal presence was dominant. In the latter, levels of abstention, as Diego Caro notes, were high. If in Spain as a whole abstention stood at 32%, there were working-class districts in Zaragoza where it exceeded 50%, sometimes even 68%, while in bourgeois neighbourhoods it stood at only 30%. The situation was similar in Jerez de la Frontera (Cádiz), where the level of abstention was also over 68%, with districts, like San Telmo, where it was as high as 79%, or Santiago, at 70%. In towns like La Felguera (Asturias), predominantly *cenetista*, abstention stood at approximately 45%. While in Catalonia, *Esquerra* went from 42 seats, obtained in 1931, to 22 in these elections. Though the causes of the distribution of abstention are complex in any kind of elections, the fact is that the vast majority of observers at the time and many contemporary historians have cited the *cenetista* abstention as one of the major causes of the conservative victory in 1933.[207]

What appears obvious is that the political wear and tear suffered by the parliamentary left in the elections was related to both the workers' frustration at the government's policies, which failed to improve the working conditions and the lives of the most vulnerable, and to the CNT's harassment of the government coalition during the first republican biennium, culminating in its particularly aggressive campaign prior to the elections. Its repeated criticism of the reformist measures promoted by the socialists amidst the economic crisis, with the consequent rise in employment and, above all, of the repression exercised by the authorities, combined with unfair sentences in high-profile trials, made an impression on a considerable number of workers, who either abstained or voted for other parties that had not been in power. In any case, the CNT, whether it liked it or not, had played an important role with its abstention, however much its conduct was in accordance with its anti-political principles.

The conservative victory forced the left to change its strategy. At least this was what Herbette advised, in reference to the socialists, because if they limited their activity to parliamentary opposition, which would be negligible given their minority status in Parliament, they would lose their influence in the workplace and on the streets at the expense of other revolutionary forces. Therefore, Parliament, in his opinion, would play a secondary role in the new phase that was beginning, because the key was to be outside, "in the semi-fascist right-wing associations, in the workers' unions, in the barracks, on the street".[208] An approach shared, for different reasons, by the anarcho-syndicalists, who appealed for union between workers and a change of strategy, because Parliament "apart from smelling of death, will smell of incense", and the work to be done would be "on the street (…) at work".[209]

But before that, the anarchists wanted to exploit the victory of the right in the elections to launch a new uprising. After the failure of the insurrection in January of that same year, the CNT was aware that it could not achieve revolution on its own. The confederal strategy was based on the "irrefutable principle", following such a high rate of abstention, that "as a consequence of the right's rise to power, the revolutionary movement would be joined by all those men of the left who aspired to a better tomorrow".[210] But one thing was not going to vote and another, quite different, embark on a revolution. The insurrection was premature. A few days after the elections, the socialists had yet to assimilate the consequences of their defeat. But the anarchists were in a hurry and once again took the initiative within the movement on their own.

The Insurrection of December 1933

The CNT now staged the most significant insurrection in republican times. The movement, as in January, had a set time and date, so the authorities were ready. The Ministry of the Interior sent a telegram to every civil governor, on 2 December, to inform them that a violent movement would take place, carried out by syndicalists and elements of the FAI, while they were advised on the 7th that it might occur that night. On the 8th, the day when Parliament resumed after the general elections, the uprising began, and on the next day, the government declared a state of alarm throughout Spain.[211] The recent secretary-general of the CNT, the *faísta* Joaquín Ascaso, was responsible for organising the movement in Zaragoza, along with a revolutionary committee that included, among others, Durruti, Cirpiano Mera, Antonio Ejarque and Isaac Puente.[212]

The figure of Durruti stood out among them all, and he was regarded as the leader of the movement. Which did not imply better organisation, coordination or planning. In fact, Horacio Martínez Prieto sent a report to the revolutionary committee, in the days leading up to the insurrection, in which he analysed the real conditions in the country and the failure that it would represent, to which Durruti replied, after reading the document: "you are quite right, but it's too late now".[213] Even his comrade in the *Nosotros* group – integrated within the FAI at the end of 1933 – and main leader of the January movement, García Oliver, expressed his misgivings vis-à-vis the new uprising.[214] Durruti's actions confirmed what the Andalusian delegate had said at the last plenum: "in any case we will act, even if we are not ready". Horacio commented that the comrades leading these actions paid no "heed to any experience or advice; they considered themselves to be a new world, superior to anything in the past, to any present comprehension; nothing was 'impossible' for them; they were 'faith' proceeding without perceiving any obstacle (...) they believed that revolutions were achieved by dint of the contagious enthusiasm of the brave minorities".[215]

But these brave minorities failed sufficiently to infect the masses, and the support for the movement was very unequal, with actions ranging from strikes to uprising with sabotage and bombs. The protests were on a larger scale in rural areas than in the big cities, and lacked, generally speaking, the revolutionary nature to which the organisation had aspired. The only places where events acquired insurrectional proportions was in Aragón and La Rioja. The city of Zaragoza witnessed an authentic pitched battle in its streets. The army employed every means available, from machine guns to tanks, to combat the rebels, sheltering behind their barricades. But it was in villages of Aragón and La Rioja where actions were particularly revolutionary. Places like Briones, Fuentemayor, San Vicente, Ábalos, San Asensio, Mas de las Matas, Alcoriza and Alcañiz proclaimed libertarian communism.[216] The sequence of events recalled, like those of January, uprisings of the previous century, with the disarming of citizens of "order", clashes with the Civil Guard, the declaration of libertarian communism, the burning of ownership deeds, etc.

Along with these collective actions, the movement was characterised by the action of groups that carried out sabotage and attacks, which lent it a more violent nature. In addition to the detonation of bombs and the burning of churches, there were a number of explosions on the railway line, with special mention of what happened in Puzol (Valencia), where the train from Barcelona to Seville was derailed as the result of an explosion, leaving 23 dead and 38 injured.[217] These kinds of acts generated such an outcry that, for Herbette, they had "contributed to the failure of the movement (…) all over Spain".[218] Another question worthy of note was the appearance of public announcements in the towns and villages controlled by the rebels. In these, the population was urged to join the movement or, if they did not, to suffer repression. The peninsular committee of the FAI had sent a document, in April 1933, stating that given the failure of earlier revolutionary attempts, it was time to prepare to defeat the enemy and "proceed with maximum energy to the nullification of all existing ecclesiastical, military and civil authorities", and if they offered "resistance to the revolution, eliminate them quickly".[219] Now, in December, the rebels posted proclamations in the villages under their control, such as Briones (La Rioja), announcing that "Libertarian communism has been proclaimed throughout Spain, those who surrender their weapons will be unharmed, those who do not will be killed. Those who oppose the new regime will meet the same fate". But these stark threats do not appear to have been fulfilled, as there is no evidence of mass shootings or widespread repression, and actions of this nature were essentially restricted to isolated cases against caciques, landowners and the odd cleric.[220]

Nevertheless, the number of victims, during the week-long uprising, was higher than on any previous occasion. According to the Minister of the Interior, Manuel Rico Avello, in his parliamentary intervention of 17 February 1934, 89 people were killed – 75 civilians and 14 members of the security forces (11 civil guards and three assault guards) – and 164 wounded – 101 of the former and 63 of the latter (45 civil guards and 18 assault guards). The figure for civilian casualties referred to "all those killed as a result of explosions or derailing, in other words who did not participate directly in the commission of the criminal acts to which I have referred". So it included the victims of the explosion in Puzol, but also, according to Rico Avello, the seven individuals that died in the village of Alfafar (Valencia), when they were handling dynamite.[221]

In addition, there were hundreds of arrests, and accusations of torture and even simulated shootings by firing squad. Among those arrested was Joaquín Ascaso, who was replaced as secretary general by Miguel Yoldi. The police also arrested the members of the revolutionary committee, while they were having dinner in a flat in Calle Convertidos de Zaragoza, except for Durruti, who was detained in Barcelona.[222] The file opened against this committee, in which were included the regional secretaries under arrest, was stolen at gunpoint by nine *faístas* from the offices of the emergency court of Zaragoza, in the presence of the judge and secretary, who were ordered not to move during the robbery. The civil governor of the city, Sr. Ordiales, attempted to play down what had occurred and said that he had several copies of the file. But years later, Ramón Álvarez, *Ramonín*, secretary of the Asturian regional federation and also arrested, maintained that the copies had not been signed – fortunately, he added, photocopiers did not yet exist – so the documents did not have the same value given the detainees' refusal to corroborate what was written by again signing the document.

In spite of everything, the prosecutor described events as "a crime against the form of government", and requested 30 years' imprisonment. A classification that ultimately led to their release from prison in April 1934, as the new government declared an amnesty that included this scenario, which saw the release of, among others, General Sanjurjo, awarded for the same offence the death penalty, later commuted. A curious circumstance because the nine anarchists who had participated in the attack on the courthouse, who were finally arrested, spent longer in prison, as the classification of their crime did not match any of those to which amnesty was applicable. So they remained in prison until they were tried by a court that acquitted them owing to a lack of evidence. In any case, according to *Ramonín*, none of the nine men arrested had taken part "in that daring strike of which they were accused". So the police continued to search for the authors, carrying out torture and arrests, as a result of which some of those detained entered prison in a "pitiful physical state". This was the cause of the major protest by the prisoners and the transfer of 99 by special train to Burgos, where, among others, Durruti, Isaac Puente and *Ramonín* himself were imprisoned.[223] Meanwhile, the political parties again spoke of large sums of money invested in financing the rebels. The right and the left accused one another of responsibility for the movement. Gil Robles, addressing the socialists, told them that "you are the moral instigators of today's events", to which the socialist Álvarez Angulo replied "and you, the material instigators".[224] Meanwhile, the anarcho-syndicalists observed the FAI. Pestaña, Peiró and Juan López were particularly harsh in their condemnation of the events of December. They said that the concept of revolution was not that which the current confederal leadership was attempting to impose, based on the violent actions of determined groups, but that which was "based upon the mobilisation of the masses upon the foundations of a state of opinion". For this reason, it was necessary to establish a clear difference between the railway catastrophe in Valencia and the revolutionary deeds in the villages of Aragón and La Rioja. The uprising had been an unqualified failure, because it had both weakened the cause of the workers and benefitted the most reactionary right by facilitating repression. The FAI controlled and dragged in its wake the CNT, while its leaders operated "on their own account, ignoring the workers, whom they claim to represent".[225]

It seems that the anarcho-syndicalists were right, for despite the fact that delegates repeatedly alluded in plenums to the allegedly revolutionary atmosphere and claimed to be prepared for the movement, both arguments were false. Spain was not on the point of insurrection, and the regional committees were not ready for action. This was acknowledged by the committees of Andalusia and Extremadura, the North, Galicia, Asturias and the Centre. In the latter, the most seasoned veterans of the struggle did not conceal the fact "that prior preparation was necessary". Galicia pointed to the shortage of funds and weaponry, which meant that under these circumstances it was "suicide to take to the streets and fight against the well-armed enemy". In Bilbao, there was "considerable confusion (...) nothing whatsoever was done". In Asturias, they could see "the haste with which all this had been done", so no action was taken in Oviedo, while in Gijón there were instances of sabotage and an all-out strike from Monday until Wednesday. Andalusia and Extremadura admitted that they had failed "to rise to the occasion", because "they were in no state to support in any way the movement agreed upon in recent plenums". Others, though they did not openly confess to as much, were not prepared either. This was the case of the emblematic Catalan federation. On 9 December, "in very few areas of Catalonia had the movement had an impact", with the exception of Bajo Llobregat, while in Barcelona there were "a few acts of sabotage of little significance". The plenum of unions agreed to encourage the movement over the ensuing days, but the 11th and 12th passed without anything special happening "in Barcelona, except for a few skirmishes in the suburbs of Sans and Coll-Blanch". So on the 12th there was a vote to return to work "in view of the impossibility of doing anything practical". After wards, the regional committee resigned and the local defence committee claimed that it had "always maintained that Barcelona was not able to undertake or initiate the attack owing to a lack of fighting resources".[226]

In conclusion, everything suggests that delegates let themselves get carried away by the impassioned atmosphere at confederal meetings, where the chosen course of action was insurrection, without respecting the agreements reached in the regional federations they represented. In other words, it was now the case not only that direct democracy, as I have been saying since the previous chapter, had shortcomings, but that representative democracy was also flawed. For example, Andalusia acknowledged that its delegate "was unable to fulfil the mandate with which he had been entrusted and exceeded the scope of his mission". But the problem existed not only in Andalusia, but in the organisation as a whole. A circumstance that led the regional federation of Aragón, La Rioja and Navarra, the most combative of all, to declare that

> always, and in all our elections, let us make a habit of sincerely expressing our labour of information and deduction, so that never shall it be the more or less heated verbosity and the cold or passionate temperament of delegates that influence or change the basis of the agreement with which they are despatched. So the regional federations might endorse or send their delegates with the

> agreements reached, in essence, without prejudice to them, and here there is room for every kind of theoretical resource, selecting the form that will produce the best results, but always without altering the essential lines and the basis of the agreements.[227]

Along the same lines, the delegate of the Pasajes Fishing Industry, at the Zaragoza Congress of 1936, Galo Díez, said that the reports compiled by the regional committees prior to the insurrections inflated the possibility of undertaking the revolution, and that the problem was that "the delegates at plenums spent their time deceiving one another". In fact, the Graphic Arts Union of Barcelona requested, at the same congress, a review of the minutes including the union agreements with regard to the *Alianza Obrera*, to check whether they corresponded with the statements uttered by delegates.[228] In other words, the problem was not a new one, and it had become chronic.

In short, the anarchists did not achieve their goals by means of the insurrections of 1933. On the one hand, because they were based on false assumptions, such as the alleged revolutionary moment that was everlastingly installed in Spanish society. On the other, because they were the actions of minorities that exuded heroism, but did not have the support of the population in general, nor of the working masses, not even of their own members. The AIT itself criticised the fact that prior to undertaking the insurrectional actions only the mood of militants was gauged, but "never then mood of the people".[229] Moreover, the fact is that the organisation never had the necessary weaponry, nor the collaboration of those who did, namely the military, to achieve its objectives. The CNT made repeated attempts to penetrate the army via young militants performing military service, but the results were disappointing. The December insurrection was joined by just one sergeant at the Villanueva de la Serena (Badajoz) recruiting office.[230] Added to these problems was the firm action taken by the government and the security forces, always united in repression. As a consequence, the anarchists never had the remotest possibility of overthrowing the republican regime.

However, the insurrections and the corresponding repression did come close to destroying the CNT. Between late 1931 and December the organisation had lost hundreds of thousands of members, while by the beginning of 1934, the number of *cenetista* prisoners had risen to 15,000.[231] The national committee issued a report announcing the end of the insurrectional cycle with

> entire CNT organisations completely devastated; local and county federations destroyed with the majority of militants imprisoned and subject to the harsh decisions of the emergency courts; trains filled with militants heading for prison (...) unions shut down by the government and with a court order from the emergency court of Zaragoza to dissolve the CNT and prosecute all its committees. Regional, county and local alike; our newspapers suspended and political events prohibited. We were the national committee of an organisation that for a hundred different reasons was sentenced to death.[232]

4

From the Workers' Alliance to the Revolution (January 1934–April 1935)

1934: Year of Changes

Spain began a new year during which the actions of political, social and economic forces, following the November election results, changed the future of the Republic. Lerroux formed a government again, in December 1933, under the watchful eye of his ally in Parliament, the CEDA, but also of the other left-wing forces, which saw in the new parliamentary majority an infringement of the "principles" inherent to the new regime. The Socialists, led by Largo Caballero, went further down the "revolutionary" path initiated with the reformist efforts of the first biennium. The purely fascist groups organised themselves and participated in street battles with left-wing groups. The employers, encouraged by the shift of power in the recent elections, proposed changes in labour relations that met with the resistance of workers and unions. All of this in the context of a Europe in which authoritarian and fascist forces were advancing at the expense of democracy.

In the CNT, after the failure of the December insurrection, the Asturian regional federation broached the need to constitute some kind of pact or alliance with other left-wing groups in view of the impossibility of achieving the revolution alone. Gijon *cenetistas* , imprisoned in Coto following the last uprising, drafted a document in which they insisted on, above all, trade union unity, with two clear objectives: halt the advance of fascism "and, in particular, to work tirelessly for the social revolution".[1] Although the organisation was averse to this type of agreement, the pro-alliance approach spread throughout the other federations, and was particularly well received in Galicia and the Centre. At the beginning of February, Valeriano Orobón Fernández wrote an article in *La Tierra* preparing the way for the union alliance between *ugetistas* and *cenetistas* that had a significant impact in confederal ranks. Orobón said that the fascist threat in Spain made it necessary to "unite the revolutionary proletariat" in order to undertake broader actions than mere defence. What was needed was "a partial proletarian victory that, without being the exclusive property of a particular movement", might fulfil, initially, the minimal aspirations that began "with the destruction of capitalism and the socialisation of the means of production". Unity would stem from the agreement between CNT and UGT, though the door was left open to the communists provided they rectified their *modus operandi.* The author was aware that each had different objectives, so he advocated shedding all that was "refractory and incompatible" so as to reach an understanding. In short, he proposed the socialisation of the means of production, in a revolutionary workers' democracy, where all executive bodies would be controlled and chosen by the people.[2]

In any case, proposing objectives that would not conflict with the ideological goals of each of the components was a complicated task. The signatories of the first *Alianza Obrera* constituted in Catalonia, in December 1933 – for the UGT, J. Vila Cuenca; for the Opposition Unions, Ángel Pestaña; the Socialist Federation of Barcelona (PSOE), Rafael Vidiella; the Workers' and Peasants' Block, Joaquín Maurín; the Libertarian Syndicalist Federation, Juan López; the Socialist Union of Catalonia, M. Martínez Cuenca; Communist Left, Andrés Nin; Unió de Rabassaires de Catalunya, José Calvet; and for the Federation of Unions Expelled from the CNT, Francisco Aguilar[3] – stressed the obligation to advance the social revolution, but without becoming a party revolution, in other words, without anyone taking exclusive control. The initial step was the destruction of capitalism in order to, subsequently, initiate a system in which no workers' movement considered it had been neglected and attain the final objective of the Federal Socialist Republic. What was needed was an organisation that would maintain the two basic conceptions of socialism: state and union. In other words, "state structure of society, superimposing political upon economic organs, and with a syndicalist structure of society, basing all social organisation upon the unions". Which clearly represented a fundamental digression from libertarian principles in the form of acceptance of the state.

Solutions that sought the common denominator in which all the left-wing forces might coincide in order to, as well as achieve the ideal society, halt the advance of fascism. In this respect, Peiró warned, exhibiting his positivism, that while they debated over whether they "were splitting hairs" the threat of fascism could become reality. Under these circumstances, he wondered: "Is it wise to maintain the irreducibility of libertarian communism? Is not fascism a thousand times worse than compromising with a revolutionary movement culminating in the destruction of the capitalist system and the establishment of a federalist-type Socialist republic?"[4] For its part, the Asturian regional federation was contemplating similar ideas when it admitted that there could "be an ideological deviation", although, first and foremost, were the interests of the working class in general, because "it would be treason to consent to the implantation of fascism just to cling onto certain principles". Considerations that, unsurprisingly, met with an angry response from the most puritan anarchists. To which the Asturians replied that it appeared, however, that "sacred principles" were not sullied when the organisation grovelled "at the feet of the craftiest politician, Alejandro Lerroux".[5] A reference to the visit paid to the Prime Minister, on behalf of the CNT national committee, by none other than

García Oliver, Francisco Ascaso and Manuel Rivas, in January, to request amnesty for those imprisoned after the December insurrection.[6] Moreover, the Galician delegates, present at the national plenum where that visit was made public, denounced the fact that the commission was accompanied by the mediation "of a leading political figure from Barcelona" and enjoyed the blessing of the authorities which, to undertake the journey to Madrid without obstacles, placed at its disposal two police escorts.[7] The contradictions abounded and roles were exchanged, since while delegations such as Asturia's expressed discrepancy with the commission's mission, Catalonia, which had always been very critical of the anarcho-syndicalists when they engaged in similar initiatives, voiced its support, and the June national plenum voted in favour of the action.[8]

Ultimately, the formation of the workers' alliance was one more source of confrontation between the libertarians, complicated by the squaring of the circle represented by adaptation to its principles. The pro-alliance persuasion forced the CNT to address the question at the February plenum. The discussion, according to the national committee, "was unusually heated and voices were raised higher than reflection and prudence recommend".[9] The alliance was supported by the regional federations of Asturias, the Centre, Galicia and the Balearic Islands, while the rest declared their opposition. The intensity of the debates made it necessary to draft a motion that clearly stated the confederal position. In it were included all the recriminations against the Socialists: labour legislation, repression, violated rights. Although it reflected their willingness to contribute with other forces to a revolutionary movement without this manifestation involving any commitment or pact with political forces or parties. Be that as it may, the CNT urged the UGT to declare "clearly and publically" its revolutionary aspirations. Bearing mind, however, that what was sought was an authentic social revolution: not "a simple change of powers, as on 14 April, but the total suppression of capitalism and the state".[10] The motion was unanimously accepted, with the insistence of the opponents of the alliance that it was not necessary to sign any document, but simply for the UGT to join the revolution in the "streets, countryside and factories", because there it would find the CNT. As one might imagine, the UGT did not accept a manifesto that, on the one hand, was strongly critical of the conduct of the Socialists in government and, on the other, established objectives that were far removed from its intentions. So the Socialist union opted for silence, and did not reply.

The point was that the *faístas* placed the blame for the situation in which the CNT found itself entirely upon the Socialists. Their responsibility began, they claimed, with the dictatorship of Primo de Rivera and continued with the Republic. This period had been an authentic "doing and undoing" for the Confederation,[11] with many spells of clandestinity and very few of calm, open work. But this new "Penelope", which the CNT had become, pending the revolution, was the work, in the main, of the anarchists themselves. They abandoned the union essence of the CNT and embarked on the attainment of immediate revolution without means, support or conditions. The Socialists had their share of the blame, but not directly for the situation of the CNT, in spite of their union-related and repressive policies, but for the situation in general of workers and peasants, for not having extended and consolidated reforms that, when they were no longer in power, would not easily be maintained.

But the situation changed for *faístas* and Socialists, early in 1934. For the FAI, the days when the union between anarchists prevailed, in the struggle against "deviationism", had gone. Once the organisation's main committees were under control, the differences widened. Thus, the Centre delegate, at the *faísta* plenum of regional committees, in September 1932, proposed that "in order to avoid suspicion and twisted or deliberate interpretations", the FAI should issue a public announcement to the effect that the Urales family had no "organic relationship" with the organisation. Although Federica acknowledged this fact, she recalled their spiritual connection and the assistance provided regarding "the propaganda needs of the so-called specific organisation". Meanwhile, Urales also alluded to the services offered, from his campaign for the holding of the FAI conference, prior to the 1931 congress, to his presidency in the closing rally at the Fuencarral Theatre in Madrid, not forgetting the publication of his daughter's famous "Yo acuso".[12]

For their part, the anarcho-Bolsheviks, with García Oliver, Durruti, Ascaso, Jover, Sanz and others, components of *Nosotros*, joined the FAI, an organisation to which, according to Oliver himself, they did not belong. Although, as he confessed, he did not participate with the greatest conviction, as in the *Específica* there were some groups whose attitude was not particularly appropriate. Referring, specifically, to both the Urales family and the anarchists assembled around Abad de Santillán and Fidel Miró, as they sought to "control the CNT via the FAI".[13] A truly surprising affirmation in view of the evidence to date. In any case, the group led by García Oliver and Durruti, in spite of the failure of the 1933 insurrections, retained a dominant position within the organisation and considerable influence among the militancy.

Meanwhile, Diego Abad de Santillán arrived in Barcelona early in 1934. In Argentina, he had edited *La Protesta*, mouthpiece of the FORA, until 1930 and General Uriburu's coup. In the Catalan capital, he formed the *Nervio* group, along with former FORA and FORU (Uruguayan) militants like Manuel Villar and Ildefonso González Gil, as well as Germinal de Sousa, Pedro Herrera and Fidel Miró. In total, according to the latter, eight people. *Nervio* had a significant influence upon other groups, such as: *Germen*, formed by, among others, Juan Manuel Molina, alias *Juanel* and Lola Iturbe; the Z group, with a strong presence in the Libertarian Youth of Catalonia; or the A group, with Jacinto Toryho, Alfredo Martínez, alias *el Cubano*, Ricardo Mestre and María Durán. Abad de Santillán's influence was very soon evident in the libertarian press. He became editor of the *faísta* weekly, *Tierra y Libertad*, with *Juanel* and Lola Iturbe on the staff, while Villar took over *Solidaridad Obrera*. Abad de Santillán himself founded in May, the journal *Tiempos Nuevos*, while *Nervio* increased his influence in the Barcelona local FAI committee and in the Catalonia regional federation. He eventually assumed control of the peninsular committee, of which *Juanel* was secretary from 1930 until 1932 and 1933–1934, with Abad de Santillán replacing him in 1935.[14] In essence, if the Nosotros group's power lay mainly in the unions and confederal committees, the *Nervio* exercised its influence, principally, via something as fundamental in libertarian media as newspapers and journals.

As far as the Socialists were concerned, the path taken towards their ideal society via the democratic regime had been interrupted without the dreamt of objective being achieved. Largo Caballero had seen how difficult it was to implement labour legislation that, albeit moderate, was radically opposed by employers and landowners. As he observed at the socialist youth summer school, in July 1933, "to implement a socialist project in bourgeois democracy was impossible". The events of the end of the year, with the defeat in the general elections, triggered conflict within the socialist family. While Julián Besteiro, at the head of the UGT, advocated maintenance of the current political strategy within the framework of legality, Largo Caballero, president of the PSOE, proposed a more revolutionary line to oppose governments that showed little respect for the reforms undertaken. At the end of January 1934, the *ugetista* leadership found itself in a minority at a meeting of the national committee in the face of the PSOE offensive, a situation that culminated in the resignation of Besteiro and his followers, while Largo recovered the post of UGT secretary general. He thus accumulated all Socialist Party and union power, as well as the unconditional support of the Socialist Youth.[15]

As a consequence, the Socialists radicalised even further a discourse that had already changed since their exit from government. There were several reasons for this shift. In the first place, disenchantment, not only on the part of militants and members, but of the workers in general, following realization that the Republic had failed to introduce the changes required in order to improve their situation.Secondly, they had been hard hit by the loss of power and, above all, finding themselves replaced on town councils and mixed juries, with the accompanying change in direction in arbitration vis-à-vis labour rules. An absence of Socialists "without whose permanent presence at the top of the new regime" they said, "the Republic is inconceivable".[16] Thirdly, the changes on the international landscape. Added to the examples, incessantly repeated by the Socialist press, of the regimes of Hitler and Mussolini, was Chancellor Dollfuss's crushing of Austrian socialism, in February 1934. The Austrian unions had risen up against the Chancellor's dictatorial actions, and the latter sent in the army and the rebellion was put down without mercy. Both Hitler and Dollfuss had attained power in their ¡countries legally, but thereafter had obliterated democracy. The Austrian chancellor represented for authoritarian Catholicism what in Spain was identified with Gil Robles, who made no secret of his sympathy for these regimes "for their openly anti-Marxist signification" and as enemies of liberal and parliamentary democracy".[17] Events in Austria appeared to confirm the worst predictions, and the Spanish Socialists issued a warning: "Rather Vienna than Berlin", in other words, better die fighting than be killed murdered with impunity.[18] And, fourthly, but no less importantly, the considerable pressure exercised by the CNT upon Socialists and *ugetistas,* both by continually mobilising workers and through the systematic condemnation of the repression suffered by workers and peasants.

The UGT had lost, as we have seen, almost 600,000 members between June 1932 and the same month of the following year.[19] The *ugetistas* saw how their unionism of negotiation and administration was questioned by another of mobilisation and action, closer to anarcho-syndicalism. They even adopted agreements that recalled the more revolutionary CNT, such as the *ugetista* resolution recommending the relegation of strikes with economic or labour-related objectives in favour of the revolutionary strike, and which were all too reminiscent of the confederal agreement of June 1933, which requested "restriction of strike action for the sake of the revolutionary movement". But rather than prepare for the revolution, what the UGT leadership aspired to was control of a movement that was getting out of hand. The workers' strikes in which its members took part did not follow, on more than one occasion, the procedure recommended by the Socialist union. In fact, in its March 1934 *Boletín* it acknowledged that the general strikes in which they participated did not comply with its statutes.[20] Herbette himself noted how in the construction sector strike in Madrid, the CNT and UGT attended meetings together in the *Casa del Pueblo*, which until shortly before had been an exclusively Socialist domain.[21]

In any case, according to the ambassador, the actions of the Socialist leaders were double-edged. On the one hand, demanding, allegedly revolutionary, appreciable, for instance, in the harsh criticism of Lerroux's government for its repression of the *cenetista* movement in December, branding it "white terror". On the other hand, however, they attempted to contain the radical yearnings of the workers and return to the trade unionism of control and negotiation. In this sense, it is essential to stress the difference between revolutionary discourse and moderate practice. Because the violent language merely concealed the prudence with which the socialist organisations acted.[22]

More real was the doctrinal shift that took place within anarcho-syndicalism, with the formation of Ángel Pestaña's *Partido Sindicalista* (Syndicalist Party). An occurrence of "clumsy inopportunity", according to Eleuterio Quintanilla, as when the PSOE began to repudiate bourgeois democracy, and with all that had to be reviewed in the libertarian world, in the words of the Asturian, all that occurred to the leading *treintista*, was the creation of a new workers' party.[23]

The Syndicalist Party

Pestaña had already flirted with the anarcho-syndicalist presence in the local elections, although he was not the only one. The municipalities had always featured along the path towards the fulfilment of the libertarian society of the future. *El Luchador*, a month before the proclamation of the Republic, in other words, in mid-election campaign, indicated that the Free Municipality would be the immediate and simplest manifestation of the state-less society, and "the start of the beginning" of the new order.[24] Anarchist José Alberola underlined, at the Conservatorio Congress, the importance of the municipality, free from anyone's control, with a view to the practical implementation of the new society.[25] Pestaña had argued that libertarian communism would not be achieved on the first day of the revolution; first there would be constructive periods during while a crucial role would be played by unions, cooperatives and municipalities.[26] Free municipalities described, at the national plenum, as "the most effective condom" against the return of the privileges previously eliminated by the social revolution.[27]

For its part, the *Federación Sindicalista Libertaria*, at its first congress held on 1 July 1934, focused in particular upon the municipal question. The motion presented assigned a prominent position to the municipality in the new federally-structured society. In the local ambit, it would be responsible for education, social welfare, public health, works of art and monuments. Operating at a regional level would be the Regional Federation of Municipalities, which would be responsible for maintaining communications, while the National Federation of Municipalities would be "the social cell par excellence", coordinating all activity. Groups as significant as Barcelona and Valencia opposed the motion, as did the national committee, with Juan López at the helm. The secretary general emphasised the difference between municipality and union. The first was part of the state and, therefore, "a political entity" with clearly defined political functions. So syndicalism could not permit "the interposition of a political organism" particularly if that organism was "a part of the bourgeois organisation". The union, on the other hand, was the basis of the organisation of society into production and distribution. Consequently, all sovereignty should reside in the union, since all organisms created should would depend upon the latter. For their part, the Zaragoza and Madrid groups expressed their support for presence in the municipalities; indeed, the former encouraged "the democratic conquest of rural municipalities", and the latter urged "acceptance of the municipality in the principle of social revolution". While militants such as Progreso Alfarache avoided what they regarded as a bourgeois term, but advocated the division of functions; in other words, the unions organising production but controlled by the unions. In the end, the motion was defeated by eight votes against, five in favour and 11 abstentions. It was the victory of a minority that revealed how the libertarians were attracted to the municipality as part of the revolution.[28]

Yet for many *cenetista* militants the municipal question transcended mere theoretical considerations. The municipality was, for agricultural workers in particular, the universe in which their entire life revolved, decisive in labour relations, fundamental for the conquest of rights and freedoms. In fact, republican legislation had turned mayors into the visible heads of the local mixed juries, of public works, of compliance with labour-related laws; they supported strikes or paralysed agricultural activities as a means of exerting pressure, and even arrested employers who did not respect legislation or agreements within labour laws.[29] As a result, it was not surprising that *cenetistas* stood in local elections in small municipalities, as was the case, among other villages of

Extremadura, in Peraleda or Malcocinado, where they occupied the councillorships in the respective town councils.[30]

In any case, libertarian organisations, both the CNT and the Opposition Unions, always called on their members not to stand in the municipal elections. Which indicated that for workers this was an option. In fact, there were militants who asked how they should act after leaving a councillorship, or referred to how local residents put pressure on them to stand again. The organisation's response never varied: loyalty to the revolutionary syndicalist path forbade them from "occupying positions in the municipality, courtesy of the popular vote". Members were thus forewarned that their actions, in this respect, were undertaken in a personal capacity, and that, in the event of being elected, they should "be dismissed immediately on grounds of incompatibility of functions".[31] Despite everything, the *feselistas*, at their first congress, moderated their position. Though they continued to prohibit the occupation of "any position of authority", they conceded that, in view of "the right to the enjoyment of collective interests denied to the working people by the ruling *caciques* (...) workers that have been councillors and for this reason have left the *Federación Sindicalista Libertaria* can re-join the latter once they have abandoned said post".[32]

So the answer was easy if one only took into account principles, the problem was when one descended into reality. Because the significance of the mayor's role in labour relations in rural areas was, as we have seen, enormous. The shift in power had been apparent since the Socialists left government, with the topping of town councils since October, with Martínez Barrio as Minister of the Interior, and had increased following the Conservative victory in the November elections. Rafael Salazar Alonso's occupation of the ministry, in April 1934, accelerated the dismissal of Socialist mayors and councillors and their replacement by Conservatives, a circumstance that intensified in the wake of the peasants' strike in June and culminated after the revolution of October.[33]

In a nutshell, the municipal question was no more than a reflection of the qualms and needs experienced by members, militants and leaders vis-à-vis the route to be taken at such a delicate moment in time, with the change of majority in Parliament and the confederal crisis arising from the last insurrectional movement in December. But it was one thing to stand, in a personal capacity, in municipal elections, and quite another to create a political party and participate in parliamentary elections. The notion of the municipality as seed of the new society, permitted by the anarchists, did not imply, by any means, acceptance of political activity. However, Pestaña took a truly courageous step and formed the Syndicalist Party.

Seeking to brand Pestaña as a reformist from the beginnings of his trade union career is to deny anyone the possibility of evolving, and to take the end result as the explanation of an entire history. It should not be forgotten that the militant *cenetistas* have been branded as both moderates and extremists, depending on the circumstances at any given time. In 1919, Pestaña was regarded as an extremist, owing to his anarchist orthodoxy, and met the opposition of syndicalists like Salvador Seguí. While in 1928 he was the moderate, and Juan Peiró assumed the role of extremist. With the advent of the Republic, these two became the moderates, while García Oliver and Federica Montseny were the extremists. With the formation of the Syndicalist Party, Pestaña was a traitor, but when the Civil War broke out, the two extremists in republican times became ministers. Although in 1938 Federica once again championed more orthodox positions.

Consequently, Pestaña's position, early in 1934, has to be understood as an ideological crisis in the light of the events of previous years. In 1932, Pestaña abandoned the post of secretary general and was expelled from the CNT. The following year, he saw how the FAI led the Confederation to relegate its union essence and launch two insurrectional attacks that had placed the organisation on the edge of extinction. Meanwhile, the Opposition Unions had not achieved their objective of regenerating the CNT. Furthermore, Pestaña complained about "the apathy of the people" in the organisation, which led to the paralysation of work "due to lack of activity and moral discipline".[34] In addition, the triumph of the centre-right in the November elections, accompanied by the first signs of social decline following the Socialists' exit from government, without forgetting the advance of fascism in Europe, was for Pestaña a source of unrest and doctrinal doubts. Doubts regarding the implementation of a project that, based on revolutionary syndicalism influenced by anarchism, side-lined political participation, so significant in the evolution of events. But also because this political activity attracted the masses, however much voices in libertarian circles insisted on citing the failure of parliamentarianism.

As a result, he signalled his intention to separate, "once and for all", purely union activity from political intervention. The union had its own mission and should not intervene in politics. It was necessary clearly to delineate "the union activity of the workers and syndicalist political activity", two parallel driving forces with the same goal. The former, via the union in its struggle for employment and economic improvements. The latter, via the party in its eminently political battle with the objective of collaborating with other forces in order, initially, to halt the advance of fascism and, subsequently, achieve the ideal society.[35] Pestaña broke sharply with libertarian principles, though he denied that his proposal was a fundamental rectification, preferring to call it "a tactical rectification", since it involved the incorporation of "a combat tactic against which we have previously fought. No more".[36] To which one should add, and no less.

Pestaña began to send a series of letters to friends and colleagues, in November 1933, describing his uncertainty with regard to the path to be followed, taking as a starting point the municipal elections. Although his real intention was to gauge the mood and recruit those comrades who were prepared to accompany him on his risky political adventure. Rather than presenting himself as the proponent of the idea, he tended to recur to the argument that "for a while now people have been approaching me asking why my friends and I don't launch the idea of forming an organisation, party or whatever of a syndicalist nature", then he raised his own questions and asked the recipient about their opinion and willingness to collaborate in this enterprise.

An attitude that, later on, militants of pedigree such as Eleuterio Quintanilla, quite rightly, condemned and described as "duplicity".

The replies, in relation to the substance of the issue, ranged from those who expressed their radical opposition, a clear majority, like Peiró, Juan López or Quintanilla himself, to those who openly supported him from the start, like Francisco Gómez de Lara, from Oviedo, or those who voiced their misgivings as to the timing of the initiative, like Marín Civera, Francisco Sabaté and José Robusté, but who eventually joined. Civera, for example, considered the PSOE to be the ideal party for the fight against fascism, although he thought it was not a bad idea to create that syndicalist party, which might function as transit and proximity to the Socialists, but without the discomfort of joining the latter "after fighting against them so long and so hard". While Sabaté acknowledged that "in the last elections I did not vote because I was not on the electoral roll, but I contributed to increasing the Socialist electoral fund".[37] José Robusté, meanwhile, admitted to having doubts with regard to "much of his ideological past", concerns that also affected "some of the most prominent members of the FSL".[38] In short, it seems that Pestaña was not the only one experiencing an ideological crisis.

Pestaña tendered his resignation from the FSL in December 1933, a decision that, in most of the letters, he associated with personal reasons, and which in the one sent to Peiró, he attributed more specifically to economic problems that could only be resolved by means of activities that might undermine the organisation's prestige, so he had chosen to leave.[39] The Syndicalist Party was legalised in April 1934. Its implantation in Spain was not particularly significant, though it had a certain presence in the Levante and Andalusia. As regards its membership, there were not many prominent militants; along with those mentioned above were, among others, Ricardo Fornells, Natividad Adalia, Benigno Bejarano, Eduardo Medrano, Benito Pabón – a lawyer close to the CNT – Antonio Viladoms, Eduardo Bellver and Martínez Novellas.[40]

The formation of the Syndicalist Party obliged the FSL to assemble all the groups with the convening of its first congress on 1 July 1934 to reaffirm its principles and clarify differences in relation to the new political formation. It was attended by 23 delegations, with a particularly strong turnout from the Levante, Catalonia and Andalusia, as well as a sizeable presence from Madrid and small groups from the North and Santander. The Federation ratified its principles based on revolutionary syndicalism, positioned itself in favour of the Alianza *Obrera* and endorsed the transfer of the weekly newspaper *Sindicalismo*, previously published in Barcelona, to Valencia, "the strongest syndicalist zone". However, the national committee remained in Barcelona, while Sebastián Flor, Progreso Alfarache and Pere Corrons were nominated for the post of secretary general.[41]

The news of the founding of the Syndicalist Party prompted a hail of criticism from the anarchists. Pestaña was the "holy man turned would-be dictator (…) hypocrite and phoney Jesuit". Federica used, as one can imagine, the sharpest pen. For her, the new party represented "the final stage of gangrene", the end of a process incubated as long ago as those distant days of 1917, of dealings with Catalan and republican politicians, "the ulcer from which the CNT has suffered the longest" and which aborted the revolutionary possibilities of 14 April. Impossible not to recall the days of the Figols protest, and take advantage of circumstances to justify old actions, when "it was necessary to descend to the same terrain that they occupied, fight with the same weapons as the impostors and the greedy". Which facilitated "a spring cleaning", of those who were never anarchists. This was the good that the Republic had done the CNT, "it has offered a hand to all those thirsty for power, for money (...) And everyone has grabbed that hand, in a frenetic ascent towards wallets and connections". Ultimately, they would all end up as corrupters of the soul and flesh do: "growing a belly, collapsed in the easy chair of bureaucrats. Growing a belly has always been the ideal of opportunists and pigs. A prosaic ending, which will bring back to us the image, one ascetic day, of Pestaña, haloed with the fat of an Indalecio Prieto".[42] Needless to say there was no "ascent", nor "money", nor "wallets", nor "connections", and Pestaña retained his "Quixotic" figure until the end of his days.

The New Government and the Strikes

The Lerroux government did not represent a shift towards the far right, as the most extremist critics claimed. Its actions revealed that it did not seek to destroy the Republic, but rather to give a Conservative twist to the new regime.[43] However, one thing was the government's conduct and another quite different the hopes and fears that the change aroused in diverse political and social sectors.

Either way, the signals emitted by the government in relation to such significant issues as the draft law on Amnesty, processed in March, gave rise to all kinds of suspicions. The law seemed to have been created with the sole purpose of releasing Sanjurjo and his fellow perpetrators of the coup in August 1932. The proposal appeared in the manifesto of the right-wing parties for the most recent elections, but not in that of the Radical Party. According to Gil Robles, the law sought to erase the unfair sentence meted out upon Primo de Rivera's ministers. So the fact that the amnesty "also extended to General Sanjurjo, whose rebellion has never inspired in us the slightest degree of solidarity – albeit we recognise the noble motives that may have led to his mistaken conduct – was a secondary question and an inevitable consequence".[44] The CNT seized the opportunity and began a campaign in defence of "full amnesty for all", in order that those comrades who had taken part in the December uprising might benefit too.

Although the President of the Republic, Niceto Alcalá Zamora, opposed the law, it was adopted. Its contents included, apart from the release from prison of Sanjurjo, who settled in Portugal pending new developments, the return to the "Spanish Grandees", involved in the coup, of confiscated estates, the readmission into the army of the rebel, and the legalisation of Calvo Sotelo's party, banned since the coup, as well as his presence in Parliament. However, for the CNT militants its application depended on the crime for which they had been sentenced. Because the amnesty was applicable to all offences committed prior to14 April 1934, when the law was passed, but the crimes of sedition and rebellion subsequent to 3 December 1933 were not included. The government's intention was to exclude from the amnesty the anarchists who participated in the insurrection of 8 December. Therefore, those that had been charged with crimes against the form of government, like the revolutionary committee, as has been indicated, were released, while the rest remained in prison.[45] The Socialists protested in Parliament against this discrimination, and the Justice Minister, Álvarez Valdés, responded with the argument that the attempted military coup was against a government because these soldiers believed that it did not represent the opinion of the nation, unlike the anarchist movement that was undertaken "against public opinion, represented by the election result".[46] As if the Republican-Socialist government, against which General Sanjurjo had rebelled, had not been democratically elected.

In parallel to the passing of the Law on Amnesty, the *Juventudes de Acción Popular* (Popular Action Youth or JAP), within the CEDA, organised a demonstration at El Escorial, on 22 April, of an unmistakably fascist complexion. The anarcho-syndicalists called it the "March on Madrid", in allusion to the "March on Roma" organised by Mussolini in 1922, and which concluded with the establishment of a fascist regime in Italia. The rally, despite the presence of around 20,000 people, was not as well-supported as its organisers had hoped, due partly "to the wind, rain and snow that began to fall in the morning" but, above all, to the general strike called in Madrid, which prevented many buses from arriving. The demonstration began with a "spoken mass", and continued with a reading of the names of "dead JAP sympathisers", to which the crowd, after hearing each name, responded by shouting: "Present!" Next to speak was Gil Robles who, upon reaching the podium, was received with cries of "*Jefe, jefe, jefe*!", and expressed his willingness to assume power when the time came, and "give his life for our God and our Spain". He declared that he was not afraid "of the nationalist movement that springs from pagan channels", a clear reference to Nazism, before ending his address with "Long live religion and long live Spain! Above all, Spain, and above Spain, God!"[47]

Under these circumstances, it is no surprise that in libertarian ranks there was suspicion of the new government, also regarded with mistrust by the more vulnerable classes and left-wing parties in general. Moreover, the recently elected government would find itself obliged to play a fundamental role in labour negotiations, which it was felt would further complicate resolution of the workers' grievances, while employers, increasingly united, would benefit from the change. But the reality of republican Spain was more complex.

Santos Juliá has analysed some of the labour disputes that arose in Madrid at the start of the year. Among the main conclusions to be drawn are, on the one hand, the unity of action between *ugetistas* and *cenetistas* which, as he noted, began in the sectors occupied by low-skilled workers, where class problems were more acute; on the other hand, the radical government's attitude to labour problems was not so favourable to employers' interests. For instance, the strike in the catering sector, in which the *cenetista* Single Union, this time of its own volition, organised a protest that was supported by the UGT members and in which the assemblies held sway. The ministry opposed management and negotiated agreements with the workers. When employers refused to accept them, and threatened to close cafes and bars, it ordered the arrest of the management committee, though its members were released a few hours later. The government's support of workers in the catering sector was repeated in the cases of construction and metallurgy.[48]

In the latter, which affected 18,000 workers, there was collaboration between UGT and CNT militants. The main demand was for a 44-hour working week, with no reduction in pay, instead of the 48 hours in force. The strike lasted three months, which made it one of the longest since 14 April. The dispute became a stalemate. Management was at its most intransigent, while the unions stood their ground, but were extremely cautious vis-à-vis the actions that should be taken. So when there was a proposed disruption of public order, the response was quite significant: with another government "more aware of its responsibility, one would have to think twice", in the case of this "reckless government" we have no doubts with regard to its conduct.

The solution for the metallurgy sector was provided by the mixed jury, which agreed to request that government should draft, within three months, labour rules for the metallurgical industry and its sub-sectors at a national level. During this period, there would be a 44-hour working week, with the same salary as for the previous 48-hour week. The decision represented a victory for the workers, while the deferment of the laws sought to allay the concerns of employers. The council of ministers on 16 June ratified the mixed jury's ruling and rejected the appeal lodged by management. So once again, the government had defended the workers. In any case, its actions cannot be separated from the need to reduce industrial unrest all over Spain, with major strikes in Valencia and Zaragoza, the aggravation of the Catalan problem with the agriculture law and the demonstrations in the agricultural sector organised by the Socialist FNTT.[49]

But one thing was what was happening in big cities and another, quite different, events in smaller towns and villages, particularly in rural areas. Mercedes Cabrera has observed how employers' organisations, with the new government, expected a swift revision of social legislation and more drastic measures to deal with social conflict. Management wanted legislation to be adapted to the possibilities of private economy, which, according to Cabrera, "was no more than an attempt to place the weight of the crisis upon the working classes". The Labour Minister, the radical José Estadella, did not agree to undertake an immediate revision of the laws, though there was a "default reaction", mainly in the agricultural sector. At any rate, some changes came with the New Year; on 11 January, the system for appointing the presidents of the mixed juries was reformed. The new appointees had to belong to the legal profession, to a state faculty or administrative body and must not have been members, during the previous four years, of any union, society or management or workers' organisation. Those who did not satisfy the new requirement were removed and fresh elections were held.[50] Thus, the improvement in workers' living conditions courtesy of the actions of the mixed juries gradually disappeared as resolutions began to favour the *caciques*.

Meanwhile, the new government maintained the agricultural reform. It should be recalled that the first peasant settlements, within the framework of the law, took place in October 1933, and that the Minister of Agriculture in the new radical government, Cirilo del Río, a member of Alcalá Zamora's Progressive Party, maintained the execution of the framework law in 1934. Furthermore, as Malefakis has noted, in the first 10 months he handed over more land to the peasants than during the whole of the previous year, with the settlement of around 6,500 workers.[51] Subsequent ministers changed policy from October onwards and, particularly, in 1935. In any case, the situation of the peasants deteriorated considerably during this period. In May 1934, the government repealed the *Ley de Términos Municipales*, a measure that, according to Cabrera, was welcomed by employers although, in fact, the balance of power had been inverted in agriculture without the need for legal changes because, quite simply, the law was not enforced. In other words, "the employers' ignorance of the legislation, protected by the changes in local powers, led to a generalised deterioration of working conditions, to a fall in agricultural wages and open discrimination against unionised labourers".[52] This was confirmed by the French ambassador, in February 1934, when he reported that agricultural wages had decreased since the political change in September of the previous year, as a result of which the peasants were "literally starving".[53] The situation worsened when Martínez Barrio was replaced by Salazar Alonso as Interior Minister in April.

The *Boletín de la UGT*, published to coincide with the holiday on May 1 1934, referred to a number of complaints in towns and villages all over Spain, denouncing the state of poverty in which workers were living. Villages in which membership of a union or left-wing party led to expulsion from work or the impossibility of being hired. All of this, in most cases, without respect for the labour rules agreed between employers and workers and in a context of non-compliance with labour legislation. Thus, for example, in Larones (Granada), "work is only offered to those who tear up their union card"; in Cantalapiedra (Salamanca), "a day's wage of 2 pesetas, with no limit on hours worked"; in Pozoblanco, "there is only work for those who belong to *Acción Popular*. The labour representative does not enforce the laws"; in Castrejón (Valladolid), "we are hungry, very hungry".[54] The confederal unions went a step further and denounced the attitude of employers, who appeared to want to force workers to go on strike. The union delegates said that often workers were so furious that the union committees themselves had to "act as firefighters" in order to restrain them.[55]

The situation was exacerbated, to a large extent, with the peasants' strike called by the National Federation of Land Workers, in June 1934. The UGT leaders were unable to prevent a strike that was the expression of the peasants' desperation and compromised the very existence of the union organisation. The leadership, fearful of finding itself overwhelmed by the grassroots members and seeing a considerable number of peasants probably abandon the federation, had no choice but to support a protest that sought only to improve working conditions. For its part, the government, at the suggestion of the Interior Minister, the radical Salazar Alonso, issued a decree, on 30 May, declaring the harvest to be a "public service", which rendered the strike illegal and prohibited stoppages during the harvest. It also banned all meetings, demonstrations and propaganda likely to hinder work, directly or indirectly, or favour the strikes; there was censorship of any newspaper articles or written documents that supported the protests, although employers were urged to pay a fair recompense for work done. The result of the strike was disastrous for the peasants, as the Ministry of Labour issued a decree annulling the employment lists drawn up by the unions and permitted employers to select workers, while it invalidated the agreed labour rules and the mixed juries practically ceased to operate. Meanwhile, the Ministry of the Interior engaged in harsh repression with the dismissals of mayors, closure of unions and Casas del Pueblo, and the arrest of between 8,000 and 10,000 peasants.[56]

CNT members claimed that the June strike had exacerbated the situation of regions such as Andalusia and Extremadura. The repression had been exceptionally "cruel and sadistic" due to the "savagery of the state's and the landowners' henchmen", who hounded and abused the peasant families. In the CNT, it was the same old story. This new wave of repression combined with the severe employment crisis, which left the organisation on the edge of extinction. The figures from the most important regional federations spoke for themselves: in 1931, Andalusia had around 400,000 members, and by June 1934 only 100,000; similar to Catalonia, where membership fell from 400,000 in August 1931 to approximately 100,000 in June 1934.[57]

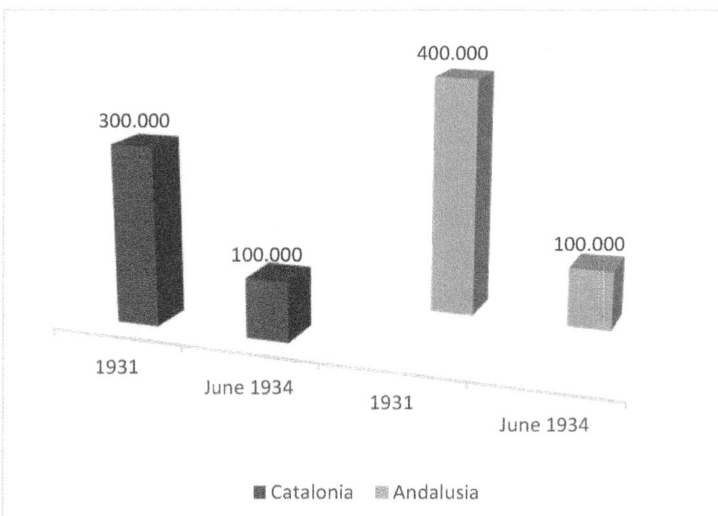

Figure 5 Membership in Catalonia and Andalusia between 1931 and 1934.

The situation deteriorated as the year progressed. In August, the regional federation of Andalusia and Extremadura took stock of the situation in their provinces. Almeria, which previously controlled 12,000 workers, now counted on about 1,000. Badajoz had "no organisation akin to our tenets". In Cadiz, nearly all the unions in the capital and the province had been closed down. In Cordoba, the local federation really existed only in name, as it was "morally dissolved", and in the province most of the unions had been shut down. In Granada, membership did not amount to "a quarter of previous numbers" and there was "not a single structured county federation". In Jaen, there was no organisation in the capital. In Malaga, union subscriptions had fallen to 3%. The same could be said of Seville, whose 40,000 membership had decreased to 15,000, while payment of the confederal stamp stood at a mere 2%.[58]

The reduced revenues from the confederal subscription also evidenced the high rates of unemployment. Ministry of Labour figures reflected a steady increase during the first months of 1934, if in December of the previous year the number of unemployed was around 619,000, by March of the New Year this had risen to 666,000 and by the following month to 703,000.[59] Figures that were almost certainly exceeded by reality. Unemployment rose and salaries fell, while employers stood together and opposed, more and more decisively, the workers' grievances. In this context, the high frequency of strikes continued, though the number of supporters and the nature of the protests changed. There was a steady increase in the number of strikers, from over 236,000 in 1931 to almost 270.000 in 1932, and a spectacular rise in 1933 to 843.000, followed by a slight reduction in 1934, to the still significant total of 741,000.[60]

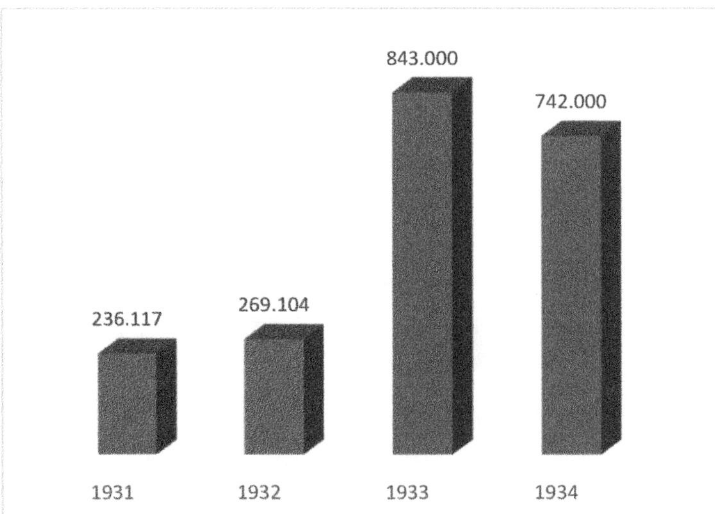

Figure 6 Number of Strikers, 1931–1934.

But the particularly radical nature of the strikes during the early republican years gave way to a more defensive strategy, aimed primarily at, rather than achieving new objectives, conserving those that had already been attained. In other words, enforce the labour rules signed with management to maintain the improvements in pay and working conditions negotiated in previous years, but also to retain jobs.[61] In short, low wages and unemployment were often the root causes of the strikes. In Toledo, a general strike was declared in solidarity with the unemployed that lasted for several days. In Avila, a strike was organised in protest against the unemployment that mainly affected agricultural workers. In Castellon, the demonstration, in which participants carried banners "for bread and our prisoners", culminated in stone throwing and the security forces opening fire in response, leaving one demonstrator dead and six wounded.[62] Of particular significance were the strike at Gas de Valencia and the general strike in Zaragoza. Both were initially work-related, but the attitude of employers and authorities transformed them into a battle against the security forces.

In Valencia, the death of a worker during the transport strike in a clash with the Civil Guard led to a sympathy strike by workers from the water, gas and electricity sectors. There were firecrackers, acts of sabotage and harsh repression by the security forces, including the arrest of the strike committee, among others, Manuel Molina Canijero, PSOE parliamentary candidate, and Domingo Torres, of the Opposition Unions. The prolongation of the strike triggered the resignation of the governor of the province, Alberto Aguilera.[63]

In Zaragoza, the origins lay in the public transport strike that resulted in the sacking of several drivers, further protests and repression. To the initial causes were added other grievances such as a demand for those sacked to be readmitted, release of detainees and re-opening of unions. Which resulted in the CNT and UGT calling a general strike on 4 April, which lasted over a month. Communities all over Spain showed their solidarity. People sent clothes, foods and money, and the strikers' children were taken in by families in Barcelona, Valencia and Madrid, in spite of the obstacles placed by the government. The authorities attempted to prevent the trucks transporting the children from reaching Barcelona and thus frustrate the example of solidarity and rejoicing of the workers awaiting them in the streets of the city. So the convoy was diverted to Tarrasa, while a number of taxis set off to meet it. The streets filled with people and the security forces of the *Generalidad*, sent by Miguel Badia, head of police in Barcelona, launched a "savage charge followed by pizzle blows and pistol shots", leaving one dead and several injured. Eventually, some 300 children arrived in Barcelona on 6 May. At which point Salazar Alonso, from the Ministry of the Interior, sent a telegram to the Civil Governor of Zaragoza ordering the suspension of "any new departure (of) workers' children" until further notice.[64] However, the following day, a new group arrived in Madrid and CNT contemplated extending the strike right across Spain. But on the 9th, the governor met the strikers and an agreement was reached that brought an end to the dispute.[65]

Ultimately, strikes during this period were essentially defensive with the objective of not losing improvements obtained in the past, and increasingly often, the UGT and the CNT collaborated in their organisation and support. The causes were work-related and economic, without forgetting unemployment, and sometimes led to sympathy strikes involving other regions of Spain. Employers, for their part, adopted an intransigent stance and did not avoid confrontation, aware of their strength in unity, but also of the power afforded them by the new parliamentary majority.

The Constitution of the Alianza Obrera

Beyond the instances of solidarity, always commendable, and of the "heroic", strikes, as Juan López described them, the fact is that the confederal organisation was in a desperate situation that forced it to change direction. The anarchists could not achieve the long-awaited social revolution on their own and needed the collaboration of other political and union forces. The Asturian CNT made this crystal clear:

> Are we going to keep on claiming our invincibility after every beating we are given? Haven't we suffered enough defeats? No, comrades, no; we alone are not enough (...) We have heroism, stoicism, audacity to spare, but we march from failure to failure, adding to the list of our martyrs with every struggle. Until when? (...) Let's not fool ourselves again (...) we would do well to dream a little less, examine more closely the state in which we find ourselves, be somewhat less adventurous.[66]

So the Asturians, on the verge of dissidence, opened negotiations with the UGT to form the *Alianza Obrera*. The truth is that the Asturian federation occupied a middle space between the CNT, dominated by the anarchists, and the opposition groups, controlled by the *treintistas*. Though a significant proportion of its leading militants felt, from an ideological point of view, closer to the latter, they were not prepared to leave the organisation in the hands of the former, who were moving further and further away from revolutionary syndicalist ideals. This was reflected in a letter sent by an Asturian militant-possibly Avelino García Entrialgo – to Juan López, in response to the latter's invitation to participate in the FSL congress. The *cenetista* said it was impossible for him to attend given "our very singular position regarding the internal confederal struggle", on account of which "it would be inappropriate officially to join the forces of the opposition, separately organised in union and specific terms". As a result, they were "more useful inside than outside for the purposes of favouring the true syndicalist and libertarian movement", although the key was for them to work as far as possible "in the same direction".[67]

Avelino himself, who took part in the Alliance negotiations, recalled years later, from his exile in Venezuela, some of the details surrounding the formation.[68] The Asturian regional committee of the CNT set up a commission formed by José María Martínez – the real promotor of the Alliance within the *cenetista* group – Horacio Argüelles and Entrialgo. The UGT was represented by Bonifacio Martín and Graciano Antuña, representative also of the PSOE to sign up to, when applicable, agreements exclusively reached by the trade unions. The first contacts took place in Oviedo, where it was agreed not to keep minutes of the meetings. However, Entrialgo, in agreement with his colleagues, decided to keep a record of the meetings. Several days later, the draft of the pact was presented to the CNT regional committee and to the UGT provincial executive committee, both of which gave it their approval. The document was signed in Gijon, on 28 March 1934, in "Casa Carmen", a "*chigre* (cider house) of a certain elegance with a restaurant on Calle Covadonga", and run by a lady of the same name "friendly, liberal, one hundred per cent trustworthy", who accommodated them in a "special little room".[69] According to Entrialgo, the original document was drawn up as signed in Oviedo at the request of the two Socialist representatives, to mislead the authorities and prevent the closure of workers' centres.

The pact declared that the economic and political situation in Spain demanded joint action with the "sole objective of promoting and implementing the social revolution". Both unions pledged to work to this end, establishing a regime of economic, political and social equality based on federalist Socialist principles. The pact included the discontinuation of all propaganda campaigns that might hinder relations between the signatory organisations, without this meaning either had to abandon their work or their doctrine. The commitment reached would end as soon as the aforementioned regime was in place. The signatory organisations would have to break any organic relationship with bourgeois parties. Finally, the promotors of the pact, UGT and CNT, indicated that the present Alliance also incorporated the Asturian Socialist Federation.[70] The following month, it was joined by Manuel Grossi's *Bloque Obrero y Campesino* (Workers' and Peasants' Block or BOC), and José Loredo Aparicio's *Izquierda Comunista Española* (Spanish Communist Left or ICE), anti-Stalinist parties with little presence in the region[71]. The *Confederación General del Trabajo Unitario* (General Confederation of Unitary Work or CGTU), linked to the PCE, not only did not participate in the Alliance, but maintained a critical stance until September 1934.[72]

The national leaderships of the two main unions displayed different attitudes towards the signatories of the pact. The UGT did not present much resistance, despite the fact that the revolutionary committee constituted by the Socialists, in January 1934, recommended avoiding alliances where they were in the majority.[73] Meanwhile, the signing of the pact triggered s major confrontation within the confederal union. Throughout the process, the CNT of Asturias was close to schism. In fact, the Asturian delegation had to confirm, in the first place, at the national plenum where the signing of the pact was debated, in June 1934, that it still belonged to the CNT. Its representatives, José Mª Martínez and Ramón Álvarez, *Ramonín*, indicated that their federation's position was the same as at the 1919 congress, where Eleuterio Quintanilla prosed union with the UGT. Motion that was defeated by another that advocated quite simply absorbing the Socialist union. Now, the Asturians firmly defended their actions and criticised the route taken by a CNT that was "in structural and revolutionary ruins", a situation it had reached by "playing the revolution game every six months". They insisted that the pact with the UGT was essential, given that in many regions, such as the North, the Centre, Galicia and Asturias, it was impossible to consider any initiatives without the support of the Socialists, while in areas like Aragón and Andalusia their collaboration was also necessary in order for strikes to be successful. Basically, the CNT was in no state to undertake revolutionary enterprises on its own.[74]

Catalonia's was the regional federation that most strongly opposed the pact. The Catalan delegation, formed by Durruti and Ascaso,[75] maintained the criticism of the Socialists and argued that if there had been a continuation of the "absorptionist criteria" of 1919 with the UGT, they would now be in a position to attract its revolutionary elements. Horacio Martínez Prieto recalled the confrontation between Durruti and "a man of about 46, strong, arrogant, who spoke with considerable aplomb and energy, without ever losing the thread of his discourse". He was referring to José Mª Martínez, who "not only did not falter for a moment but described Durruti as a big child and his speech as mundane".[76] Be that as it may, the plenum agreed that the Asturian regional federation had violated, "via the pact with the UGT and the procedure employed, the agreements reached at the last national plenum". But, as it was not authorised to decide on this issue, it proposed to hold, "within a non-renewable period of two months, a national conference of unions" in order to discuss the *Alianza Obrera*.[77]

Although the intended conference never actually took place, the subject of the Alliance was the cause of a major confrontation within the Confederation, including mobilisation of militants in organised campaigns. The FAI peninsular committees bragged that "José Mª Martínez's views" were not triumphing in Asturias, and hoped that the *faístas* in the region "would continue the offensive against any more or less veiled political persuasion". The same thing happened in other parts of Spain, like Galicia, where the FAI attempted to influence CNT militants by sending "instructions to see if we can counter" the actions of militants like José Villaverde – secretary general of the Galician regional federation who had abandoned his position at the end of 1932 under pressure from the *faístas* – who argued successfully in defence of the formation of the alliance at the last regional plenum.[78]

In other parts of Spain, the formation of alliances did not include the presence of the CNT. In Valencia, anarcho-syndicalist representation corresponded to the Opposition Unions, while the official CNT did not participate.[79] In Catalonia, in February 1934, Largo Caballero endorsed the pact signed at the end of the previous year by the UGT, the BOC, *Izquierda Comunista*, the Unión of Socialists of Catalonia, the Union of Rabassaires, the Opposition Unions and the Federation of Unions Expelled from the CNT. The UGT leader sought, in this way, to mitigate the weakness of his organisation in Catalonia. But the CNT was in the majority in this region and its absence from the alliance condemned any popular mobilisation to failure,[80] as was seen in October 1934.

In short, the issue of the Alliance divided the Confederation between those who advocated revolutionary action on their own and those who favoured union with other forces to promote an insurrection with possibilities of success. Any attempt at rapprochement between both positions appeared to be virtually impossible, as per usual. The fact is that this question presented an organisation that was divided own the middle. This seemed evident at the plenum of the regional federation that had travelled the furthest along the road towards the Alliance. Asturias endorsed its committee's handling of the issue with 39 unions voting in favour, 35 against and 4 abstentions. The plenum also voted on whether the Alliance should be with only the UGT or if the pact should also include the PSOE. The latter option received 21 votes in favour, while the former obtained only 16.[81] The main opposition came from the sections in La Felguera, a decidedly anarchist area.

The recently constituted Alianza Obrera in Asturias faced considerable challenges. In the first place, it had to heal the wounds opened during the first two years of the Republican-Socialist government, which was no easy task. However many calls there were for a "fraternal embrace" or lists of all the questions that had led to its formation such as "the development and articulation of the phalanges of Spanish fascism, the desperate economic situation of the country (...) the systematic violent repression against workers".[82] So only the real presence of the enemy facilitated confraternisation. This came when Gil Robles convened an event at the Sanctuary of Covadonga, on 9 September. A rally that was interpreted as the start of a new *reconquista* (in the image of that undertaken by the Christians against the Arabs in Spain some 1,200 years earlier), which now targeted the left-wing in Spain. Although nearly 6,000 people attended the act, the general strike organised by the Alliance was a great success, both because it was almost general and because it served to unite militants from both organisations. But not those who defended opposing positions within the CNT. Entrialgo recalled how, in the days prior to the rally, he and José Mª Martínez spent their time littering the roads leading up to Covadonga with thumbtacks, "forced to do this work by the sabotage" visited upon them by "those who proclaimed themselves to be blue chip revolutionaries", in clear allusion to the anarchist groups and Libertarian Youth, who took no part in the action.[83]

However, other groups changed their attitude after the September strike. The communists, in the summer of 1934, continued to advocate the grassroots single front, and criticised the formation of workers' alliances, describing them as a "manoeuvre by the bourgeoisie and its agents, socialist bosses and anarchists, *treintistas* and *bloquistas* and other renegades to impede the organisation of the revolution". Claiming, in short, that the *Alianza Obrera* was really a "counter-revolutionary alliance".[84] But in September, they requested the incorporation of their union, the CGTU. However, the Alliance committee did not accept their immediate inclusion, mainly in order to be certain of the "seriousness of so swift a conversion". To the extent that on 5 October, the starting date of the Asturian insurrection, they did not form part of the union. Which did not prevent the communists from joining the uprising in the streets and participating in the revolution.[85]

The October 1934 Movement

Lerroux had lost the confidence of the President of the Republic, Alcalá Zamora, as a consequence of the adoption of the law on amnesty. His resignation led to the appointment of Ricardo Samper, also of the Radical Party, as Prime Minister. He immediately found himself under considerable pressure from the CEDA to allow it to join the government. Alcalá Zamora was reluctant, but his options were limited. He could either accept the CEDA's incorporation or dissolve parliament, when less than a year had passed since the last elections, so he opted to accede to their demands. Samper resigned, and Lerroux formed a new government, on 4 October, which included three ministries for the CEDA, namely, Rafael Aizpún, in Justice, Manuel Jiménez Fernández, in Agriculture and José Oriol Anguera de Sojo, in Labour. In view of the crisis facing the Samper government, the CNT anticipated that there would probably not be a fall "all the way into fascism", but that the new government would mean "a new phase of rapprochement".[86] So the CEDA's entry into government set off all the alarms. In fact, the Socialists were awaiting this signal to launch themselves into a general strike that, in places like Asturias, developed into an insurrectional uprising.

The preparations had been going on for some time. At the end of January 1934, the PSOE, the UGT and the Socialist Youth had set up a mixed commission whose task was to organise the movement. The guidelines issued by the new body stressed that the movement had to be predominantly Socialist, avoiding alliances with other forces, but accepting them where the Socialist presence was minority. The objective of the movement, according to the commission, was none other than the conquest of political power by means of an armed uprising. For which the Socialist organisations would train militia and seek to incorporate into the movement members of the armed forces.[87]

All these plans developed in diverse fashion. The Socialists seemed to move between looking upon as examples and disdaining previous uprisings, like the Bolshevik Revolution of 1917 and the more recent insurrections involving the anarchists. From the former, they understood the need for a movement of this nature to count on the collaboration, at the very least, of a significant part of the army. But, although some of its members were contacted, the truth is that, when the time came for action, there was hardly any military cooperation. With regard to the latter, the Socialists appeared to think, like the anarchists, that they alone were more than capable of leading a popular uprising and attaining power. For although they encouraged contact and even alliances with other forces, everything suggests that they were wary of the movement escaping their control and leadership.

Either way, serious doubts exist as to the Socialists' real intentions, which could have been a general strike the success of which would force the President of the Republic to call new elections, or an insurrectional movement that would involve the seizure of political power. Both strategies had a negative impact on the *cenetista* collaboration, because not only were they objectives alien to the CNT leaders but they met with their most absolute opposition and disdain. However, the libertarian militants found themselves caught between their revolutionary concerns and their mistrust of the Socialists' intentions. The confederal organisation faced a serious dilemma: support a movement the goal of which was not in line with their objectives, and which moreover was directed by those whom they held responsible for the repression suffered, or maintain a distant position, which could lead to a boycott, and miss the appointment on the street to which it had repeatedly summoned the rest of the political forces. In the confederal actions there was a bit of everything.

In most cases, the Socialists did not involve the CNT, but not only in the organisation of the movement; they did not even inform about the uprising or seek their collaboration. However, in many parts of Spain, the confederal militants needed no invitation, nor even instructions from their organisation, and took to the streets as soon as the action began. In many towns and villages across Spain, the solidarity of workers and peasants prevailed over the reluctance and disputes within the union leaderships. So it came as no real surprise when the *cenetistas,* as had occurred during previous uprisings, assaulted town halls and proclaimed libertarian communism, as was the case in Alcudia and in Banyeres (Alicante), in Villanueva (Cantabria) or in Aguilar del Campo (Valladolid).[88] Sometimes there was a clear lack of coherence between *ugetistas* and *cenetistas,* for example in the important workers' centre of Alcoy, where the movement did not begin until the 8th, according to Civil Guard reports, "due to the initial confusion between syndicalists and Socialists". Although once this had been overcome, the hostilities continued until 12 October.[89]

The rebellion spread right across the country, according to the reports sent to Madrid every day by Civil Guard commands. In Cantabria, a revolutionary general strike was declared in the capital and the province. There were violent clashes in Reinosa, Laredo, Cabárceno, Torrelavega....In León, apart from the uprisings in the capital, the miners of Santa Lucía de Gordón began a strike that lasted 15 days, and there were attacks on Civil Guard garrisons in Matallana de Torío and Páramo del Sil. In Ciudad Real there were clashes in Corral de Calatrava, Campo de Criptana and La Sierra de los Molinos. In Gerona, uprisings in Palamós and Palafrugell. In Baeza (Jaen), six high voltage pylons were blown up, while in Villarrobledo (Badajoz), the members of the Casa del Pueblo occupied the Círculo Mercantil. In Épila (Zaragoza) and Tarazona (Albacete), the rebels took control of the town hall, and in San Clodio (Lugo) there were clashes between the strikers and security forces. In Alguazas (Murcia), the rebels cut the telephone and telegraph lines, and arrested and imprisoned civil and ecclesiastical authorities in the village.[90]

In other places, like the Basque Country, the Socialists, who were majority, intended to undertake the uprising on their own. The *cenetistas* reported that they refused to give them weapons.[91] In Bilbao, the railways were paralysed, and there were major clashes in Baracaldo, Portugalete, Sestao and Erandio, while in Mondragon, the town hall was occupied and the Socialist Republic was proclaimed.[92] In the Levante, the armed clashes spread across localities like Elche, Alicante, Novelda and Villena, where there were several deaths and injuries, while in Valencia a general strike was declared.[93] In this area, the CNT maintained a passive attitude, owing to, they argued, a real lack of revolutionary action, and because "they did not want to be the vanguard of sacrifice".[94] So libertarian participation was down to the Opposition Unions, who denounced the CNT's attitude, since while they were called reformists, the confederal leaders had abandoned their revolutionary stance and occupied a position "alongside the enemy". Now it was they, so they said, who were intoning "the 'Yo acuso' against the CNT" – in reference to the famous article by Federica Montseny .[95]

Another emblematic place for the CNT was the regional federation of Aragon, La Rioja and Navarra. After all, the organisation's national committee was based in Zaragoza, which had been the centre of the last anarchist insurrection. Well, the *cenetistas* in this region had no knowledge of the action, just as in many other cities, until the general strike was declared. Then the UGT tried to convince the CNT to join the movement, but mutual mistrust made unity of action impossible. In Logroño a general strike was declared. The *cenetistas* were awaiting instructions from the confederal leadership, though they requested weapons from the socialists, who refused. So within 48 hours the strike was over. In Pamplona, circumstances were repeated, and action consisted in the main of peaceful strikes. In any case, the movement in the smaller localities, where class solidarity prevailed over decisions taken by the leaders of the organisations, was very different. In Uncastillo, socialists and *cenetistas* faced the security forces together. In Cervera del Río Alhama, the *cenetistas*, without waiting for orders from anybody and seeing how the socialists were calling a revolutionary general strike, threw themselves into the struggle.

The regional leadership's assessment of the October movement, equally applicable to other regions, acknowledged that most localities perceived the magnitude of the movement and looked to the regional committee for guidance. But the latter, without instructions from the national committee, advised them to wait. However, many militants were caught up in the heat of the moment, and the general strike took place throughout the region with the exception of Zaragoza, which was waiting expectantly. This circumstance determined the general course of action, as the stance adopted by the capital conditioned, to a large extent, the actions of the rest. The towns and villages, disorientated by the lack of direction, desisted. The regional federation ended its report by calling into question the conduct of the confederal leadership.[96]

Conduct that, as one can easily imagine, was marked by what occurred in such important places for the uprising as Madrid and Barcelona, towards which much of Spain turned its gaze.

Madrid: Strike and Boycott

On 6 October, General Virgilio Cabanellas Ferrer, General of the 1st Organic Division, declare the state of war in the provinces of Madrid, Toledo, Ciudad Real, Cuenca and Badajoz, a situation that spread to the rest of the national territory.[97] This was in response to the general strike that had begun the previous day in the Spanish capital. A strike that had been conceived as one of the most important in the history of Madrid. There were violent clashes between the security forces and workers with barricades, gunfire and explosions. However, for the strike to develop into an insurrection, and thereby threaten the stability of the regime, it required both the backing of the armed forces and the presence and guidance of the Socialist leaders.[98] As had been the case with the anarchist insurrections, the absence of the army meant the failure of the movement. An uprising of this nature could never triumph while the military remained loyal to the established power. The Socialists, like the anarchists before them, were in contact with high-ranking officers in the armed forces and carried out propaganda activities to attract soldiers to the cause, but all these efforts ended in abject failure.[99] As for the Socialist leaders, they simply did not appear. While the workers occupied the streets and fought against the security forces, their leaders hid in the houses of friends, waiting for the violence to finish. This was true of the main leader of the movement, Largo Caballero, who toured around the homes of various colleagues until he was arrested on the 14th, in other words, over a week after the uprising began. Other leaders of the movement, like Santiago Carrillo and Hernández Zancajo, of the Socialist Youth, Enrique de Francisco, José Díaz Alor and Felipe Pretel were detained three days after the start of the disturbances.[100]

As had occurred in other regions of Spain, the Madrid Socialists began the movement on their own. The PSOE and the UGT were majority forces in the capital and, in accordance with the directives issued by the Socialist commission, their participation in the action had to be exclusive. Another question was whether or not, once out in the streets, the rest of the workers would join the movement. In any case, the Madrid *cenetistas* acknowledged that they were "apprised of the Socialist activities". They knew what was being prepared, though not the exact date of the action. The local Madrid federation attempted, the day after the strike declaration, to contact the UGT executive and formalise the Madrid CNT's participation in events. But confederal rules were an obstacle to conducting procedures that corresponded in an organic sense to the national leadership. So the organisation recognised the impossibility of taking a decision, while the revolutionary committee, created for the occasion, imposed the condition of not beginning any action while a delegate was sent to Zaragoza to inform the national committee.

The days went by without the organisation taking any decision. A quite incomprehensible circumstance when *cenetista* militants were battling on the streets of Madrid and, as the Talavera county federation reported, news was arriving from Asturias to the effect "that this was a social revolution". Underlying all this indecision was the internal conflict within the CNT, between those who were willing to take to the streets and collaborate with any political force in pursuit of the revolution, and those who had no desire to participate with the Socialists in a movement the objectives of which were very unclear, and from which, from the very beginning, the cenetistas had been excluded.

On 8 October, three days after the start of the strike, the Secretary General of the National Committee, Miguel Yoldi, arrived in Madrid with the intention of holding a national plenum to make a decision with regard to the CNT's participation in the movement. Convening a national plenum, in the current situation, with strikes and insurrections in a good many towns and cities of Spain, in order to decide whether or not to take part in the movement, was, to say the least, bizarre. So only three regional federations were able to attend: the Levante, Aragon and the Centre. But even the latter declared that it had not reached an agreement vis-à-vis the question and therefore could not take a decision. As the Madrid *cenetistas* were out on the streets taking part in the struggle, the revolutionary committee had no choice but to negotiate with the Socialists. But the talks were over before they even began, because the latter did not even turn up. So the CNT published a flyer, on the 11th, when the strike was practically over, denouncing "the villainy" to which the workers had been subjected. In spite of everything, militants from Zaragoza continued to exert pressure on the national committee to consult the organisation as to whether or not to participate in the movement. So the leadership called a new plenum, which was held on the 14th, in which it was agreed that the CNT would not intervene because it was now too late to take that decision.[101]

However, perhaps the most important aspect of what happened in Madrid was the information that came out of the capital and conditioned the confederal leadership's decision-taking – or rather lack of decision-taking – and therefore the organisation's actions at a national level. The Confederation decided, in September 1934, to change the editorial team of the CNT newspaper in Madrid, and appointed Liberto Callejas as director, along with Horacio Martínez Prieto, José Ballester and Juan García Oliver as editors.[102] All the evidence suggests that during the first days of October, with the new team in place and the strike in full swing, the phone calls from the newspaper influenced the decision-making of both the national and the Catalan regional committee. That at least was the accusation made by the revolutionary committee of the Centre, which claimed that García Oliver had deceived the leadership with regard to what was occurring in Madrid. According to this committee, the information he provided, to the effect that some businesses were open and some trams running, was not true, because the strike had a 100% following.

But the revolutionary committee's accusation went much further. It invited the members of the editorial team to join the committee, but the invitation was refused because they did not agree with the latter's stance, as their approach was much more radical and, in their own words, they were not prepared "to be the Socialists' assault guards". During the meeting, they noticed that via the newspaper's telephone the national committee and the Catalan organisation were being informed of the situation in Madrid. In fact, the former acknowledged that on Saturday the 6th, in a telephone conversation with the editorial team, they had been told "that the strike Madrid was incomplete and insignificant and that in Asturias there were some outbreaks that would soon be quelled".[103]

In libertarian circles, there was criticism of the conduct of García Oliver, who was accused of being responsible for discouraging the CNT from joining the movement.[104] A circumstance that led him to resign his union membership until the matter was clarified. The accusations were also directed against another *CNT* editor, Horacio Martínez Prieto. It was not until the national plenum of May 1935 that what had actually happened came to light. Madrid militants, like Máximo Palomar, Feliciano Benito and Pedro Falomir, among others, signed a document, addressed to the Madrid local federation, accusing García Oliver, in the first place, of having wanted to publish the *CNT* when there was a general strike in Madrid and comrades were fighting in Asturias and the North. Secondly, of undertaking a defeatist and counter-revolutionary campaign, by saying that "by any means possible, the movement had to be made to fail". One of the signatories Ángel Rodríguez, claimed that in a meeting with Martínez Prieto and García Oliver and, after "rather a violent argument", the latter said they were "playing the Socialists' game, and that what they should do was give the order to return to work. That the movement was planned by the Socialists and it had to be made to fail". While Horacio criticised the actions of the Asturian regional committee, and advocated its expulsion once everything returned to normal. Thirdly, they said Oliver had given false information to the national and the Catalan regional committees in telling them that the strike was peaceful in Madrid and that in Asturias everything had been contained. Finally, he was accused of having convinced the secretary general, Miguel Yoldi, of cancelling a telegram he was going to send to the comrades in Zaragoza and which read as follows: "Sister seriously ill, come now", which, apparently, was the signal to support the movement.[105]

García Oliver admitted that he attempted to publish the paper on the first days of the insurrection "but with the idea of strengthening the building and violently taking it out onto the streets". He also said that the expression that they were going to be "the Socialists' assault guards" was "more than justified", particularly when *Mundo Obrero*, the Communist newspaper, had declared on the eve of the uprising that "they would not act as pawns for the Socialists". But he refuted the rest of the accusations levelled against him. For his part, Horacio Martínez Prieto acknowledged what had been said about the Asturian regional federation and criticised the latter's indiscipline. Although he said "that as later it became known that the Asturian regional federation had no knowledge whatsoever of the Socialist machinations", he admitted "his error" and took back what he had said. Meanwhile, the third *CNT* editor, José Ballester, acknowledged the rumours that were circulating about the confederal newspaper's attempt to influence the Catalan regional federation not to intervene in the movement. A question that tied in with the fact that while *Mundo Obrero* was closed down, *CNT* was published as per normal; and that while the revolutionaries were arrested, the confederal editors remained free.

The commission ended its deliberations without establishing any firm conclusions. There was no definitive evidence and it was basically the word of one group against that of another. So in these circumstances, with an organisation dominated by *faístas* and bearing in mind the importance of García

Oliver, the organisation's decision was highly unlikely to go against the accused. As a result, it was taken as proven that the entire accusation was a lie, and though there were even those who demanded that the accusers be sanctioned, the national committee requested "high-mindedness" since everyone had acted "in excessive good faith, though interpreting things differently". In short, García Oliver was reinstated and his accusers pardoned. These agreements were reached , curiously enough, on 28 December 1935, day of the *Santos Inocentes* (Spain's equivalent to April Fool's Day), although the committee did not make them public until much later, specifically, 22 February 1936, in other words, a few days after the victory of the Popular Front in the elections.[106] A moment when the joy at the end of the Conservative government and the release of prisoners painted a more optimistic scenario.

Underlying this resolution was the important internal division within the CNT, but also the diversity that always characterised the libertarian movement. There were cenetistas that, without awaiting the committees' instructions, took to the streets, no longer in search of revolution, but of any action that might improve their living conditions. There were others who understood that it was time to change the organisation's essentially solitary and insurrectional tactics. Lastly, there were anarchists and *faístas* who were not prepared to support a revolution that was not theirs, and much less so if it was led by the Socialists, responsible for such oft-repeated wrongs. Which renders more than possible many of the arguments employed by García Oliver's accusers, and which the latter accepted, such as publishing the confederal newspaper in the middle of a general strike or not wishing to become the assault guards of the Socialists. To which needed to be added, according to his words, included in the same report, the personal attack by the Socialists themselves when they indicated that they did not want a person like him involved in the movement. So, score settling with the Socialists, but also personal slight. Questions that translated into hostility towards a movement alien to the CNT and which could be undermined simply by issuing information that was not false, but which concealed the whole reality.

Because news of what was happening in Madrid was crucial to the activities of the organisation in general. This was what was understood by Falomir, for whom the Catalan regional federation issued the order to return to work on the basis of information received from Madrid. In addition to which were the events in Asturias, if we take into account the statement made before the commission by Francisco Ascaso, head of the Catalan regional, who acknowledged that, if he had known was happening in that region, he would have joined in the revolution. But the circumstances surrounding the Catalan organisation during those days of October were far more complex.

Catalonia: On the Streets, But Against Everyone

The CNT had a good relationship with the leaders of *Esquerra Republicana de Catalonia*, as we have seen, in the early days of the Republic. But by October

1934, that harmony was a thing of the past. The deterioration had been steady since the anarchists and *faístas* assumed control of the union. From that point onwards, the confrontation between *Esquerra* and the confederal union was permanent. So there was no shortage of accusations in *L'Opinió*, a newspaper linked to *Esquerra*, which accused the anarchists of being robbers, of imposing "a dictatorship upon the CNT" and of living off the workers' subscriptions. Meanwhile, the anarchist press accused the Catalan leaders, along with judges and the police, of mistreating their imprisoned comrades and of themselves being – politicians, bourgeoisie, bankers, soldiers, moneylenders – the real robbers, "Al Capones of the treasury and the tax office".[107]

From the spoken confrontation to the facts. The insurrectional movements undertaken by the anarchists in 1933 met with a corresponding response from both central government and the *Generalidad*. The repression exercised by the Catalan government against the CNT was relentless. So the Confederation identified *Esquerra Republicana* with a fascist group, "the '*esquerran*' Ku Klux Klan". While the *escamots*, the riot squad of *Estat Català* (a schism group from *Esquerra*) – led by Josep Dencás, Interior Minister of the *Generalidad*, and Miguel Badia, Barcelona Chief of Police – were likened to Hitler and Goering's Nazi militias, beating people up "when the victims are not Catalan", or shooting them. Which recalled what had happened in Mussolini's Italy with Giacomo Mateotti,[108] an Italian Socialist militant killed by fascist militia. Catalan nationalism was becoming authoritarian, antidemocratic and xenophobic, in a word, fascist, proof of which was to be seen in its actions, but also in its publications. *Solidaridad Obrera* echoed the news that appeared in La *Nació Catalana*, in July 1934, saying that the 80 *presos gubernativos* in the Modelo prison were 80 Spaniards and that therefore they should remain in prison. The inmates wrote a letter in which they pointed out that many of them had been born in Catalonia, while repudiating "that stupid nationalism", before wondering what La *Nació* would say if Catalans were "abused and humiliated" on the other side of the Ebro. *Solidaridad* mediated in the dispute, and commented that libertarians did not recognise "nations large or small", only "man as a thinking and acting individual (who) is above this bourgeois nonsense".[109]

Identification of this Catalan nationalism with fascism was not exclusive to the CNT and the anarchists. Dencás himself exhibited it, as Juan Avilés has described, before the Chancellor of the Italian Consulate General in Barcelona, Alessandro Majeroni. The Catalan minister expressed "his enthusiastic admiration for the ethics of fascism", the main principles of which he hoped "to put into practice in Catalonia". *Esquerra*, continued Dencás, had "exploited the two arguments that could bring us political success: the nationalistic sentiment of Catalans and democratic sentiment". Although, "in confidence", continued Dencás, "democracy has had its day". Catalonia was returning to its history, to its traditions, while "Spain has been, is and always will be, apathetic, Saracen, a vassal". His party had assumed power, but was not orientated

> In any way towards the extreme left. Discreetly, without any jolts, we will go backwards (...) But we have to move slowly; for my part, organising the Catalan

> youth, disciplining them, making soldiers of them without them realizing (...) you are aware that I am the organiser of the *Escamots*, shock troops of pure fascist essence. You will have seen that my police now act with decision. Soon Catalonia will have neither bank robbers nor gunmen, let alone political strikes.[110]

A repression that crushed left-wing groups and in particular the CNT. After the uprising in December 1933, confederal premises were shut down, while in September 1934 almost 8,000 libertarian prisoners were crammed into the jails of Catalonia.[111]

The *Generalidad* foresaw, with the CEDA in government, a more than possible reduction of its autonomy. Companys, President of the *Generalidad* following Macià's death at Christmas of 1933, had attempted to extend Catalan self-government. But the crop contract law – aimed at preventing the expulsion from Catalan land of non-land-owning wine growers – passed in the Catalan Parliament, had led to a clash with the central government from the moment when the Court of Constitutional Guarantees the Parliament declared it incompetent to legislate in this matter and, therefore, declared the law to be unconstitutional. *Esquerra* withdrew its MPs from parliament, while Dencás took advantage of the situation to denounce the anti-Catalan attitude of the Spanish right. So the regional parliament, ignoring the court's ruling, passed the law again. The Spanish Prime Minister, Samper, tried to mediate with Companys, but the CEDA, through its party in Catalonia, *Acció Popular*, convened almost 2,000 Catalan rural landowners to protest against the actions of the *Generalidad.* Samper managed to negotiate an agreement with the Catalans, but the CEDA opposed it and brought down the government. Lerroux's new government, as we have seen, included three CEDA ministers, which for the *Generalidad* was tantamount to a declaration of war.[112]

The libertarian movement regarded this entire polemic through different eyes. On the one hand, because for the FAI the crop contract law was the law of the "*caseta*" and "*hortet*", in other words, the materialisation of a "petit bourgeois programme" which had always been an inspiration for Catalan republicans. What the *Generalidad* sought was to make peasants owners with their house and allotment, and thus distance them from "more dignified and revolutionary solutions". The libertarian vision, on the other hand, essentially internationalist, was in favour of breaking down borders and against nationalist singularisms. This was evidenced by the Tierra *y Libertad* editorial entitled "Catalan Republic? Spanish Republic?" which situated the conflict between Madrid and Barcelona in the political sphere and, consequently, removed from the proletariat and the peasantry: "Catalan Republic? Spanish Republic? No!, Libertarian Communism, Free Iberia. Reduce the boundaries of the national cage? No, extend them, beyond Catalonia, beyond Spain, beyond all Iberia, as far as the universal Confederation of free peoples. That is our programme, that is what we are fighting for".[113]

A fight that also resulted in them having a different vision with regard to the CEDA's participation in the government. According to their interpretation, the experience of recent republican years had reaffirmed their belief that rulers were all "the same in the persecution of the proletariat, all are fascists when it comes to defending privileges". So in relation to the movement being prepared, they recommended that nobody should support movements alien to the organisation, "everything for the CNT. Nothing for the politicians".[114]

So on the morning of 5 October, when the general strike was declared in Catalonia, the movement, according to the confederal, was a struggle that had to be placed in a nationalist context, lacking the masses and the proletariat and imposed by the pistols and rifles of the *escamots*. This situation did not prevent the anarchists, as had occurred in many parts of Spain, from taking to the streets and trying to lend the uprising a revolutionary character. According to official figures, in the towns of Montbrio, Monferri, Salomo and Lidemolins, the revolutionaries took control of the town councils and proclaimed libertarian communism. In San Sadurní, the FAI had taken over the town, while in Villafranca the anarchists had burnt three churches, and directed their anger against the premises of the *Partido Radical*, the *Lliga* and the *Casino Católico*.[115]

The CNT militants waged a conflict on two fronts: on the one hand, against *Catalanistas* and members of the workers' alliance formed in Catalonia and, on the other, against the armed government forces. Initially, the confederal headed for their union offices, closed down since the last insurrection in December, and opened them, but the *Generalidad* security forces began to make arrests and closed them again. On the morning of the 5th, in places like Lerida, the *Alianza Obrera* declared a general strike and the train service was interrupted. When the railway bosses asked the *Generalidad* to send security forces to keep the service running, they were advised that this was impossible. A circumstance that indicated, according to the *cenetistas*, that the political forces controlling the Catalan government were behind the movement.

At the same time, representatives of the Socialist Youth and the Workers' and Peasants' Block harangued the population vis-à-vis the threat to Catalan freedoms and the fascist tendencies of the central government. Although there was contact between members of the CNT-FAI and the Alliance, it proved impossible to reach an understanding. So while Companys proclaimed "the Catalan State, in the Spanish Federal Republic", *Solidaridad Obrera* was banned, CNT militants persecuted and their premises closed down. The regional committee issued a document saying that they did not rule out taking part in the action, but only in a manner corresponding "to their revolutionary and anarchic principles".[116]

Ultimately, the CNT participated in neither the *Catalanista* movement nor the general strike promoted by the Alliance with the blessing of the Catalan government, so both initiatives were condemned to failure as they lacked the support of the working masses who, in Catalonia, were to a large extent controlled by the confederal organisation. The intervention of the armed forces of the 4th Division, commanded by General Batet, quelled the rebellion in a matter of hours. The army occupied the main buildings, such as the Town hall or the Palace of the *Generalidad*, while Companys and the Mayor of Barcelona,

Carlos Pi y Suñer, along with advisors and councillors were arrested and transferred to the S.S. *Uruguay*; except for Dencás, who escaped through a tunnel connected to the city sewer system and escaped to France.[117] A more than symbolic escape for a "seemingly insurrectional coup" which from anarchist ranks was seen as an alibi concealing *Esquerra's* inability to solve Catalonia's problems, as a result of which "the choice was a heroic fall, which rather than heroic proved utterly ridiculous".[118]

Although the actions of the CNT leaders in Catalonia might also be described as, if not ridiculous, nonsensical. On the night of Monday, 8 October, the regional and local committees of the Confederation not only brought an end to a strike that they had not called, asking workers to return to factories and workshops, but did so via the radio microphones installed in the headquarters of the 4th Division. However much they attempted to justify the "suspension" in order "to avoid sterile sacrifices",[119] the anarchists themselves acknowledged that it was, at the very least, "not a particularly noble action".[120] The truth was that anarchists and *faístas*, leaders of the organisation in Catalonia, opposed this movement for the same reasons cited in the case of Madrid. In fact, the Catalan regional federation had led the opposition to any rapprochement with other forces, and had been intransigent in their refusal to accept criticism from the Opposition Unions, who were quick to see the possibility of shaming those who had always branded them as reformists and were now involved in such shady conduct.[121] The local and regional committees had no choice but to resign. The FAI, meanwhile, commented that among the lessons learnt from the movement was, beyond organisation, planning and tactics, the need to "possess a radio station".[122]

Of course, as Ascaso himself observed, everything would have changed if they had known what was happening in Asturias. What the Catalan secretary perhaps had not given any thought to was the very fact that the Asturian regional federation had followed a completely different path to that taken by the organisation in Catalonia. A path that had led to criticism from and confrontation with the immense majority of the Confederation, mainly with the Catalan federation, and had left the Asturians on the verge of expulsion. However, that path, so heavily criticised by *faístas* and anarchists, had led them to where they wanted to arrive, but they had not been able to take the CNT with them.

Asturias: Alliance and Revolution

The workers' alliance formed in Asturias represented a differentiating element in comparison with the rest of Spain. An important point to make, given that if historical analysis of the events of October 1934 always highlights the eminently Socialist authorship and organisation, it is no less true that the main reference has always been what happened in Asturias, the only place where the actions were of a truly revolutionary nature. Well, this reference makes it obligatory to place the emphasis on the element that marked the main difference from other places, in other words, unity of action, initially, between *ugetistas* and *cenetistas*, who were joined, later on, by the other left-wing organisations.

Other circumstances played a fundamental role in the uprising having such exceptional importance in Asturias; like the situation in which miners and steelworkers lived, with the closure of mines and factories. A consequence, to a large degree, of the major economic crisis, but also of the attitude of the mine owners who, if in the first biennium had shown little respect for labour legislation, now, with the change in power following the November 1933 elections, hardened their position. As a result, the massive layoffs and consequent rise in unemployment, the lack of help for families and an uncertain future made the region a likely venue for the uprising.[123] An illustrative example is what happened in La Felguera, a town in the municipality of Langreo. La Felguera was an industrial centre in the Valle del Nalón, home of the Duro-Felguera steel-metallurgical company, with a majority presence of CNT members among its workers. There had been drastic cutbacks in the company's workforce, from over 2,300 employees to around 1.900. The workers responded to the layoffs with strikes, such as the one held from November 1932 to August 1933. The town council, as the situation of the population was unsustainable, set up a charity commission, with a medical/pharmaceutical service and even financial assistance for those most in need, which was often overwhelmed. The desperate plight in which many families found themselves encouraged child labour, a circumstance that resulted in empty classrooms, according to their teachers.

To this critical social situation was added the political pressure exercised in the Langreo Town Council. On 31 March 1934, for instance, Socialist and Radical-Socialist councillors requested an end to the searches to which people known to be loyal to the Republic were subjected. On 14 May, Councillor Julián Muñiz reported intimidation by the Civil Guard Captain Alonso Nart. On 10 September, the same councillor spoke of several people's resistance to pay taxes and the disappearance of copies of the town's last land census. On the 15th, the decision was taken to suspend the session following the arrest of Socialist Berlarmino Tomás. Meanwhile, during the following days, the Communist minority reported an attack on a demonstration by the security forces and the death of a worker.[124]

To this politically and socially heated atmosphere was added the introduction of weapons. According to the official Civil Guard report from the San Esteban de Pravia command post, on 11 September 1934, members of the *Benemérita* and policemen, commanded by Sergeant Ferreiros Preire, "confiscated 70 boxes of rifle ammunition stowed aboard the S.S. *Turquesa*, while other trucks loaded with weapons escaped". Some of these weapons were found later in the Valduno-Las Regueras-Grado Church. And on the same day, at 11 p.m., at the Muros de Nalón post, the Municipal Guard, accompanied by civil guards, seized various vehicles that were transporting hunting guns and pistols.[125]

According to the testimony of Jenaro Álvarez, socialist and chief engineer of the *Turquesa*, Indalecio Prieto was in charge of this operation. The Socialist leader was supported, in Asturias, by the MPs Amador Fernández and Ramón González Peña, among others, and Manuel Vilasó, UGT delegate in Gijon. For some time, Prieto had been looking for a boat to transport weapons. The boat chosen was the fishing vessel *Turquesa*, owned by Ramón de Carranza, noble man, mayor of Cadiz during the Primo de Rivera dictatorship, who undertook the relevant administrative procedures and converted the fishing boat, without any changes, into a cargo ship.

The *Turquesa* was registered in the name of Manuel Atejada, the captain, and Jenaro Álvarez, the chief engineer. These two alone, according to the latter, knew the purpose of the voyage. The remainder of the crew, though recruited from socialist ranks, were unaware of the mission. In any case, knowledge or ignorance, according to Jenaro, depended on what each individual wanted to know, "as the boxes carried the stamp of the Seville Weapons Factory, had arrived with a military escort and the operation was performed at Cadiz docks in broad daylights". The crew was told that the shipment was for Djibouti (Abyssinia) – the capital of Somaliland – "where the Portuguese republicans would take possession of the weapons", and that, following the delivery, they would begin fishing. The Portuguese exiles, who for economic reasons had been unable to obtain these weapons, loyally supported these plans, appearing as purchasers until they were taken aboard the *Turquesa*.[126] The weapons formed part of a batch acquired from the Consortium of Military Industries by Basque industrialist Horacio Echevarrieta, before they were bought by Indalecio Prieto for the sum of half a million pesetas. This fact was denied by the Socialist leader.[127]

The *Turquesa* sailed from the port of Cadiz, supposedly on its way to Djibouti, though in truth it was heading for Estaca de Vares, where they dropped anchor to await final orders regarding where to disembark. It was typical for vessels to arrive here when the weather was bad or they were in need of minor repairs. They were joined on board by Amador Fernández, who instructed them to proceed to San Esteban de Pravia. Close to this Asturian port, part cargo was transferred to motorboats and taken onshore. The *Turquesa* waited for them to return to continue unloading, but they did not come back. The security forces had been tipped off and they thwarted the operation. Supervising the disembarkation was the man behind the operation, Indalecio Prieto, who was recognised by the police, but not arrested. The Socialist leader, in the wake of such a fateful night, headed for Bilbao and eventually fled to France, where he spent over a year.

After a long wait, continued Jenaro Álvarez, the boat returned to high sea, those aboard convinced that something serious had occurred. An odyssey began, in search of information, taking them to Musel, Candas and a port near Bilbao, before finally being ordered to make for Bordeaux, where they docked. The French police inspected and confiscated the cargo. The Spanish Navy took possession of the *Turquesa*, while the crew members were arrested and extradited to Spain, where they were imprisoned.[128]

Later there was an attempt by the Right to use the *Turquesa* incident to discredit the person regarded as their main political rival, Manuel Azaña.

Ninety-three MPs, including Gil Robles and Nicasio Velayos, presented a document in Parliament requesting that the investigation into Azaña's alleged responsibility in his functions as Minister of War and President of the Council of Ministers be referred to the Court of Constitutional Guarantees; specifically, because of his involvement in the sale and delivery contracts for the weapons supplied, according to his version, to the Portuguese revolutionaries to help them overthrow the Portuguese government. Actions that, they warned, might possibly extended to other members of the provisional government of the Republic.

In the parliamentary session held to this end, in March 1935, Azaña delivered a speech, which lasted over three hours, in which he explained the creation of the Consortium of Military Industries, the objective of which was to revive the weapons industry in Spain and promote exports. He said that the investigation was undertaken in order to link him with the October movement and thus incriminate him, since when the arms cache was discovered in San Esteban de Pravia someone said: "Echevarrieta, a contract from '32, Azaña was the minister (...) we've got him". He admitted to having helped the Portuguese political refugees, which he described as a normal aspect of relations between Spain and Portugal. In short, he dismantled the accusations against him and ended by attacking his persecutors amidst the "republican enthusiasm". José Antonio Primo de Rivera himself declared that "if the monarchists' intention was for Azaña to confront the radicals and the CEDA so as to demonstrate his superiority, they have completely succeeded. But if their goal was to eliminate him, they will have seen that they have achieved quite the contrary".[129]

The weapons cache on the *Turquesa* was not the only one seized by the security forces. During the previous months, newspapers reported the discovery of various deposits, like the one found in the Casa del Pueblo in Madrid.[130] In any case, the weapons possessed by the rebels early in October 1934 did not appear to be many in number. Azaña himself, in the parliamentary session that sought to involve him in the *Turquesa* affair, stressed that it was "pure fantasy to think that a revolution can be achieved with 500 Mausers and 24 machine guns. No parliament that takes itself seriously could say that".[131] Neither could the Socialist leaders who had spent months preparing the movement. Which begs the question, once again, as to whether the Socialists aspired to a genuine revolution, or, rather, a general strike in much of Spain with armed uprisings in designated places, like Madrid and Asturias. In fact, in other areas, with a strong Socialist presence, such as Badajoz, local leaders acknowledged the fact that they had not prepared anything more than a strike, and that insurrection did not form part of their plans.[132] However, the Socialists wished to demonstrate that they were ready for a course of action that, in reality, they were incapable of undertaking, but which would force the President of the Republic to change the government or call new elections.

But these objectives were surpassed in Asturias, where events culminated in an authentic revolution. Although the leadership of the movement was initially socialist, the circumstances already alluded to – higher unemployment, industrial conflict, formation of the alliance – and the encouragement offered by local leaders had the effect of fragmenting the movement and taking it out of the leadership's control. As the towns and cities of Asturias fell into the hands of the revolutionaries, committees were formed the orientation of which reflected the majority organisation in the locality. Thus, the CNT, with around 22,000 members in the region, had its principal strongholds in Gijon, where it had some 13,000 members, and La Felguera, with approximately 4,000.

Avelino González Entrialgo, an Asturian *cenetista* who played a prominent role in events, wrote a detailed report on what happened in Gijon. According to Entrialgo, on the night of 4 October, the CNT components of the committees and of the alliance – José Mª Martínez, Horacio Argüelles, Ramón Álvarez, *Ramonín*, Margaride and Entrialgo himself – held a meeting, once it was known that three CEDA members were going to enter the government, and agreed upon the constitution of a local revolutionary committee. They also considered sending a delegate to Zaragoza to contact the national committee, but the development of events made this impossible. So the only information they received about what was happening elsewhere was through Horacio Argüelles, who cycled to Oviedo when the movement had already begun.

The main concern was the lack of weapons, since at the beginning of October they only had 120 rifles and 3,000 cartridges. There were repeated requests for material to be sent from Oviedo, but to no avail. In fact, the lack of weapons delayed the outbreak of the insurrection in Gijon. On the 5th, when the entire city was on strike, in a field "near la Nuria, Tremañes", 300 assembled, waiting to be armed. But they were only given 70 rifles, so the decision was taken to postpone any action. Although the situation the next day was identical, Argüelles's return with the information that Oviedo was "a revolutionary volcano" and that "the mining basin was already in the hands of the working people", changed the outlook and they decided to advance towards Gijon.

The committee divided the men into groups formed by "colleagues of different ideological sympathies". In the forces, there was a predominance of *cenetistas*, followed by *ugetistas* and, finally, communists from the CGTU. Entrialgo noted in his report that although the leadership of the groups fell to the most committed, among the confederals "most were colleagues who as CNT members were not usually regarded as idealists". A telling detail that reveals a much more popular participation than in previous insurrections, and which the most radical were able to convert into a state of revolution. Because what happened in Asturias was much more than an uprising caused by generalised discontent, as used to be the case in the outbreaks of violence that, sporadically, had for centuries occurred all over the Spanish countryside. What took place was an insurrectional movement, understood as a first necessary and inevitably violent step, the ultimate objective of which was social revolution. This at least was the approach taken by the *cenetistas* as they advanced through Gijon executing the violent aspect of the insurrection, with shots and bombs, in order after the destruction to proceed to the constructive work of revolution.

Consequently, the taking of buildings and seizure of food warehouses was followed by the formation of neighbourhood supply committees to avoid looting and to provide the population with food. Measures that were imperative "since every liberal citizen's support of the movement depended in part on well directed and energetic organisation against those seeking to take advantage of the confusion ". This happened with "Biribí", who was arrested for stealing in a house and sent to the front, though there were those who wanted him shot. The new organisation included the generalised use of vouchers for the fair distribution of supplies.[133]

In La Felguera, another CNT stronghold, the militants had made clear their opposition to the workers' alliance. However, they put into practice what had so often been defended by the anarchists, and, no sooner had the movement begun, took to the streets. The Socialists had not reckoned with their participation but, as one of the *cenetistas* observed, they overlooked "recent grievances", took up arms and laid siege to and eventually captured the Civil Guard headquarters... Other groups of men and women "formed a single insurrectional torrent", which occupied public buildings, the Dominican convent, took possession of the town hall, burnt "the registry files" and raised "the red and black flag". They then headed for the church, which, doused with petrol and set fire to "was completely destroyed". A revolutionary committee was set up that decided to occupy and maintain active the Duro-Felguera steel-making and metallurgy plant. The general manager and the other engineers in the Company were arrested, while brigades were organised in each of the workshops, furnaces and the electricity cooperative. The factory was operative throughout the short-lived revolution. Trucks drove out, protected by steel plates against the fire of the army's machine guns.

The revolution in La Felguera had its own particular characteristics; for example, a popular assembly was held in the town's park to choose the social regime to be introduced. Although, with the major CNT presence and the maelstrom of events, this could only be libertarian communism. As a result, money was abolished and a supply committee set up which, by means of a system of vouchers, attended the needs of the population. Another characteristic was the relatively peaceful nature of the revolution. There were no reprisals or killings, as had occurred in other towns and villages. The *cenetistas* insisted on highlighting this aspect once the movement was over. The example was very representative if compared with what happened in other places like Sama de Langreo, with a Socialist majority; while in La Felguera two members of the security forces died, in Sama the figure was 69. Though it is true that the situation in this locality prior to the outbreak of the insurrection was, as we have seen, one of major confrontation, and there was greater resistance from the security forces. In any case, there were acts of extreme violence, like the shooting of 22 guards after they had surrendered.[134] According to the version of the Asturian Civil Guard headquarters, Belarmino Tomás, president of the revolutionary committees in the area, telephoned Captain Nart and asked him to surrender the garrison, but he refused. The besieged guards exited the building, early in the morning on the 6th, and attacked the revolutionaries, leaving several dead, but then there "began a real guard hunt, and many were gunned own" or were finished off "with shots and knives".[135]

The majority forces in each locality assigned their ideological orientation to the revolution. Thus, in line with what happened in places like La Felguera, where libertarian communism was established, in others like Sama or Langreo the revolution was of a more socialist order, while in Muros de Nalón it was communist. Although, initially, the characteristics were very similar; in Langreo, a revolutionary committee was formed and patrols organised to keep the new order, with warnings of exemplary punishments for those who stole or looted. Products were acquired with "bankbook, money or vouchers, duly authorised"; in Muros, they began the construction of a proletarian regime, "the same as the Soviet Regime". The village mayor, secretary, priest and caciques were imprisoned, and the locality fell under the control of revolutionary committee that flew the Communist Party flag from the town hall. A soviet (council) was formed along with a local red army, and food and other objects were distributed among the population.[136]

The revolution began to lose impetus on 10 October, with the news of the army's disembarkation. The relative absence of disturbances in the rest of Spain facilitated the despatch of troops to Asturias. Nonetheless, while Civil Guard reports from all over Spain indicated, the following day, a return to normality in the vast majority of provinces, in Asturias the struggle continued. General Ochoa advanced with considerable difficulty in the face of rebel resistance.[137.] With the army's advance and the harsh repression came the order to retreat. On the 12th, there was a wholesale flight into the mountains and those who could left Spain. These were moments of confusion and desperation, but also of clashes between the revolutionary forces, with changes in the leadership committees and accusations of treason. As occurred with *cenetista* José Mª Martínez, the driving force behind the workers' Alliance in Asturias, whom the revolutionary committee of Oviedo made responsible for communicating to towns and villages the order to retreat. This led those who refused to admit defeat to regard his undertaking as an act of treason. So when Martínez was found dead in Sotiello, many *cenetistas* believed the Socialists to be behind his murder. However, as was discovered years later, he actually did accidentally when his own gun went off while he was cleaning it.[138]

A metaphor for a movement that was as confusing as it was varied, and for which Asturias, in its revolutionary solitude, paid a high price. The insurrection, and the ensuing repression, left over 1,000 dead and almost 30,000 behind bars, and many others in flight or exile, and thousands of workers expelled from their jobs.

Repression and Revolutionary Violence

In the first place, it should be remembered that the government assigned the military the task of repressing the movement. The Minister of War, the Radical Diego Hidalgo, and the CEDA ministers tried to appoint General Franco head of the troops deployed in Asturias. But opposition from part of the government prevented this from happening. They then attempted to have him appointed Chief of General Staff, a post he was also denied. The appointment as head of operations went to General López de Ochoa. Although the minister placed Franco, unofficially, in charge of the entire campaign, above General Masquelet, Chief of General Staff. Franco sent the Army of Africa to Asturias, formed by Legionnaires and Regulars, commanded by his colleague at military academy, Lieutenant Colonel Yagüe, who had his differences with Ochoa during operations.[139]

Ochoa flew from Madrid to Lugo on 6 October, in order to lead the troops that were going to assault the main square in Oviedo, held by the rebels. The forces under his command "totalled 18,000 men". The General occupied the entire mining basin and succeeded in entering the Pelayo Garrison in Oviedo. On the 22nd, he informed the Minister "that the operational territory was completely under control".

In any case, Franco tried to have him replaced by Yagüe as head of operations. Ochoa, according to his military record, had several run-ins with superiors during his career, one of them with Franco. In 1925, he was placed under 14 days' arrest for "performing actions contrary to military dignity". The reason was that, already on reserve duty in Barcelona, he had been receiving advance payment of his salary from the Alcántara regiment, by deference of Colonel Franco, who was his commanding officer. So when the latter heard about Ochoa's arrest and trial, he interrupted the payment. Ochoa, annoyed by this decision, wrote Franco a letter "in which he said that his conduct could only be described as cowardly and despicable". Moreover, he condemned his behaviour, "unworthy of a friend and colleague", and invited him to "settle the business in the field of honour". But Franco, instead of attending the appointment, made the fact known "to the Military Authority of the Region and avoided the challenge, making his excuses to the witnesses sent to meet him". As a result, the Captain General initiated proceedings against Ochoa and ordered his arrest. This incident came to light again when he was being investigated prior to his admission into the Order of San Hermenegildo. So he presented a statement of disclaimer declaring that "in the event of there being any doubt with regard to the conduct of both adversaries, in this case, and under the concept of the most refined repute, it would be ascribed to he who flees the field of honour and never to he who issued the invitation, to he who takes refugee behind Military Authority, and not to he who foregoes all hierarchical superiority". The confrontation with Franco appears to have continued after the events of Asturias. Ochoa complained that in spite of his actions against the rebels he had received no reward, although the government had recommended his promotion to lieutenant general. Moreover, he protested because he had not been supported in the question of the arrest and trial of Lieutenant Colonel Yagüe, who had instead been granted a command.[140]

Yagüe had confronted Ochoa in Asturias, and communicated "his dissatisfaction with Franco on account of the General's treatment of the rebels". The Lieutenant Colonel went as far as to "draw his pistol, with the safety off" against the General.[141] However, Ochoa's conduct, according to his own written documents, was not so humanitarian or honourable. The General negotiated the rebels' surrender with Gabriel Torrens, lieutenant in the Civil Guard, as an intermediary of the Socialist Belarmino Tomás, president of the revolutionary committee of Sama. Torrens proposed as a condition for the soldiers to be able to enter the mining basin without resistance the avoidance of reprisals on the part of the troops "and especially of the use of Moorish troops, who inspired genuine terror". Ochoa declared the absence of retaliation to be conditional upon the surrender of all weapons and ammunition and the presence as hostages of a quarter of the provincial committee. An offer that, according to the document, was guaranteed by the General's word of honour. Torrens returned with Belarmino Tomás, who informed Ochoa that it was not possible to fulfil the condition vis-à-vis the committee because it no longer existed, but that he would take responsibility or the other conditions imposed. On the day after the agreement was reached, General Ochoa led the advance of four columns, which succeeded in taking control "in a few hours of the entire mining basin without a shot being fired". The rebels also handed in their weapons as had been agreed, leaving them in the Casas del Pueblo and public buildings. Nowhere to be seen was Belarmino, who had fled. Ochoa, meanwhile, did not respect the terms of the agreement and the army went on the rampage. The General himself argued "sincerely", in his own words, that

> the execution of a few death penalties would be suitably exemplary, without this being the same as the government cruelly executing many or all of the death sentences issued. As an enemy of the spilling of blood beyond the field of combat, as I make clear in this proclamation, I believe it is absolutely necessary for examples to be made.

Alejandro Lerroux awarded him the Gran Cruz Laureada de la Orden Militar de San Fernando, in February 1935. But during the elections of February 1936 he was sent to a military prison, accused of unlawful execution by firing squad in the Pelayo garrison in Oviedo. He was killed during the first few days of the Civil War on 17 August 1936, whilst hospitalised.[142]

The truth is that in Asturias the army and the security forces acted more like a colonial army than a peacekeeping force. The air force bombed areas held by the rebels. In Carabanzo and Vega del Ciego, "they dropped incendiary bombs (and) shrapnel bombs".[143]During the final days of the insurrection, while the rebels were reported to be escaping to the mountains, groups of people wandered the streets trying to avoid repression, hungry and determined to return "to their homes, come what may".[144] Though they all knew what was going to happen. To a large extent, because the army itself had already warned them in the thousands of leaflets that were scattered everywhere, demanding unconditional surrender and announcing the intention to crush them "without mercy, as just punishment for your criminal madness. All the damage done to you by the aerial bombings and the troops' weapons are a mere warning of what remorselessly awaits you (...) Then, we will come after you and destroy you, without truce or forgiveness".[145] Which is exactly what happened.

Legionnaires were photographed "exhibiting with obvious delight the heads of decapitated miners" and another showed "the pathetic moment when a group of wounded and hospitalised workers, after being dragged from Oviedo hospital, (had) been shot against a wall".[146] Legionnaires who wore their victims' strung on pieces of wire by way of necklaces or prisoners placed in front of troops to offer protection as they advanced. This was how the *ugetista* Bonifacio Martín met his death, one of the signatories of the workers' Alliance in Asturias, when he was in the vanguard of Ochoa's troops. As the general himself stated, acknowledging that he had "died when accompanying my column in the vicinity of Corredoira".[147] Those under arrest made allegations of torture, as was reflected by the letter signed by 564 prisoners in Oviedo's Modelo Prison, which the Socialist MP Álvarez del Vayo passed on to Lerroux, which included a detailed description of the abuse received:

> blows and beatings were the norm in all actions, accompanied by insults and harassment (…) Twisting of testicles, application of fire to sexual organs and other parts of the body; hammer blows to hands and knees; toothpicks forced under fingernails; naked bodies doused with boiling water (…), simulations of execution by firing squad.[148]

There were also executions without trial, like the 19 militiamen killed by the African troops on the esplanade of the Pelayo barracks, according to allegations made in Parliament by Socialist MP Félix Gordón Ordás. The murder of nine neighbours from the working-class district of La Tenderina, who did not belong to any political or union organisation and were stripped of their money and watches. Arrests of women, miners' wives and daughters who were terrorised with the threat of being handed over to the regulars and the legionnaires if the guerrillas on the run did not surrender. The death of communist Aida de la Fuente, 16 years old, in San Pedro de los Arcos, where she was shot after attempting to advise the rebels of the enemy's position. Among her killers was the Legion officer Dimitri Iván Ivanov, of Bulgarian origins.[149]

The very same Legion lieutenant Ivanov (or Ivanoff) was also involved in the murder of journalist Luis Higón, known as Luis Sirval, which became a symbol of the repression. The trial proceedings noted, as proven facts, that on 27 October 1934 a lieutenant in the Second Legion, Ramón Pardo, discovered that Sirval had information about the crimes committed by the legionnaires when they arrived in Oviedo, so he decided to go to the police station where the journalist was under arrest and interrogate him. On the way, he met two colleagues of similar rank, Rafael Florit Togores and Dimitri Iván Ivanoff, whom he invited to accompany him. When they reached the police station, they took the prisoner out of his cell and into a corridor, and when Pardo began the conversation, Sirval ran towards an interior courtyard, at which point Ivanoff drew his gun and tried to fire into the air, but

> when he was attempting to move the gun slide, in order to load the weapon, it slipped, resulting in all the rounds being fired off in rapid succession, because of

> a special device on the gun , which converts it into a machine pistol, leading to shots being fired automatically and quickly, without it being necessary to squeeze the trigger, shots which, fired by the defendant with no desire whatsoever to kill or injure, hit Mr Higón, who had at that moment turned to face the defendant, producing six almost simultaneous wounds in different parts of the body, all suffered before he fell to the ground, causing almost instantaneous death.[150]

In short, the pistol slipped in his hands and shifted into machine-gun mode, and fired six bullets, all of which hit the fugitive who, moreover, in full flight, turned around and faced his pursuers. Well, in an initial trial, Ivanoff was sentenced to six months and a day of imprisonment and payment of 15,000 pesetas in compensation to the victim's family, for a crime of manslaughter through negligence with the extenuating circumstance of having reported the incident to his superiors. It was not until the triumph of the Popular Front that there was a certain rectification of the case, since, as Republican Álvaro de Albornoz observed, revision was impossible because the existing law of criminal instruction did not allow for it.[151] So the Supreme Court admitted a complaint, presented by the Prosecutor of the Republic, against the actions of the judges that issued the first sentence. The Prosecutor maintained that neither the contents of the proceedings nor the evidence given daring the oral proceedings established as proven the facts laid out in the sentence, so he accused booth judges of a crime of prevarication, and described Lieutenant Ivanoff's act as wilful homicide.[152]

Specific cases apart, the October repression filled the prisons, which were bursting at the seams. A glance at telegrams sent by military commanders in different areas suffices to bear witness to the exceptional number of detainees. The officer in command of Pontevedra reported that "provincial prisons are full to excess" and requested that a ship be dispatched urgently to "normalise prison services"; the commanding officer in Valladolid hoped to reduce overcrowding by transferring prisoners to Avila; his counterpart in León reported that he had 868 prisoners and lacked "indispensable means (of) accommodation and sustenance". Those arrested all over Spain amounted to around 30,000. A circumstance that leads one to think of indiscriminate action by the state, which arrested any citizen who was singled out or had participated in any strike or demonstration and thus had nothing to do with the insurrectionist movements. This was acknowledged by the 2nd Division Chief of Staff when he referred to the accumulation of "a large quantity of prisoners with regard to whom there is no evidence of subversion". He therefore recommended their gradual release, "thus reducing congestion in extremely overcrowded prisons".[153]

Later came the colder, more calculated repression. Then it was "the Civil Guard – according to its records – significantly reinforced, which, led by Commander D. Lisardo Doval Bravo and Captain D. Nilo Tella Cantos, (undertook) an efficient labour of policing and purging".[154] Doval, like many soldiers, had sworn loyalty to the Republic in April 1931. Which did not prevent him from taking part in General Sanjurjo's coup, in August 1932, for which he was tried. In 1934, be benefitted from the amnesty, and in June of that same year was promoted to Civil Guard Commander. On 20 October he left for Oviedo, and via a 1 November decree was appointed the Minister of War's delegate for Public Order in the provinces of Asturias and León. A position he occupied until 13 December.[155] His dismissal was related to the "ferocity" he employed in order to obtain statements from prisoners. Even the Director General of Security, José Valdivia, went to the office of the Minister of the Interior, on 30 November, to inform him of the abuses being committed by Doval, according to reports reaching him from the police in Asturias. Valdivia threatened to resign unless the situation were addressed. The Minister admitted that he was aware of what was going on, and dismissed Doval.[156]

In spite of the heavy censorship imposed by the government, news of the repression and mistreatment transcended Spain's borders, and European public opinion mobilised governments. The Belgian Socialist Vandervelde, for example, denounced the "ruthless sentences", and demanded that the Belgian government grant "asylum to Spanish political refugees".[157] Meanwhile, the left-wing press in France reported the arrest in Madrid of lawyer Thades Oppman, member of the Paris Bar Association and delegate in Spain of the International Legal Association, while he was "compiling reports on the situation of political prisoners and repression of the revolutionary movement".[158] In a similar vein, a commission of English Labour MPs, led by Wuilxinston, travelled to Asturias to gather information about the repression. The Ministry of War advised its delegation in Oviedo that it should not "permit any action" that was not "authorised for citizens be they national or foreign".[159] Meanwhile, town councils in France passed motions of solidarity with Spanish political refugees, and the International Red Cross organised meetings, published leaflets and in Paris set up a "Popular Committee of aid for all the victims of fascism in Spain".[160]

In this context, Doval was dismissed, and his deputy, Nilo Tella, replaced him. Tella had participated in the executions at the Pelayo garrison in Oviedo, on 13 October, and had been awarded the Military Medal, in December 1934, for undertaking a supposedly heroic action in those barracks. Specifically, according to his file, Tello left the building at the head of a group of soldiers "under enemy fire, and opened the gate to allow in the column" commanded by General Ochoa. However, a later investigation found "no evidence whatsoever that Captain Tella has taken part in the events referred to", since witnesses declared that he was inside the building observing the entry of the troops. As a result, the concession of the medal was rescinded in 1935.[161]

As for Doval, in 1936 he was in America on an official mission, but once this was completed he failed to report for duty, so a case was brought against him on 2 July. However, that same month, he was notified "by telegram from Portugal of the Movement that was being prepared", so he travelled to Lisbon, via Gibraltar. There, on 7 July, he joined "the Glorious General Sanjurjo, and was appointed by the latter as his Assistant Secretary during the planned Movement". The day after Sanjurjo died in an aeroplane accident, Doval crossed the border into Spain at Fuente Oñoro, "accompanied by 85 *falangistas* who appointed him as their leader". He organised, along with the military authorities in the region, the so-called "Mobile Column of Salamanca". Doval was promoted to lieutenant colonel of the Civil Guard in July 1938.[162]

In Parliament, the far-right groups demanded exemplary punishments, while the Prime Minister, Lerroux, was more moderate in his application of the law. In fact, he supported many of the pardons for those sentenced to capital punishment, among them the Socialist González Peña, despite the fact that the CEDA opposed any pardons. In any case, on October 9 the government presented Parliament with a draft law re-establishing the death penalty, which was adopted with the absence of the opposition. The war councils issued around 30 death sentences, four of which were carried out, specifically, José Guerra Pardo, in Léon, José Moredo Corrales, in Asturias, both as soon as military operations ended; and those of Jesús Argüelles and Sergeant Diego Vázquez, on 1 February 1935.[163]

For too long Lerroux denied the illegal repression exercised by soldiers, guards and police in Asturias and Léon. MP Félix Gordón Ordás highlighted Lerroux's contradictory behaviour when he recalled how he "bravely denounced the disgraceful torture of Montjuich", at the end of the 19th century, but now opted for silence or denial. Gordón noted, with good reason, that it was perfectly feasible that those who staged a revolutionary uprising wished to take the law into their own hands, but "when that someone who rides roughshod over the law is obliged by authority to see that everyone obeys the law, the social damage caused is immense". Revolt, sedition, rebellion and revolution were different degrees of the same criminal act that the laws defined and punished, and nobody could argue against that. One could debate the greater or lesser justice of the severity of the penalty but nobody could deny the state's right and duty to apply it, though always "according to the law, in no other way". The state should respond to an uprising against the law, with the law, which was not what had occurred in Asturias. There was no questioning the actions of the security forces in the struggle against the revolutionaries. But this was not the case in the Pelayo barracks or before the walls of the cemetery of San Pedro de los Arcos, or with the executions in private homes of Cabaña, Tendorina, Villaira or San Esteban de las Cruces, or the removal of 20 inmates from the prison of Sama to murder them and bury them in Tuilla y Carbayin, or the torture and murder in Sabeto, Barruelo, Aguilar de Campo, etc.[164]

The repression reached, significantly, the teaching profession, a prelude to the "cleansing" that would come years later. The permanent commission of the National Association of Primary Teachers visited the Minister of the Interior and requested clarification of the situation of teachers under arrest without trial, "in order to regulate teaching in the schools where they work". In fact, the primary teaching inspector in the province of Asturias asked the new town council of Langreo, established after the insurrection, for "the list of teachers involved" in the events of October.[165]

With regard to the revolutionary violence, the proclamations published by the committees formed in different areas urged citizens to join the movement and hand in their weapons, otherwise they would be punished. Some lent a philosophical air to what was simply death and violence. The revolutionary committee of Grado, in the hands of the anarchists, warned that the birth of a new society

> is evidenced by physical wounds and moral pain. These are natural laws from which no-one is free. The most illustrious man produced by Humanity was born of a dying mother, submitting to the pain of her torn womb (...) Death brings life. The agony of a dying man, his final breath, will strengthen the lungs of a new-born baby. It will give them life (...) It will be a question of hours; those necessary in order to convince those formerly privileged that their privileges have ended forever.[166]

A major part of the revolutionary violence was exercised against the security forces, in the main, the Civil Guard. In most cases, the rebels headed for the barracks and appealed to the guards to surrender and on occasions even to join them. When they refused, there ensued an armed confrontation that ended with the guards being arrested or killed, depending on how much resistance they offered. In Ujo, the revolutionaries surrounded the barracks and, in the subsequent gunfight, one of the guards was wounded and one of the attackers, Juan Vázquez Villanueva, a local resident, killed. The guards eventually surrendered and were led "by the working mass to the Mieres Municipal Morgue, where they were held until 28 October"; in Riosa, the revolutionaries employed dynamite, causing damage to the barracks. The guards' families were then evacuated, "the shooting continuing, this humanitarian gesture having been completed". The guards finally surrendered, and some of the rebels proposed "the shooting en masse of all the guards (...) with the opposition of the mayor of the town council, who in clear and categorical fashion staunchly defended the security forces and their families", who were taken to Mieres under arrest". Elsewhere, resistance led to the death of civil guards, for instance, in Ablaña, all the members of the garrison were killed or wounded by their assailants; in Olloniego, the commanding officer died while defending his post; in Campomanes, the rebels entered the barracks, disarmed and arrested the guards. When the army took control of the town they found the bodies of nine guards, while Lieutenant Halcón was found on the side of a mountain, "horribly mutilated, his legs amputated and his body full of stab-wounds, with a bullet in his forehead and eye sockets emptied by the knives that had been plunged into them"; or the aforementioned events in Sama.[167] Added to all this were selective killings, such as that of Carlist Marcelino Oreja in the Basque Country, or the 33 clergy members killed by the revolutionaries during the movement. Worthy of particular mention is the cold-blooded murder of six young seminarians in Oviedo and the shooting of nine priests in Turón.[168]

The closing balance of the insurrection, and the consequent repression, was, according to official figures, 1,050 civilians killed and 321 members of the army and security forces, with 2,015 of the former and 871 of the latter wounded. Approximately 30,000 were arrested.[169]

Ultimately, the events of October 1934 cannot be considered, broadly speaking, to have been a revolutionary movement. It would be more accurate to speak of diverse actions, such as strikes, uprisings, nationalist movements and, in the case of Asturias, an insurrection that attained revolutionary status during a short period of time. The movement was a serious error that saw the democratic rules of the Republic broken by those who had played a fundamental role in its advent and consolidation, in other words, the Socialists. But the vengeful repression was even more calamitous than the uprising itself. October 1934 represented a before and an after in the evolution of the Republic, with an exceptional increase in political and social tension

As far as the CNT was concerned, there was very strong criticism of its conduct at both national and international level. The main argument was that the confederal organisation could not miss an appointment with revolution, irrespective of who initiated it. All the more so when in confederal plenums it had been repeated ad infinitum that if the Socialists wanted revolution all they had to do was take to the streets, where they would find the confederals. But the anarchists found themselves caught between this defiant discourse and hostility towards the protagonists of the uprising. An uprising that, in most cases, was perceived as something alien, on account of both its unclear objectives and its postponement in the organisation and deployment of the action.

These circumstances contributed decisively to the disorientation that dominated the conduct of the CNT. Because while there were militants that supported strikes and uprisings, driven by their class consciousness, the confederal leaders were divided between those who were prepared to forget recent affronts and take part in the action and those who did not want to collaborate in a movement that not only was not theirs, but the protagonists of which were, in their view, responsible for the disastrous situation in which the CNT found itself. Amidst this chaos, the confederal leadership was left without answers.

The CNT's revolutionary prestige was tarnished. Although, ironically, the actions of the Asturian regional federation would save confederal honour. I say ironically because the Asturian *cenetistas* took a completely different line to that defended by the national leadership, to a degree bordering on rupture. Their signing of the *Alianza Obrera* with the UGT, against the majority view of the organisation, and their participation in the insurrectional movement, without waiting for instructions from the national committee, was tantamount to rebellion. However, these actions would subsequently become the great example to be followed. A circumstance not unrelated to the Conservative government's solution to the conflict, with both the despatch of troops that were all too reminiscent of a colonial army, and the excessively ruthless and illegal repression undertaken by those who should have re-established the rule of law rather than that of vengeance. The government's mixture of authoritarianism and clumsiness, ignoring illegal conduct and endorsing the expulsion of thousands of workers from their jobs, helped the Left, in the ensuing months, to turn defeat into triumph and identify unity as the prime objective, which would take the form of the creation of the Popular Front. The CNT was faced with "old" and troubling dilemmas. On the one hand, the agreement with the Opposition Unions and the UGT was regarded, after the Asturian experience, as the only possible path to revolution; on the other, the organisation would have to reconsider, once again, significant questions, such as its abstentionist stance in future elections. The thousands of confederal prisoners crowded inside the republican jails left it with no other option.

5

Between Rectification and Continuity (May 1935–July 1936)

The Government after the October Movement

The government, with the presence of the Radicals, Liberal Democrats, the Agrarian Party and *cedistas*, imposed heavy censorship, which not only created problems for the parties and unions that had participated in recent events, but also in other spheres of national and international life. The difficulty in sending telegrams abroad hindered commercial transactions and undermined the national economy. At the same time, the foreign media were also affected, and their embassies lobbied for the news agencies to be able to inform freely. The German ambassador asked for the censorship of his country's media to be lifted, arguing that the information provided by Germany's newspapers had been "objective and neutral". A different case to that of the French communist newspaper *L'Humanité*, banned in Spain "owing to biased information and campaigns".[1]

Meanwhile, the government increased the pressure in the political and social terrain. In the former, the conservative groups wanted to involve Azaña and, by extension, members of the Republican-Socialist government in the *Turquesa* incident, as we have seen. In the latter, the changes in social and labour-related areas were evident, beginning with those that were fundamental in negotiations. Municipal corporations were replaced by more conservative formations. This was the case, for example, in Langreo (Asturias), where an administrative body, formed by prominent industrialists and business people, assumed control of the town council.[2] But also in places where the strike had been completely peaceful, like La Granja de San Ildefonso (Segovia), where the councillors from the Socialist Group and the Republican Left, as Eduardo Juárez has noted, were dismissed and replaced by Radicals, members of groups that have joined the CEDA or by independents.[3] Dismissals and appointments that, as I have noted on numerous occasions, influenced the decisions of the mixed juries.

Although by now these juries were mortally wounded. In the main because most of their members had been disqualified, but also because employers opposed the continued existence of agencies that they had always rejected. Moreover, right-wing and fascist organisations attempted to organise workers into unions that they called anti-Marxist and counter-revolutionary. Thus, the Falange formed the *Central Obrera Nacional Sindicalista* (Workers' National Syndicalist Union or CONS), while the Catholics created the *Frente Nacional del Trabajo* (National Labour Front or FNT). The *cedista* Federico Salmón, Labour Minister since May 1935, encouraged the presence of Catholics in the juries via the introduction of minorities in the appointment of members. But even management was wary of this initiative, because these unions, in truth, barely represented anybody. The Minister tried again, in July 1935, with a decree establishing new rules for the completion of the electoral roll, which met with the UGT's opposition, given the difficulty in registering associations that had been closed down, suspended or dissolved. Ultimately, the aim was to replace class-based trade unionism with another that was more subservient to the interests of employers; in Mercedes Cabrera's words, "the reform was seen for what it was: the reinforcement of anti-Marxist worker representation".[4]

Management preferred to act without conditions of any kind, taking advantage of a following wind. The government issued a decree, in December 1934, which declared any strike undertaken for non-labour-related reasons, or in the absence of legal formalities, to be "abusive". In this case, employers could terminate contracts, leaving wide open the doorway to dismissal. In any case, it made it obligatory to respect negotiated work rules, a question that, as we shall see, was also ignored. Although the law was passed after the uprising, it was applied retroactively, which was illegal. There were mass redundancies, but in selective fashion, with the discretional expulsion of those who had supported the October strike, whether in a violent or a peaceful manner, but also of those most outspoken in their criticism of management. Dismissals that intensified confrontation, when what was needed was for people to be kept in work as a path towards repairing the shattered peace. The Catholic unions collaborated shamelessly in the recruitment of workers, even hastening to fill the vacancies left by those condemned to unemployment with the corresponding sentence of hunger for their families. Such was management's abuse of the situation that the government had to remind them, by means of a decree in August 1935, that contracts for new workers had to respect work rules agreed to previously; this point had to be reiterated via another decree, in October of the same year.[5] In other words, employers took advantage of the dismissals of employees on an individual basis in order to make general changes to work rules.

Thus, rights won by dint of long and bitter struggles were soon lost: metallurgical workers, who had succeeded, along with other sectors, in reducing the working week to 44 hours, saw it return to 48 hours, courtesy of a decree issued by the Labour Minister, the *cedista* Anguera de Sojo; employees of the Asland Company denounced the fact that "improvements obtained via considerable struggle and heartache" were trampled upon by management; workers at the Ter Company, in Catalonia, reported that "wages had been cut in two weaving mills"; shipping companies in Las Palmas violated "existing commitments" and increased the working day from 8 to 12 hours, while sailors were turned into goods loaders and unloaders; work rules signed in the construction sector, in Tenerife, were not respected, and wages were reduced, "4 pesetas for labourers and whatever they wanted for masons". It was impossible to find work if you were a member of the CNT, so if you did not want to "starve to death" you had to "think as the contractor wished" and do whatever you were ordered to do. The authorities claimed to be undertaking public works to alleviate unemployment, but there were no jobs for those who did not carry "a card provided by a certain political formation or by gentlemen of a specific political leaning". The unions denounced the actions of the Modern Tannery F.E., which had introduced a new system: "workers are 'hired' per hour and paid accordingly".[6] A circumstance described as scandalous, and food for thought today. A change in labour relations that was favourably received by foreign governments, always concerned about their investments in Spain. American diplomat Douglas Little commented that "the Spanish government controlled labour unrest and moderated the economic regulations that had made life so difficult for Río Tinto, ITT and other foreign companies".[7]

The situation within the Ministry of Agriculture merits particular attention. The policies encouraged by the *cedista* Jiménez Fernández upset landowners and even his colleagues. He promoted a leasing law that made it easier for peasant leaseholders to become owners of the plots that they farmed. But his project did not sit well with Conservative groups in Parliament, from the Agrarians to traditionalists, including his fellow CEDA MPs, who altered the law by reducing the minimum contract from six to four years and adopting a transitional provision enabling owners to recover the land and farm it themselves. There were evictions right across the country. The situation deteriorated further when the PAE's Nicasio Velayos took over the ministry in May 1935, and made it possible for landowners directly to exploit their farms, and reduced salaries to levels prior to the advent of the Republic.[8]

The uprising and the subsequent repression had left Spanish society deeply scarred and divided. While some remembered those killed in the uprising and faced prison, exile, unemployment and hunger, which they tried to escape by obtaining certificates of "good conduct" issued by traders and clerics;[9] others paid tribute to the fallen members of the security forces and raised money for their families. Letters and telegrams from all over Spain piled up in the War Ministry, with information about these initiatives; in Catalonia, for instance, where the not inconsiderable sum of 1,027,300 pesetas was donated in honour of those who took part in the October repression.[10]

Such was the atmosphere when Portela Valladares, new Minister of the Interior, initiated the path towards the end of censorship in April and authorised public events, although rights and freedoms were not fully recovered until the dissolution of Parliament and the calling of new elections, at the beginning of January 1936.

The CNT: Between Defence and Rectification

The actions of the unions, in the wake of the October uprising, were mainly directed towards avoiding repression, facilitating escape help those being persecuted, with attention later being focused on prisoners and their families. During the first days of November, the CNT called strikes all over Spain, which unfolded quite peacefully, aimed at preventing the execution of death penalties.[11]

The Confederation, apart from the almost spasmodic reaction against the repression, was stunned. The anarchists at the head of the organisation had spent over two years participating in uprisings and protests but, when it came to the crunch, had not been equal to the challenge. The national committee itself, in a manifesto issued in October, admitted that for many confederal and for public opinion in general "the CNT's passive and expectant attitude towards recent events was something of an enigma. Those who are like us are simply flabbergasted". For its part, the FAI said that "forgetting recent, shocking actions" it had joined the movement, albeit "without enthusiasm". Although it had no option but to confess to "an absolute lack of revolutionary action (…) (placing it) in an erroneous, ambiguous situation". While the AIT pointed to overseas criticism of the CNT's actions.[12] Amazement gave way to defensiveness, with criticism of the Socialists for the earlier repression and the omnipresent memory of Casas Viejas, but also for their promotion of a movement exclusively directed towards political change. Followed by the attempt to impose a narrative, as desperate as it was implausible, which maintained that the objective of the uprising was "the annihilation of the CNT". This was the opinion expressed by the national committee, in the aforementioned manifesto, but also by individuals like Abad de Santillán who, after criticising all the groups that took part in the uprising, insisted that the October movement had been more against the CNT than against the Right.[13]

But however much the CNT denied any need to "rectify its programme or its methods",[14] circumstances forced a change of tack. In the first place, owing to the criticism of the Asturian organisation in both form and content. The former, because the lesson to be drawn from October included, in particular, the need to unite the working class, which involved not only getting along with other left-wing forces, but beginning at home with the Opposition Unions. The latter, because Asturias "the villain", with a very different approach to that of the organisation, became the "hero", and José Mª Martínez, now a martyr, became an example of militants who defended "ideas and the organisation from the rostrum and in the press", who were "both excellent organisers and men of action".[15]

The CNT national committee attempted, in spring of 1935, to bring "order" to a dismembered and leaderless organisation. The previous committee, with Miguel Yoldi at the helm, handed in its resignation on 7 January 1935. This was a consequence of its conduct during the October movement, although, as usual in these cases, the plenary sessions of 14 October and 12 November endorsed its work. The secretary general of the new national committee was Horacio

Martínez Prieto, who presented a plan to right wrongs. In the first place, he criticised the apathy within the organisation, since a general strike had been called for 6 November, and there was barely any response "in the entire country"; a call went out due to the harrowing economic situation, and nobody took any notice; a questionnaire was sent to the regional committees, and it was completed by "an insignificant minority". As a result, decision-making was prolonged indefinitely, in light of the merely representative nature of the national committee, so the new secretary aimed to assign it more power. The rigid system of decision-making via successive committees and unions necessitated "as a rule, a margin of one month – the minimum period – during which time the possibilities of success (vanished)". In short, the national committee was "little more than nothing", and no longer wished to be "the Cinderella of the organisation". However, the regional representatives opposed his proposals at the plenum held in May, understanding the national committee to be a liaison body, which had no executive powers.[16]

Meanwhile, the conduct of the committees adjacent to the CNT, such as the prisoners' aid and defence committees, continued to be a source of problems. They were parallel organisations that, on too many occasions, acted as if they were the Confederation itself, as has been seen, when they were supposed to be dependent upon it. The situation was more complicated because, in spite of all the previous agreements, there were militants whose responsibilities overlapped with those of members in similar positions on other committees. A circumstance with regard to which the May plenum again expressed its opposition. In this respect, the national committee decided to incorporate commissions from both committees, in order to strengthen its role in directing and controlling activities via direct delegates, but maintaining its autonomy.[17]

The national committee also expressed its concern at what had become an "endemic illness" within the organisation, in other words, decision-making based on the delegates own criteria, but without taking into account the opinions of members. In this respect, it pointed to the need for the minutes of national plenums to be ratified or rejected by the CNT grassroots, as the agreements reached might "not faithfully reflect the prevailing mood in the organisations that the delegates obey and interpret". The situation had been further complicated by the repression. Andalusia acknowledged, at this May 1935 plenum, that in view of the irregular scenario within the organisation, agreements brought by delegations may have been reached "in meetings of leaders and militants", not by the unions. So "to be honest, we have to acknowledge that the agreements reached here cannot faithfully reflect the mood of the workers". While Catalonia understood the agreements to be necessary "even if they were only the product of militants and committees". But the question transcended the difficult circumstances in which the CNT found itself, since, for example, the North denounced the fact that its delegate at the previous plenum had voted against the national committee on account of its actions in October, as this decision was purely individual. And the Levante, whose delegate voted in favour of the commission that was going to visit the government "on a personal basis"; even Catalonia admitted that its delegate "was guided by personal criteria, a fact that forced the Regional Committee to stand down".[18]

On another note, the national committee engaged itself, as Peiró acknowledged,[19] in the task of bringing an end to the schism, and he noted the impact this had had upon the organisation, in terms of both the "fall in numbers" and the "lack of competent comrades".[20] Although there are no figures available with regard to membership at that time, as well-informed an observer as Herbette estimated, in February 1935, a total of around 200,000, and put the circulation of *Solidaridad Obrera* at approximately 20,000 copies.[21] If the CNT had, as I have commented, some 800,000 members in the autumn of 1931, membership had fallen by around 75% in just over three years. With regard to the newspaper, this represented a reduction of almost 50%, if compared with the 39,000 copies printed in May 1931. Although, above and beyond numbers, if unity between workers' organisations was of undeniable value in order to address the future, the CNT could not sidestep the problem of the schism.

The AIT was also a source of concern for the national committee given its "steep decline". In fact, the International had scheduled a congress for June that was far from certain to be held, since the CNT, on account of its situation, could not participate and, in its absence, the convocation made no sense, because all the unions revolved "around this organisation". The limited deployment of the AIT on a global scale could not be unrelated to the maximalism it exhibited. Its secretariat criticised what it called the "theory of the lesser evil", in other words, choosing between fascism and socialism, or between democracy and fascism or communism, which, it said, was like choosing "between the plague and cholera".[22] It is hardly surprising that, with reflections of this nature, with what was happening in Spain, after the events of October, and in the rest of Europe, in Germany, Italy and Austria in particular, membership of the International was little more than testimonial.

The national committee also attempted to address the ideological challenges looming on the horizon, among them, future general elections. After the abstentionist campaign in the previous elections in November 1933, with the subsequent victory of the centre-right and the ensuing criticism for having, according to the accusations, paved the way to fascism, the committee acknowledged the "multitude of discrepancies" within confederal ranks. The organisation was not going suddenly to change its anti-political approach, so abstentionism continued to be an unalterable principle. But, no matter how many times it was said that the CNT's attitude during the previous elections had been "a greater moral triumph than some revolutions", the organisation recognised that the new situation was different, and that sooner or later it would have to consider, among others, the "mantra of amnesty". The question was whether the CNT would be capable of promoting some kind of action leading towards the release of prisoners, or whether the only option was the ballot box.

The issue of the prisoners was fundamental. In fact, one of the first actions taken by the new national committee had been the constitution of a commission that would meet the President of the Council of Ministers, Alejandro

Lerroux, to demand freedom for prisoners and the legalisation of unions. Meetings with the government that, as we have seen, had become a "classic" element of confederal conduct. The situation at the time was doubly complicated, on account of both the number of prisoners and confederal fugitives, and the actions of the prisoners' aid committee. Thousands of comrades were behind bars, but the income raised by the committee was practically "nil". Its funding depended on the "magnanimous effort of colleagues in America" and France, without which "wouldn't even raise enough money to pay for postage". Added to economic problems were those related to principles, as the legalisation of the prisoners' aid committee, necessary to render it more effective, caused certain misgivings among those who, as a matter of principle, preferred it to remain in clandestinity. In short, the committee itself pointed to the chaos resulting from the shortage of money and its lack of legality, but also on account of the "incompetent lawyers" who defended them and were responsible, according to the organisation, for most of those tried being issued clearly disproportionate 12-30 year sentences. Consequently, the national committee decided to recruit lawyers Benito Pabón and Eduardo Barriobero, who accompanied the confederal commission to the meeting with Lerroux, in April 1935. The organisation eventually accepted the legalisation of the prisoners' aid committees, but retained commissions responsible for fugitives and other questions that needed to be dealt with in clandestine fashion.[23]

Ultimately, the new national committee wished to address old, deep-seated problems, but also new ones presented by complicated issues. Prominent among all these challenges was that of prisoners and fugitives, who not only traversed the peninsula, but crossed Spain's borders and chose the path of exile.

Different Places, Same Problems

The Spaniards who entered France did so as political refugees. The French government issued an order for the internment of Spaniards north of the Loire, with the exception of the region of Paris[24], which meant that they were denied the right to legal exile, previously available to refugees from other countries. According to José Cenitagoya, a communist member of the revolutionary committee of Muros del Nalón, there was a certain tendency, with the complicity of the authorities, to take advantage of the Spaniards' situation, and give them the "worst jobs with lowest wages". In Orleans, for example, they were paid 21 francs to unload coal wagons, when other workers earned 25–30 francs per day.[25]

The French police monitored the Spaniards continuously, sometimes on a daily basis. Leaders such as Montagut, Duran, Dencas and Badia, among others, tried to escape the surveillance, as the police themselves observed, "Suddenly jumping into a taxi" or "going for a run". Police reports were most disparaging, describing the refugees "as dangerous elements" who spent "many nights in the capital's whorehouses". The police insisted that all of them were engaged in political activity, except Dencas – who declined the company of his exiled comrades – so they were regarded as undesirables and, pursuant to the ministerial circular of 31 October 1934, were to be expelled lest they created problems of public order.[26]

But while the police exhibited their hostility towards the refugees, France's left-wing parties and unions demonstrated their solidarity. Newspapers like *Le Peuple* recalled that France was a democracy and, along with *L'Oeuvre*, demanded the right of exile for the Spaniards, an ancient French tradition, while the communist *L'Humanité* recalled that their expulsion would mean prison and, for more than one, the death penalty. For its part, the Socialist parliamentary group, led by Léon Baylet and Jean Longuet, met the Foreign Minister, Pierre Laval, and the Minister of the Interior, Paul Marchandeau, to defend the rights of the refugees.[27] In a similar vein, the Belgian Socialist Émile Vandervelde demanded that his country's authorities grant the right of exile to the Spanish refugees, while he publically denounced the "demands by Spanish right-wing elements and military elements in favour (...) (of) the ruthless execution (of) sentences".[28] At the same time, aid committees were formed and there was fund-raising for the "brave fighters of Spain". Especially prominent was the International Red Cross, organised by the Comintern, which, as well as providing money, convened rallies and meetings where it denounced the advance of fascism in Spain and its implications for workers all over Europe.[29]

The main support for the Spanish refugees was provided by this communist organisation. While European social democracy contributed in far more discreet manner, since it did not identify with the revolutionary movement of October. As Elorza and Bizcarrondo have noted, the communists provided considerably more aid than the socialists: while the latter sent four million francs to their German comrades after the Nazis' rise to power in 1933, and seven and a half million to the Austrians after the February 1934 uprising, their Spanish brethren received only 106,000 francs of the 230,000 raised, sharing the rest between Germany, Austria, Latvia, Dantzing, Hungary and Italy. Meanwhile, the communist aid totalled three million francs. A policy that was not unrelated to the attempt to recruit militants to the cause.[30]

The distribution of money by aid organisations led to confrontation between the *cenetista* refugees and the (Spanish-speaking) anarchist groups in France, with the involvement of the Spanish CNT. The Federation of Anarchist Groups of the Seine (Paris) denounced the actions of the Asturian refugees who accepted the help offered by a committee formed by socialists and communists, and even suggested that they join them to manage the aid. Asturian *cenetista* Horacio Argüelles was one of those who advocated actions that would enable the regional federation to show its worth, which meant unity of action with other left-wing groups. Although the CNT in Spain cited the revolutionary example of the Confederation in Asturias, the truth was that it had not forgiven the latter for embarrassing the rest of the organisation. So the CNT accepted the version given by the "Parisian" anarchists because they had shown their "*cenetista* love" and because they were thought to be incapable "of a felony", while Argüelles, apparently lacking these qualities, was urged to explain himself. But not only that: only other anarchist groups resident in France were authorised to assume control of the CNT fugitives.[31]

The situation reached the point where, when the Asturian *cenetistas* that had sought refuge in Holland requested aid to survive, from the "pro-CNT funds" created in the International to help the victims of repression in Spain, the CNT national committee expressed its opposition and urged the Dutch NSV union to send the money straight to the AIT. Furthermore, it refused to "advise any kind of solidarity, neither moral nor economic, with the Asturian comrades Avelino Martínez, Horacio Argüelles, Harmodio Argüelles, Ramón Álvarez, Aurelio Permia, Manuel Sánchez, José Arriba, Emeterio Díaz and Luis Meana", because, according to a report sent by the Federation of Anarchist Groups of the Seine, "those comrades were in receipt of simultaneous solidarity from the Prisoners' Aid and the Aid Committee, comprised of republican and Marxist elements". But also because when asked to stop collaborating with the latter committee, "they refused". Essentially, the NSV could not involve itself in the internal affairs of another section of the AIT and should "follow the indications issued by the CNT national committee", in spite of the conditions in which the *cenetista* refugees found themselves.[32] The reaction was swift, and the Asturian regional federation undertook a campaign in which it accused the CNT national prisoners' aid committee of abandoning its militants. An action that reduced the amount of money arriving from the other side of the Atlantic, which was no small matter, given that, as will be recalled, a substantial part of its income came from America.[33]

The underlying problem was none other than the confrontation dividing the CNT with regard to the events of October 1934 and its stance vis-à-vis the workers' alliance. Ramón Álvarez, *Ramonín*, secretary of the Asturian federation and a refugee in France, declared that the anarchist groups in Paris "attempted to sow confusion in relation to our activities in a unitary organisation", just like the other enemies of the alliance sealed in Asturias.[34] Because, in this respect, the Asturians were not only in confrontation with the Parisian groups and the CNT, but also with the leading representatives of the AIT. In June 1935, Horacio Argüelles met Schapiro, Bernard and Müller in Paris to inform them about the formation of the alliance and events in Asturias during the revolution. The differences between the Asturian and the International leaders were vast. The latter presented themselves as "irreconcilable enemies of any understanding with the Marxists", while their questions focused in the main upon social laws, Casas Viejas or whether the socialists were given rifles during the insurrection. As Argüelles said, "the same old story, trying to reduce a problem that involved the happiness of the people to such ridiculous details". In a nutshell, the Asturian made it clear that he would fight to extend the Alliance right across Spain, to which Schapiro replied that he would do the very opposite.[35]

The agreement between the CNT and the AIT was affected by the earmarking of the funds received by the Spanish organisation from other unions to help prisoners and other victims. Both the Swedish SAC and the Dutch NSV refused to allow the funds raised in their campaigns to this end to be employed for other purposes. The Swedes, after meetings with the CNT delegate who travelled to Sweden to take part in the 7th SAC Congress, abandoned "such a closed" position and accepted a broader destination for the funds, although always for the organisation's "needs". The problem was, as the *cenetista* delegate himself acknowledged, that the Swedes did not regard as "an organic necessity the revolutionary preparation of the defender committees, with the meaning and the scope that we in Spain give to the word". In other words, not only was the CNT spending part of the money it received for victims on other questions, strange enough in itself for the Swedes, but in addition, it was spending it on preparing the revolution at a time when it was barely structured as an organisation, a circumstance that made things even more incomprehensible. But if the Swedes became more "flexible", the Dutch were another story. The NSV refused to permit the money raised for prisoners to be diverted elsewhere, as "it was extremely embarrassing to risk the fraud being discovered one day, if they authorised modification of the use that should be made of the florins donated".[36]

The whole controversy surfaced again at the Zaragoza Congress in 1936 at the behest of the Asturian federation, which came out in defence of comrades who had been compromised in exile. The national committee attempted to avoid the discussion, but the Asturians' insistence made this impossible. Unions like the Miners Union of Asturias or the Food Union of Gijon accused the national committee of having opposed their receiving aid in an "extremely critical" situation and of treating Asturian *cenetistas* as traitors, when neither they "were traitors to the Asturian movement, nor were the socialists", as libertarians inside and outside Spain insisted on repeating. The national committee defended itself by pointing out that the decision to deny help to the Asturian exiles was taken at the national plenum in May 1935, and revoked at a new plenum in January of the following year, in the belief that they had been too strict. But the Asturians were not satisfied with the explanations of the abandonment suffered, and even denounced that they had been branded with "the nickname of 'alliance members, applied with pejorative criteria as if they were crooks". The congress settled the controversy, as on so many other occasions, without anybody assuming any kind of responsibility. The Manufacturers' Union of Barcelona, of which García Oliver, Durruti and Ascaso were members, proposed a motion to the effect that as the new national committee had amended its decision and endorsed the aid, and as the Asturian federation was present with its exiles at the congress, the demand had been met and the issue resolved. The congress, without further ado, passed the motion.[37]

Syndicalism on the Defensive

In May 1935 there was a government reshuffle. Lerroux assigned five ministries to the CEDA. The rest of the cabinet was formed by three members of the Radical Party, two from the Agrarian Party, two independents and a member of the Democratic Liberal Party, in other words, the government had a majority of ministers belonging to parties on the non-republican Right. Among the members of CEDA was Gil Robles as Minister of War, which influenced the role to be played by the armed forces. The republican elements of the military were beating a retreat, unlike those colleagues opposed to the regime. The Minister strove, in the words of Gabriel Cardona, to "turn the army into a political instrument". While in the police, according to Gerald Blaney Jr., "if the intention of the governments of the first biennium was to attempt to create a professional police force controlled by the civil authorities of the Ministry of Interior, those of the second tried to create a militarised police to protect its position in power".[38] The anarcho-syndicalist warned against Gil Robles's actions in pursuit of a dictatorship, both from outside power, with demonstrations and acts of violence in overtly fascist style, and within, with the appointment in significant army posts of officers who had always been "distinguished by their reactionaryism".[39]

Meanwhile, the CEDA sought a constitutional reform that it failed to achieve, partly, due to its differences with the Radicals, but also because it required a majority of two thirds of parliament for any change that might take place during the first four years of the Constitution, in other words, until December 1935. In any case, the right-wing exerted pressure in order to repeal, as we have seen, many of the reformist measures adopted during previous years. At the same time, the more powerful groups took advantage of the new circumstances to impose their will and crush the humbler classes. In this context, the roles played by workers and bosses changed radically in comparison with previous years: if the former had been on the offensive, in the quest for labour-related rights and pay rises denied them for years, and the latter, outmanoeuvred by the arrival of the new regime, simply weathered the storm, with the election victory in November and, above all, in the wake of October 1934, roles were reversed. The unions were well aware that circumstances had changed. During the CNT national plenum held in May 1935, the Centre regional federation proposed the launching of a propaganda campaign in defence of a six-hour working day, a long-lasting grievance; the organisation rejected the suggestion because "the national scenario requires us to direct our activities via other channels more in line with the demands of the moment".[40] Which meant, in other words, that work-related grievances took second place to other more pressing problems, such as those related to prisoners and redundancies. A defensive approach that was also apparent in the editorial line of *Solidaridad Obrera*, as the national committee acknowledged, explaining that the newspaper could not act with "the pugnacity of previous occasions (...) (due to) current circumstances".[41]

Circumstances that were determined by, among other factors, the forced closure of unions that, in random fashion, was taking place all over Spain, which resulted in the disorganisation of workers and an increase in their vulnerability. According to the strike data published in the Labour Ministry Bulletin, in 1935 there were 181 strikes involving 33,000 strikers, very different figures, not only from the previous year, with 594 strikes and 742,000 strikers, but from 1931, with 734 strikes and 236,117 strikers, or 1932, with 681 strikes and almost 270,000 strikers, and light years away from the peak of industrial unrest in 1933, with 1,127 strikes and 843,000 strikers. The statistics for 1935 were below those corresponding to the years prior to the advent of the Republic, such as 1930, when there were 402 strikes and 247,000 strikers.[42]

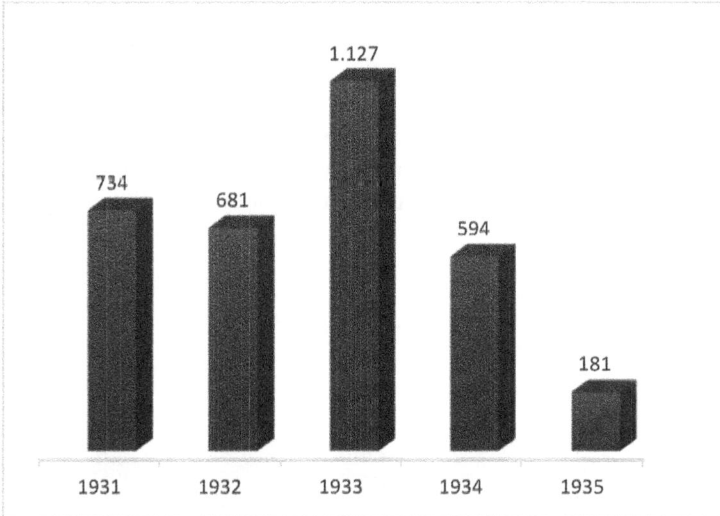

Figure 7 Number of Strikes, 1931–1935.

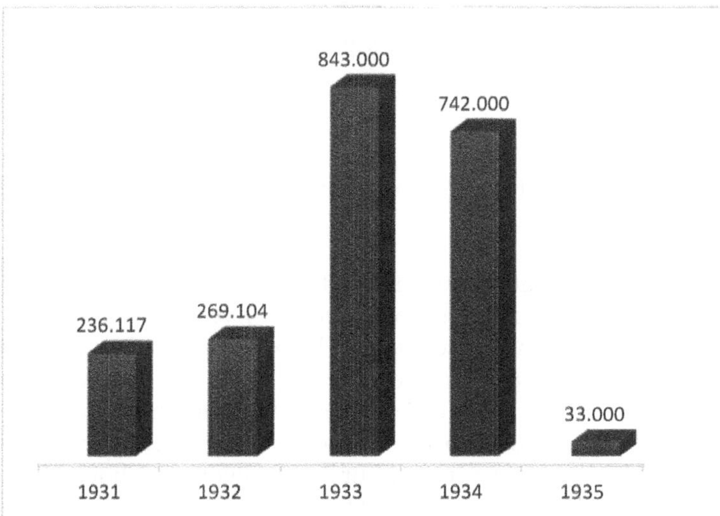

Figure 8 Number of Strikers, 1931–1935.

In a similar and significant vein, Civil Guard HQ records corresponding to 1935 reflect few labour disputes. Although they echoed the "growing civil unrest: unemployment rose every day, as did the Provincial Authorities' lack of assistance to tackle this problem".[43] Unemployment that stood in March 1935, according to official figures quoted in the confederal press, at 711,184, up from 619,000 in December 1933 and 666,000 in March of the following year.[44] While, according to Francisco Comín, public spending as a percentage of GDP fell, in 1934 and 1935, to 12.4%, back to the level in 1932.[45] Similarly, wages also decreased. According to the National Council of Chambers of Commerce, the salary index, taking as a base 100 from 1924–1926, was 116.5 in 1931; 122.0 in 1932; and 123.6 the following year, while in 1934 and 1935 it stood at 119.7.[46] Data that reveals the change of cycle in the evolution of the Republic.

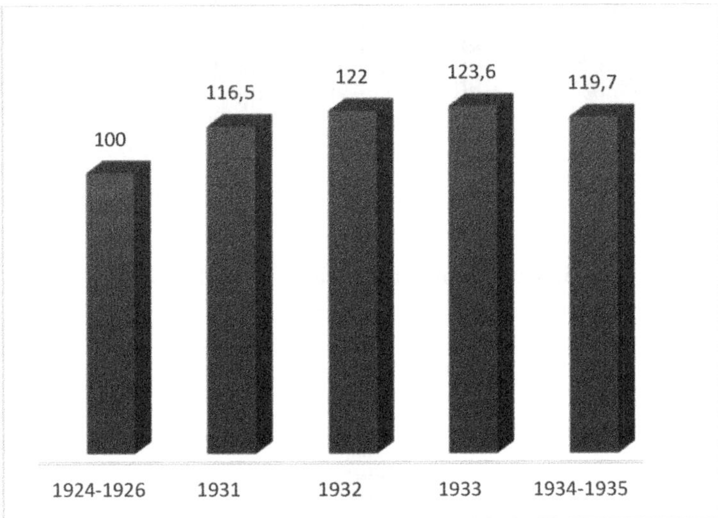

Figure 9 Evolution of Salaries.

The new labour situation was reflected in factories, workshops and fields. Weaving looms, for example, were operated by 14-year-old children, and most female workers earned two pesetas a day; labourers in the Levante used to be paid 13 pesetas for planting orange trees and 8 was the daily wage, while in September 1935 they received 6 or 7 pesetas for planting and 4.5 as a day's wage, and only if employers did not bring in workers from other towns and villages, who were paid less for eight or nine-hour days, previously 5-hours' long; in the port of Burriana (Castellón), wages fell from 12.75 pesetas to 5.95; in Tarrasa, bosses and the town council did not respect work rules in the construction sector and anyone who complained was fired; in Huelva, peasants worked 12-hour days for 2 or 3 pesetas; the Huelva Fishing Industry Union reported that all the improvements achieved in previous years had been lost. Unions, closed until November 1935, aimed to return "to where we were in 1931".[47]

Political Ups and Downs

The Left was increasingly aware of the need to form an electoral front to defeat the Right in the next general elections. But, while Azaña manoeuvred to unite republicanism, the PSOE need to travel the path that would take it from the "revolutionary" approach, defended Largo Caballero, to the coalition with the republicans, supported by Indalecio Prieto.[48] For the libertarians, rather than transit, there was only opportunism, as the Socialists always rode two horses. From one, they spoke of a united front and of revolution; from the other, they negotiated with the republicans in order to revive the combination of the first biennium.[49] The communists, meanwhile, had also pursued their own particular route from the single front, with its criticism of the workers' alliances, to their participation in the latter on the eve of the October movement. Their latest move was the formation of the Leftist Bloc, which enjoyed particular support from the more radical wing of socialism, represented, above all, by its youth organisation, led by Santiago Carrillo.

The conversations between socialists and communists bore fruit in November 1935, with the integration of the unions that formed the CGTU, a minority group within the UGT. As Elorza and Bizcarrondo have pointed out, for the communists this was the surrender of a secondary piece (in chess-playing terms), behind which lay more important aspirations, namely union as a single party. In any case, while the communists continued to shift their position with the acceptance of a popular front that integrated the bourgeois parties, in the style of the French Communist Party, Largo Caballero refused to accept it so as to avoid a repeat of 14 April.[50] But his resignation as secretary general of the PSOE, in December 1935 – on account of the parliamentary minority's dependence upon the executive commission and the national committee – had a crucial impact upon the future. Prieto assumed control of the executive, which precluded convergence with the communists but facilitated the agreement with the republicans to form an electoral front.[51]

In this regard, the internal disagreements within the government and the cases of corruption that affected, in the main, the Radical Party, encouraged rapprochement between the left and the republicans. A consequence of the former was the Lerroux, government crisis in September 1935, which led to the appointment of the independent Joaquín Chapaprieta as Prime Minister. During his government two corruption cases came to light that played a decisive role in the calling of new elections: the "*straperlo*" case and the Nombela-Tallá incident. The former corresponded to the bribes that Daniel Strauss, a Dutch businessman, and his partner, Perlowitz, had allegedly offered to members of the Radical Party in return for the introduction in Spain of a fixed roulette machine. The accusations of regularities in various casinos led to its withdrawal and the subsequent complaint by Strauss. The case was known by the name "*straperlo*", a combination of the first part of the surnames of the two foreigners. Parliament appointed a commission to investigate the facts, which reported irregular conduct by prominent individuals such as Aurelio Lerroux – Lerroux's adopted son – Emiliano Iglesias, Joan Pich i Pon – General Governor of Catalonia during the suspension of the *Generalidad* – Sigfrido Blasco Ibáñez – leader of the PURA – Eduardo Benzo and ex-minister Salazar Alonso. Although the courts found no evidence to prosecute those involved and the supposed bribes were relatively modest in quantity, Alejandro Lerroux and his colleague Juan José Rocha, Minister of State, had to leave the government.

More serious, though with less impact in the media, was the second case in which the Radical Party was involved. Antonio Nombela, Inspector General of Colonies, denounced the intervention of some Radical Party leaders in the fraudulent resolution of a compensation claim filed by the *África Occidental* shipping company, owned by Catalan businessman Antonio Tallá, following the loss of two ships in Guinea. Nombela refusal to pay the corresponding compensation, which he considered to be illegal and which had been approved by the Lerroux government in July, led him to present the case to the ministers Gil Robles and Luis Lucia, which resulted in his dismissal. Nombela then lodged a complaint before Parliament, which set up a commission at the end of November. Although the House plenary exonerated Lerroux, his party was discredited.[52]

Gil Robles attempted to take advantage of the corruption cases in the Radical Party in order to become prime minister. The CEDA opposed the fiscal reform project that the new Prime Minister, Joaquín Chapaprieta, presented before Parliament, so, lacking support, he handed in his resignation. The CEDA leader believed the time had come for him to take over the reins of government, but the President of the Republic, Alcalá Zamora, prevented this by charging Manuel Portela Valladares with forming a new government, dissolving Parliament and calling new elections. Seemingly, Gil Robles attempted to carry out a coup d'état, but various generals persuaded him that there was no guarantee of success.[53] Gil Robles himself recalled in his memoirs how General Fanjul offered to take part in an uprising but, after extolling and admiring "his patriotism, demonstrated on so many occasions", informed him of his democratic convictions. Although, "however – continued Gil Robles – if the army, assembled around its natural commanders, believes it should temporarily assume power in order to protect the spirit of the Constitution and prevent a massive revolutionary fraud, I shall be no obstacle whatsoever and shall do everything necessary so the continuity of action of public power remains unbroken". In any case, the CEDA leader concluded by acknowledging that "the army was still far from being the powerful force that could safeguard genuinely national interests, of which I had dreamt and which I was unable to forge".[54] In the end, Alcalá Zamora dissolved Parliament on 6 January 1936.

Earlier, in mid-November, Azaña sent a document to imprisoned socialist leaders, including Largo Caballero, presenting them with a programme for the upcoming elections. The Socialists offered their support on condition that other left-wing formations participated, including the Communist Party and the UGT. Largo's resignation as PSOE secretary facilitated negotiations in which the Socialists, represented by Prieto, and the Republicans, by Azaña, were mainly responsible for drafting the programme of the Popular Front, and they just informed the other left-wing groups.[55]

The programme reflected the principal concessions to the left-wing formations: the amnesty and the readmission of workers sacked after the events of October 1934. But it omitted the social and work-related demands of the workers' organisations which transcended the legislation of the first biennium, namely, the nationalisation of banks, workers' control of factories and workshops and a new land ownership regime. The agreement represented a return to the republican concepts of the first biennium, with the maintenance of the economic and political principles of bourgeois democracy. The Popular Front pact was signed on 15 January by Amós Salvador, of Republican Left; Bernardo Ginés de los Ríos, of Republican Union; Manuel Cordero and Juan Simeón Vidarte, for the PSOE; Largo Caballero, for the UGT; José Cazorla, on behalf of the National Federation of Socialist Youth; Vicente Uribe, for the Communist Party; Ángel Pestaña, for the Syndicalist Party and Juan Andrade, of the Workers' Party of Marxist Unification (POUM).[56]

For the CNT, the programme was "reactionary". Laws on vagrancy, public order and mixed juries were still in force, the land had not been nationalised, or placed under the workers' control, and it "merely referred to defending the state, principles of authority and ownership, public order (...) the exploitation of man by man. As for the amnesty, it was no more than a "sentimentalism, in order to gain the support of the working class".[57] In fact, amnesty represented the fundamental base for union in the Popular Front since, beyond this question, each formation had its own interpretation of the likely scenario in the wake of a possible election victory for the coalition. For the republicans this was a second opportunity, by way of a new 14 April, while for the left-wing groups, victory meant a return to the reformist path, rectifying mistakes, until the start of the revolution. In the first case, Prieto's socialists, in the second, with different nuances, Largo Caballero's followers, with *ugetistas* and the youth associations, members of the POUM or the Syndicalist Party. Others outside the coalition, like some of the anarcho-syndicalists, saw in the possible triumph of the Left a prelude to resuming the journey begun in October1934 and channelling the revolution.[58]

The CNT, naturally, was also thinking of revolution, but without the prior step of an election victory, or any kind of alliance. The difficulties most libertarians had in accepting the popular front resulted, in part, from the experience of the first biennium. Spain needed a radical, revolutionary change, nothing to do with the actions of the republican-socialist government, which had consisted in "undertaking a revolution without attacking anything fundamental", which was impossible.[59]

The CNT and the February Elections

Although it has been said that the CNT conducted a less forceful abstentionist campaign than in 1933, the fact is that one needs to differentiate between, and qualify, the "official" position, the approach adopted by the leading militants and the confederal masses. Because reading the libertarian newspapers, examining the minutes of meetings and analysing the organisation's official communiques, one reaches the conclusion that the propaganda was intense and categorical, with little margin for interpretation. In any case, as voting day drew nearer, messages became ambiguous, the internal conflict grew and confusion spread throughout the organisation.

The national plenum of CNT regional federations, held at the end of January 1936, confirmed federal principles and refuted bourgeois democratic and parliamentary procedures, criticising "all parties" without recourse to stridency or "pernicious demagoguery".[60] The FAI, meanwhile, adhered to its abstentionist line and criticised the workers' organisations that established the revolutionary route in 1934 – the same one that they had boycotted – and were now becoming allies of the bourgeois parties. Their recipe was as familiar as it was generic, namely, not to consent to exploitation of man by man, promote the international struggle against fascism and employ the tactics of insurrection; in short, the FAI had "nothing to rectify".[61] For its part, the AIT reminded the CNT that there was no solution other than revolution. Any other recipe, including an election victory for the Left, was no "more than an illusion full of bitter disappointment".[62] What neither the CNT, nor FAI nor the AIT said, beyond the call for an impossible revolution, was how to get the thousands of prisoners out of jail, how to help unfairly sacked workers recover their jobs, how to restructure unions in order to continue the struggle against management and put an end to the loss of wages and employment rights, or how to escape hunger. To all these questions the three organisations had no answers.

In February itself, *Solidaridad Obrera* ran with the headlines: "The proletariat (...) should abstain"; "Elections distract popular attention (…) Electoral abstention!"; "Against criminal fascism, now and forever, not at the ballot box: in the streets"; "We have to fight the state, far from politics, within our own defence agency: the unions".[63] The national committee issued a manifesto, on 3 February, clearly indicating its abstentionist stance. The CNT was not worried about a victory for the Right because, in an explanation all too reminiscent of the 1933 elections, "this would lead all the enemies of the dictatorship to rise up once again",[64] in other words, the same strategy that led to the failure of the insurrection in December of that same year.

But beyond the official discourse, and however many times they repeated that "the Confederation has nothing to rectify", however many times they pointed to the "triumph" represented by the abstentionism in the 1933 elections[65] and the organisation's "revolutionary" actions in October 1934, these were still the wounds from which the organisation was bleeding. Wounds that immersed the movement in a sea of confusion, in "a multitude of discrepancies", as the national committee admitted, but also of contradictions.

General, maximalist considerations, which equated one government with another, democracies with dictatorships, because both were different forms of the apparatus that maintained "economic and state privilege".[66] Difficult positions to sustain given what had happened in Spain after the October uprising, but also in Europe, where the absence of rights and freedoms shaped the references of countries where democracies were falling and dictatorships advancing.

For their part, the Opposition Unions maintained their apolitical stance. Although their approach, in general, differed considerably from anarchist maximalism. Peiró, for example, stressed the difference between a reactionary, conservative government, and a liberal and democratic one. It was the latter that favoured the proletariat, because "the tyranny of the governments of the biennium, though great, (was) was incomparable to that of the Lerroux–Gil Robles government". All the monstrosities committed by the former, Casas Viejas included, were ridiculous in comparison to the repression in Asturias. The problem, as Peiró acknowledged, was how to remove the government without betraying one's convictions. The best thing was to "leave the working masses free of all moral coercion", but also to tell them: "Workers, if you are going to vote, vote against fascism!" At this point, Peiró was crystal clear, and once again showed his courage by declaring: "I have said, and I repeat it here, that if in opposition to the fascists governing us now a working-class electoral front were to appear, I would vote for the first time in my life". Although he was also guilty of contradiction when he said it was an "aberration" to advise the working masses to participate in the elections, when he was urging them to vote.[67] In this respect, Pestaña had been clearer, less "political".

The real problem was that neither the CNT nor the Opposition Unions were in any condition to free the prisoners, to force the readmission of sacked workers, never mind implement the revolution. However much militants as important as Durruti argued at rallies that they had to "pull the prisoners out of the jails", as this required strength they did not have, necessitated, he said, "organisation".[68] Which was what the CNT lacked at that time. Because, apart from the freefall in membership, its presence in society was on the wane. Rallies, conferences and meetings that during the early years of the Republic were crowded, now, at the end of 1935, offered a sorry sight. This was the case, for example, at the November rally organised by the CNT in the bullring in Valencia. *Solidaridad Obrera* only referred to the messages transmitted by the speakers who endorsed the confederal line against the *treintistas*, the "they're all the same", in reference to Lerroux and Azaña, or the never-ending revision of events in Catalonia in October 1934 in which everyone fought against the CNT and the FAI. But the newspaper maintained a telling silence, in comparison with its traditional headlines, in relation to the people who "crowded" the venue. A "multitude" that El *Combate Sindicalista* estimated to be "only (...) around 3,000 people", and which Villaverde, in a personal letter addressed to Avelino G. Entrialgo, described as "a dismal failure. It was pitiful seeing the Plaza completely empty".[69]

And once again, the repression showed no mercy with the confederal organisation. The police arrested the CNT national committee in a raid in early

December 1935, except for the secretary general, Horacio Martínez Prieto, who managed to escape. Prieto referred to "the scene of disarray" in which the main confederal body found itself, given the impossibility of providing the regional federations with confederal material, the dire shortage of membership cards, the absence of a postal address to receive correspondence and money transfers and the shortage of comrades to travel to regions where plenums were being held.[70]

In spite of its obvious weakness, there was no change in the CNT's official discourse. Barcelona trade unions, such as food and construction, urged the organisation to remain faithful to apolitical principles, "without intervening, either directly or indirectly, in the electoral contest". It was the "slogan of today, yesterday and always: Do not vote! Revolution!"[71] A strategy echoed by the extraordinary regional conference of unions of Catalonia, held at the end of January, which advocated carrying "out an apolitical and abstentionist campaign (...) (since) neither the contention of fascism, nor the release of the prisoners could be successfully achieved by voting". But one had to query the extent to which the abstentionist stance exhibited by the militants occupying positions on the confederal committees coincided with the CNT membership as a whole, a question hanging in the air at the conference of unions. Because apparently, the organisation was reluctant to consult its members, lest their opinion did not coincide with that expressed by their leaders. In fact, the Catalan regional committee hesitated to convene the conference, acknowledging that

> some comrades are somewhat apprehensive with regard to the possible threat to the ideals always maintained by the CNT if, after a long period of repression (...) (there were a) weakening of convictions, a turnaround, which not only jeopardised the anarchist effectiveness of our ideals, but harmed the opposition of members . . .[72]

In fact, the plenum addressed the accusation that agreements were reached in meetings of militants and not in union assemblies, in spite of which an attempt was made to "give the impression that these agreements reflected the will of the working class en masse". The atmosphere was so bad that the conference, aware that this was in violation of confederal rules, resolved not to ask delegates how the agreements being debated had been reached, in other words, in meetings of militants or union assemblies. In view of which many delegations understandably questioned the validity of the meeting itself.[73]

The official discourse, defended by the leaders, and that of the membership, clashed most clearly over the issue that attracted much of the public's attention, namely, the October repression, with particular reference to the "30,000 prisoners".[74] Which, basically, was a call to vote. In fact, many *cenetistas* saw no likely solution until elections were held, and mistrusted their leaders, since "if the CNT committees, as appears to be the case, encourages abstentionist comrades, the people will respond to such dire leadership with a gesture of scorn (that) would be disastrous for the organisation".[75] To a large degree, because the CNT would be seen to be disconnected from the population, as most of the proletariat would go to the ballot box and would vote for left-wing men to get the prisoners out of jail, but also because of the "wages of hunger". In short, for "fear that this state of things might persist".[76] It seemed, as the mother of a CNT prisoner said, that the CNT leaders were paving

> the way for the enemy. What happens to these people is incomprehensible; they rail against the established tyranny, the danger the latter represents to the small freedoms still enjoyed by the people, and then when it comes to providing solutions they play the same old record, increasingly impotent and amidst a sea of contradictions.[77]

Even the Galician *cenetista* José Villaverde, who took part in the occasional confederal rally before the elections, revealed himself in his personal correspondence to be very pessimistic about the resurgence of the CNT, and predicted that "if we do not make amends (...) the future will close its doors and open those of our tombs".[78]

The abstentionist position struck not only confederal members as negative, but also workers in general. The CNT speakers that took part in rallies had to be careful what they said, as in many towns they found it "difficult to comply with the agreements adopted by the Organisation" and had "to sidestep many questions in order not to give rise to divorces between unaware workers (sic)".[79] The conference of Catalan unions requested that the regional committee "avoid contradictions in acts of propaganda" and make it clear to participating comrades how "to focus their speeches", which led some of them to refuse to take part. Francisco Isgleas, opposed to the organisation's stance, refused to participate in rallies "until March, at which point he resumed apolitical and revolutionary propaganda".[80]

The Andalusia delegate at the confederal plenum, in January 1936, acknowledged that among the workers there was a current of sympathy towards left-wing parties "and a predisposition to go to the ballot box and vote for these parties"; the Aragón delegate, meanwhile, described the abstentionist propaganda as clumsiness, since "the popular mood is decidedly contrary"; and the Galician delegate added that: "we would make fools of ourselves". Catalonia differed most with all these stances, and called for abstention, although less vigorously than in 1933, declaring that the solution to problems would be provided by the unions; to which the Aragón representative replied by asking whether "Catalonia will make the revolution after the elections", to which the Catalan replied, "no". Well then, concluded the former, an abstentionist campaign was not possible. In spite of everything, as we have seen, the plenum reiterated the official position of abstention in the elections[81]. A debate that was repeated in the same terms in the FAI, with an identical result, since, as everyone knows, the anarchist organisation had "nothing to rectify".[82]

Although the official position appeared to be unalterable, the libertarian movement reached the final days of the campaign with discordant strategies, amidst confusion and ambiguity. *Solidaridad Obrera* argued, on the same day as the elections, that beyond the appropriateness of being "a voter or an abstentionist", if you want to create "a new world, then don't vote. Fight, redeem yourself, rebel and triumph". The Barcelona local federation insisted on abstention and disowned any manifesto published, including the sheets that appeared on the city's buildings, with the CNT's name, calling on people to vote. However, Badalona Manufacturing and Textile Union said that every worker was of legal age and knew how to "interpret the organisation's agreements", so the "freedom to think and act belongs to each individual".[83] The local federation of Hospitalet de Llobregat, at the 1936 congress, admitted that the position maintained was "confusing, so much so that it would have been better to tell people to vote".[84]

Prominent militants, from the Opposition Unions, the CNT and the FAI, advocated, beyond the official campaign, voting or abstaining, or both actions at the same time. Domingo Torres favoured voting, Peiró insisted on his "class" conditions, while Mascarell, secretary of the Opposition Unions national committee, advocated abstention.[85] There was also ambiguity on the part of some of his colleagues, like Juan López, who wanted to eradicate from workers' minds the illusion that the solution lay in Parliament, but counted on the electoral victory of the left – without saying who was going to vote – to unite the proletariat in workers' alliances and "channel the revolution".[86]

Faístas and *cenetistas* experienced a similar situation. Floreal Ocaña published an article, on the same day as the elections, in which he said that depositing one's voting paper in the ballot box contributed only to "the legal persecution, imprisonment and machine gunning of comrades engaged in a courageous struggle".[87] Isaac Puente spoke of "siren calls" that sought to seduce workers, but whoever voted helped "to strengthen the state" and those who abstained contributed "to undermine it".[88] However, Durruti announced, according to *Ramonín*, in *La Humanitat*, on 5 February, that he could not advise anybody not to vote.[89] Although Abad de Santillán went further and said that "only one working-class militant dared publically to recommend in a confederal rally a vote to obtain freedom for the prisoners: Buenaventura Durruti", before ending the paragraph with a fine dose of irony: "the hero of the ballot box boycott in 1933".[90] Abad de Santillán himself also contributed to the confusion, as he both regretted the identification of "progress and advance towards social justice with a political triumph of the so-called Left", and claimed that "not voting is just as pointless as going to the ballot box".[91] A confusing reflection that must have baffled a number of libertarians. Ultimately, it was the ambiguity tactic to avoid dirtying oneself in the "sludge" of voting and placing the responsibility of the membership; a circumstance arrived at out of pure impotence, as, in order to secure release of the prisoners, the ballot box was really the only route open.

Francisco Ascaso admitted after the election that he had "experienced misgivings about voting for this or that left-wing name (...) But he had voted for them because in this way he clearly expressed his solidarity with those waging the revolutionary struggle".[92] Others, like Abad de Santillán, exhibited their ideological "cleanliness" by declaring that some "of us do not go (to the ballot box) so as not to become accomplices of slavery", and maintaining that "right, left, centre, have the same program".[93] However, during the Civil War, he attacked "dogmatic inflexibility" as something artificial, "a foreign body within our beautiful ideal and within the flexibility required by all vital thinking in order to expand and assert itself in everyday events". The problem was, he now said, that "anti-election propaganda had become a routine that was not easily transcended", in which "principles and tactics were capriciously" shuffled by militants who failed to understand that a repeat of the November 1933 campaign would lead to the triumph of the Right, which was "fascism endorsed by the law and the people". Militants who presented themselves "as custodians of principles and intended to lecture us on Revolution and Anarchy". So he said that did not advocate abstention, but neither did he favour participation, because "it would have been interpreted as an abandonment of principles". Abad ended the article with a memorable sentence: "fortunately we were aided by the good instinct of the great masses" [94](...), who voted.

Ultimately, the official abstentionist campaign changed, in the days prior to the election, to messages in favour of voting, messages against and ambiguous messages that advocated the one and the other, the opposite and vice versa, everything and nothing. As Cesar M. Lorenzo has observed, the February 1936 election campaign placed a disorientated CNT in the tortuous maze of "apolitical politicking".[95]

Thankfully, most *cenetistas*, ignoring the official message, but also the most puritan militants and those who urged people to vote, but advocated both this and the opposite, voted for the Popular Front, and secured the release of the prisoners. Because the coalition achieved victory thanks to the general mobilisation of workers, largely motivated by the call for amnesty. The Right had obtained more votes than in 1933, but was surpassed by the Left. Although the difference in votes was not great, in terms of the number of MPs (on account of the electoral law) it was, and the Popular Front won 278 of the 450 seats in Parliament.[96] Two of these corresponded to members of the Syndicalist Party: Pestaña, who was elected as Member for Cadiz, and Benito Pabón, a lawyer who had defended the cenetistas in the trials following the December 1933 uprising, who was elected as an MP for Zaragoza, though as an independent.[97]

If the mobilisation of the workers, in general, was fundamental, the *cenetistas* voted in particularly large numbers. According to Diego Caro, the CNT's participation in Barcelona, Seville and Cádiz was decisive, while in Asturias, Valencia, Madrid, Huesca and Badajoz it had a significant influence. The CNT turnout was evident in places like Santa Coloma where, in 1933, abstention was as high as 59.2%, while in 1936 it fell to 37.3%; in San Adrià it dropped to 15%; and in Badalona it went from 44% to 24.8%. César M. Lorenzo notes that in Barcelona abstention was 27%, compared with 40% in 1933, while in Zaragoza it fell from 38% to 31%.[98]

Contemporary analysis of the election results attributed pride of place to the participation of the cenetistas. Gil Robles himself said that the anarchist and anarcho-syndicalist vote had been fundamental. One of the electoral keys for the Right was confederal abstention. The anarchist weekly *Tierra y Libertad* denounced the attempts by "Jesuit and fascist hordes" to bribe confederals, placing "at their disposition half a million pesetas to prevent a left-wing triumph on 16 February".[99] A fact to which Gil Robles also referred in his memoirs. Firstly in the case of the 1933 elections, when "somebody, who knew what they were doing from a conspiratorial and electoral point of view, subsidised the odd CNT leader so he would accentuate his suppressive tactics" in towns and villages of Cadiz; then, in the elections of February 1936, negotiations were aimed at "ensuring the CNT's abstention, by means of the payment of a sizeable sum of money".[100] An attempted bribe that Abad de Santillán said was directed at *cenetista* Vicente Ballester, whom "the Right approached with half a million pesetas so we would engage in the usual anti-electoral propaganda".[101]

For his part, Herbette identified the *cenetista* participation as primarily responsible for the electoral turnaround, since, despite the fact that the union maintained its abstentionist position, the Popular Front, with the promised amnesty, "obliged" it to vote. Other factors, in his opinion, had been crucial: the success of the left in mobilising the workers' and peasant masses and the question of the autonomies, in reference to Catalonia and the Basque Country. Both areas with different political realities: in the former, the dominance of the left, in the latter, of the right. Gil Robles's party failed to respect their autonomous rights, showing an exclusive interest in championing the unity of Spain.

The women's vote deserves special mention. In the 1933 elections, it had been seen as crucial to the victory of the centre-right, and now, in February 1936, it received a different interpretation. Women had increased their presence in the political life of the nation, a circumstance evidenced by the protests and demonstrations on the streets of Spain. The right-wing parties had thought that women's religious convictions would guarantee that their vote always went to the more conservative formations, closely linked to the Catholic Church. But reality eventually proved the Socialists right when in Parliament they supported female suffrage. Ultimately, Gil Robles had hoped, according to the French ambassador, to establish a regime similar to Portugal's, but conditions in republican Spain did not lend themselves to an imitation of Salazar, just as the Spain of Primo de Rivera could not mirror the Italy of Mussolini. Because Spain was "an individualistic nation" that had "major collective problems to resolve", a task that could only be accomplished "by freedom or revolution".[102]

The Right interpreted the latter as what happened in Spain when there was any kind of mobilisation of the popular masses. So no sooner had the Popular Front triumphed, than pressure was put upon the Prime Minister, Portela Valladares, to declare a state of war in Spain, something that did indeed occur in Zaragoza, Valencia, Oviedo and Alicante, although the order was revoked.[103] "Sabre rattling" could also be heard. Azaña alluded, in his memoirs, to the rumours of a military rebellion, like those which pointed to Franco and Goded, but which the republican leader played down because he saw "no.one prepared to take a serious gamble".[104] Meanwhile, the upper classes showed their fear when , a few days after the election, a number of members of Spanish right-wing parties crossed the border into France, where they crossed paths with left-wing compatriots, exiled since October 1934, who were returning to Spain.[105] Most of these new refugees remained in the south of France, while other "notable travellers" went to Paris, among others, according to the French police, Francisco Cambó, the Duke of Alba, Count Gonzalo Mora, the Count of the Andes, the Marquis of Viana, Antonio Goicoechea, Ángel Escaudon and Eduardo Aunos.[106] In the financial world, concern had reached "panic level", and the government had to intervene in the Stock Market to arrest the fall in value of government bonds.[107] The unions, meanwhile, denounced capital flight and the closure of factories, examples of the "capitalist boycott".[108]

At an international level, the Popular Front's victory was also a cause for concern. Britain and the USA were fearful of the impact upon their companies in Spain, mainly, on salaries and employment rights, but also vis-à-vis the possible readmission of sacked workers, as will be seen later. The US ambassador, little, spoke of "Bolshevik subversion", a very similar term, curiously enough, to the "triumph of Moscow", used by the German press to refer to the victory of the left-wing coalition.[109] For its part, the Vatican had made no secret of its hopes for a right-wing victory, so after the results were announced confessed to being "surprised and disappointed". Meanwhile, the Spanish Catholic Church expressed concern over the possible repetition of the events of May 31, and even the Bishop of Madrid voiced his intention to evacuate the convents. In any case, neither the Vatican nor the Spanish ecclesiastical hierarchy had concealed their support for the Right, nor hesitated to exhibit this during the election campaign, as had the Cardinal Archbishop de Toledo, whose sermons included an order to vote for conservative forces.[110]

In short, the Right acted without restraint, with a lack of balance, as Herbette observed, when he used Goethe's phrase: Hammer oder Ambose (Hammer or Anvil), to explain its situation, in other words, dominate or be dominated, there were no half measures. So "many people who had dreamed of being a hammer" did not resign themselves to acting as an anvil. Although the French ambassador, always worried about an uprising of the masses, acknowledged that workers and peasants expected changes that it was "impossible not to call revolutionary".[111]

Reconquest or Revolution

Azaña's return as prime minister had occurred, as he himself admitted, in the worst possible way. Portela Valladares had practically thrown in the towel, while "almost all the governors" had fled, "abandoning the provinces". Once again, as he put it, "the wheat had to be reaped before it was ripe".[112] Moreover, the new government was composed exclusively of republicans, following the PSOE's refusal, under pressure from Largo Caballero, to participate in a new government that might tread the same reformist path as in the first biennium.

So it was that the Popular Front, as such, disappeared after the election victory. Although the popular masses, who occupied the streets, conserved the spirit out of which it had been born.

Cities were filled with expressions of joy. 20,000 people, for example, took to the streets of Valencia and, when they passed the French consulate, saluted its flag with "applause and the Marseillaise", which recalled the first days of the Republic; and other celebrations, like the one held in Madrid, with some 25,000 people, substantially different from those, so distant, of 14 April. The presence of the political forces that had formed the electoral front was very unequal. The republicans, with tricolour flags – hegemonic in April 1931 – were few in number in comparison with the union delegations, socialists, communists and popular associations carrying red flags. Meanwhile, "the anarcho-syndicalists were barely in evidence". Those who were present, and particularly demonstrative of their joy, were women, "not only the wives of workers, but also women and girls belonging to the petite bourgeoisie". Enthusiasm that was also evident in other demonstrations where what predominated was a sense of justice. Like the crowd that accompanied around 900 inmates that left the prisons of Gijon and Oviedo, "most of the heading for the stations of Langreo and the North, to wait for the trains that would take them home".[113] Though there were also instances of churches and convents being burnt down, or uprisings in prisons, usually involving ordinary prisoners seeking to take advantage of the amnesty, like the mutiny in San Miguel de los Reyes prison, in Valencia, where various galleries were set fire to.[114] In this respect, the CNT led an important campaign in favour of a pardon for these prisoners, considering them also to be victims "of the capitalist social organisation".[115]

The atmosphere of jubilation, one might say of euphoria, which flooded the streets of the principal towns and cities of Spain, was even reflected in the confederal press. It is surprising that the CNT expressed its enthusiasm at the result of the elections when it had advocated abstention, attributing to the vote an importance that it had systematically denied. *Solidaridad Obrera* ran the headline: "the ballot boxes have accomplished their mission", and even congratulated the Confederation on being "the axis of the popular movement in Spain"; which was somewhat surprising, since the very same newspaper that invested rivers of ink to promote abstention, was now virtually proclaiming the CNT as winner of the elections. The point was that the organisation's interpretation of the significance of the Popular Front's election victory fluctuated between hope and reality. Because the coalition's victory, it was said, was not a political triumph, "however paradoxical and incomprehensible that might appear", but the triumph of the revolution. However, a minimum analysis of the CNT's situation and the primary objective of the popular demonstrations, which was none other than the release of the prisoners, made it necessary to qualify the stubbornly repeated discourse on the revolutionary moment. Thus the confederal press, while still "whipping up the masses for the revolutionary event", added a differentiating nuance vis-à-vis the past: "to begin the assault on our immediate goals".[116] It was obvious that "immediate goals" connected far better with workers' aspirations than the exclusively revolutionary end pursued without success over recent years.

Immediate goals amongst which amnesty occupied pride of place. In fact, it seemed almost impossible, as Azaña himself acknowledged, for people to wait "one month, until the new Parliament could vote on it".[117] So it was necessary to resort to the parliamentary standing committee, of the previous legislature, to adopt the amnesty decree on 21 February. The sense of urgency was a fair reflection of what was happening at the time, as those who had voted for the Popular Front mobilized and demanded that the government fulfil its electoral promises, starting with the amnesty; but they also wanted "justice to be done" regarding events in Asturias. The victims of which were not content with the proposed material compensation, and demanded prison sentences for the instigators and authors of the killings in Villafría, La Cabaña, the Pelayo garrison, the Modelo prison, Carbayín and Vega del Rey, among others, "places inhabited by bloody shadows" who cried out for "Justice!".[118]

The government, overwhelmed by the protests, tried to recover control by means of decrees. On the 21st, the amnesty decree, and on the 28th, the decree readmitting workers sacked, in the main, after the events of October 1934, but also the settlers and sharecroppers that had been evicted for defaulting on payments. This was followed by the re-appointment of town council members suspended without charges. But the mobilisations continued. Approximately 80,000 peasants from Andalusia, la Mancha and Extremadura, convened by the FNTT, and tired of waiting for land that never arrived, rushed to occupy land. Poverty drove these workers, part of the 428,000 unemployed in the countryside, out of a total of 800,000 in Spain.[119] The Ministry of Agriculture, headed by Ruiz Funes, issued a decree legalising the peasants' actions, in other words, the pressure bore fruit. As Edward Malefakis noted, "finally, land reform was becoming a reality", because from May to July 1936 seven times more land was distributed than during the previous five years, around 550,000 Ha, where some 110,000 peasants settled.[120]

In short, the spring of 1936 was not April 1931. Among other reasons, because the Socialists were not in government, and the confederal unions, together with the UGT and other workers' organisations, were in effervescence. Workers were applying pressure in the streets to achieve necessary changes, but also to recover improved salaries and working conditions already obtained during previous years but which employers, with the acquiescence of the authorities, had recently reversed. On 18 February, two days after the elections, the taxi section of the transport sector union initiated a struggle in pursuit of an eight-hour day. The single union of bakers requested "the recovery of stolen improvements" and proposed a set of work rules that were "another edition of those already propounded on countless occasions, a revised but not extended edition". The construction unions demanded a six-hour day, unification of salaries and tools provided by employers. The timber union succeeded in obtaining the improvements it had been fighting for four years , namely, a 44-hour working week and a new pay scale. In short, doing and undoing, in many cases starting again, as expressed in the demands submitted by the metallurgy single union, which contemplated "the reconquest of the 44 hours", as a question of dignity, added to which was the suppression of piecework.[121] The government, facing the possibility of a metallurgical strike that could affect almost 40,000 workers, addressed these demands via a decree, on 5 March, which restored the 44-hour week, which the radical governments had revoked in November 1934, returning to 48 hours.[122]

Among all the demands, the readmission of those sacked in the wake of the October movement occupied a prominent position. The word employed in the working-class press to refer to them was *seleccionados* (selected), which, in truth, clearly explained the reason for their expulsion from factories and jobs, in other words, those who had stood out in the union struggle. Although the government issued a decree, at the end of February, providing for the readmission of those sacked because of their ideas or for participating in political strikes since 1 January 1934 – a date imposed, apparently, by the Madrid unions in order to reinstate the typographers sacked by the *ABC* newspaper for staging a strike that month[123] – its application met with all kinds of resistance. On the one hand, on account of the compensation imposed: a minimum of 39 working days, a maximum of six months' salary. On the other, due to management's refusal to reinstate the most politicised workers. Management that was now expressing its concern for the workers it was going to have to dismiss, those scabs who, according to *Solidaridad Obrera*, "devoted themselves to breaking the October strikes and all the others staged in recent years", who took the jobs of and "condemned to hunger and desperation thousands of workers". Defence of jobs, as undertaken by *El Debate*, the CEDA mouthpiece, which the confederal newspaper described as "self-righteous Christianity", as then it went silent, with no reference to the suffering experienced by the families of sacked workers.[124]

So the reinstatement of the *seleccionados* was a slow process and became "a struggle from factory to factory". For example, in the Vulcano workshops, in the Casa Hierros Mateo and in Pirelli, which refused to reinstate the sacked workers that had gone on strike on 6 October, but also in 1930 and 1932. The railway workers demanded the "immediate reinstatement of those selected as a result of political and social incidents", while the Barcelona water unions demanded the readmission of all the *seleccionados*, including those who had been amnestied. The CNT union in Telefónica requested that a commission be set up to review the files of those sacked since October 1931.[125]

The international financial media criticised the compensation and readmissions, and came out in defence of the multinationals based in Spain. Thus, for example, the French rubber factory Klein Frères, located in Segovia, was forced to reinstate 60 workers, whilst the Agence de Crédit Lyonnais, in Madrid, and also French, had to do the same with 50 employees.[126] Companies that had benefitted from the government repression after the events of October, and now had to make amends. As occurred with the Anglo-Saxon company Río Tinto, which reached an agreement with its workers, during the first years of the Republic, to give heads of family a supplement of four pesetas in compensation for the reduction of the working week to five days. In 1934, both parties agreed to eliminate this supplement to prevent the expulsion of 1,000 workers, but after the events of October the company dismissed 3,000. Now, the tide had turned in the wake of the February elections, and the company had to reinstate some of the sacked employees, while the workers denied the validity of the company's unilateral rupture of the agreement in 1934, and demanded the re-establishment of the supplement for heads of households. The dispute concluded with an arbitrated sentence in favour of the workers that obliged the company to undertake retroactive payment of the quantities not paid between October 1934 and March 1936.[127]

Basically, there was no revolution under way. In the first place, because no organisation, and least of all the CNT, its main advocate, was in any condition to launch one. Secondly, because the vast majority of workers had voted, essentially, to free the prisoners, reinstate sacked employees and improve their own situation, not to achieve the revolution; thirdly, because the new government, formed exclusively by republicans, was not revolutionary, as was reflected in the Popular Front's programme. And, ultimately, because the main artifice of the election victory, in other words, Azaña, was not, in spite of right-wing accusations, a revolutionary, as was confirmed when, as Herbette had predicted, back in power, he once again fought against the most radical forces.[128] The republican leader wanted, at most, to recover the ideological foundations of the Republic and develop the reforms that it had been unable to conclude.

However, the experience accumulated by parties and unions, by bosses and workers, over the last four years, but also the advance of fascism in countries that, like Spain, had a democratic regime, exercised considerable influence when it came to deciding how to proceed. With the exception of the occupation of farms, more related to poverty and the needs of the peasantry than to a revolutionary movement, the objective of workers' actions was, beyond amnesty and the reinstatement of those who had been sacked, the recovery of the improved working conditions and pay rises obtained during the first years of the Republic and revoked in recent times. There were no widespread assaults on institutions of power, or attempted uprisings, or occupation of factories; there was legitimate and legal pressure, because legitimate and legal were the demonstrations and strikes to improve their living conditions. Protests that were not exclusive to Spain, for in France, the victory of the popular front, led by León Blum, occurred in the middle of a major wave of strikes called for similar reasons – poor working conditions, low wages, unemployment – in which French workers occupied factories, and which resulted in the signing of the Matignon agreements, with significant pay rises, paid holidays and the adoption of collective contracts.[129] Of course, there were isolated unlawful incidents, but they were not part of a revolutionary plan preconceived by any organisation. Including, obviously, the CNT, which, despite the usual revolutionary discourse, acted with a degree of caution and exhausted the channels of negotiation with employers.

In any case, the Confederation faced a major obstacle, which it would have to overcome immediately if it did not wish to be excluded, which was none other than the unity of the movement.

Reunification

The CNT national committee recognised, in April 1935, that, after the events of October of the previous year, the issue of the schism within the organisation had moved to a different level. If the union of the working-class forces had been fundamental, as had been demonstrated, in the greatest revolutionary effort of the republican period, any action required, as a prior step, the reunification of the movement itself.

Both organisations, CNT and Opposition Unions, arrived at this point with major problems, since neither had attained their primary objectives. The former had not been capable on its own of achieving revolution. What happened in October called into question its policy of opposing alliances and, therefore, the isolationism advocated by the anarchists. Added to which was the organic fragmentation and the loss of a considerable number of members. The Opposition Unions, meanwhile, were unable to capitalise on the industrial action and, in this way, occupy the ideological position inherent to revolutionary syndicalism. That which, without losing sight of the quest for an ideal society, maintained the struggle to improve workers' living conditions. In other words, the space that existed between the reformist syndicalism of the UGT and the anarchism that prevailed in the CNT. A space that gradually narrowed as the Socialist union encouraged a "revolutionary" discourse and the confederal organisation moderated its message after the events of October. Consequently, the Opposition Unions did not attract those thousands of workers lost by the CNT, and its membership remained modest in number, added to which there was a crisis of militancy similar to that which affected the Confederation. Its own press complained, in July 1935, that the revolutionary syndicalists did not provide "the necessary heat (…) Those who know how to write, do not (…) Those who can occupy positions in the organisation, retract, and the bulk of our members (…) do not express their concern regarding the present state of our affairs (…) Come down from your ivory towers and do something!".[130] Abandonment, laziness, which Pestaña described in graphic fashion in relation to events in the *feselista* organisation in Barcelona, where "they agreed to abandon the premises and share out the furniture that was in storage".[131] It was clear that both the CNT and the Opposition Unions were in crisis, but there was an important difference: the former had the strength of its initials. No trivial matter when both presented themselves as depositaries of the organisation's fundamental principles.

The confederal leadership had repeated it ad infinitum, while accusing the Opposition Unions of being traitors to the movement. The problem was that the latter maintained the same discourse, and accused the CNT of abandoning the principles of revolutionary syndicalism and not respecting the resolutions adopted in previous congresses. The Opposition Unions were not prepared, according to Peiró, to return liker the prodigal son "repentant, humiliated, begging forgiveness", because the prodigals were those who had tutored the CNT, and because they had squandered their inheritance. So they argued in favour of a return to "a CNT free of the burden of the anarchist groups", but not forgetting the insults and affronts of "reformists, politicians, traitors", a problem that demanded a rectification, without which unity would be a lie that would deceive "nobody, except ourselves".[132]

Ideological problems, perhaps the least difficult, and personal ambition, the worst, which ended up determining the form and the content of the reunification. The national committee stated, in April 1935, that "very little or nothing was done for a return to normality", instead of dissolving, the problem of the schism had become entrenched, exacerbated, even. Thus, for instance, at the plenum in May of that year, while Galicia was in favour of admitting those who had left and the Levante accepted a return without humiliation, Catalonia opposed "admissions of a collective nature" and advocated selection "with the filtering required by the moral abyss between both organisations", because they could not "accept the generalised admission of these collectives without delousing them". As simple as that. Therefore, the plenum's agreement, granting each regional federation freedom to resolve the issue as it saw fit, did not enjoy the support of Catalonia; a place where personal clashes dominated much of confederal life.[133]

For its part, in October 1935, the Opposition national committee, located in Catalonia, expressed its opposition to the reunification taking place on the basis of individual unions, as if it were the consequence of a stampede, denying them their status as organisation, with their committees and governing bodies.[134] Meanwhile, the CNT national committee, in its report for the May 1936 congress, called for an end to intransigence and avoidance of "giving preference to the prosecution and punishment of personal processes", disregarding "the detailed narration of the incidents that intensified the struggle between militants". Basically, the committee advocated "maximum discretion and tolerance, listening calmly and respectfully to the fundamental reasons that led those comrades to split from the Confederation", and gave the same advice to the Opposition Unions.[135]

In spite of everything, reunification, prior to the congress, was in the hands of each regional committee, which addressed the situation taking into account what had occurred at the time of the schism, but also the strength wielded by each group in its zone. Thus, for example, in places, like Galicia, where the clashes had not been particularly violent, the Union Oppositions agreed to rejoin the CNT on an unconditional basis. In the Levante, meanwhile, where the opposition was in the majority, the CNT regional committee needed to act very differently to in other places, like Catalonia, where the cenetistas formed a majority. The Levante federation was in favour of convening a regional plenum, also attended by the opposition, in order to analyse the causes pf the schism and attempt to find a solution.[136] In any case, it maintained a stance that cast doubts as to the true scope of its intentions or, at least, sought to maintain the power conferred upon it by its initials. A letter of January 1936, addressed, significantly, to the Opposition Union workers, not to its committees, invited them, in a paternalistic tone, to return "without records or ridiculous penance"; on an individual rather than a collective basis, however.[137] The Levante opposition unions and their secretary general, Juan López, were in favour of unity so avoided any kind of controversy. The agreement was adopted at the regional plenum of Levante CNT unions, held at the beginning of February 1936, which approved the entry of the opposition unions, given that they observed and accepted the agreements reached at the congresses, as well as the CNT's principles and tactics. The regional federation proposed to the national committee that all the Opposition and Autonomous Unions with a voice and a vote should be invited to the next congress for their definitive incorporation.[138]

In Catalonia, the situation was very different. With good reason, it had been the cradle of *treintismo* and of the ensuing schism. The origins were to be found in a major confrontation during which some unions left of their own will, but others were expelled. The solution was doubly complicated because it remained to be seen, on the one hand, whether the expelled unions wished to return and under what conditions, and, on the other, how they would be re-admitted. An issue rendered even more complex by the fact that the opposition unions were in the minority in the regional federation, so could only exercise a very limited amount of pressure.

The CNT union conference in Catalonia, in January 1936, revealed the different sensibilities in this respect. The Igualada local federation presented a document according to which the rivalry between "*faístas* and *treintistas*" had given rise to a "an acrimonious campaign of hatred and insults (that) transcended the original causes of the discord", resulting in "a fratricide brawl". But it regarded as erroneous the method being employed in an attempt to resolve the problem, in other words, trying to establish harmony in each locality, because in every town and village the conflict had been more personal and therefore "self-esteem" precluded reconciliation. This differed from the attitude of the Barcelona local federation, which was in favour of allowing each locality to act in autonomous fashion, with individual circumstances prevailing. Although the conference passed the motion proposed by Igualada – which consisted in unconditional acceptance of confederal principles, forgetting egocentricity and mutual renunciation of any kind of sanctions with the automatic merger in each locality of confederal and opposition unions – a caveat was added, at the suggestion of the construction union, granting localities autonomy to resolve the problem while the unions were informed of Igualada's proposal.[139] A ploy designed to defer the agreement *sine die* so unification took place locality by locality, with all that this implied.

It was obvious that the situation in the Levante and in Catalonia was very different, on account of both past history and the balance of power between the two sides in each regional federation, which affected the way in which the opposition was integrated. The situation reached a point where it resulted in a heated confrontation within the opposition unions, leaving them on the verge of their own schism. The Catalan opposition unions, assembled at a plenum in mid-March 1936 voted against entry, in spite of the CNT's demands to the contrary; moreover, they exceeded their own limits and went further than they had ever dared during the long years of schism, forming a union, namely, the *Federación Obrera Catalana* (Catalan Workers' Federation). The new union would occupy the space between the UGT and the CNT, with the aim of integrating all the previously excluded federal groups and on e or two other organisations from the region.[140]

For its part, the Levante organisation, where reunification was a fact, exerted pressure on the CNT with a view to its integration at the next congress. A circumstance that led to a clash between the national committee, headed by Manuel Mascarell, in Mataró, and the Levante regional federation. The Opposition Unions held a national conference at the end of March, which the Catalan organisation did not attend, a situation the Levante took advantage of in order to impose its pro-unity approach and oust the Mataró committee. As a result, the Levante regional committee occupied the national committee's position, while the conference unanimously approved a return to the CNT, prior to the confederal congress, which it would attend with the same rights as the other *cenetista* unions. The readmission procedure would be the same as that laid out at the Levante CNT union plenum at the beginning of February, described earlier. The new committee's first objective was to resolve the "schism of Catalonia".[141] A task that was sabotaged, as was revealed by the opposition unions' national committee circular, when it noted that "certain elements" in Catalonia did not issue their communiques so as to prevent the committees learning of the decisions taken at the conference held in Valencia; added to which was the disappearance of copies of *El Combate Sindicalista*, which they sent to Catalonia.[142]

The fact is that reunification had its detractor son both sides. If it was going to take place, it was, largely because of the need for unity, due to the events of October, and indispensable for the CNT's recovery; but also because workers demanded that unity in order to improve their working conditions. So the Catalan opposition unions' obstructionist tactics were replicated in the CNT. Germinal Esgleas recommended, in readiness for the next congress, "sharpening all the senses to avoid being victims of crafty deceit", although, employing his signature tone, he commented that it was "far from our intention to arouse suspicion (…) Salutary warnings, of the purest and most honourable purpose of our words, lest there be any shady element intent on poisoning issues". But maintaining the same as during the schism, in other words, the backbone of the CNT was formed by "the anarchist workers with the endorsement and support of the nuclei of workers". But what mattered was that comrades were "more anarchists than revolutionary syndicalists (…) and that their moral unity is not broken and is entrenched". Considerations recalled by Esgleas himself during the first months of the schism, when he declared that "if in order to safeguard principles and tactics, so as not to deviate from the revolutionary path, we lose almost all our members, we would prefer this to seeing the organisation become a shapeless leviathan".[143] Ultimately, the CNT as an anarchist organisation in the hands of anarchists "entrenched" in their principles, more as a sect than what it really was, a union.

But the misgivings about, if not to say opposition to, unity were not only apparent in the more extreme positions. Even Horacio Martínez Prieto said, recalling the moment, "I personally would never have re-admitted the opposition unions; but as CNT secretary general I abided by the organisation's needs".[144] So circumstances forced the national committee to invite the opposition and the autonomous unions to attend the confederal congress.

Wherever it occurred, as in the case of the Levante, the effects of reunification were immediate, as unions that had disappeared as a consequence of past events "re-emerged with more strength (...) in Valencia, in Alicante, Murcia, etc." The regional committee needed 5,000 membership cards, for Valencia alone, and warned that more would be needed "at once"; in fact, it had orders for 16,000. Workers turned up "en masse at their respective unions" and the committees found it impossible, they said, to attend all those asking to be reincorporated.[145] In spite of the likely exaggeration of the numbers, the fact is that the CNT recovered part of its lost membership. The Levante CNT had paid a high price for the schism, with membership falling from 99,741 in January 1932, to 70,295 in summer of the same year, and to 13,612 in February 1936; in other words, it had lost over 85% of its members in four years.[146] Reunification brought a degree of recovery, as at the Zaragoza confederal congress in May 1936, the Levante regional confederation membership stood at 48,950.[147]

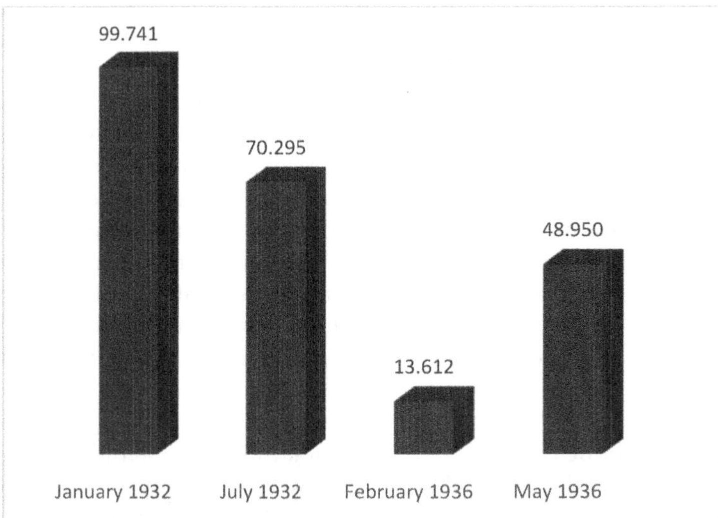

Figure 10 Membership in The Levante, 1932–1936.

The mise-en-scène of confederal unity took place at a rally held at the Monumental bullring in Barcelona, on 25 April, presided over the CNT secretary general, with the participation of Domingo Torres and Juan López, from the opposition unions. But each organisation's stance vis-à-vis the event was very different. The Opposition Unions' national committee accepted with resignation the only option open to it, hoping that the future cull of comrades in Catalonia would not disclose its policy of unity. Consequently, it insisted in its discourse on "drowning the attempts to promote states of passion", on the part of those who showed no desire for unification, for these attempts did not reflect the feelings of the working masses, but were "the results of egocentricity and passions that, though very human, (were) not in keeping with the demands of the moment".[148] Meanwhile, *Solidaridad Obrera* took advantage of its report on the meeting to demonstrate who the clear victor was: "the Opposition Unions have purged themselves. The elements corrupted by politics left the field of union ideas via direct action", those that have remained "faithful to the libertarian revolutionary cause are returning to our ranks".[149]

A return that would take place at one of the most important congresses in the history of the CNT.

The Zaragoza Congress

The CNT assembled at the Iris Park Theatre in Zaragoza on 1 May 1936. 550,595 members were represented – 60,621 of whom belonged to the opposition unions – with 649 from 982 unions.[150] Membership was slightly less than at the Conservatorio Congress, in 1931, which totalled 602,986, and far from the peak of autumn 1931 of approximately 800,000. However, it represented a sizeable increase after the steady decline in membership of the organisation since the spring of 1932, which led to a low of around 200,000 members in February 1935.[151]

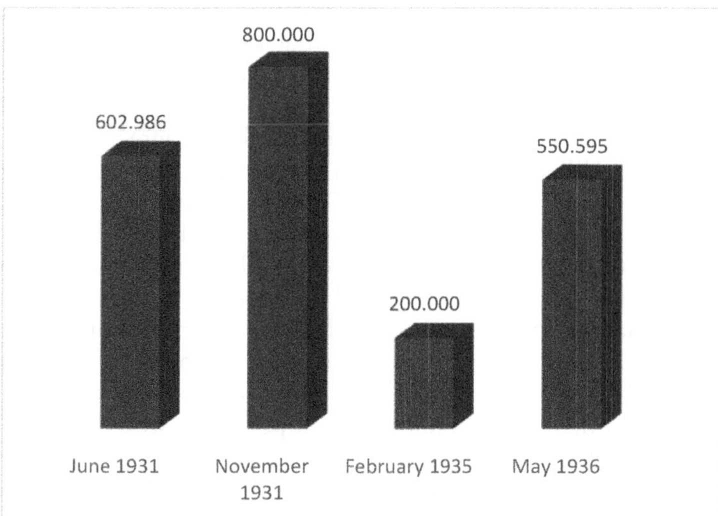

Figure 11 CNT Membership During the Second Republic, 1931–1936.

The CNT's recovery was mainly due to the circumstances of the moment, more than to the actions of the confederal leadership. The enthusiastic response to the Popular Front's victory had seen thousands of workers take to the streets. They saw how their protests succeeded in correcting the course taken by the Republic, and turned up at the unions en masse, seeking strength in numbers to recover what had been lost. Meanwhile, the confederal leaders had done little to improve the CNT's situation. Their main activities, such as insurrectional movements, repeated calls for strikes and protests, isolationism and even its conduct during the key revolutionary moment experienced by the Republic, resulted in abject failure, without the slightest evidence of rectification. The real problems facing both the organisation – prisoners, falling membership, division, disorganisation and destructuring of the unions – and workers – unemployment, pay cuts and loss of rights – were circumvented by hanging onto principles, without offering any practical solution beyond the illusion of revolution. Principles that had become the spar of driftwood to which its shipwrecked leaders clung, unaware that they might also be the burden that threatened to sink the organisation. The solution to this extreme situation came, contrary to their strategy, with the "disobedience" of the working class and the ensuing election victory. However, the principal CNT leaders arrived at the Zaragoza conclave bolstered by a recovery that had little to do with them, but which they knew how to exploit.

Facing the congress was the challenge of tackling fundamental issues: some from the recent past, which required analysis; others pertaining to the future, which would have to be addressed. Among the former, most importantly, the two failed insurrections and the confederal actions in October 1934. Among the latter, the reunification of the movement, the union alliance and the concept of libertarian communism. The agreements reached in relation to all these questions revealed an organisation that invariably followed the same criteria that it had maintained during recent years, without the reality of experience altering its approach or its actions. Because, though the debates were intense and things were said clearly and firmly, the agreements evidenced an organisation indifferent to criticism, in which each group was satisfied with implementing its short-term strategy. Thus, for example, the Opposition Unions, aware of their inferiority and with the significant absence of Juan Peiró, who was unable to attend the congress, settled for their reincorporation into the CNT, in a manner that disguised their failure. Those in the majority, anarchists and faístas, maintained their "ideological purity", isolation from the exterior and indifference to any criticism, aware of the position of strength afforded them by control of the main committees. As a result, the resolutions adopted reflected their strategy and, more importantly, would have effect for as long as they wished.

The focal point of the congress, as has been indicated, was reunification, which unsurprisingly was the first item on the agenda. All the sessions, and this one in particular, "unfolded in an atmosphere charged with tension". The opposition unions arrived in a state of disunity, since although those from the Levante and Huelva had resolved their situation within the respective regional confederations and, therefore, were present as CNT members and not as Opposition Unions, in other words, with voice and vote, their Catalan counterparts, far from reaching an agreement in their regional committee, continued in opposition so their presence was merely informative, and their intervention restricted to this question. The Opposition Union delegates took stock of the events of recent years, with strong criticism of the actions of the anarchists in the CNT, while they insisted that they had been the staunchest supporters of confederal principles and congressional agreements.

Their reply underlined the importance of the revolutionary moment squandered on 14 April and the change imposed upon the CNT by the anarchists. This was pointed out by the Barcelona Manufacturing and Textile Union, to which Durruti, Ascaso and García Oliver belonged, which played a leading role throughout the congress. The latter argued that the schism had been no more than the "launch" of the two currents that had simmering in the organisation for some time, and which had clashed, in the main, owing to differences vis-à-vis the optimum moment for the revolution. The winners of the conflict, anarchists and faístas, had given the organisation a new perspective, promoting "national struggles on a grand scale" at the expense of individual trade union struggles against management. In short, the CNT had become "the global hope for a libertarian communist society".

But the general recommendation was "not to look to the past", because memory and analysis of the past was an obstacle to unity. This was the ultimate objective to which any action had to be subordinated. So the anarchist majority adopted an opinion in line with its approaches and ignoring those of the opposition. The motion stated given there was agreement that the conditions necessary for the revolution now existed, a revolution that appeared to be the main source of discord, there was no longer any obstacle to unity; that said, it was emphasised that the solution depended on the Opposition Unions' compliance with the principles and tactics approved in confederal congresses. In other words, the opposition unions' arguments fell on deaf ears. The latter expressed their displeasure at the procedure approved, including the fact that the regional federations, where the schism continued, had to convene assemblies to implement mergers in each locality and, subsequently, hold a congress to seal unity. The proposal left the door open to the purges that were perceived to be inversely proportional to the size of the decision-making body.

The congress had allowed the opposition unions to rant and rave and proclaim their truths, but without admitting any of their arguments. Ultimately, the agreement was no more than a parody in order to muddle through which neither of the two parties believed in, but which they accepted given the particular circumstances. For this reason, it was approved by a majority but not unanimously, as would have been desirable.[152] The "Phantom Federation" itself, headed by Federica Montseny, declared, after the congress, that "everything else was forgotten and ignored for the sake of unity". Federica, who had played such a prominent part in the schism, repeated an age-old discourse that, without reflecting upon her own role in the decline of the CNT, stressed what had been the essential problem: the power struggle within the organisation. So she urged the anarchists to "ensure the prestige of our ideas and their influence within the CNT". Because the internal division, she insisted, continued, and the objective remained the same. In other words, "let us deploy the necessary activity for positions of responsibility to remain in the hands of those who have guided the CNT during periods of persecution and who logically have the right to continue guiding it".[153] Federica placed the accent, once again, on control of the steering bodies, committees that, in theory, had no executive power but which, in reality, had a decisive influence in confederal life.

In this respect, one only has to remember the *Federaciones Nacionales de Industria* (FNI) which, in spite of being approved at the previous congress, had a minimum impact. The anarchists employed every possible ruse to hinder their constitution.[154] The Centre regional federation, at the national plenum in April 1932, attempted to bring about their constitution, and achieved acceptance of the implementation of the agreements reached at the last congress,[155] as if the regional federations could rule upon the implementation or not of what had been approved by the supreme confederal decision-making organ. But Progeso Alfarache said, in February 1933, that there was not yet "one single note from the National Committee pointing in this direction. Not one letter". Alfarache himself provided the explanation: "those who took over on the Confederal Committee (…) did not share (…) the criteria that prevailed in the Congress", in other words, the new national committee, in anarchist hands, imposed its particular convictions and ignored its responsibilities.[156] Two months later, in May 1933, the national committee asked the regional federations if they regarded the FNI as necessary and, if so, what should be their true function or whether it should continue as agreed by the previous congress. [157]In short, agreements reached at the highest level were not respected, which the opposition union press described as "absolute sabotage" that equated to the virtual non-existence of the FNI.[158]

These federations, forgotten in a drawer, were presented with another of the main issues at the congress: the workers' alliance. In this respect, it should be noted, on the one hand, that emphasis was placed on its evolutionary nature, which overshadowed its other purpose, detaining fascism; and, on the other hand, the essence of the example of Asturias was forgotten, despite the fact that the spectre of the CNT's conduct in October 1934 was omnipresent at the meeting. The national committee itself recommended, once again, no focusing on individual events, so as to address this issue from a doctrinal and tactical point of view.[159] Although it has always been said that the approval of this point was a consequence of what happened in Asturias, the fact is that both analysis of the minutes and the agreement reached, and the actions subsequent to the congress, question this interpretation and take the organisation far back in time.

The motion on the workers' alliance (which was entitled *Alianza Revolucionaria*) began with an attack on the UGT and the PSOE as servants and collaborators of republican democracy. A collaboration that had divided the proletariat and seen it lose some of its revolutionary courage. The solution was unity between the two major union organisations in order to achieve revolution, bearing in mind the working-class's fervent desire to overthrow the existing political and social regime. Consequently, the CNT had to convince the UGT to accept a revolutionary pact under the following conditions: implicit acknowledgement of the failure of the system of political and parliamentary collaboration and implementation of a genuine social revolution, in other words, complete destruction of the political and social regime that regulated the life of the country. The form of coexistence born of the revolution would be freely decided by the workers and its defence would require unity of action, putting aside the interests of each movement.

Beyond considerations regarding responsibility for the division of the proletariat or the working-class's fervent desire to overthrow the existing regime, the fact was that an alliance between different organisations made it necessary to compromise, to abandon some of one's own ideas for the sake of a common good. However, the motion was based on anarchist principles that were considered indisputable, whilst those of the UGT were ignored. A strange method of seeking to reach an agreement with another organisation, if indeed that was really the intention. Because, as we shall see later, the motion was addressed not to the socialist union, but to its members. Thus, in contrast with a syndicalist proposal that aspired to revolutionary union with all the workers' parties, the anarchist motion rejected not only the pact with parties but with any organ connected to them, which in this case meant the UGT. Furthermore, the Barcelona Manufacturing and Textile Union, with García Oliver at the helm, proposed and additional article, which reflected the prevailing mistrust – in truth, a precaution against a future change in committee leadership – by attributing to the aforementioned points a provisional nature. So that when the Alliance were formed, two national liaison committees would be appointed which would define both organisations' points of view and draft a joint motion that would be discussed and put to referendum before the unions of both organisations. The result would be accepted, as a definitive agreement, provided it received at least 75% of votes. Ultimately, it had to be the unions, and not their leaders, "or what we could call bosses", who would approve the union.[160] The Congress adopted the motion, which it extended with the additional article, in a vote with the following results: unions against, 12; in favour without the addition, 62; in favour with the addition, 822.

Such a clear result did not preclude suspicion vis-à-vis two long-standing issues, namely the authenticity of the representation and the voting system. The Graphic Arts Union of Barcelona requested that the minutes of the agreements with the unions be examined to check that they corresponded with the views expressed by the delegates at the congress. Meanwhile, some unions, like the Construction Union of Madrid, protested because the agreements were being adopted outside confederal regulations, since one vote was assigned to each union when they should have applied the system of `proportional representation approved at the last congress. A circumstance that, as one recalls, had been very present in more than one assembly that had ended in schism. The national committee intervened to say that congresses were places for compromise.[161]

Solidaridad Obrera spoke, straight after the vote, of the union "that we call for now", as in truth it bore little resemblance to its predecessor. Because, far from the teachings of the Asturias CNT and its pact with the other workers' organisations, it refuted any agreement with political parties, and should only pact with the UGT when it had accepted "the revolutionary concepts proposed by the CNT".[162] The national committee sent a letter to the UGT leadership in order to "open negotiations", detailing the reflections and fundamentals of the adopted motion, including the PSOE's and the UGT's alleged responsibility in the division of the proletariat, the need openly to admit their failure and to end collaboration with the prevailing regime. The UGT opted for moderation, and accepted the proposal in principle, but postponed the definitive decision until a future congress. Meanwhile, the CNT decided to goad the *ugetista* members into challenging their leadership. The highest confederal body advised the regional federations to conduct a propaganda campaign "in skilful fashion (and) instil in the UGT workers the desire for that congress to be held so as to reveal the real and public thinking of the UGT leaders". By real thinking, it was referring to a supposed agreement with government to prevent strikes from being convened. Consequently, the CNT committee sought to promote "social conflict wherever need produced it and thereby convince *ugetista* workers to defy the orders issued by their executive committee". A strategy designed to present "the UGT leaders with the following dilemma: in favour of the Revolutionary Alliance or of collaboration with bourgeois society".[163] The CNT appeared to be returning to the approach approved in 1919, when instead of unity, the decision was taken simply to absorb the socialist union.

The question of the workers' alliance was related to the October 1934 movement which, along with the uprisings of January and December 1933, was also a matter for consideration by the congress under the heading of "Examination of Activities". The arguments employed by delegates have already been described in earlier pages. But it is worthwhile briefly considering the intervention by the representative of the Pasajes Fishing Industry – possibly Galo Díez -[164]as an example of how the congress addressed questions in clear and open fashion, but also how, despite the bitter criticism, the organisation appeared not to listen or, at the very least, did not react. Díez commented on how the CNT organised protests with no support other than that provided by its militants. This was the case in the insurrection of January 1933, with the participation "of everyone except the workers". According to Díez it was necessary to promote, in contrast to García Oliver's approach, local (trade) movements, based on the latter's vital need to "recover from seven years of dictatorship", instead of "spending all their time organising revolutions". Because the proletariat, in the wake of the dictatorship, needed to fan democratic hopes and required time in order to disabuse itself and "join the ranks of the revolution". However, the revolutions promoted were more Jacobin than anarchist; more related to the action of groups than to "a revolution of the People". Revolutions that lacked the necessary convergence between a set of circumstances and organic preparation. Thus, given the failure of the insurrections of January and December and the advance of the Right, there was a desire for collaboration with other parties, resulting in the workers' alliance. But that action, which was logical, was not understood within the organisation, and the consequence was "war between comrades". Díez ended his intervention, sounding like a voice in the wilderness, with the October 1934 movement in which, beyond the false revolutionaryism of Largo Caballero, the CNT should have appreciated the coincidence in immediate objectives, instead of attacking the socialists and "not giving signs of life" or, at least, declaring a general strike.

Indeed, the October movement was the source of much of the criticism that the Asturian regional federation directed at the national committee headed by Yoldi, which attributed its actions to the plenary agreements at the time and the information sent by delegates from Madrid and Barcelona. The debate displayed the weaknesses, contradictions and, above all, the failure of the insurrections. Which did not prevent García Oliver, who had been particularly involved in the January 1933 movement, from continuing to advocate the creation of armed militia in the unions. This was what he proposed during the motion on libertarian communism. The congress rejected the proposal, after Cipriano Mera, representing the Madrid Construction Union, declared: "Let comrade García Oliver tell us what colour he wants the insignia!"; to which Oliver replied, years later, that later it was Mera who, during the Civil War, accepted militarisation and the army insignia.[165]

As well as the insurrectional movements, the hard-hitting analysis of events also addressed the CNT's abstentionist during the elections, the strikes organised and the lack of commitment in compliance with congressional agreements, as was the case of the FNI. However, in spite of everything, and as usual, the congress expressed its approval of the national committee's work.[166]

Finally, participants addressed the question of the definition of libertarian communism, one of the most eagerly awaited subjects, given that it would lay the foundations of the libertarian society of the future. For while socialists and communists could contemplate the real existence of their kind of society, the anarchists and anarcho-syndicalists had yet to see theirs. The libertarians had engaged in an intense theoretical debate, over decades, with regard to what should be the nature of that new society that would follow the violent action that precedes any revolution. In this, as in so many other debates in the libertarian world, there were many different positions. Suffice it to recall that at the Zaragoza Congress there were 150 proposed definitions of libertarian communism.

Ideas that can be condensed, briefly, into two stances: on the one hand, the anarcho-syndicalist position, with Juan Peiró at the helm; on the other, the one defended by individuals such as Isaac Puente or Federico Urales – with their differences – that can be described as anarchist. The former supported the union, not only as fundamental element of the economic struggle against capitalism, but as the only entity capable of replacing the governing bodies of the capitalist economy and fulfilling the fundamental role of agent of social transformation. In this respect, Peiró was particularly keen to separate the act of initial force, which would be the insurrection per se, from the revolution. In a series of articles he published in *Sindicalismo*, in mid-1933, influenced no doubt by the insurrectionist course that the CNT was steering, he criticised thinking that placed the emphasis more on destroying than building. Peiró wrote that "anarchism is set on destroying that which it is unable to overcome"[167]. For him the revolution was not the fact of violently taking to the streets against the power of capitalism and the state. Revolution was not only "taking possession of factories, land, mines, railways, means of production", that was only the first part. True revolution came after that violent phase. The unions should concentrate on the task of organising the production and distribution of the articles required by society.[168] Organisation of production that he would assign to factory committees, industry unions, local, county and regional federations and the national federations of industry, the supreme authority that would articulate production, work and consumption.[169] Ultimately, the constructive solution of anarcho-syndicalism, within the ideological tenets of revolutionary syndicalism, was the central instrument of social transformation. In this construction, as has already been noted, the municipality, federatively structured, would be the political complement to the economic system built upon the union and the industry federations.[170]

But it was the anarchist strategy advocated by Urales and Puente that eventually shaped the essence of the definition adopted at the Zaragoza Congress. They were of the opinion that both insurrection, in other words, the violent phase, and revolution involved a fair degree of improvisation and spontaneity, not everything had to be planned. The revolution would have its origins in rural, not urban areas. Hence, the pre-eminence of the free commune as a basic element in the new society, which Puente completed with the union. Once each locality was well managed and organised, the whole would be harmonious and national consensus perfect. Urales, meanwhile, placed particular emphasis upon individual independence, as the basis for new society. He also preferred the rural environment to the industrial urban one because, he said, Spanish anarchism was modest. He did not believe in the anarchism of great industrial federations, his "was of municipalities, first, counties, next, and of nation, later. We are in love with a very simple anarchism".[171]

The opinion on the confederal concept of libertarian communism adopted at the congress advocated the abolition of private property, the state and the principle of authority; a libertarian commune would be created in each locality, would seize all the bourgeoisie's possessions and would be where producers from all sectors, assembled in unions, would freely decide the way in which work was to be organised. In the communes there would be workshop and factory councils; in the countryside, farm councils, which would federate until all the producers formed "the Iberian Confederation"; and the communes, "the Libertarian Communes of the Peninsula". The opinion included sections that developed these communes and their functioning in very generic fashion: the individual, the commune and the federation; relations and exchange of goods; the family and sexual relations; the question of religion; the teaching of art, science and free experimentation, etc. A society in which all its components would prepare to "fulfil the voluntary task of making their contribution to the collective". The opinion was adopted unanimously, and was put to referendum before the unions with an additional proposal declaring that the motion considered it necessary to create a commission of five comrades to articulate it in more complete fashion and with the necessary technical guidance.

In conclusion, the opinion prioritised educational questions and personal relations over economic issues, which, to a large degree, were side-lined. In fact, some unions voiced their misgivings. For example, the Gijon Graphic Arts delegate said that "spiritually, we endorse the opinion. As the representative of an organisation that is not anarchist I cannot endorse it, as neither is the Organisation"; the Valencia water, Gas and Electricity asked that "the Motion not forget, nor the delegates, that this is not an anarchist congress. It is a CNT congress".[172] The truth is that such important issues were ignored as the way of achieving this keenly awaited libertarian society, but also how to organise the production and distribution of products, generalities apart. Spontaneity and improvisation were the pillars of the construction of libertarian communism. This was the opinion of Abad de Santillán, who, after describing as "poor and unsustainable" the concept adopted, criticised the fact that there was discussion "of the family, of crime, of jealousy, of nudity and of many other things", but barely "a word about work, the work place, the organisation of production".[173] Horacio Martínez Prieto, secretary general of the national committee, criticised the utopian nature of the opinion[174]. Utopian and seemingly incomprehensible to most, as the CNT itself, at the AIT congress, in 1953, requested a text that provided a clear explanation of libertarian communism, which could be understood by all and not only by "great minds".[175]

Beyond the opinion adopted and the anarcho-syndicalist, I should like to add a third project, advocated by Abad de Santillán, who had initially supported essentially anarchist positions. In fact, at the AIT congress held in Madrid in 1931, to which I referred in the first chapter, he clashed with the anarcho-syndicalists who defended ruralism and improvisation. However, his stance underwent significant modifications depending on the actions of the anarchists during the republic. The change began to be evident in 1933, and was obvious after the events of October 1934. In his book, *El organismo económico de la revolución*, he outlined the economic structure that, in his view, the new society should have, ranging from factory councils to the federal council on economy, the main coordination centre in the country, with unions, branch councils, local councils and national federations of branch councils.[176] In his evolution, he rejected the anarchist ruralist conception and began to accept the necessary intervention of the unions in the management of the revolutionary economy.

But there is one aspect of Abad de Santillán's vision that merits particular attention: the "harmonious cooperation" between all currents of socialism. As early as 1934, he published an article in *Tiempos Nuevos* indicating the need for revolutionary forces to be united with regard to the economy, though admitting diversity in social organisation. In other words, after the revolution there would be "equitable production and distribution created by all", but each person would promote "the form of social coexistence" that it preferred.[177] An approach that, to a large extent, was corroborated by the events of October 1934 in Asturias, where each political force organised life in the locality under its control, for example, in Sama de Langreo, in socialist fashion, or in La Felguera, along anarchist lines. Abad de Santillán appeared to be seeking a synthesis that would be indispensable given the need to unite the working-class forces in order to achieve the revolution.

But while that libertarian society was arriving, the CNT had to tackle problems of the moment that, spite of their importance, were the subject of rather brief discussion. In the first place, the problem of unemployment, which had risen steadily since the advent of the Republic; from the approximately 300,000 unemployed in June 1931, to 389,000, in January of the following year, 619,000 in December 1933, 666,000 in March 1934, 711,000 year later, and over 800,000 in June 1936.[178]

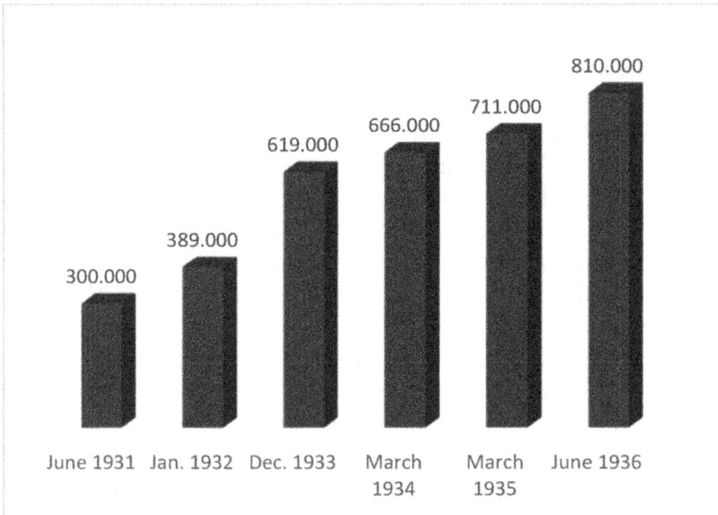

Figure 12 Unemployed in Spain, 1931–1936.

The motion indicated two clearly identifiable problems, "the growing development of machinism and the increasing emergence of women in the world of production". The latter a somewhat surprising affirmation if we bear in mind that it was precisely the libertarian world that had always argued in favour of the emancipation of women. But these notions have to be situated in the context of the time in order to be understood in their true dimension. In any case, the definitive solution was none other than, as was repeated time and time again, eliminating the capitalist regime by means of social revolution. But until then, the proposal continued to be the reduction of the working day: a 36-hour week, without cutting salaries and in the hope that employers would take on more workers; combined with the abolition of piece-work, bonuses and overtime and the creation of labour exchanges in the unions, without ruling out the seizure of factories, to be exploited by the unions, in the event of closure. To all this were added two approaches to be taken into account: on the one hand, it demanded "of the State, Municipalities and Provincial Councils the intensification of public works", which was a change of stance in comparison with early republican times, when any request to the state was seen as treason; and, on the other, it expressed opposition to unemployment benefit, which had been introduced in England, and which the CNT had no hesitation in describing as an "utter failure", because it meant economic ruin for the country "with millions of unemployed people having to be parasitically sustained" with miserable sums that were no more than investments in a work of philanthropy "that neither reproduced nor created wealth".[179] Although, almost certainly, rather than thinking of the nation's economy, the aim was to avoid the possible "numbing" of that vanguard represented by the unemployed in uprisings and protests.

With regard to the agricultural question, the CNT had not yet been able to create a body at a national level, as the UGT had with the FNTT. The national federation of peasants – in the image of the national federations of industry – did not yet exist, in spite of the agreements that had been signed. So agricultural workers still belonged to the mixed unions. Added to this situation, which revealed the organisation's weakness in the rural spheres, was the opposition to land reform, so attractive to a collective of millions of workers that lived in hunger and poverty. The motion acknowledged that it was not possible to reject the benefits the land reform offered the peasantry, because those who suffered from deprivation took advantage of those benefits. The reappearance of Peiro's fatal law, which questioned any action depending on need and convenience. The organisation was aware of the reality but ideology conditioned the solution, which led to a "blind alley". The way out, in accordance with principles, was to accept the reform, but collectively rather than individually; "the land should not belong to those who work it", as the Marxists claimed, "but for the collective". In the end the congress approved expropriation without compensation of estates of over 50 Ha. to be handed over to the unions for collective exploitation.[180]

The congress was drawing to a close. The meeting had served to evidence the strength of anarchists and *faístas* who, despite having taken the CNT to the edge of extinction, still controlled the organisation and emerged victorious from such an important conclave. The schism and the insurrections had occupied much of the debate, but, in spite of the harsh criticism received, there was not the slightest gesture suggesting a change of direction. Reunification in Catalonia, the main anarchist stronghold, was going to take place in accordance with their wishes, in other words, locality by locality, which meant the likelihood of personal clashes that would complicate the process; the country's situation was once again described as revolutionary, just as at each and every previous moment; the solution to unemployment or the agrarian crisis pointed, invariably, to revolution. All this without the least consideration of whether the workers approved of this objective and, therefore, necessary assessment of how much support they could count on. Support that, obviously, required the participation of other organisations if things were going to be changed. But the issue of the workers' alliance, which seemed to be moving towards a rectification, ended up being a ratification of what had been advocated during previous decades, with requirements, conditions and actions that were unlikely to culminate in any kind of coalition. Until they succeeded in implementing their concept of libertarian communism, to the detriment of other solutions more in line not only with the real situation of the CNT, a union, but with its ideological foundation, which was none other than revolutionary syndicalism. Meanwhile, the anarcho-syndicalist opposition, beyond the proclamation of "its truths", did little and, consequently, achieved nothing. They neither went to battle nor defended projects that were fundamental for the organisation, like the union structure approved at the 1931 congress, which was simply disregarded. They surrended for the sake of a unity that was more fictitious than real.

The *faísta* victory was also reflected in a national committee that had revealed too many difficulties in its pre-congressional strategy. Horacio Martínez Prieto resigned as secretary general after the closing rally. Mariano Rodríguez Vázquez, alias *Marianet*, took over leadership of the new committee that was set up in Madrid. According to Horacio, *Marianet* had moved from Murcia to Catalonia as a child, and later joined the Barcelona Construction Union, "where it was said that he was the leader of the hard men, of the extremists who purged the union of its '*treintista*' residue and of ambushed communists", and situated in the "Oliverista and *faísta* clan in *Solidaridad Obrera*".[181]

Despite the clear victory, Federica Montseny argued that the congress had been "in a way disastrous for anarchist ideals, which had lost ground, influence and purity (...) We have been forced to make a series of compromises for the sake of a lesser evil, which, at the end of the day, may be the beginning of an elimination of the anarchist spirit within the CNT". A return to the false victimhood that, ultimately, did not conceal her ambition for power and control of the organisation, when she said that "never has it been as necessary as it is now for us to take action in the confederal media, on the podium, in the press (...) To prevent the great dream of freedom and justice (...) from being shattered, once again, with the destiny of Spain's proletariat falling into the hands of the usual profiteers".[182] The power struggle continued within the CNT.

The Last Republican Months

The government had responded quickly to the protests that filled the streets, such as those demanding an amnesty. But it maintained a far more lackadaisical attitude in employment issues. Pay rises, readmission of sacked workers and recovery of lost rights continued to be the main demands that fuelled disputes during the months following the confederal congress. The government asked for patience, but the workers were in a hurry to recover what he been taken away from them. Largo Caballero himself, no advocate of calling strikes, said that "when the Right triumphs we are persecuted and when democracy triumphs we are asked for patience, common sense and reflection".[183]

Strikes broke out everywhere, which led those months to be regarded as the most unstable of the entire republican period. However, the number of strikes recorded by the Ministry of Labour, between 1 May and 18 July 1936, was 192,[184] in other words, an average of 2.43 per day. We do not, unfortunately, know the number of strikers or days lost, which are far more telling statistics. In any case, if these numbers are compared with the first republican years, with 734 strikes in 1931, 681 the following year and 1,127 in 1933,[185] the average number of strikes per day was 2.01, 1.86 and 3.09, respectively, so there were more labour disputes during those two and a half months of 1936 than during the first two years, but considerably fewer than during the most conflictive year, 1933; in spite of the fact that the number of unemployed, as we have seen, exceeded, in 1936, 800.000, the highest figure throughout the period.

The CNT was involved, of course, in calling the vast majority of strikes, but did not have exclusive responsibility. Because the organisation was not at its best, and showed signs of weakness in those areas with a strong anarchist tradition, where there was most unrest during the early republican years. In Andalusia, according to the minutes of the last congress, membership stood at 116,753, a figure far removed from the 325,000 of April 1932. The Levante had 48,950 members at the time of the same congress, half as many as the 99,741 of January 1932. While Catalonia, with 142,789 members in May 1936, was a long way from the 198,764 of 1933.[186]

In this context, some confederal unions adopted a more cautious stance than during the years of maximum unrest. Thus, for example, the Manufacturing and Textile Union of Badalona wanted to go beyond revolutionary maximalism and demanded a "study of viable solutions". The Barcelona Transport and Water Union advocated negotiation, despite the lack of agreement with management and the prolongation of the differences over the reinstatement of the *seleccionados*, and explicitly expressed its desire not to return to "bombs and the burning of trams".[187]

The strikes were obviously called by the workers, but management had its own share of responsibility in the disputes. A person "of order" like Herbette noted in June how Madrid employers were beginning a phase of firmness that included their opposition to the work laws established by the government in different disputes. In fact, employers all over Spain issued manifestos, that month, calling on management "to be organically strong and stand up to workers".[188] Even Civil Guard reports acknowledged that Marxist doctrine had gained a foothold among workers "due to the scant interest owners showed in things that affected workers and to the exploitation to which they were submitted in the payment of daily wages, (which) obliged the working classes to enrol in unions or left-wing organisations, where they imagined that their interests would be well looked after".[189]

For their part, workers had seen how protests were bearing fruit in issues such as the release of prisoners, the amnesty and the agrarian problem, solutions that were an example to be followed. In any case, demands continued to concern a return to previous salaries, the reinstatement of sacked workers and the recovery of lost rights. While the means of reaching agreement continued to be very varied, from consensus to the collapse of negotiations with ensuing strikes, and sometimes mediation by the state. Thus, the Manufacturing and Textile Unions of the Catalan region proposed "moral" foundations the content of which was nothing new but, rather the opposite, was a return to the past. Specifically, recognition of the union committees and delegates, acceptance of the job exchange, the total abolition of piecework, a ban on night shifts for women and minors, the provision of clean changing rooms, toilets, showers (...). Meanwhile, the Seville Construction Union presented management with proposals for a series of improvements "accompanied by the corresponding strike notification", which did not have to be activated because the collective bargaining agreement was signed that included economic improvements, a 36-hour week and recognition of the union. While the Alicante construction union had been on strike for two weeks over the demand for a 36-hour week and other "moral questions". In Villamayor de la Vega (León), landowners paid peasants six reals a day for working from dawn until dusk; cigarette and match sellers went on strike to force the return to work of their sacked colleagues . . .[190]

The solution of disputes, as had happened earlier, was based on the needs and interests of workers and employers, but also on the mediation of the state, however much there were incessant calls from confederal ranks for direct action. In this respect, it is worth recalling that the return of the mixed juries occurred as late as June 1936, amidst major unrest, and was received by the CNT with the same disdain and affirmation of principles as in previous periods. Nothing new. Neither was there anything new about the fact that the workers, the *cenetistas* included, accepted the mediation. This was was the case in the dispute involving the coal and oil unions, when "after some incidents and paralysis of road traffic due to fuel shortages", the solution took the form of a judgement issued by the special delegation sent by the government. And in the strike called by the miners of Río Tinto, brought to an end when a commission formed by UGT and CNT members met the Minister of Labour.[191]

In spite of the latter example, CNT and UGT continued with their struggle for supremacy in the workers' movement. In this regard, one should not forget the confederal strategy, which was based upon the agreement reached at the Zaragoza Congress in relation to the workers' alliance, which involved making approaches to workers belonging to the socialist union with a view to setting them against the leadership. Approaches that, apparently, were bearing fruit. I have already noted how during earlier periods the CNT's tactics had penetrated the UGT's actions. Now, in the spring of 1936, *El Socialista* evidenced a degree of perplexity in asking whether "the tactic that has been employed in recent strikes, can we recognise it as our own?" to which it replied "we wish, clearly and categorically, to say no (...) The system is anarchist".[192]

An approach that gave rise to an interesting debate between the socialist newspaper *Claridad* and the *cenetista Solidaridad Obrera.* The latter accused the government and the socialists of acting in favour of the bourgeoisie and being intent "on undermining the CNT's peculiar tactics". For its part, *Claridad* attacked the "syndicalist myth of direct action", because, contrary to what its advocates believed, it was not a negation of the state, but an "old idea of the liberal state, of 'laissez faire, of the economic doctrine of the previous century, which asked the state to abstain from intervening in disputes within society". An explanation that *Solidaridad* had no hesitation in describing as "childish and capricious", as the state did indeed intervene, but "in the service of the ruling classes", before finishing by recalling that Marx proposed the destruction of the state, and that it had been Marx and Engels who referred to the modern state as "the bourgeoisie's instrument of force and repression against the proletarian class"[193]. Behind the whole debate was the struggle between *ugetistas* and *cenetistas* in the construction strike in Madrid, which could serve the CNT as an example of the effectiveness of its tactics and "unmasking" of the socialist leaders.

CNT membership in Madrid had increased significantly, rising from 14,535 in February 1935 and to 32,162 in May of the following year.[194] In fact, Azaña was concerned "about the CNT upsurge in Madrid", a situation to which, according to Herbette, Madrid employers themselves had contributed.[195] The dispute had started when the Madrid construction workers, members of the UGT and CNT, agreed upon work rules to be presented to management, including, among other questions, a pay rise, the 36-hour week, the admission of workers with the consent of both unions and improvements in hygiene standards. Management refused to accept these conditions, so a strike was called at the end of May, and supported by 80,000 workers. The mixed jury's verdict did not solve the problem either, as it was not accepted by the employers. The *cenetista* union denounced the actions of the Madrid employers, branding it "political", since in Seville an agreement had been reached that included a pay rise, the 36-hour week and recognition of the union, without needing to go on strike. After a 42-day stoppage, the Ministry of Labour issued a ruling that did not address all the workers' claims, but which the UGT accepted. Which triggered the confederal strategy of attracting UGT members that wanted nothing to do with the political deals made between "their leaders and the petite bourgeoisie". While *El Socialista* accused the CNT of recruitment and domination of members, *Solidaridad Obrera* spoke of "purification, disinfection, cleansing", of definitively removing them "from the ranks of social reformism", of rejection of "their leaders' political suggestions". But it was not only the CNT that opposed the ruling. Employers did not respect it either and, consequently, shut down work centres. Under these circumstances, the CNT urged UGT members to switch to its form of struggle and refuse to accept government mediation, so the strike continued. There was no shortage of calls for solidarity, both to fight against the bourgeoisie, as a victory for the latter in Madrid would lead to a general offensive throughout Spain, and for the children of strikers to be received in other proletarian homes. In mid-July, the ministry ratified the ruling, which the UGT and management abided by, but did not approve of; for this reason, the CNT continued with the strike, since, it argued, it was the employers who had to approve the agreement, not a body unrelated to the negotiations. The hardening of the CNT's attitude and the government's response, with the closure of its unions, was only eclipsed by the rumours of a fascist coup.[196]

Rumours that had been constant during the first biennium and which returned and intensified following the Popular Front's election victory. General Franco himself denounced, in a letter addressed to the Minister of War, Casares Quiroga, in June, those who presented "the Army as disloyal to the Republic".[197] But the fact is that there was a civil and military conspiracy in progress, already evident in August 1932, and which, in July 1936, was repeated by the military and right-wing groups. Ángel Viñas has documented "the fascist collusion with the uprising" in the four contracts, dated 1 July 1936, signed by the monarchic representative Pedro Sainz Rodríguez – and the more than probable participation of some member of the rebel military leadership – with fascist Italy. Contracts detailing the purchase of planes, bombs, machine guns (...) indicating preparation for a more than probable war, should the coup fail.[198]

Rumours of the fascist coup were mixed with other information about political, social and work-related violence, but also state repression. González Calleja has provided exhaustive quantification and classification of the violence between February and July 1936, and arrived at a total of 384 fatalities. Of these, with regard to those he has been able to identify, left-wing organisations and their militants would have been responsible for approximately 28% of the deaths; right-wing groups, 29%; and around 22% resulted from the actions of the security forces.

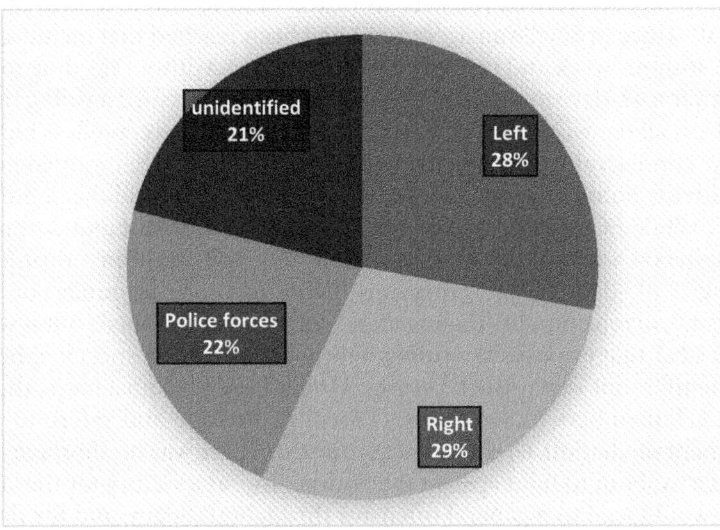

Figure 13 Authors of Fatal Attacks, February–July 1936.

Victims associated with the Right are estimated at 29%, with the political centre at 1%, while those associated with unions and left-wing parties are calculated to represent 42%. A calculation that, as the author acknowledges, is quite conservative, as among the 23% of unidentified victims are a number of workers and labourers killed in clashes with the security forces during social or work-related protests involving supporters of the Popular Front.[199] Violence that was related to the political and social struggle, and which peaked, as we have seen, in the repression of strikes and demonstrations, with victims among workers, syndicalist and members of left-wing parties.

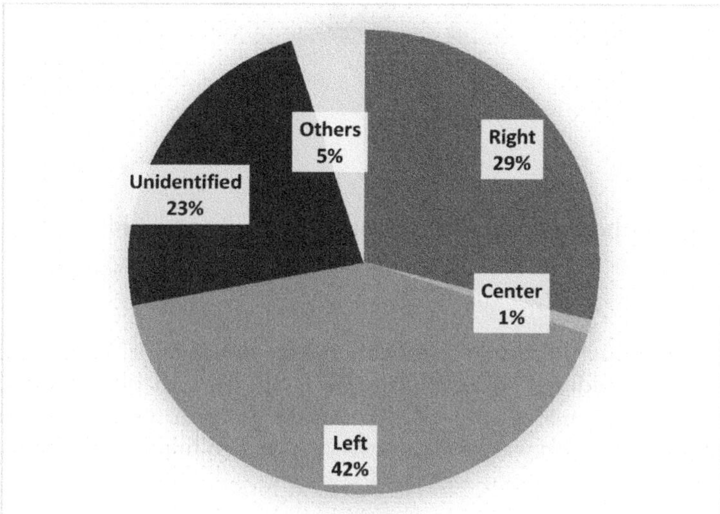

Figure 14 Fatalities, February–July 1936.

If the analysis is extended to socio-political violence in Spain for the entire republican period, with the exception of Asturias in October 1934, González Calleja refers to 1,607 fatalities. Militants from the CNT, FAI and the Libertarian Youth were responsible for 159 deaths, almost 10% of the total; above these were the 226 victims that the author has been unable to identify and, standing out, the 631 caused by soldiers, police and Civil Guard, in other words, almost 40% of the total. Below the libertarians is the Falange – with SEU and CONS – which was responsible for 108 deaths, almost 7%; in proportional terms, considerably higher figures, bearing in mind that the fascist party was formed in October 1933 and, in other words, was present during only half of the republican period. For their part, communist organisations accounted for 35 fatalities. As regards the victims, 174 of those killed were libertarians, in other words, almost 11% of the total. Above them were the socialists – PSOE, UGT and the Socialist Youth – with 191 victims, around 12%; higher still, the 291 unidentified left-wing victims, representing 18%; and, most numerous, the

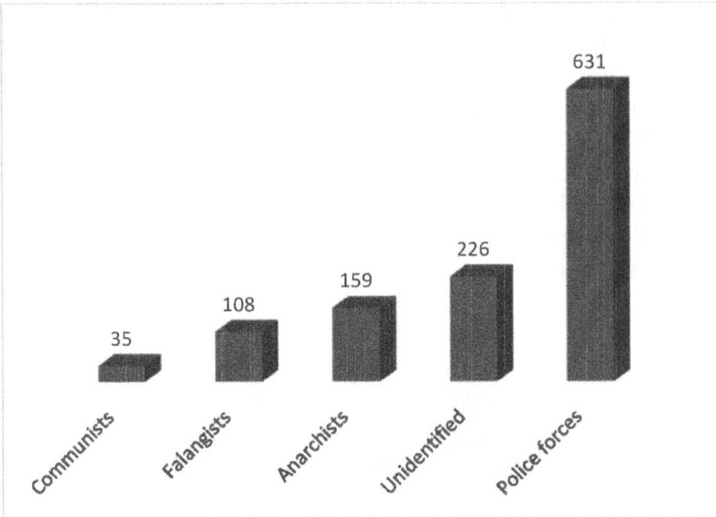

Figure 15 Authors of Fatal Attacks During the Second Republic, 1931–1936.

387 dead without political identification, accounting for 24%; below the libertarians are soldiers, police and the Civil Guard, with 148 fatalities; while the 108 Falange members were killed, around 7%; again, a significant number for an organisation that was less than two years old. While the communists lost 93 militants.

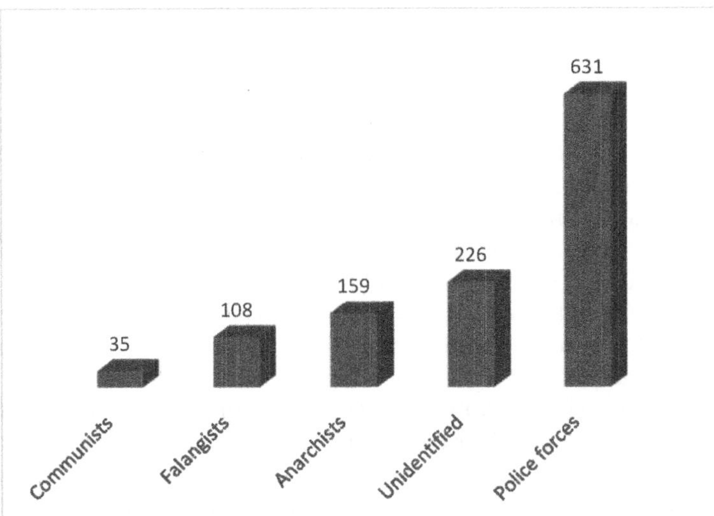

Figure 16 Political Affiliation of Fatalities During the Second Republic, 1931–1936.

Finally, the study reveals that soldiers, the police and the Civil Guard were responsible for the greatest number of victims in libertarian organisations, with 126 deaths; while the security forces suffered 53 fatalities at the hands of the former; although unidentified victims of libertarian violence were higher in number, with 60 dead.

These statistics highlight the fact that, on the one hand, state repression was the principal cause of violent deaths; and, on the other, that the greatest number of victims corresponded to workers and peasants, along with unions and left-wing parties. In the specific case of the libertarians, their major presence in demonstrations, strikes, uprisings and insurrections is confirmed by the fact that they are the group with most victims of the security forces; an involvement in the conflict that also meant they were the organisation responsible for most violent deaths, with the aforementioned exception of the Falange.

Violence of a particular nature in attacks on individuals, like those against Socialist MP Luis Jiménez de Asúa, from which he escaped unharmed, but which resulted in the death of his bodyguard, Gisberg; or the attack on the assault guard Lieutenant José Castillo and his colleagues' revenge against far right-wing leader José Calvo Sotelo. The anarchists also resorted to individual attacks during this period, like the one that took the life of the ex-police chief of Catalonia, Miguel Badia, at the end of April 1936. Fidel Miró recalled that, in private conversation with Abad de Santillán, the latter commented that Badia had got what he deserved, given his brutal treatment "of our militants whenever he had the opportunity and in particular of García Oliver when he was arrested following the frustrated revolutionary uprising in Barcelona". When asked if he knew the author of the attack, Abad de Santillán answered that he did not, though his reply, according to Miró, did not sound very convincing.[200]

The government presented before Parliament, at the end of June, a draft anti-terrorist law with severe penalties for the possession of weapons and explosives. For the CNT, the proposal was just one more attempt at repression against the more vulnerable classes, however much it was disguised as a law against acts of terror committed by fascist and monarchic organisations. For its objective was none other than to "leave workers defenceless against reactionary and fascist provocation", and favour those who could "use their influence and money to supply weapons and authorise their use". So, "faced by such a counter-revolutionary project" only the staunchest opposition would serve.[201]

The Civil Guard yearned for "the calm of 1935", and the "security of Public Order".[202] A circumstance that was not the result of any relaxation on the part of the government, since the actions of the security forces in 1936, as we have seen, caused a considerable number of victims. Protests continued to be repressed in no uncertain manner, with similar episodes to the most tragic events of previous years. Inn Yeste (Albacete), 17 peasants were killed and many more injured in clashes with the Civil Guard, which lost one agent and saw 16 injured. The inhabitants of the parish of la Graya, close to Yeste, had earned their living from cutting down pine trees and taking them downriver to the mine, but some construction work in the Segura Confederation changed their lifestyle and, as a result, unemployment and hunger made their presence felt. The villagers invaded the mountains belonging to the state and to ex-Radical Party MP Edmundo Alfaro – described by *Solidaridad Obrera* as a *cacique* – where they cut down "pines without any economic motives, but simply to express their dismay at the distressing situation" in which they had found themselves for some time. The Civil Guard arrived and arrested six peasants. When the Civil Guard began to transfer the detainees to Yeste, around 200 men – 3,000, according to the Civil Guard report – followed them. The mayor of Yeste convinced the agents, in order to prevent further unrest, to release the prisoners. However, this did not calm the situation, and a struggle ensued in which the first shots were heard. The fray led to the first deaths, while some fled into the countryside. Three MPs, Prat, Socialist, Mije, Communist and Martínez Moreno, of Republican Union, travelled to the area to investigate events. The controversy surrounded not those who had died during the clash, but the fact that "there were subsequent deaths and some quite some distance away", as the incident occurred at 12.30 p.m., and the pursuit of those who escaped continued until nine at night.[203] The Minister of Interior promoted Félix Velando Gómez, the Civil Guard warrant officer in command of the post at the time, to the rank of second lieutenant, on 2 June 1936. But the judge directing the proceedings concerning the incident issued an order for his arrest and prosecution, on June 23. In other words, on the one hand he was promoted and on the other he was tried for the same actions. On 5 July, he was taken to Albacete prison.[204]

In other Civil Guard headquarters, like Huelva, arrest warrants were also issued, but this time against those involved in the military rebellion, like the one issued on 17 July for the arrest of General Queipo de Llano. However, agents José Díaz Cano and Tomás Sorio Parriego ordered "the General's car to stop, conversing with him, without arresting him". Sorio, who showed "true love for the profession" and was described in his file as an "excellent guard", joined the movement "with great enthusiasm".[205] Meanwhile, in the press, there were repeated rumours of a fascist coup, and the confederal masses took to the streets. The CNT was surprised when the government ordered the closure of its centres in Madrid instead of promoting unity between anti-fascists, because "the forces of the popular front" could not on their own tackle the danger that threatened everyone.[206]

But not everybody identified the danger in the same place. Herbette expressed his agreement with Azaña with regard to its origins. The President regarded anarchism as "a cancer" that it was "necessary to remove". But he also knew, continued Herbette, that it was not possible to apply repression of the type that Lenin and Dzerjinski – founder and director of the TCHÉCA, the political police in the new Bolshevik state after the revolution of 1917 – deployed in Russia, because it was "particularly dangerous to shed blood in as sensitive a nation as Spain". His concern about revolution caused him to err, like so many others, when it came to identifying the principal enemy of the

Republic, and declare that "the main danger comes from anarchism".[207] In the same sense, Asturian *cenetista Ramonín* recalled how José Maldonado, last President of the Republic in exile, told him how in a Republican Left meeting, in the spring of 1936, Azaña told him that "you look too often to the right when the danger lies on the left".[208] The President was unconcerned about the rumours that pointed to the army, "coffee shop conversations between monarchic officers", he said.[209]

"Coffee shop conversations" that got out of hand with the military rebellion initiated in North Africa, in which "fascism has appeared in violent fashion (...) in order to bring an end to all the freedoms achieved so far". The CNT placed itself at the head of the resistance, with a "they shall not pass", and in the hope "that the organisation will adopt strategic positions in the struggle that lies ahead in Alliance with other anti-fascist sectors", albeit attempting to direct that resistance "in favour of our ideological conception, based on libertarian communism".[210]

The CNT, which had sought via every means possible to bring about the revolution, would see how a military rebellion paradoxically cleared the road to anarchy.

Conclusions

In summary, and by way of conclusion, one can say that the CNT's relationship with the Republic was substantially altered by the change in confederal leadership. The anarcho-syndicalists, who initially controlled the main confederal committees, understood that the strengthening and improvement of the union necessitated the survival of the Republic, with the freedoms and rights inherent to any democratic regime. However, historiography has identified the CNT in particular as the organisation most responsible for destabilizing the Republic as a consequence of its involvement in social and industrial unrest. But not only did the confederal union not promote, during the first months, any kind of uprising in opposition to the new regime, it actually supported its consolidation. It should be borne in mind that the working classes received the Republic, to a large extent, as a revolutionary regime destined to redress the social injustice that had existed in Spanish society for decades. As a result, the workers were the first to demand "moral" and economic improvements denied them for years. The struggle for the recognition of unions, improved working conditions and pay rises were the demands most voiced by the thousands of workers that flooded the unions in search of strength in unity so as to attain their objectives. Unions that, like the CNT, struggled not only to organise the entry of this torrent of people, but also to control their legitimate demands in order to obtain a positive result. So while the confederal press issued calls not to systematically harass the new regime, the confederal leadership asked the thousands of workers for calm in order to present employers with new work rules. In this context, there was support for negotiations with management, but also demonstrations and strikes, legal actions that were necessary in order to improve the social situation of the most vulnerable. The Republic, with its democratic legitimacy, made it possible to wage the union struggle where under the dictatorship this had been prohibited.

However, while the anarcho-syndicalists believed that the new democratic period could serve to prepare the new libertarian society by increasing worker awareness and strengthening the union, the anarchists thought that the revolutionary moment had already arrived and that all that was missing, therefore, was action. But they needed the workers en masse to take to the streets and bring about the social revolution. Consequently, the anarchists began to join forces in the FAI with the aim of removing the anarcho-syndicalists from the governing bodies, and from that vantage point channelling the CNT's activities. In this undertaking, they received the unwitting help of the Republican-Socialist government, whose labour and public order policies provided ammunition for the anarchists in both their assault on the new regime and their internal battles

The state's intervention in labour negotiations via joint committees, initially, and mixed juries, later, improved the situation of workers, but, at the same time, made it impossible to collaborate with the CNT, reluctant to abandon one of its basic principles – direct action. Moreover, neither were employers keen on this kind of mediation, which presumably favoured workers' interests. So aspiring to social change, with the opposition of both employers and the other major union, was highly unrealistic. If the Republican-Socialists wanted to change things in Spain, it was necessary, at the very least, to reach an agreement with the union that represented practically half of the workers' movement. A viable situation while confederal leadership was in the hands of the anarcho-syndicalists. In fact, although the latter's' ultimate goal was the creation of a libertarian communist organisation, including the destruction of the state, they acted in accordance with the reality of the moment. In other words, they continued to acknowledge the state's existence and to demand of the authorities their necessary involvement in improving the living conditions of the poorest and in extending rights and freedoms. And neither did they hesitate to establish contact with the government when it was necessary to intervene on behalf of prisoners or deportees, in spite of continuous criticism by the anarchists. But the government not only passed labour legislation that favoured the UGT and divided the unions; the actions of the security forces in the repression of strikes and demonstrations led to widespread disenchantment among the poorer classes and facilitated the anarchist discourse seeking a change in CNT leadership.

After the Conservatorio Congress, the scene of an unqualified victory for the anarcho-syndicalists, the confrontation within the confederal organisation was no different from the typical power struggle within any political party. The anarchists made the most of the historical ascendancy of men of action in the libertarian movement to recruit the young immigrants arriving in Barcelona who, owing to their lack of qualifications, had the least stable and worst paid jobs. Anarchist activity was particularly significant at syndicalist grassroots level, but also in the like-minded press, with the purpose of discrediting the anarcho-syndicalists. The latter, meanwhile, issued a manifesto signed by thirty militants – the *treintistas* – denouncing anarchist interference in the union and pointing to their revolutionary inconsistency. But the anarchist campaign, full of smears that were particularly hurtful in the libertarian world, with words like bureaucrats and "politicians", was mixed with accusations of "sold out" and traitors to the movement. Accusations that were never proven and, moreover, were shown over time to be false, but which enabled the anarchists to take control of the confederal press and of the main committees within the organisation. Crucial in this respect was the conduct of the Republican-Socialist government in the repression of the protests in Figols, in January 1932.

Although historiography has always identified three insurrections led by the CNT during the Republic – January 1932 and January and December 1933 –

the fact is that the first of these cannot be regarded as the CNT's, because it neither directed, planned nor organised the uprising. And neither was it planned, designed or conceived by the FAI. A self-serving interpretation by an anarchist ruling group, which lent a disproportionate dimension to the protest, transformed into a *cenetista* insurrection what was no more than a local uprising by workers suffering from a long-lasting situation of poverty and social injustice. The anarchists wanted to demonstrate that their hopes for an imminent revolution were realistic, while at the same time attacking the CNT leaders with the sole objective of attaining confederal power. Once they had reached their goal, the Figols uprising was relegated to its true dimension, and not even the libertarians of the day acknowledged it as a CNT insurrection at the famous congress in Zaragoza in 1936.

The repression exercised by the Republican-Socialist government, which included sending in the army and deporting over one hundred people to the African colonies, facilitated the anarchist strategy. Although the repression in Casas Viejas has always been cited as an example of brutality and continuism in the actions of the security forces in republican times, the truth is that what occurred in Figols is far more representative of the absurd behaviour of the government in this respect. The decision to quash the uprising at any cost, ignoring the root of the problem, which was none other than compliance with the law on the part of the ruling classes, constituted an exercise of power that continued to prejudice the most underprivileged classes, the very classes that had contributed most to the advent of the new regime. The government clearly had the right to repress any kind of uprising against the Republic, but it is no less true that the authorities also had an obligation to see that employers obeyed the law. However, many of them systematically failed to comply not only with republican decrees and laws, but also with the labour agreements negotiated within the mixed juries. A repression that lacked, moreover, a long-term political vision and intelligent direction. An absence that gradually undermined the support of the working classes and which, in the CNT's case, facilitated the change in leadership and control of the organisation in favour of those who advocated confrontation, bringing instability to the Republic. In fact, the anarchists' arrival in power led to a radical change within the CNT, which, from that point onwards, side-lined its essence as a union to embark on the road to insurrection.

At the same time, the anarcho-syndicalists, *treintistas* in particular, were expelled from the confederal organisation in both individual and collective fashion. Their leaders were unable to counter a campaign that was as false as it was unfair, and pinned their hopes on showing themselves to be the true defenders of CNT principles and on the response of members who, they hoped, would not abandon the reality of the union struggle for the revolutionary dream. But the anarchists enjoyed considerable support among the union's grassroots, where the assemblies were highly radicalised and anyone who opposed this current might be branded a *treintista*, "politician" or traitor and, as result, be expelled from the organisation. The anarcho-syndicalists eventually organised themselves into the Libertarian Syndicalist Federation, which gathered together like-minded revolutionary syndicalist militants, and the Opposition Unions, a working-class organisation where all workers were welcome. Although its objective was to recover control of the CNT, its strategy was basically that of demonstrating loyalty to revolutionary syndicalist principles, an approach that was obviously insufficient. It had a significant presence in Catalonia, the Levante and Huelva, but no more than 55,000 members.

For their part, the anarchists launched two uprisings, in January and December of 1933, and both failed. In the first place, because both were based upon the false premise that the revolutionary moment had arrived, when it had not; secondly, because they never had enough weapons, nor the backing of those who did, the military; thirdly, because they did not have the support of the general population or of the working masses, not even that of their members, for these were the actions of minorities; brave, heroic, but alone. In fact, all the evidence suggests that the decisions to promote not only these insurrectional deeds but also other protests were taken by a minority rather than a majority within the organisation's membership. The delegates attending the national plenums let themselves get carried away, on more than one occasion, by the revolutionary atmosphere, or felt coerced by the prevailing mood to communicate agreements that did not correspond to those adopted at their respective regional confederations; furthermore, the supposed preparation of and support for these actions that they transmitted in the plenums became an ambiguous response when they were asked by the confederal leadership to participate when the time came for action. And militants held meetings before the assemblies in order to deploy a specific strategy that would favour adoption of such agreements, which to a large degree was a manipulation of the assembly itself; not to mention cases in which the decisions taken at these prior meetings of militants were presented in the plenums as if they had been adopted at union assemblies, something even more serious, since it completely distorted the reality in which the organisation moved. All of this resulted in a crisis of representation, if not of principles themselves, within CNT, which explains why all those involved in the struggle were so obsessed with controlling the confederal committees. Committees that, in theory, had no decision-making power, but which in practice had a broad remit that could include organising a protest or preventing the application of agreements reached in confederal congresses, as occurred with the FNI. Questions that all needed to be taken into account when analysing the significant difference between the support and the participation that delegates claimed to have in plenums and assemblies and the subsequent difficulties experienced by regional confederations when attempting to put into practice what their delegates had advocated or the limited presence on the streets of the confederal masses. Ultimately, these insurrections had no possibility of bringing down the Republic, although they did create a degree of instability. However, they did almost succeed in bringing an end to the CNT itself. The various waves of repression left a destructured organisation, with unions closed down, almost 15,000 militants in prison and the loss of hundreds of thousands of members.

The advance of fascism at the expense of democracy in Europe and the worsening of the economic crisis on a global scale, along with the rise to power of the Radical Party, with the parliamentary backing of the CEDA, the tougher stance adopted by employers in negotiations and the consequences of the repression in response to the most recent uprising forced the CNT to change tactics. This at least was the thinking of part of the organisation, with the Asturian confederation in the van, which advocated the constitution of a workers' alliance. It seemed clear that on its own the CNT could neither address the new situation nor bring about the long-awaited revolution, so the collaboration of other left-wing forces was required. However, the confederal leadership maintained an isolationist and defiant stance that only endorsed collaboration with other organisations where, they said, revolutions took place, in other words, on the streets. As a result, the question of the workers' alliance became another bone of contention that divided the organisation. In fact, when the time came for the main attempt at revolution during the Republic, in the shape of the October 1934 movement, the CNT's involvement was as diverse as one could possibly imagine, from collaboration with other forces to non-involvement, boycott included. Consequently, October left the CNT battered and bruised, in the first place, because the confederal leadership had opposed the alliance, an agreement that proved to be crucial in the unfolding of events, and, on the other hand, because their hostility towards the socialists led them to miss an appointment that they themselves had organised, a fact that was difficult to justify. In any case, although the emphasis has always been placed on the socialists' responsibility for and organisation of the movement, it is no less true that the main reference has always been what happened in Asturias, the place where events took a revolutionary turn and where the alliance formed by *ugetistas* and *cenetistas*, joined by the other left-wing organisations, set it apart from the rest of Spain. Thus, ironically, the Asturian confederation, on the verge of schism on account of its pro-alliance stance, turned out to be the saviour of "confederal honour" and indicated the path to be taken in the immediate future.

However, and in spite of everything, the CNT struggled to make amends. Long gone were the early republican years when workers went on the offensive to obtain labour rights and pay rises denied them on previous occasions. The Radical Party-CEDA election victory in November 1933 and, above all, the repression of the October movement the following year, placed workers on the defensive, not only in order to conserve wages and rights, but even just to keep their jobs. The imprisonment of militants and the closure of unions resulted in workers being disorganised and vulnerable. Which materialised in the sacking of those regarded as most conflictive, wage cuts and the loss of improved working conditions. In fact, salaries fell below the level in 1932, while the defensive attitude of the workers was reflected by the number of strikes and strikers, which dropped to levels prior to the advent of the Republic.

Releasing the prisoners crowded into the republican jails became an undeniable need. The CNT was insufficiently prepared to carry out any kind of action that would facilitate their release, so, once again, it faced the dilemma of choosing between principles and reality, in other words, maintaining, above all, abstentionist anti-politicism, or voting for those who included amnesty in their election manifesto. The debate within the organisation covered everything, from the maximalism that argued against voting under any circumstances, to those who defended the vote to secure the release of the prisoners, and including those persuaded by the experience of recent years that not all regimes were the same and that the Republican-Socialist government, despite its unjustifiable actions, could in no way be compared to the repressive Radical-CEDA coalition. In spite of the official abstentionist campaign and the ambiguity of the messages emitted, most confederal militants turned out to vote and collaborated in the victory of the Popular Front.

The working classes took to the streets again, but the spring of 1936 was not 14 April 1931; among other reasons because of the experience accumulated in the interim, but also because the Socialists were not in government. Many of them took to the streets along with confederals, communists and other left-wing organisations in demonstrations demanding that the government kept the promises made during the election campaign. The demonstrations in favour of amnesty and the reinstatement of sacked workers combined with demands for the recovery of salaries and improved working conditions that had been lost in recent years. The working class was set on the reconquest of what had been lost, without there being any revolution under way, because there were no generalised attacks on institutions, or occupation of factories, or insurrectionist movements. There was legitimate and legal exerted via strikes and demonstrations, just as in any democratic nation. No organisation conceived of a revolutionary plan, the CNT included, which had enough on its plate with recovering its organic structure and winning back the hundreds of thousands of disenchanted members. The confederation focused its attention, above all, on immediate objectives, with no sign on the horizon of even a would-be insurrectionist uprising.

The CNT recovered its strength and thousands of workers returned to the unions. The organisation's exceptional recovery was courtesy, above all, of the Popular Front's victory, and had less to do with the conduct of the confederal leadership. Nevertheless, the improvement intensified the anarchists' control of the organisation. Although everything pointed to the need for a change of direction in crucial areas for the future, such as the reunification of the movement and the workers' alliance, the agreements adopted at the Zaragoza Congress, in May 1936, maintained, in essence, the leadership's criteria in recent years. Unity was the result more of the dispersion and rendition of the opposition, given the failure of its organisation, than of examination and critical analysis of past events. The agreement was little more than a parody in which neither of the parties really believed, for the differences remained, but which they accepted for the sake of necessary unity. Regarding the formation of a workers' alliance with a view to halting fascism and working for the revolution, the agreements reached maintained the same approach that had been followed for years. In other words, there was no assumption of responsibility for the failed uprisings and, instead of promotion of an alliance with other left-wing organisations, there was a return to the criterion of plain and simple absorption of the UGT, approved in 1919.

The dazzling spectacle of thousands of workers on the streets, taking part in demonstrations and strikes, blinded the confederal leadership, which failed to see that a change of direction was needed. Just as it blinded many others, including Azaña himself, who, when it came to identifying the true enemy of the Republic, pointed the finger at the anarchists, when the danger really lay in the union between the military and the far right. Ironically, the failure of the rebellion made it easier for the CNT to find the road to anarchy.

Notes

1 Anarchists and Anarcho-syndicalists in the Early Days of the Republic (April 1931–June 1931)

1. See, among others, Juliá, Santos (1984), *Madrid, 1931–1934. De la fiesta popular a la lucha de clases*, Madrid, Siglo XXI; Townson, Nigel (2002), *La República que no pudo ser. La política de centro en España (1931–1936)*, Madrid, Taurus; Gil, Julio (2006), *Segunda República Española (1931–1936)*, Madrid, Biblioteca Nueva; Casanova, Julián (2007), *República y guerra civil*, Madrid, Crítica-Marcial Pons; González Calleja, Eduardo, Cobo, Francisco, Martínez, Ana and Sánchez, Francisco (2015), *La Segunda República Española*, Barcelona, Pasado y Presente.
2. Lorenzo, Anselmo (1974), *El proletariado militante. Memorias de un internacional*, Madrid, Zero; Termes, Josep (2000), *Anarquismo y sindicalismo en España (1864–1881)*, Barcelona, Crítica, (primera publicación en 1965); Lida, Clara (1972), *Anarquismo y revolución en la España del siglo XIX*, Madrid, Siglo XXI; Paniagua, Javier (2008), *La larga marcha hacia la anarquía. Pensamiento y acción del movimiento libertario*, Madrid, Síntesis; Herrerín, Ángel (2011), *Anarquía, dinamita y revolución social. Violencia y represión en la España de entre siglos (1868–1909)*, Madrid, Los libros de la Catarata.
3. Hennessy, C.A.M. (2010), *La República Federal en España. Pi y Margall y el movimiento republicano Federal, 1868–1874*, Los libros de la Catarata, Madrid, pp. 201–220; Lida (1972), pp. 212–227.
4. Herrerín (2011), pp. 36–39.
5. See Álvarez Junco, José (1976), *La ideología política del anarquismo español (1868–1910)*, Siglo XXI, Madrid.
6. *El Perseguido*, Buenos Aires, 15-9-1895.
7. Maitron, Jean (1975), *Le mouvement anarchiste en France, Vol. I : Des origines à 1914*, Gallimard editions, Paris, pp. 286–309; Cuadrat, Xavier (1976), *Socialismo y anarquismo en Cataluña. Los orígenes de la CNT*, Madrid, Revista del Trabajo, pp. 96–111; Paniagua (2008), pp. 170–171; Bar, Antonio (1981), *La CNT en los años rojos, del sindicalismo revolucionario al anarcosindicalismo (1910–1926)*, Madrid, AKAL, pp. 54–80; Francesc Bonamusa (ed.) (1991), *La Huelga General, Ayer*, nº 4.
8. Antonio Bar (1981), pp. 41–43; Herrerín (2011), pp. 202–203.
9. Navarro, Francisco Javier (2013), "Diversidad y dualismos. La(s) cultura(s) política(s) del movimiento libertario español", in Bosch, Aurora, Carnero, T. and Valero, S. (eds.), *Entre la reforma y la revolución. La construcción de la democracia desde la izquierda*, Granada, Comares, pp. 183–200.
10. See, among others, Pestaña, Ángel (1979), *Terrorismo en Barcelona. La autodestrucción del movimiento obrero por el terrorismo*, Barcelona, Planeta; González Calleja, Eduardo (1999), *El máuser y el sufragio. Orden público, subversión y*

violencia política en la crisis de la Restauración (1917–1931), Madrid, CSIC; García Sanz, Fernando (2014), *España en la Gran Guerra. Espías, diplomáticos y traficantes*, Barcelona, Galaxia Gutenberg.

11. On all these questions see: Elorza, Antonio (1973), *La utopía anarquista durante la guerra civil española*, Madrid, Editorial Ayuso; the prologue by Antonio Elorza in Pestaña, Ángel (1974), *Trayectoria Sindicalista*, Madrid, Tebas, pp. 5–77; See also, Vega, Eulalia (1987), *Anarquistas y sindicalistas, 1931–1936*, Valencia, Edicions Alfons el Magnànim; Barrio, Ángeles (1988), *Anarquismo y anarcosindicalismo en Asturias (1890–1936)*, Madrid, Siglo XXI.
12. *Tierra y Libertad*, 12-4-1931.
13. *Solidaridad Obrera*, 12 y 14-4-1931.
14. *Solidaridad Obrera*, 15-4-1931.
15. *Tierra y Libertad*, 19-4-1931.
16. *Solidaridad Obrera*, 23-4-1931.
17. *Solidaridad Obrera*, 23-4-1931.
18. *El Combate Sindicalista*, 6-9-1935.
19. International Institute of Social History of Amsterdam (henceforth IISH), sig. CNT, 93 B. Confederal Defence Organisation. National Committee. Revolutionary Orientations.
20. Aróstegui, Julio (2013b), "Una izquierda en busca de la revolución (El fracaso de la segunda revolución)", in Sánchez, Francisco (Coord.), *Los mitos del 18 de julio*, Barcelona, Crítica, pp. 183–220.
21. IISH, sig. CNT, 93 B. Report National Confederal Defence Committee. Revolutionary Orientations.
22. Elorza, Antonio and Bizcarrondo, Marta (1999), *Queridos camaradas. La Internacional comunista y España (1919–1939)*, Barcelona, Planeta, pp. 146–148.
23. Elorza (1973), pp. 448–449; Vega (1987), p. 64.
24. IISH, Ramón Álvarez Archive, box 431. Regional Confederation Plenary Session, Asturias, León and Palencia, May 1931.
25. Proceedings National Plenary Session, Madrid, of 28/30-8-1932, *CNT Bulletin*, September 1932.
26. See: Navarro, Francisco Javier (2002), *Ateneos y grupos ácratas. Vida y actividad cultural de las asociaciones anarquistas valencianas durante la Segunda República y la Guerra civil*, Valencia Generalitat Valenciana.
27. Pestaña, Ángel (1973), *Lo que aprendí en la vida II*, Bilbao, Zero, p. 64.
28. See: Herrerín (2011).
29. Termes, Josep (2011), *Historia del anarquismo en España (1870–1980)*, Barcelona, RBA, pp. 402–404; Pestaña (1973); Elorza (1973).
30. García Oliver, Juan (2008), *El eco de los pasos*, Barcelona, Backlist (1st edition: París, Ruedo Ibérico, 1978), p. 156.
31. Archives Diplomatiques de France (henceforth, ADF), series Z, 151. Report by Fleuriau, French Ambassador to London, for Briand, 29-4-1931.
32. Gil (2006), pp. 89–95–114; Casanova (2007), pp. 16–17.
33. Juliá, Santos (1997), *Los socialistas en la política española, 1879–1982*, Madrid, Taurus, pp. 126–131.
34. Vega (1987), pp. 76–77.
35. Cabrera, Mercedes (1983), *La patronal ante la II República. Organizaciones y estrategia (1931–1936)*, Madrid, Siglo XXI, pp. 203–204. González Calleja, Eduardo (2014), *En nombre de la Autoridad. La defensa del orden público durante*

la Segunda República (1931–1936), Granada, Comares, p. 75; Macarro, José Manuel (2011), "Los socialistas en la Segunda República", in Álvarez Junco, José and Cabrera, Mercedes (eds.), *La mirada del historiador. Un viaje por la obra de Santos Juliá*, Madrid, Taurus, pp. 95–104.

36. National Historical Archive (henceforth, NHA), Interior, series A, dkt. 6 A. Telegram from Civil Governor of La Coruña to Ministry of Interior, 17-7-1931.
37. *Solidaridad Obrera*, 29-5-1931.
38. Data from the Ministry of Labour Bulletin, Madrid 1934–1935, in Vega (1987), pp. 113–114.
39. Vega (1987), pp. 39–41; Elorza (1973), pp. 444–445; Ruiz, David (2008), *Octubre de 1934. Revolución en la República española*, Madrid, Síntesis, p. 41.
40. *Solidaridad Obrera*, 7-5-1931.
41. Gil (2006), p. 99.
42. Bizcarrondo, Marta (2008), *Historia de la UGT. Entre la democracia y la revolución, 1931–1936*, Madrid, Siglo XXI, p. 29.
43. Azaña, Manuel (1981), *Memorias políticas y de guerra, I*, Barcelona, Crítica, pp. 176–179.
44. Cabrera (1983), pp. 196–201.
45. NHA, Interior series A, dkt. 6 A, 3. Similar telegrams in other provinces, like Caceres.
46. *Solidaridad Obrera*, 7-5-1931.
47. Salvador Seguí Foundation in Madrid (henceforth, FSS), archive: Workers' Union Prat de Llobregat.
48. *Solidaridad Obrera*, 8-7-1931.
49. Historical Memory Documentation Centre of Salamanca (henceforth, CDMHS), sig. Madrid, 989, 62. Police reports on the telephone strike, 15-7-1931.
50. *Solidaridad Obrera*, 24-6-1931.
51. IISH, archive, Ramón Álvarez, box 442. Report by Jacinto Toryho; Juliá (1984), p. 198.
52. *Solidaridad Obrera*, 7-5, 8-7-1931.
53. *Solidaridad Obrera*, 7-5, 1-7-1931; *El Luchador*, 22-5-1931.
54. ADF, series Z, 151. Charles Corbin, French Ambassador to Spain, to Briand, Foreign Ministry, 3-6-1931.
55. See: Herrerín, Ángel (2010), "De la lucha por la revolución a la defensa de los derechos. El 1º de Mayo en España a través de sus manifiestos", in Rivas, Lucía (dir.), *El Primero de Mayo en España. 120 aniversario (1890–2010)*, Madrid, Fundación Primero de Mayo.
56. *Solidaridad Obrera*, 1-5-1931.
57. García Oliver (2008), pp. 157–159. VV.AA. (1990), *Colección de Historia oral: El movimiento libertario en España*, Madrid, Fundación Salvador Seguí, pp. 8–11. Interview with García Oliver by Freddy Gómez, París, 29-6-1977.
58. *Tierra y Libertad*, 8-5-1931.
59. García Oliver (2008), p. 160.
60. *El Luchador*, 8-5-1931; *Tierra y Libertad*, 8-5-1931; and FAI note announcing the funeral of metal worker, Bienvenido Giménez, following the injuries suffered in the Plaza de la República on May 1, in *Solidaridad Obrera*, 19-5-1931.
61. *El Luchador*, 8-5-1931.
62. Gil (2006), pp. 60–62.

63. ADF, series Z, 158, Reports by Jean Herbette to Boncour, 22, 27-11-1933.
64. See, Álvarez Junto (1976); Herrerín (2011).
65. NHA, series A, dkt. 16 A, file 16. Telegrams from Justice Ministry to Ministry of Interior, 14-5, 21-10-1931.
66. *La Libertad* y *Heraldo de Madrid,* 12-5-1931, in Según, Manuel, "El anticlericalismo de la cerilla y la gasolina: la quema de conventos de mayo de 1931 en Madrid", *Alcores,* nº 16, 2013, pp. 181–203.
67. Azaña (1981), pp. 373–374.
68. Ballbé, Manuel (1983), *Orden público y militarismo en la España constitucional,* Madrid, Alianza Editorial, p. 319. A measure that, according to Gabriel Cardona, was excessive as it left repression in the hands of the Army without the events representing an attempt to overthrow the Republic, Cardona, Gabriel (1987), "Estado y poder militar en la Segunda República", VV.AA., *La II República. Una esperanza frustrada.* Congress Proceedings: Valencia Capital de la República (abril 1986), Valencia, Edicions Alfons El Magnànim, pp. 49–64.
69. NHA, series A, dkt. 16 A, file 16. Telegrams from Ministry of Interior to Civil Governors, 12, 14, 17-5-1931.
70. NHA, series A, dkt. 16 A, file 16. Telegram from Captain General of Seville to Ministry of Interior, 14-5-1931; and Ballbé (1983), p. 319.
71. *Solidaridad Obrera,* 13, 14-5-1931; *El Luchador,* 22-5-1931.
72. Gil (2006), pp. 64–65; Casanova (2007), pp. 25–26.
73. Ballbé (1983), pp. 338–339.
74. Azaña (1981), p. 74.
75. Cardona, Gabriel (1893), *El poder militar en la España contemporánea hasta la guerra civil,* Madrid, Siglo XXI, p. 161; and Cardona (1987), p. 52.
76. Ballbé (1983), pp. 347–358.
77. Casanova (1997), p. 37.
78. *Boletín de la UGT* nº 35, November 1931, in Bizcarrondo (2008), p. 72.
79. *El Luchador,* 5-6-1931; Ballbé (1983), p. 319.
80. NHA, Interior series A, dkt. 49 A, file 35. Letter from Civil Governor of Gipuzcoa to the Ministry of Interior, 5-6-1931. My underlining.
81. Maura, Miguel (1995), *Así cayó Alfonso XIII, Barcelona,* Ariel (first edition of 1962), p. 279.
82. NHA, series A, Dkt. 16 A, file 16, Telegram from Ministry of War to Ministry of Interior, 13-6-1931.
83. *Solidaridad Obrera,* 30-5-1931.
84. *El Luchador,* 12-6-1931.
85. See: Lorenzo (1974); Herrerín, Ángel (2004), *La CNT durante el franquismo. Clandestinidad y exilio (1939–1975),* Siglo XXI, Madrid.
86. Lorenzo (1974), pp. 340–344.
87. *Solidaridad Obrera,* 25-4-1931.
88. Martínez Lorenzo (1969), p. 48; Martínez Lorenzo (2006), pp. 106–109; VV.AA (1990), interview with García Oliver by Freddy Gómez, Paris, 29-6-1977, p. 15.
89. Martínez Lorenzo (1969), p. 55; García Oliver (2008).
90. Vega (1987), pp. 89–90.
91. FAI Peninsular Committee Newsletter, *El Luchador,* 10-4-1931; and note from Regional Federation of Anarchist Groups, Catalonia, *Tierra y Libertad,* 12-4-1931.
92. *Tierra y Libertad,* 30-5-1931.

93. *Tierra y Libertad*, 12-4-1931.
94. *Tierra y Libertad*, 26-4-1931.
95. Lorenzo (1974), p. 408.
96. *El Luchador*, 15 and 29-5-1931.
97. *Tierra y Libertad*, 30-5-1931.
98. FAI Conference, *El Luchador*, 19-6-1931; *Tierra y Libertad*, 20-6-1931.
99. *El Luchador*, 3-7-1931.
100. This number of members in *El Luchador*, 24-7-1931; same figure in last contribution by Elorza (2013), p. 194; however, Julián Casanova and César M. Lorenzo quote 535,565, Casanova (1997), p. 84; Martínez Lorenzo (2006), p. 100; while Elorza, in an earlier book, indicated 548,310 members, since, he maintained, there was a mistake in the document that referred to 535,565, Elorza (1973), pp. 447–449.
101. *El Luchador*, 10-7-1931.
102. Elorza (1973), p. 444; Termes (2011), p. 406.
103. CNT, *Congresos Anarcosindicalistas en España, 1870–1936*, Ediciones CNT, Toulouse (France), 1977.
104. See: CNT (1977); *El Luchador*, 3-7-1931; Elorza (2013), p. 195.
105. *El Luchador*, 3, 10-7-1931.
106. *El Luchador*, 10-7-1931; and CNT (1977).
107. My underlining, *El Luchador*, 10-7-1931. On the "political deviationism" of the members of the CP of FAI, Brademas (1973), p. 50.
108. *El Luchador*, 10-7-1931.
109. CNT (1977); and *El Luchador*, 10-7-1931.
110. Martínez Lorenzo (1969), p. 37; Brademas (1973), p. 45; Elorza (2013), p. 197.
111. IISH, Horacio Martínez Prieto archive, sig. Utopistas.
112. The debate over the FNI in: CNT (1977); and *El Luchador*, 24-7, 28-8, 4-9-1931. Result of the voting in *El Luchador*, 18-9-1931, 316,649 in favour, from 183 delegations, 112,416 against, from 61 delegations, and 10.947 abstentions.
113. The pronouncement was endorsed with the signatures of Valentín García, Galo Díez, F. Subero, Enrique Melchor, Eduardo Collado, Segundo Blanco, Niceto de la Iglesia, José Corbella, Pedro Cané, José Villaverde, José Margalef, Miguel Mendiola and the Cement Union of Madrid, although there was one dissenting vote in response to the pronouncement, deeming it collaborationist. This vote against was signed by Feliciano Benito and Cipriano Mera, of Cement and Builders of Madrid, respectively, with the adhesion of Joaquín Ramos, of Steelmaking of Sagunto. CNT (1977).
114. *El Luchador*, 17, 24-7-1931.
115. CNT National Plenary Session, December, 1931, *CNT Bulletin*, January, 1932.
116. *El Luchador*, 2-10-1931.
117. Brademas (1973), p. 65.
118. See: Monjo, Anna (2003), *Militants. Participació i democràcia a la CNT als anys trenta*, Barcelona, Laertes; Vilanova, Mercedes (1996), *Las mayorías invisibles*, Barcelona, Icaria.
119. CNT (1977); *El Luchador*, 26-6-1931.
120. *El Luchador*, 10-7-1931.
121. See: Paniagua, Javier (2001) (edition and preliminary study), *Orto (1932–1934), revista de documentación social*, 2 vols., Valencia, UNED, vol. 1, pp. XXVIII–XXIX.

122. CNT (1977).
123. *El Luchador*, 16-10-1931.
124. Federico Urales, "Por la vida de la C.N. del T.", *El Luchador*, 2-10-1931.
125. FSS, archive, prior to Civil War, box 1. The voting: Peiró, 46 votes; Clará, 12; Pestaña, 6; Alaiz, 3; Gibanel, 1; Cano Ruiz, 1. Regional Conference of Unions, Catalonia, 31-5, 1-6-1931.
126. *Solidaridad Obrera*, 21-6-1931.
127. CNT (1977).
128. *Tierra y Libertad*, 20-6-1931.
129. Regional Committees Plenary Session Proceedings, Madrid, 13/16-4-1932, *CNT Bulletin*, May 1932; and article by José Villaverde, in *Sindicalismo*, 2-5-1934.
130. FSS, archive, prior to Civil War, box 3. Proceedings 4th IWA World Congress, Madrid, 16/20-6-1931. Attended by: IWA secretariat, Rudolf Rocker, Augustin Souchy and Valeriano Orobón Fernández; representing the International Antimilitarist Office, A. de Jong; the Relief Fund, Poliakoff; the German Organisations: FAID, Rüdiger and Karl Windhof; Portugal: Confederaçao Geral do Trabalho, Manuel Joaquín de Souza; South America: Asociación Continental Americana de Trabajadores (ACAT), Diego Abad de Santillán and Juan Miranda; Bolivia: Federación Obrera Boliviana, Jerónimo Rodríguez; Uruguay: Federación Obrera Regional Uruguaya, Joaquín Cortes; France: Confederación General del Trabajo Sindicalista Revolucionaria (CGTSR), Pierre Bernard and Lucien Huart; Spain: CNT, Avelino González and Eusebio C. Carbó; Costa Rica: Agrupación Obrera de Estudios Sociales, José Alberola; Bulgaria: various groups, P. Wassilief; Suecia: Sveriges Arbetares Centralorganisation (SAC), A. Jensen; Holland: Nederlandsch Syndikalistich (NS), Wolthuis Rosseau and J. Woaci; and representing Poland: Polish Anarchist Federation, Soundy. The CNT regional delegates were: Ramón Acín, de Aragón; Feliciano Benito, from both Castiles; Miguel Mendiola, Andalusia; Diego Parra, Levante; José Robusté, Catalonia; Manuel Pérez, North; José Villaverde, Galicia; and Francisco Arín, Balearic Islands.
131. Bar (1981); Martínez Lorenzo (1969).
132. Elorza (1973), pp. 391–397.
133. Pronouncement: "La lucha de clase internacional", *La Revista Blanca*, 1-7-1931
134. FSS, archive; prior to Civil War, box 3. Proceedings 4th IWA World Congress, Madrid, 16/20-6-1931.
135. Pronouncements: "La actitud del sindicalismo revolucionario frente a la democracia política"; "La AIT, el problema agrario y los campesinos"; and other resolutions in *La Revista Blanca*, 1-7-1931.

2 The Struggle for Power: From Syndicalism to Insurrection (July 1931–April 1932)

1. On joining the CNT, *El Luchador*, 24-7-1931; the "Federación Fantasma", in article by José Domingo, *El Luchador*, 6-5-1932.
2. See: Juliá (1984), pp. 183–184; Bizcarrondo (2008).
3. See: Tuñon de Lara, Manuel (1972), *El movimiento obrero en la Historia de España*, Taurus, Madrid; and Bar (1981).
4. NHA. Interior series A, dkt. 6ª. 3. Telegram from Civil Governor of Cadiz to Minister of Interior, 3-5-1931.

5. *En Marcha*, 3-12-1932.
6. NHA, series A, dkt. 58 A, file. 29. Telegram from Civil Governor of Seville to Minister of Interior, 4-8-1933.
7. *En Marcha*, 3-12-1932.
8. Articles from La *Voz* compiled in *El Luchador*, 17, 24-7-1931.
9. *El Socialista*, "El objetivo principal de las huelgas sindicalistas", 10-7-1931; "¿Por qué hay tantas huelgas?", 22-7-1931.
10. *El Socialista*, 22-7-1931.
11. *El Luchador*, 17-7-1931.
12. *Solidaridad Obrera*, 14-7-1931.
13. ADF, series Z, 151. Herbette to Briand, Foreign Minister, 21-7-1931.
14. *El Socialista*, 22-7-1931.
15. *Solidaridad Obrera*, 24-7-1931.
16. Juliá (1984), p. 210.
17. Bizcarrondo (2008), p. 80.
18. NHA, Interior series A, dkt. 7 A. Telegram from Civil Governor of Seville to Minister of Interior, 22-8-1931,
19. NHA, Interior series A, dkt. 6 A. Telegrams from Civil Governor of La Coruña to Ministers of Interior and Labour, 17-7-1931.
20. *El Socialista*, 14-7-1931.
21. Azaña (1981), p. 48, note 21-7-1931.
22. Juliá (1984), p. 211.
23. *Solidaridad Obrera*, 10-7-1931.
24. *El Socialista*, 3-7-1931.
25. Azaña (1981), p. 64.
26. *Solidaridad Obrera*, 2-8-1931.
27. FSS, archive; prior to Civil War, box 1. Regional Plenum Unions Catalonia 2/4-8-1931.
28. Note Regional Committee Andalusia, 23-8-1931. *Solidaridad Obrera*, 27-8-1931.
29. NHA, Interior series, dkt. 7 A. Telegrams Civil Governor of Barcelona to Ministers of Interior and Labour, 20, 26-8-1931.
30. Archive of Historical Studies of the Civil Guard (henceforth, AEHGC). Records Huesca Military Command, September 1931.
31. Pestaña (1973); Elorza (1973), p. 439.
32. IISH, CNT 93 B. Report Regional Pro-prisoners Committee Catalonia, May 1934.
33. Archive of the Paris Police Prefecture (henceforth, APPP), dossier: Ascaso-Durruti, 2-11-1931.
34. *Solidaridad Obrera*, 19-6-1931.
35. Sender Ramón J. (2005), *Siete domingos rojos*, Barcelona, Virus, 2005, p. 102.
36. IISH, Horacio Martínez Prieto archive, sig. Anake, pp. 134–139.
37. De los Santos, Mercedes (1996), "El devenir revolucionario de Buenaventura Durruti", pp. 13–54, in Morales, Antonio y Ortega, Javier (eds.), *El lenguaje de los hechos*, Madrid, Los libros de la Catarata.
38. *Solidaridad Obrera*, 28-2-1933.
39. *Solidaridad Obrera*, 6-7-1933.
40. *Solidaridad Obrera*, 23-7-1931.
41. Preston, Paul (1978), *La destrucción de la democracia en España. Reacción, reforma y revolución en la Segunda República*, Madrid, Turner, p. 112; Fontana,

Josep (1987), *La II República. Una esperanza frustrada.* Minutes of the Congress Valencia Capital of the Republic (April 1986), Valencia, Edicions Alfons El Magnànim, pp. 9–22.

42. Azaña (1981), pp. 51–55, annotations 22, 23-7-1931.
43. CDMHS, sig: PS Madrid, 989, 62. Police reports on telefónica strike, 8-7 al 7-8-1931; IIHS, archive: Ramón Álvarez, box442, Jacinto Toryho estimated 2,000 arrested throughout Spain; Juliá (1984), pp. 198–205.
44. Azaña (1981), p. 48, annotation 21-7-1931.
45. *El Luchador*, 7-8-1931.
46. Azaña (1981), pp. 55–56, annotations, 23, 24-7-1931.
47. *El Luchador*, 28-8-1931.
48. Cabrera (1983), p. 209.
49. AHN, Interior series A, dkt. 7 A (Seville). Edict of General of the 2nd Division, 22-7-1931.
50. Azaña (1981), p. 57.
51. Azaña (1981), pp. 93–95.
52. *El Socialista*, 27-8-1931.
53. Ballbé (1983), pp. 322–323.
54. *Solidaridad Obrera*, 31-7-1931.
55. *El Luchador*, 31-7-1931.
56. CDMHS, sig: PS Madrid, 989, Barcelona police report on Construction Union, 30-7-1931.
57. *El Luchador*, 4-9-1931.
58. FSS, archive; Anterior Guerra civil, caja 1. Regional Plenum Unions Catalonia, 2/4-8-1931.
59. Termes (2011), p. 402.
60. *Solidaridad Obrera*, 25-4-1931.
61. FSS, fondo; prior to Civil War, box 1. Regional Plenum Unions Catalonia, 2/4-8-1931.
62. Brademas (1973), p. 77.
63. Termes (2011), p. 413.
64. CDMHS, sig. PS Santander HA, C 12, file 2. Circular nº 1, CNT NC, Barcelona, 11-08-1931.
65. Elorza (1973), pp. 444–445.
66. Manifesto signed by: Ángel Pestaña, CN secretary; Juan Peiró, editor of *Solidaridad Obrera*; Sebastián Clará, Ricardo Fornells and Agustín Gibanel, members of newspaper editorial team; Pedro Massoni, newspaper manager; Francisco Arín, president Transport Union Barcelona; Joaquín Cortés, board member SU Textil and CN delegate; Juan López, SU Construction board; Camilo Piñón, SU Transport board; Progreso Alfarache, president SU Graphic Arts; Pere Canet, SU Glassworkers Badalona; Espartaco Puig, FL Tarrasa; Mariano Prat, president SU Transport Manresa; along with other prominent militants: José Girona, Daniel Navarro, Jesús Rodríguez, Antonio Vallabriga, Miguel Portolés, Joaquín Roura, Joaquín Llorente, Antonio Peñarroya, Isidoro Gabín, José Cristiá, Juan Dinarés, Roldán Cortada, Ramón Viñas, Federico Uleda, Narciso Marcó and Jenaro Minguet. Various Authors. (1974), *El movimiento libertario español. Pasado, presente y futuro*, Cuadernos de Ruedo Ibérico, pp. 300–302; Vega (1987), p. 88; Vega, Eulalia (1980), *El treintisme a Catalunya, Divergències ideològiques en la CNT (1930–1933)*, Barcelona, Curial.

67. APPP, Ascaso and Durruti files, sig. 1 W 1184; Interview in *Le Tempos*, 2-9-1931.
68. Durruti's response in *La Nau*, VV.AA. (1974), pp. 304–305.
69. *El Luchador*, 11-9-1931
70. CDMHS, sig. PS Madrid, 989, 62. Report by Police Chief Inspector Social Investigation Zaragoza, 13-9-1931.
71. Note by prisoners in Modelo prison, Barcelona, signed by Vicente Vidal, Santiago Bilbao, Manuel Damians, José Moreno, Luzbel Ruiz, Guillermo Granades, *El Luchador*, 4-9-1931.
72. *Solidaridad Obrera*, 6, 8, 11-9-1931; *Batalla*, Communist weekly, 10-9-1931; *El Luchador*, 2-10-1931; Elorza indicates 6 dead and 25 or 30 wounded among the strikers and 6 civil guards wounded, Elorza (2013), p. 208.
73. Elorza (2013), pp. 207–208.
74. *Solidaridad Obrera*, 10-9-1931
75. *Solidaridad Obrera*, 6, 10-9-1931.
76. Different personnel in the editorial team: Vega (1987), p. 95; Termes (2011), p. 421; Brademas (1973), p. 84.
77. ADF, serie Z, sig. 240. Informe Herbette.
78. *Solidaridad Obrera*, 20-11-1931.
79. Ballbé (1983), p. 325.
80. NHA, Series A Interior, dkt.18 A, nº 8. Law on Defence of the Republic; see: Gil (2006); Ballbé (1983), pp. 324–335; González Calleja (2014), pp. 191–197.
81. NHA, Series A Interior, Dkt.18 A, nº 8. Telegram Ministry of Interior to Civil Governors, 4-1-1932.
82. Herrerín (2011), pp. 245–248.
83. *El Socialista*, 23-10-1931.
84. NHA, Interior series A, dkt. 49 A, nº 37. Telegram Ministry of Interior to Civil Governor Barcelona, 23-10-1931.
85. NHA, Series A Interior dkt.18 A, nº 8. Telegrams Civil Governor Cadiz, 9-11-1931, and Civil Governor Vitoria, 18-11, 2-12-1931, to Ministry of Interior.
86. Azaña (1981), p. 321.
87. Letter CN of CNT to Azaña, *Solidaridad Obrera*, 3-12-1931.
88. Minutes Regional Plenum Anarchist Groups., Levante, Valencia, 5/6-12-1931. *Tierra y Libertad*, 23-1-1932; *Sindicalismo*, 14-7-1933.
89. *Tierra y Libertad*, 23-1-1932.
90. National Plenum, Madrid, 13/17-12-1931, *CNT Bulletin*, January 1932.
91. *El Luchador*, 23-10-1931.
92. Minutes Regional Plenum GG.AA. Levante, Valencia, 5/6-12-1931 and GGAA Catalonia, 24/25-12-1931. *Tierra y Libertad*, 23-1-1932, 6-2-1932.
93. *El Luchador*, 8-1-1932.
94. *El Luchador*, 8-1-1932.
95. National Plenum, Madrid, 13/17-12-1931, *CNT Bulletin*, January 1932.
96. FSS, archive prior to Civil War, box 1. Document meeting with Sochy; Martínez Lorenzo (2006), pp. 101–102.
97. *El Luchador*, 4, 8-12-1931
98. AEHGC, Records Civil Guard Military Command Cuenca, 28-1-1931.
99. *Solidaridad Obrera*, 31-12-1931, *El Socialista*, 1-1-1932.
100. ADF, series Z, sig. 154. Report Herbette to Aristide Briand, 6-1-1932; Bizcarrondo (2008), pp. 76–77; Preston (1978), p. 120.
101. *El Socialista*, 6-1-1932.

102. *Solidaridad Obrera*, 5-1-1932.
103. *El Socialista*, 1-1-1932.
104. *El Socialista*, 2-1-1932.
105. ADF, series Z, sig. 154. Declarations to *El Sol*, in report Herbette to Aristide Briand, 6-1-1932.
106. González Calleja (2014), pp. 100–101.
107. *El Socialista*, 6-1-1932.
108. Trullén, Ramiro (2015), "Castilblanco como sinécdoque. El discurso contrarrevolucionario de interpretación de la Segunda República", *Historia Social* nº 83, pp. 55–71.
109. *El Socialista*, 6-1-1932.
110. Azaña (1981), pp. 362–364.
111. *El Socialista*, 6-1-1932; *Solidaridad Obrera*, 5, 6, 7-1-1932.
112. NHA, series A dkt. 16 A, file. 19. Telegram Governor Caceres to Minister of Interior, 4-1-1932.
113. Gil, Carlos (2002), *La República en la plaza: los sucesos de Arnedo de 1932*, Logroño, Government of la Rioja.
114. Gil (2002), pp. 78–81.
115. AEHGC, Records Civil Guard Command, Logroño.
116. Gil (2002), pp. 111–112.
117. Azaña (1981), p. 365.
118. Archive Congress of Deputies (henceforth, ACD), Session record. Historical series, 6-1-1932.
119. *El Luchador*, 15-1-1932.
120. Azaña (1981), pp. 382 and 365.
121. Gil (2002), pp. 133–145.
122. Azaña (1981), pp. 368–369.
123. Cardona (1987), pp. 49–64.
124. Azaña (1981), pp. 368–371.
125. ADF, series Z, 141. Report Herbette to Aristide Briand, 30-12-1931.
126. ADF, series Z, 153. Report by Jean Herbette, for Aristide Briand, 23-12-1931.
127. *El Socialista*, 7-1-1932.
128. Bizcarrondo (2008), p. 77; González Calleja (2014), p. 104.
129. Gil (2002), pp. 156–167.
130. AEHGC, Civil Guard Command Records, Logroño.
131. *El Luchador*, 1-1-1932.
132. Borderías, Cristina and Vilanova, Mercedes (1983), "Cronología de una insurrección: Figols en 1932", *Estudios de Historia Social*, nº 24–25, pp. 187–199; Giráldez, Jesús (2009), *Creyeron que éramos rebaño. La insurrección del Alto llobregat y la deportación de anarquistas a Canarias y África durante la II República*, Malaga, publishers: Zambra, Libreando and Balandre, pp. 34–40.
133. Giráldez (2009), p. 39.
134. Borderías and Vilanova (1983), pp. 187–199.
135. *El Luchador*, 5-2-1932.
136. IISH, sig. CNT, 93 B. Minutes Local Barcelona Federation analysis insurrection January 1932. Copy signed by secretary on 3-3-1932.
137. National Plenum, Madrid, 13/16-4-1932, *CNT Bulletin*, May 1932.
138. *Tierra y Libertad*, 16-1-1932.

139. IISH, sig. CNT, 93 B. Barcelona Local Federation Records, January 1932; *CNT Bulletin*, May 1932. National Plenum, Madrid, 13/16-4-1932.
140. Borderías and Vilanova (1983), pp. 187–199.
141. *El Luchador*, 29-1-1931.
142. Herrerín (2011), pp. 76–82.
143. Eduardo de Guzmán, "Los sucesos de Figols", *La Tierra*, in *Tierra y Libertad*, 6-2-1932. Many of these claims have been qualified by historical research, which, without denying the revolutionary nature of the movement, has pointed out that "neither money nor private ownership was abolished, nor was that of others shared out. . ." Borderías and Vilanova (1983), pp. 187–199.
144. *Tierra y Libertad*, 6-2-1932; *El Luchador*, 5-2-1932.
145. NHA, Interior series A, dkt. 7 A (Barcelona). Telegram Civil Governor to Ministry Interior, 28-5-1931; Solidaridad Obrera, 27-5-1931.
146. Azaña (1981), p. 402.
147. Azaña, Manuel (1992), *Discursos parlamentarios*, Madrid, Congress of Deputies Publications, pp. 132–133.
148. ACD, Parliamentary Daily Sessions. Historical Series, pp. 3712–3714. Intervention José Grau, parliamentary session 10-2-1932.
149. NHA, Interior series A, dkt. 7 A (Barcelona). Telegram Civil Governor to Ministry Interior, 10-8-1931; *Solidaridad Obrera*, 27-8-1931.
150. *El Socialista*, 26-1-1932; Ballbé (1983), p. 342.
151. Borderías and Vilanova (1983), pp. 187–199; *Solidaridad Obrera*, 2-3-1932.
152. *CNT Bulletin*, February–April 1932; *El Luchador*, 19-2-1932; Borderías and Vilanova (1983); Giráldez (2009).
153. The deportees numbered 118, according to *Solidaridad Obrera*, 4-3-1932; 117, according to Giráldez (2009), pp. 128–135.
154. *El Socialista*, 22-1-1932.
155. *El Luchador*, 29-1-1932.
156. *El Luchador*, 19-2-1932.
157. *Cultura Libertaria*, 5, 26-2-1932, in Elorza (1973), p. 452; Giráldez (2009), p. 90.
158. Azaña (1981), p. 417, annotation 27-2-1932.
159. *El Socialista*, 6-8-1931.
160. ADF, series Z, sig. 240. Report Herbette, 15-12-1931.
161. Vega (1987), p. 95.
162. *El Luchador*, 25-3-1932.
163. VV.AA. (1990), p. 13.
164. *El Luchador*, 4-3-1932.
165. *CNT Bulletin*, May 1932. National Plenum, Madrid, 13/16-4-1932.
166. *Solidaridad Obrera*, 20, 21-1-1932.
167. Paz, Abel (1996), *Durruti en la revolución española*, Madrid, Fundación Anselmo Lorenzo, pp. 314–315.
168. *El Luchador*, 24-4-1931.
169. IISH, sig. FAI, 36 A. Regional Plenum Records FAI, Madrid, 31-7, 2-8-1932.
170. *El Luchador*, 15-4-1932.
171. IISH, Horacio Martínez Prieto archive, sig. Anake, p. 148.
172. CNT (1955), *El Congreso Confederal de Zaragoza*, Toulouse, CNT Publications, pp. 118, 57.
173. ADF, series Z, sig. 154. Report Herbette to Pierre Laval, Council President, 25-

1-1932; and G. Le Lorrain, French Consul in Malaga to the Foreign Minister, 26-1-1932.
174. Ruling signed by: Miguel Mendiola, for Andalusia, Juan Font, Catalonia, Miguel González, Centre and Marcos Alcón and Manuel Rivas, National Committee. *CNT Bulletin*, May 1932. National Plenum, Madrid, 13/16-4-1932.
175. National Plenum, Madrid, 13/16-4-1932, *CNT Bulletin*, May 1932.
176. *El Luchador*, 5-5-1932.
177. *El Luchador*, 25-3, 6-5-1932.
178. *El Luchador*, 1-4-1932.
179. *El Luchador*, 1-4-1932
180. *El Luchador*, 1-4-1932.
181. FSS, archive, prior to Civil War, box 1. Regional Plenum Unions Catalonia, 2/4-8-1931; Elorza (1973), p. 453.
182. *Solidaridad Obrera*, 30-4, 1-5-1932, Regional Plenum Catalonia, Sabadell, abril 1932.
183. *El Luchador*, 15-4-1932.
184. *Solidaridad Obrera*, 4, 5-5-1932.
185. *El Luchador*, 6-5-1932.
186. FSS, archive; prior to Civil War, box 1. Regional Union Conference, Catalonia, 31-5, 1-6-1931.
187. *Solidaridad Obrera*, 2-3-1932.
188. *El Luchador*, 15-4, 20-5-1932.
189. *Solidaridad Obrera*, 27, 30-4-1932.
190. Peirats (1971), p. 72; Elorza (1973), p. 453.
191. *CNT Bulletin*, September 1932. National Plenum Regional Delegates, Madrid, 28/30-8-1932.
192. IISH, CNT, 93 B. Report RC Catalonia, 24-6-1932.
193. *CNT Bulletin*, July 1932. Circular nº 14.
194. FSS, archive, prior to Civil War, box 1. Letter SU Construction Barcelona to CN, 27-11-1932.
195. *CNT Bulletin*, January 1933. Minutes Extraordinary Assembly Single Food Union, 16-11-1932.
196. *CNT Bulletin*, March 1933.

3 To the Barricades! (May 1932–December 1933)

1. *CNT Bulletin*, February–April 1932.
2. *Solidaridad Obrera*, 8-3-1932.
3. National Plenum, Madrid, 13 to 16-4-1932. *CNT Bulletin*, May 1932.
4. Note from NC of CNT, 24-3-1932, *CNT Bulletin*, February–April 1932.
5. National Plenum, Madrid, 13 to 16-4-1932. *CNT Bulletin*, May 1932.
6. Bizcarrondo (2008), p. 27.
7. Azaña (1981), p. 465, annotation 7-5-1932.
8. NHA, Interior series A, dkt. 6 A. Newsletter Ministry of the Interior to Civil Governors, 1-6-1932, telegram, 1-7-1931.
9. Newsletters 17 and 19 of the NC. *CNT Bulletins*, August and October 1932.
10. IISH, CNT 93 B. Newsletter RC Catalonia, 22-7-1932.
11. *Solidaridad Obrera*, 19-8 and 13-9-1932.
12. *CNT Bulletins*, September and October 1932.

13. Azaña, Manuel, *Diarios, 1932–1933, "los cuadernos robados"*, Barcelona, Crítica, 1997. p. 151.
14. Figures from different publications: Bizcarrondo (2008), pp. 3, 18–24; Ruiz (2008), pp. 36–39; Preston (1978), p. 99; Gil (2006), p. 210.
15. NHA, Interior series A, dkt. 7 A, file 16. Telegrams governors of Malaga and Granada, 19 y 21-4; 8 y 16-5; y 5-7-1932.
16. ADF, series Z, 173. Report French Consulate in Seville, 18-4-1932.
17. Report Regional Federation of Andalusia and Extremadura on the strike of 19-5-1932. National Plenum of Regional Delegates, Madrid, 28/30-8-1932. *CNT Bulletin* (September1932).
18. *CNT Bulletin*, September 1932, and *Sindicalismo*, 29-9-1933.
19. *Solidaridad Obrera*, 4-6-1932.
20. ADF, series Z, 173. Report French Consulate in Seville, 9-6-1932.
21. Preston (1978), p. 125.
22. NHA, Interior series A, dkt. 6 A (Cordoba). Telegrams Ministry of the Interior, 16-6 and 10-11-1932.
23. Bizcarrondo (2008), pp. 55–58.
24. Azaña (1981), p. 443.
25. ADF, series Z, 258. Report French Embassy in Spain, 24-5-1932.
26. Bizcarrondo (2008), p. 73.
27. *CNT Bulletin*, July 1932.
28. NHA, series A dkt. 16 A, file 18. Telegrams civil governors to Ministry of the Interior, 29, 30, 31-5 and 1-6-1932.
29. *CNT Bulletin*, July 1932.
30. Data from the following sources: FSS, archive, Anterior Guerra civil, box 1. Regional Plenum of Unions of Catalonia 2/4-8-1931; Levante Regional Congress, summer 1932, in *Sindicalismo* 14-7-1933; Elorza (1973), pp. 448–449; Vega (1987), pp. 65 and 110; Casanova (1997), p. 84.
31. National Plenum, April 1932, *CNT Bulletin*, May 1932.
32. Casanova (1997), p. 68.
33. Cardona (1983), p. 187; Ballbé (1983), pp. 345–347.
34. AEHGC, Huelva General Command Records.
35. Minutes NC meeting 10 and 11 August, *CNT Bulletin*, August 1932; Regional report Andalusia and Extremadura, National Plenum Delegates, 28/30-8-1932, *CNT Bulletin*, September 1932.
36. ADF, series Z, sig. 154. Report Jean Herbette to Edouard Herriot, Council President.
37. Cardona (1987), pp. 49–64.
38. This figure in Giráldez (2009), *Creyeron que éramos rebaño. La insurrección del Alto Llobregat y la deportación de anarquistas a Canarias y África durante la II República*, Malaga, editoriales Zambra, Libreando and Balandre, p. 209; 145 according to Ballbé (1983), p. 346.
39. NHA, series A, dkt. 2 A, nº 22. Telegrams to the Ministry of the Interior.
40. Giráldez (2009), pp. 150–178; Pérez, Guadalupe (2002), "La colonia penitenciaria de Villa Cisneros. Deportaciones y fugas durante la Segunda República", *Historia y Comunicación social*, vol. 7, pp. 169–186.
41. *El Luchador*, 15-4-1932.
42. ACD, Diary Court Sessions. Historical Series, 8-7-1932.
43. Guadalupe (2002), pp. 169–186.

44. *Solidaridad Obrera*, 20-8-1932.
45. ACD, Diary Parliamentary Sessions. Historical Series, 28-12-1932.
46. Azaña (1997), p. 197.
47. On these questions, see: Malefakis, Edward (2001), *Reforma agraria y revolución campesina en la España del siglo XX*, Madrid, Espasa Calpe; by the same author (1987), "El problema agrario y la República", in VVAA. *La II República. Una esperanza frustrada*, Minutes of the Congress Valencia Capital de la República (April 1986), Valencia, Edicions Alfons El Magnànim, pp. 37–48; Gil (2006), pp. 100–107; Avilés et al Juan (2002), *Historia política, 1875–1939*, Madrid, Istmo.
48. Conservatorio Congress, June 1931, *El Luchador*, 17 and 24-7-1931; and National Plenum, December 1931, *CNT Bulletin*, January 1932.
49. Martínez Lorenzo (1969), p. 51.
50. *El Luchador*, 1-5-1932.
51. Martínez Lorenzo (1969), p. 51; Termes (2011), p. 402.
52. Azaña (1981), pp. 191–192.
53. *Tierra y Libertad*, 23-9-1932 y *El Luchador*, 14-10-1932.
54. IISH, CNT, 93 B, Sabadell unions report, 28-10-1932.
55. FSS, archive; Anterior Guerra civil, box 1. Regional Plenum Single Unions Catalonia, Barcelona 5/13-3-1933. Letter from Pere Robert (possibly Arturo Parera) to the RC, 15-5-1932 and Gilabert's reply 18-5-1932, reproduced in the plenum minutes.
56. FSS, archive; Anterior Guerra civil, box 1. Letters between Rivas, Gilabert and Virgili, 18-5, 2 and 5-7-1932, reproduced in the minutes of the Regional Plenum Single Unions Catalonia, Barcelona 5/13-3-1933.
57. IISH, CNT, 93 B. Report RC Catalonia, 29-9-1932.
58. According to Termes 1,000 members, Termes (2011), p. 442.
59. FSS, archive: Frank Mintz, Shapiro report; Elorza (1973), pp. 453–454; Peirats, José, *La CNT en la revolución española*, vol. 1, Cary-Colombes, Ruedo Ibérico, 1971. p. 72.
60. IISH, CNT, 93 B. Extract minutes Regional Plenum, Madrid, 30-1-1933; Single Unions Assembly Valencia, 8-2-1933, in *El Combate Sindicalista*, 4-3-1933.
61. National Plenum Regional Delegates, Madrid, 28/30-8-1932, *CNT Bulletin*, September 1932.
62. CDMHS, sig. PS Barcelona 512/2. Letter Juan López to Pestaña, 9-11-1932.
63. Elorza (1973), pp. 453–454.
64. CDMHS, sig. PS Barcelona 512/2, Letters Palafrugell Single Union, 10-10-1932, and from the LF of the San Sebastian Single Union, 1-3-33, to Pestaña.
65. CDMHS, sig. PS Barcelona 512/2, Letter Juan López to Pestaña, 9-11-1932.
66. *Solidaridad Obrera*, 26-10-1932
67. *Tierra y Libertad*, 4-11-1932; *El Luchador*, 4-11-1932; *Sindicalismo*, 24-3-1933.
68. CDMHS, sig. PS Gijon, JC 11, 6. Meetings regional militants of Asturias, León and Palencia, 6 and 8-11-1932.
69. CDMHS, sig. PS Gijon, JC 12, file 11. Letter Ateneo Sindicalista Libertario, Barcelona, Pestaña to the Asturian militants, 19-11-1932.
70. *Solidaridad Obrera*, 18 y 20-11-1932.
71. "On the Sheep", article by Federica Montseny in *El Luchador*, 2-12-1932; Martínez Lorenzo (2006), p. 118.
72. *Solidaridad Obrera*, 21-11-1932 and *En Marcha*, 26-11-1932.

73. IISH, sig. CNT, 93 B. Minutes CNT Regional Plenum, Madrid, 2-12-1932 and minutes local and regional plenums RC Catalonia, 10-12-1932.
74. IISH, sig. CNT, 93 B. Extract minutes National Plenum, Madrid, 30-1-1933.
75. CDMHS, sig. F-1511. Levante RC report, insurrection January 1933.
76. NHA, Serie A Gobernación, dkt. 4, 13. Telegram Civil Governor Barcelona to the Ministry of the Interior, 3-1-1933; FSS, archive, Frank Mintz, Shapiro Report, 15-4-1933; *Solidaridad Obrera*, 3-1-1933.
77. Azaña (1997), pp. 122 and 128.
78. García Oliver (2008), *El eco de los pasos*, Barcelona, Backlist (1st edition: Paris, Ruedo Ibérico, 1978), p. 174.
79. Martínez Lorenzo (1969), pp. 48 and 111; Peiró's "Imperio callejero" in *El Combate Sindicalista*, 10-6-1933.
80. *Solidaridad Obrera*, 10 and 12-1-1933; FSS, Frank Mintz archive, Shapiro report, 15-4-1933; IISH, sig. CNT, 93 B. Extract minutes National Plenum, Madrid, 30-1-1933.
81. CNT (1955), pp. 123–124.
82. IISH, sig. CNT, 93 B. Extracto Minutes National Plenum, Madrid, 30-1-1933.
83. IISH, CNT, 93 B. Extract minutes National Plenum, Madrid, June 1933.
84. CNT (1955), p. 120.
85. FSS, archive: Anterior Guerra civil, box 1. Letter from Sender to Carbó, 11-10-1932.
86. The underlining is mine, CNT (1955), pp. 120 and 128.
87. García Oliver (2008), p. 176.
88. ACD, Diary Parliamentary Sessions. Historical Series, 2-2-1933.
89. Domingo Torres, "La verdad sobre la última huelga general", *Sindicalismo*, 14-2-1933.
90. AEHGC, Civil Guard Command Records, Valencia, January 1933.
91. NHA, series A, dkt. 58 A, file 29. Telegrams Civil Governor of Seville to the Minister and Director General of Security, January 1933.
92. *La Libertad*, 21 and 22-1-1933; De Guzmán, Eduardo, *La tragedia de Casas Viejas, 1933*, Madrid, Vosa, 2007, pp. 18–37.
93. AEHGC, Civil Guard Command Records Cádiz.
94. Sender, Ramón J. (2004), *Casas Viejas*, Zaragoza, Larumbe, pp. 71–94.
95. Azaña (1997), pp. 130–136.
96. Ramos, Tano (2012), *Casas Viejas: crónica de una insidia (1933–1936)*, Barcelona, Tusquets, pp. 341–342 y 350.
97. CDMHS, sig: PS Santander HA, C 12, file 2. Newsletter II, CPPN, 20-6-1934; *Solidaridad Obrera*, 1-7-1934; *Tierra y Libertad*, 30-6-1934. The sentence was read out on 26 June 1934. Antonio Cabañas Salvador was sentenced to six years in prison; Salvador Jurado, Francisco Rocha, Sebastián Pavón, José Toro and Manuel Murube to five; José Muñoz, Juan Jiménez, Manuel Vera, Francisco Cantero, Francisco Durán and Miguel Pavón to three; Estebán Jiménez to two; José Moreno, Antonio Durán and José Rodríguez to one; Diego Fernández, Francisco Quijada, Juan Pérez, José González, Manuel González, Antonio Pérez, Antonio Conejero, Antonio Vinués, José Conejero and Sebastián Rodríguez were acquitted.
98. Juliá, Santos (2008), *Vida y tiempo de Manuel Azaña (1880–1940)*, Madrid, Taurus, pp. 324–327; Ramos (2012).

99. Segovia General Military Archives (henceforth AGMS), CG: R-228. Personal file Manuel Rojas Feigenspan.
100. AGMS, B-633. Personal file Bartolomé Barba Hernández; Cardona (1987), pp. 49–64.
101. Herrerín (2011a), pp. 185–186.
102. CNT (1955), pp. 120 y 57.
103. Sender (2005), p. 119.
104. IISH, sig. CNT, 93 B. Extract minutes National Plenum, Madrid, 30-1-1933.
105. IISH, sig. CNT, 93 B. Extract minutes National Plenum, Madrid, 12-6-1933.
106. *La Libertad*, 21 and 22-1-1933; also in ADF, series Z, sig. 156. Report French Consulate in Barcelona to President French Government, 9-1-1933.
107. Azaña (1997), p. 145.
108. ACD, Diario Sesiones Cortes. Historical Series, 2-2-1933.
109. *La Libertad*, 26 and 27-1-1933.
110. Azaña (1997), p. 160.
111. Azaña (1997), p. 173, 13-2-1933.
112. FSS, Frank Mintz archive, Shapiro Report. IWA Secretariat report by Carbó and Shapiro.
113. García Oliver (2008), p. 176
114. *La Libertad*, 21-1-1933.
115. IISH, archive Horacio Martínez Prieto, sig. Utopistas, p. 104.
116. IISH, CNT, 93 B. Extract minutes National Plenum, Madrid, 30-1-1933.
117. Appeared in *Cultura Libertaria*, 15-1-1933; summary in *El Luchador*, 3-2-1933.
118. Elorza (1973), pp. 352 and 403.
119. *El Combate Sindicalista*, 4-3-1933.
120. *Sindicalismo*, 21-7-1933.
121. FSL note to regional secretaries and Local Associations, *Sindicalismo*, 19-12-1933.
122. *Sindicalismo*, 14-2-1933; *El Combate Sindicalista*, 13-5-1933.
123. Emiliana Morin, "El cometido de la mujer en la lucha social", *Solidaridad Obrera*, 26-7-1931; IISH, CNT, 68 B. Minutes Regional, Local and County Plenum, Andalusia and Extremadura, August 1934; La Agrupación Femenina de Educación Libertaria, in *El Luchador*, 3-2-1933.
124. Termes (2011), pp. 445–446.
125. *Sindicalismo*, 1-8-1933; El *Combate Sindicalista*, 23-2-1933.
126. Minutes Administrative Assembly Single Unions Valencia, 8-2-1933, *El Combate Sindicalista*, 4-3-1933.
127. Vega (1987), pp. 180–181.
128. Vega (1987), p. 188.
129. *Sindicalismo*, 14-2-1933.
130. *El Combate Sindicalista*, 1-4-1933.
131. CDMHS, sig: PS Barcelona 512/2. Letter San Sebastian LF to Pestaña, 2-3-1933.
132. FSS, archive; Anterior Guerra civil, box 1. Regional Plenum Single Unions Catalonia, 5/13-3-1933; *Solidaridad Obrera*, 9-3-1933; *Sindicalismo*, 24-3-1933; Termes (2011), p. 444.
133. IISH, archive: FAI, 36 A. Letter Local Federation of Anarchist Groups of Barcelona to FAI peninsular committee, 16-2-1933.
134. *Solidaridad Obrera*, 9-3-1933.
135. *Sindicalismo*, 9-6, 1-8 y 25-8-1933; Brademas (1973), pp. 117–119.

136. FSS, archive; Anterior Guerra civil, box 1. Regional Plenum Single Unions Catalonia, 5/13-3-1933.
137. Constituted 9-12-1933, signed, on behalf of the UGT, by J. Vila Cuenca; on behalf of the Opposition Unions, Ángel Pestaña; Socialist Federation of Barcelona (PSOE), with Rafael Vidiella; the Workers' and Peasants' Block, with Joaquín Maurín; on behalf of the Libertarian Syndicalist Federation, Juan López; on behalf of the Socialist Union of Catalonia, M. Martinez Cuenca; on behalf of Communist Left, Andrés Nin; Unió de Rabassaires de Catalunya, with José Calvet; and on behalf of the Federation of Unions Expelled from the CNT, Francisco Aguilar, *Sindicalismo*, 3-11 and 15-12-1933.
138. Bizcarrondo (2008), p. 69; Gil (2006), p. 214.
139. Bizcarrondo (2008), p. 56; Gil (2006), p. 99.
140. NHA, serie A, dkt. 40 A, dkt. 10, Telegrams Civil Governor Zaragoza, 9, 11 y 12-5-1933.
141. *Solidaridad Obrera*, 24 y 28-10-1933; *Sindicalismo*, 17-11-1933; Juliá (1984), pp. 234–236; Bizcarrondo (2008), pp. 73–75.
142. Azaña (1997), pp. 411–412.
143. ADF, serie Z, sig 157. Report Herbette to Paul Boncour, Foreign Minister.
144. Bizcarrondo (2008), pp. 18 and 24.
145. Ruiz (2008), p. 86; Bizcarrondo (2008), p. 83.
146. *El Combate Sindicalista*, 4-3, 1 and 15-4-1933.
147. *El Combate Sindicalista*, 29-4 and 6-5-1933.
148. Cabrera (1983), pp. 206–207.
149. Information about the strike in *Solidaridad Obrera*, 4, 21, 22 y 24-4, 9-6, 2, 6, 8 y 12-7, 5 y 16-8-1933 y *Sindicalismo*, 8-9-1933.
150. Bizcarrondo (2008), p. 68; Cabrera (1983), p. 132.
151. *Solidaridad Obrera*, 12-7-1933.
152. NHA, Serie A Gobernación, dkt. 4, 13. Telegrams Civil Governors of Alicante, Almeria, Barcelona, La Coruña, Huelva and Huesca to the Ministry of the Interior, 1933.
153. NHA, series A, Interior, Seville dkt. 58 A, file 29; ADF, series Z, sig. 156, Herbette report, 1-5-1933.
154. *Sindicalismo*, 28-4-1933.
155. IISH, archive FAI, 36 A. Local Federation Anarchist Groups of Barcelona to the FAI Peninsular Committee 16-2-1933.
156. Azaña (1997), pp. 183–184, 21-2-1933.
157. APPP, sig: BA 2156. French police report, June 1933.
158. NHA, series A, dkt. 58 A, file. 27. Telegram Minister of the Interior to Civil Governors.
159. NHA, Series A Interior, dkt. 4, 13. Telegram Civil Governor Barcelona to the Ministry of the Interior
160. ADF, series Z, 173. Report French Ambassador to Spain, 17-5-1932.
161. *Sindicalismo*, 23-6-1933.
162. *El Combate Sindicalista*, 8-4-1933; and *Sindicalismo*, 28-4-1933.
163. *Sindicalismo*, 2-6-1933.
164. NHA, Interior series A, dkt. 51 nº 16, April 1933.
165. Ballbé (1983), pp. 359–363; González Calleja (2014), pp. 205–211.
166. González Calleja (2014), pp. 209–215; on anarchist propaganda, Herrerín (2011a), p. 78.

167. NHA, series A, dkt. 58 A, file 29. Telegram Civil Governor Seville to the Ministry of the Interior, 6-9-1933; *Solidaridad Obrera*, 14 and 26-9-1933.
168. NHA, series A, dkt. 58 A, file 29. Telegram Civil Governor Seville to the Ministry of the Interior, 28-8-1933.
169. *Solidaridad Obrera*, 17-9-1933.
170. ADF, series Z, sig. 157. Herbette report for Paul Boncour, Foreign Minister, 25-8-1933.
171. NHA, series A, dkt. 58 A, file 29. Telegrams Governor Seville to Ministry of the Interior, July and August 1933; *ABC*, 27-7-1933, in ADF, series Z, sig. 157. Herbette report to Paul Boncour.
172. *Solidaridad Obrera*, 1-9-1933.
173. *Solidaridad Obrera*, 7-10-1933.
174. See, for example *Sindicalista*, 25-6 and 7-7-1933.
175. *El Combate Sindicalista*, 8, 15-4-1933; *Sindicalismo*, 12-5-1933.
176. IISH, CNT, 93 B. Extract National Plenum, Madrid, June 1933.
177. *Sindicalismo*, 20-7-1933.
178. IISH, CNT, 93 B. Minutes CNT Regional Plenum, Madrid, 30-10-1933.
179. FSS, archive Anterior Guerra civil, box 1. Carta CN CNT a AIT, 17-11-1933.
180. NHA, serie A, dkt. 40 A, dkt. 10. Telegrams Civil Governor Barcelona, 7 y 8-5-1933.
181. NHA, serie A, dkt. 40 A, dkt. 10. Telegram Civil Governor Barcelona, 19-6-1933.
182. IISH, CNT, 93 B. Extract National Plenum, Madrid, June 1933.
183. Andalusia CNT Regional Congress, April 1933, in *Sindicalismo*, 7-4-1933.
184. IISH, CNT, 93 B. Extract National Plenum, Madrid, June 1933.
185. NHA, serie A, dkt. 58 A, file 29. Telegram Civil Governor Seville, 4-8-1933; *El Combate Sindicalista*, 17-6-1933; *Solidaridad Obrera*, 21-6 y 26-8-1933.
186. FSS, Archive Frank Mintz, Shapiro Report.
187. IISH, CNT, 93 B. National Plenum, Madrid, June 1933.
188. FSS, archive, Frank Mintz, Shapiro Report, Regional Conference Unions of Catalonia, 31-5 and 1-6-1931.
189. IISH, CNT 93 B. Callejas letter of resignation, 24-6-1933, and RC negotiations in search of director in Catalonia RC report to unions, July 1933; *Solidaridad Obrera*, 2-7-1933 and *Sindicalismo*, 21-7-1933.
190. IISH, CNT, 93 B. Report RC Catalonia to unions, 9-8-1933.
191. *Sindicalismo*, 21-7 and 1-12-1933.
192. IISH, Archive Ramón Álvarez, box 449. Pleno Regional CNT Asturias, mayo 1931; Elorza y Bizcarrondo (1999), p. 178; Barrio (1988), pp. 324–325.
193. FSS, archive, Anterior Guerra civil, box 1. Manifiesto Frente Antifascista; Elorza and Bizcarrondo (1999), pp. 176–181.
194. *Solidaridad Obrera*, 28-3 y 9-11-1933; *El Combate Sindicalista*, 18-3-1933 y *Sindicalismo*, 12-5, 28-7 y 4-8-1933.
195. Gil, Julio (1994), *Conservadores subversivos: la derecha autoritaria alfonsina (1913–1936)*, Madrid, Eudema; Gil (2006), pp. 259–265.
196. ADF, series Z, 157. Herbette report for Paul Boncour, 31-8-1933.
197. Gil Robles, José María (1998), *No fue posible la paz. Memorias*, Barcelona, Planteta, p. 90.
198. *ABC*, 9-9-1933, Herbette mentions this in: ADF, series Z, 157. Herbette report for Paul Boncour, 11-9-1933.
199. ADF, series Z, 157. Interview in report by Herbette for Paul Boncour, 16-9-1933.

200. *Solidaridad Obrera*, 9-9-1933; *Sindicalismo*, 15-9-1933.
201. *Solidaridad Obrera*, 10, 11, 21, 22-10-1933 y 7, 14, 16, 17 y 18-11-1933.
202. IISH, CNT, 93 B. Minutes CNT Regional Plenum, Madrid, 30-10-1933.
203. *Sindicalismo*, 10 and 24-11-1933; see also, Brademas (1973), pp. 111–112.
204. Gil (2006), pp. 254–257–283.
205. ADF, series Z, 158, Herbette report for Paul Boncour, 22 and 27-11-1933.
206. See: Caro, Diego (2013), "El anarcosindicalismo y la victoria del Frente Popular en las elecciones de 1936", *Historia Social*, nº 76, pp. 45–66; and Villa, Roberto (2011), *La República en las urnas. El despertar de la democracia en España*, Madrid, Marcial Pons.
207. Caro (2013), pp. 51–53; Ruiz (2008), p. 371; Martínez Lorenzo (1969), p. 62; Preston (1978), pp. 155–156.
208. ADF, series Z, 158. Herbette report for Paul Boncour, 22-11-1933.
209. *Sindicalismo*, 24-11-1933.
210. IISH, sig. CNT, 93 B. Minutes National Plenum, Barcelona, February 1934.
211. NHA, series A, dkt. 58 A, file 27. Telegrams Ministry of the Interior to Civil Governors, 2, 7 and 12-12-1933.
212. Different versions of the formation of the Revolutionary Committee. Peirats names only Cipriano Mera and Isaac Puente, Peirats (1971), p. 77; According to Casanova, it was formed by: Durruti, Cipriano Mera, Rafael García Chacón, Rafael Casado Ojeda, Isaac Puente, Felipe Orquín, Ramón Andrés and Antonio Ejarque, Casanova (1997), p. 117; Meanwhile Martínez Lorenzo lists Cipriano Mera, Durruti, Antonio Ejarque, Isaac Puente and Francisco Foyo, who is the person from whom he obtained the information in an interview in Toulouse in 1971, Martínez Lorenzo (2006), pp. 118–119.
213. IISH, archive Horacio Martínez Prieto, sig. Utopistas, p. 120.
214. Brademas (1973), p. 115; Martínez. Lorenzo (1969), p. 62.
215. IISH, Horacio Martínez Prieto archive, sig. Anake, p. 151.
216. AEHGC, Civil Guard Headquarters Records, Logroño and Zaragoza.
217. AEHGC, Civil Guard Headquarters Records, Castellón.
218. ADF, series Z, sig. 158. Report Herbette to Paul Boncour, 12-12-1933.
219. IISH, archive: FAI, 36 A. FAI Peninsular Committee to regional federations, 15-4-1933.
220. AEHGC, Civil Guard Headquarters Records, Logroño, 9-12-1933; Elorza (1973), pp. 462–463.
221. ACD, Diary Parliamentary Sessions. Historical Series, 17-1-1934. Roberto Villa provides other figures: 125 dead and 186 injured; of the rebels: 65 dead and 38 injured; other civilian victims: 44 dead and 85 injured; security forces: 16 dead and 63 injured, in Villa, Roberto (2011b), "La CNT contra la república: La insurrección revolucionaria de diciembre de 1933", *Historia y Política*, nº 5, January-June, pp. 177–205. However, González Calleja puts the number of dead during the month of December, including civilians and the security forces, at 114. My thanks to Professor González Calleja for generously sharing with me the results of his research.
222. IISH, sig. CNT, 93 B. Minutes National Plenum, Barcelona, February 1934; accusations of repression, *Ahora*, 17-12-1933; Those arrested were: Cipriano Mera, Rafael García Chacón, Rafael Casado, Isaac Puente, Felipe Orquín Aspas, Ramón Andrés Crespo and Antonio Ejarque. With them were three women, the owner

of the flat, María Castañeda, and two servants: Francisca Santos Clemente and Dolores Lerín.

223. IISH, Archive Ramón Álvarez, box 443. Documento de Ramón Álvarez, *Ramonín*; *La Voz de Aragón*, 25-1-1934.
224. ADF, series Z, sig. 158. Report Herbette to Paul Boncour, 12-12-1933.
225. *Sindicalismo*, 15, 19 and 29-12-1933.
226. IISH, sig. CNT, 93 B. Minutes National Plenum, Barcelona, February 1934.
227. IISH, sig. CNT, 93 B. Minutes National Plenum, Barcelona, February 1934.
228. CNT (1955), pp. 120–156.
229. IISH, sig. FAI, 36 B. Minutes National Plenum, Madrid, June 1934.
230. IISH, CNT, 93 B. Extract National Plenum, Madrid, June 1933; Cardona (1993), p. 197.
231. *Tiempos Nuevos*, II, 1, 10-1-1935; Elorza (1973), pp. 448–449; Casanova (1997), p. 84.
232. IISH, sig. CNT, 93 B, Report CNT National Committee, 20-1-1934, signed in Barcelona 26-2-1934.

4 From the Workers' Alliance to the Revolution (January 1934–April 1935)

1. IISH, Ramón Álvarez Archive, box 443. The document was signed on 26-1-1934 in Coto prison by: Avelino González Mallada, A. Bartolomé, Segundo Blanco, Horacio Argüelles, José D. Doraño, Avelino Martínez, Pelayo Cifuentes and José Mª Martínez; See, also, Barrio, Ángeles (1984), "La CNT de Asturias, León y Palencia y la Alianza Obrera de 1934", *Estudios de Historia Social* nº 31, pp. 123–129.
2. Article by Valeriano Orobón Fernández in *La Tierra*, in Martínez Lorenzo (1969), pp. 63–65.
3. *Sindicalismo*, 15-12-1933.
4. Mitin en La Bohemia por el Comité Regional de Alianza Obrera Cataluña. Speakers: Juan López, on behalf of the FSL; Jaime Miravitlles, representing the unions expelled from the CNT; Rafael Vidiella, PSOE; Andrés Nin, Communist Left; Francisco Arín, Opposition Unions; Joaquín Maurín, Workers' and Peasants' Block; and J. Vila Cuenca, UGT. Absent: J. Calvet, Unió Rabassaires de Cataluña, *Sindicalismo*, 7-3-1934.
5. IISH, CNT, 68 A. Regional Report Asturias, León and Palencia, 10-3-1934.
6. IISH, CNT, 68 A. NC Report, 20-1-1934, contacts with Lerroux, 26-2-1934.
7. *Boletín de la Regional Galaica*, April–May 1934.
8. IISH, FAI, 36 B. Minutes National Plenum, June 1934.
9. IISH, sig. CNT, 50 A. CNT National Committee Report to Secretariat AIT, 30-7-1935.
10. IISH, sig. CNT, 93 B. Minutes National Plenum, Barcelona. Motion adopted, 12-2-1934.
11. IISH, sig. CNT, 50 A. Sentence in National Committee report, 30-7-1935.
12. *El Luchador*, 30-9-1932.
13. CNT (1990), *Colección de Historia oral: El movimiento libertario en España*, García Oliver interviewed by Freddy Gómez, 29-6-1977, Paris, Madrid, Fundación Salvador Seguí, pp. 15–16.
14. IISH, Fondo Ramón Álvarez, box 385. Letter Fidel Miró, Mexico, to Ramón Álvarez, *Ramonín*, 21-11-1992; Martínez Lorenzo (2006), pp. 110–111;

Foreword Antonio Elorza in Abad de Santillán, Diego (1976), *El anarquismo y la revolución en España. Escritos 1930/1938*, Madrid, Ayuso, pp. 10–11.

15. Juliá (1997), *Los socialistas en la política española, 1879–1982*, Madrid, Taurus, pp. 197–203; Bizcarrondo (2008), pp. 99–103.
16. *El Socialista*, 1-5-1934.
17. Avilés, Juan (2008), "Los socialistas y la insurrección de octubre de 1934", *Espacio, tiempo y forma* nº 20, pp. 129–158.
18. *Solidaridad Obrera*, 17-10-1933; Juliá (2008), pp. 347–348; Bizcarrondo (2008), p. 88.
19. Bizcarrondo (2008), pp. 18 and 24.
20. Juliá (1984), note 34, p. 356.
21. ADF, series Z, 159. Herbette report for Edouard Daladier, President Council of Ministers France, 2-2-1934.
22. ADF, series Z, 160. Herbette report for Louis led by Largo Caballero, did everything possible to contain the strikes, Juliá (1984), note 34, p. 356.
23. CDMHS, sig. PS Barcelona 272/1. Letter Eleuterio Quintanilla to Pestaña, undated.
24. *El Luchador*, 13-3-1931.
25. CNT Congress, June 1931, in *El Luchador*, 14-6-1931.
26. *Sindicalismo*, 10-3-1933.
27. CNT National Plenum, December 1931, *Boletín de la CNT*, January 1932.
28. First FSL Congress, 1-7-1934, *Sindicalismo*, 11, 18, 24-7-1934; Vega (1987), pp. 177–179.
29. González Calleja (2014), p. 75.
30. See: Olmedo, Ángel (1997), *El anarquismo extremeño frente al poder. Estudio de un periódico libertario. El Amigo del Pueblo, 1930–1933*, Cáceres, Institución Cultural "El Brocense"; Quijada, Domingo (2015), "Los conflictos políticos sociales en Navalmoral durante la II República", in *Revista de Estudios Extremeños*, vol. LXXI, p. 529; both in Reyes, Esmeralda (2016), *Anarcosindicalismo en el norte de Extremadura durante la II República. Navalmoral-Plasencia- Peraleda de la Mata. Diciembre 1933*, Trabajo Fin de Máster, unpublished.
31. *Sindicalismo*, 29-12-1933.
32. First FSL Congress, 1-7-1934, *Sindicalismo*, 11, 18, 24-7-1934.
33. González Calleja (2014), pp. 75–85.
34. CDMHS, sig. PS Barcelona, 272, 1, 41. Letter Pestaña to Peiró, 8-1-1934.
35. See: Pestaña, Ángel (1970), *Por qué se constituyó el Partido Sindicalista*, Madrid, Zero ZYX; Pestaña (1973) and Pestaña (1974).
36. CDMHS, sig. PS Barcelona 272/1. Letter Pestaña to Eleuterio Quintanilla, 31-3-1934.
37. CDMHS, sig. PS Barcelona 383, folder. 272, file 18. Letter Pestaña to Marín Civera, 24-11-1933, reply, 26-11-1933; CDMHS, sig. PS Barcelona 272/1. Letter Pestaña to Francisco Sabaté, 18-12-1933, reply, 22-12-1933.
38. Regional plenum Catalan groups, *Sindicalismo*, 7-2-1934.
39. CDMHS, sig. PS Barcelona 272, 1, 41. Letter Pestaña to Peiró, 8-1-1933.
40. Pestaña (1974), foreword by Antonio Elorza, pp. 67–71; Martínez Lorenzo (2006), p. 105;
41. First FSL Congress, 1-7-1934, *Sindicalismo*, 11, 18, 24-7-1934; Vega (1987), pp. 177–179.

42. *Solidaridad Obrera*, 17-4-1934.
43. Townson (2002).
44. Gil Robles (1978), p. 139.
45. ADF, series Z, sig. 159. Report Herbette to Louis Barthou, Foreign Minister; Ballbé (1983), pp. 364–366; Cabrera (1983), pp. 21–22; Cardona (1993), p. 201.
46. Ballbé (1983), p. 365.
47. ADF, series Z, sig. 159. Telegram Herbette, 22-4-1934; *Sindicalismo*, 24-1-1934; *Solidaridad Obrera*, 24-4-1934; Preston (1978), p. 185.
48. Juliá (1984), pp. 345–346.
49. CDMHS, sig. PS Madrid, 926, 24. On the conflict: *Boletín de huelga de la metalurgia*, UGT-CNT; CDMHS, sig. PS Madrid, 1003, 66. Local Federation Single Unions CNT; ADF, series Z, sig. 259. Report Herbette to Louis Barthou, 19-6-1934.
50. Cabrera (1983), pp. 21 y 219.
51. Malefakis (1987), pp. 37–48.
52. Cabrera (1983), pp. 21, 160–161, 171–172, 218–219.
53. ADF, serie Z, sig. 159. Herbette report to Louis Barthou, 19-2-1934.
54. *Boletín de la UGT*, May 1934, in Bizcarrondo (2008), pp. 104–105.
55. *Boletin de la Región Galaica*, April-May 1934.
56. Bizcarrondo (2008), pp. 110–113; Ballbé (1983), p. 367; ADF, series Z, sig. 259. Herbette report to Louis Barthou, 30-5-1934.
57. IISH, sig. FAI, 36 B. Minutes National Plenum, Madrid, June 1934; *Solidaridad Obrera*, 8-8-1934; IISH, sig. CNT, 68 B; FSS file, prior to Civil War, box 1. Regional Plenum Cataluña, 2/4-8-1931.
58. IISH, sig. FAI, 36 B. Minutes National Plenum, Madrid, June 1934; IISH, sig. CNT, 68 B. Minutes Regional, Local and County Plenum, Andalusia and Extremadura, August 1934.
59. Bizcarrondo (2008), pp. 64–65; Preston (1978), p. 159.
60. Gil (2006), p. 214.
61. Eulalia Vega cites the electricity and transport strikes in Valencia, and metallurgy in Alcoy, Vega (1987), pp. 200–201.
62. ADF, series Z, sig. 159. Herbette report to Edouard Daladier, President Council of Ministers, 2-2-1934.
63. *Solidaridad Obrera*, 20-4-1934; *Sindicalismo*, 9-5-1934; ADF, series Z, sig. 259. Herbette report to Louis Barthou, 16-4-1934.
64. NHA, series A, dkt. 17 A, file. 19. Telegram Minister of the Interior to Civil Governor Zaragoza, 7-5-1934.
65. ADF, series Z, sig. 259. Information on the strike in Zaragoza, in Herbette to Louis Barthou, 16-4-1934; IISH, archive: FAI, sig. 4.1-18, *FAI*, 15-5-1934; IISH, CNT, 68 A. Minutes County Plenum Aragón, Rioja and Navarra, June 1934; *Solidaridad Obrera*, 20-4, 6-5-1934; *Sindicalismo*, 9-5-1934; *Boletín de la Regional Galaica*, June 1934; Martínez Lorenzo (2006), pp. 131–132.
66. IISH, CNT, 68 A. Regional Report Asturias, León and Palencia in minutes County Plenum Aragón, Rioja and Navarra, 17-6-1934.
67. FSS, archive; prior to Civil War, box 3. Letter CNT militant, unsigned (possibly García Entrialgo), Gijon, to Juan López, 26-6-1934.
68. IISH, Ramón Álvarez archive, box 384. Letters Avelino González Entrialgo, Mérida (Venezuela) to Ramón Álvarez, Paris, 1970s.

69. According to David Ruiz, the agreement was signed on 30 March in a room in the Gijon inn "Casa Manfredo", Ruiz (2008), pp. 145.
70. IISH, CNT, 68 A. Asturias Pact between CNT and UGT, 28-3-1934.
71. FSS, file; prior to Civil War, box 3. Report Commission Alianza Obrera to CR Asturias; Barrio (1984), pp. 123–129; Ruiz (2008), p. 170.
72. IISH, Ramón Álvarez archive, box 384. Letter Avelino González Entrialgo, 19-1-1975.
73. Bizcarrondo (2008), pp. 115–117.
74. IISH, FAI, 36 B. Minutes National Plenum, Madrid, June 1934.
75. IISH, Ramón Álvarez file, box 449. Note on the plenum by Ramón Álvarez.
76. IISH, Horacio Martínez Prieto archive, sig. Utopistas, Horacio Martínez Prieto, *Utopistas*, p. 23.
77. IISH, FAI, 36 B. Minutes National Plenum, Madrid, June 1934.
78. IISH, FAI, 36 B. Letter FAI Peninsular Committee, Barcelona, to CNT National Committee, 3-8-1934.
79. *El Combate Sindicalista*, 27-9-1935.
80. Bizcarrondo (2008), pp. 116–17; Brademas (1973), p. 123.
81. IISH, Ramón Álvarez archive, box 431. Minutes Regional Plenum Asturias, León and Palencia, 16-9-1934.
82. IISH, Ramón Álvarez archive, box 441. Manifesto *Alianza Obrera.*
83. IISH, Ramón Álvarez archive, box 384. Letters Avelino González Entrialgo, Mérida (Venezuela), to Ramón Álvarez, París, 1970s.
84. Elorza y Bizcarrondo (1999), p. 190.
85. IISH, Ramón Álvarez archive, box 384. Letters Avelino González Entrialgo, Mérida (Venezuela), to Ramón Álvarez, París, 19-1-1975.
86. *Solidaridad Obrera*, 2-10-1934.
87. The mixed commission was formed by: Juan Simeón Vidarte and Enrique de Francisco, PSOE; Pascual Tomás and José Díaz Alor, UGT; Carlos Hernández Zancajo and Santiago Carrillo, Socialist Youth; the president was Largo Caballero, Bizcarrondo (2008), pp. 115–117.
88. AEHGC, Records Civil Guard headquarters Alicante and Cantabria; Avila General Military Archive (henceforth AGMA), Political background, leg. 4, folder. 1. Reports 7-10-1934.
89. AEHGC, Records Civil Guard headquarters Alicante.
90. AEHGC, Records Civil Guard headquarters Huelva, León, Levante, Cantabria, Murcia, Asturias, Ciudad Real, Gerona and Alicante; AGMA, Political background, leg. 4, folder. 1. News received at headquarters, 7-10-1934.
91. Martínez Lorenzo (1969), pp. 69–70.
92. AGMA, Political background, leg. 4, folder. 1. Reports, 7-10-1934; Ruiz (2008), pp. 138–142.
93. AEHGC, Records Civil Guard headquarters Alicante y Castellón.
94. IISH. Fondo Ramón Álvarez, box 444. CNT Manifesto CNT on October 1934. Signed, January 1935.
95. *El Combate Sindicalista*, Opposition Unions National Committee Manifesto, 27-9-1935, and article "Contestación obligada", 18-10-1935.
96. IISH. CNT, 68 A. Report Regional Committee Aragón, Rioja and Navarra on the October movement 1934. Prepared in 1935.
97. AGMA. Political precedents, leg. 2, folder. 1. Proclamation signed General Virgilio Cabanellas Ferrer.

98. See: Souto, Sandra (2004), *Y ¿Madrid? ¿Qué hace Madrid?: movimiento revolucionario y acción colectiva (1933–1936)*, Madrid Siglo XXI; Juliá (1997), pp. 205–218; Ruiz (2008).
99. AGMS, box 2637, File. 21106, sec. 9. War councils against peasants for inciting troops to rebel.
100. *Revolución Social*, 1-11-1934; Juliá (1997), pp. 215–218; Souto (2004), p. 414; Bizcarrondo (2008), pp. 129–130; Ruiz (2008), pp. 127–129; Martínez Lorenzo (1969), p. 70.
101. IISH. CNT, 68 B. Centre Regional Committee Report on events October 1934 for Regional Plenum, held February 1935; Report Regional Committee Aragón, Rioja and Navarra on October 1934, written February 1935; Minutes, Plenums of the Central Federation's local, county and regional committees, 25-2-1935.
102. García Oliver (2008), p. 215.
103. IISH, CNT, 68 B. Minutes, Local and County Plenum Center Regional, Madrid, 25-2-1935.
104. García Oliver (2008), p. 222.
105. IISH. CNT, 50 A. NC report on García Oliver and events October 1934, 22-2-1936.
106. IISH. CNT, 50 A. NC report on García Oliver in October 1934, 22-2-1936.
107. *Tierra y Libertad*, 4-11-1932; *FAI*, 15-5-1934.
108. *Solidaridad Obrera*, 23-8-1934.
109. *Solidaridad Obrera*, 22-7-1934.
110. Avilés, Juan (2016), "Una República anacrónica, una derecha reaccionaria y un fascismo incipiente: España en los informes diplomáticos italianos, 1931–1936", *Alcores*, nº 20, pp. 69–90.
111. Brademas (1973), p. 144.
112. Avilés et al. (2002), p. 360.
113. *Tierra y Libertad*, 30-6-1934.
114. *Solidaridad Obrera*, 3-10-1934, Brademas (1973), p.142.
115. AGMA, Political background, dkt. 4, folder 1. Catalonia in October 1934.
116. IISH. CNT, 68 A. Lerida Single Unions Local Federation Report on October 1934; and Cataluña Regional Committee manifesto, 6-10-1934, in Peirats (1971), pp. 101–102.
117. AGMA, Political background, leg. 4, folder. 1; Ruiz (2008), p. 131.
118. Abad de Santillán, "Los anarquistas españoles y la insurrección de octubre", *Tiempos Nuevos*, II, nº 1, 10-1-1935.
119. Abad de Santillán, "Los anarquistas españoles y la insurrección de octubre", *Tiempos Nuevos*, II, nº 1, 10-1-1935.
120. *La Revista Blanca*, 12-10-1934.
121. *El Combate Sindicalista*, 27-9-1935.
122. IISH. FAI Archive, sig. 4.1-18. Letter FAI Peninsular Committee, Barcelona, to the Comité Relaciones Grupos Anarquistas de Lengua Española, Francia, 27-10-1934.
123. Ruiz (2008), pp. 233–235.
124. IISH, Ramón Álvarez Archive, box 444. Langreo Town Council Archive.
125. AEHGC, Records Civil Guard Headquarters, Asturias.
126. IISH, Ramón Álvarez Archive, box 443. Letter Jenaro Álvarez, México, to Ramón Álvarez, August 1974.

127. Ruiz (2008), pp. 120–121; IISH, CNT, 72 D. Article by Indalecio Prieto in *El Socialista.*
128. IISH Ramón Álvarez Archive, box 443. Letter Jenaro Álvarez, México, to Ramón Álvarez, August 1974.
129. IISH, CNT, 72 D, Parliamentary minutes. Accusation proposal formulated by Sr. Moutas and other MPs against Azaña and Casares Quiroga; *La Vanguardia,* 21-3-1935, see also Juliá (2008).
130. *ABC,* 29-9-1934; see also Bizcarrondo (2008), pp. 120–121; Ruiz (2008), pp. 122–123.
131. *La Vanguardia,* 21-3-1935
132. Bizcarrondo (2008), p. 130.
133. IISH. Ramón Álvarez Archive, box 385. Report Avelino González Entrialgo, Gijon, 25-10-1934.
134. IISH, Ramón Álvarez Archive, box 443. "La Felguera en la revolución asturiana de 1934". CNT document, edited in France, 1973; Ruiz (2008), pp. 293–297.
135. AEHGC, Asturias Civil Guard headquarters records.
136. IISH, Ramón Álvarez Archive, boxes 358 and 441. Revolutionary proclamations in Sama and Langreo; FSS, File AHNS Ps-Gijon, F, C.97. Account by José Cenitagoya Echeondia, Revolutionary Committee Muros del Nalón, signed in Rennes (France), 31-7-1935.
137. AGMA, Political Background dkt 4, folder 6. Central General Staff Information Services.
138. *Tiempos Nuevos,* 4-4-1935, stated that the information about the alleged murder of Martínez by the socialists was false; the version describing Martínez's accidental death was provided by journalist and researcher Paco Ignacio Taibo, *La Voz de Asturias,* 29-10-1981; See also: IISH, Ramón Álvarez Archive, box 443. "La Felguera en la revolución asturiana de 1934". CNT document, published in France, 1973.
139. Cardona (1993), pp. 203–207; Cardona (1987), pp. 49–64.
140. AGMS, L-1152. Personal file Division General Eduardo López de Ochoa Portuondo.
141. Cardona (1993), p. 205; Bizcarrondo (2008), p. 137.
142. AGMS, L-1152. Personal file Division General Eduardo López de Ochoa Portuondo, Documents signed by General Ochoa, 18 and 22-10-1934, Oviedo; *La Época,* 22-4-1936.
143. AGMA, Political background, dkt. 4, folder 6. Air Force Command report.
144. AFSS, AHNS file PS-Gijon, F, C.97. Account by José Cenitagoya Echeondia, Muros del Nalón Revolutionary Committee, signed in Rennes (France), 31-7-1935.
145. Institute of Military History and Culture (henceforth AIHCM) files, political background, dkt. 4, folder8.
146. *El Combate Sindicalista,* 8-11, 12-12-1935.
147. AGMS, L-1152. Report from General Ochoa to the Minister of War, 22-10-1934.
148. "Documentos de la Revolución". Published by the Madrid Socialists in 1935. Biblioteca Fundación Pablo Iglesias. Document signed by 564 inmates in the Modelo prison, Oviedo, 24-1-1935.
149. Ruiz (2008), pp. 315–317; Bizcarrondo (2008), pp. 137–140.
150. Intervention by the Republic prosecutor in the first trial, regarding the events of 27-10-1934, *Ahora,* 28-4-1936

151. *El Combate Sindicalista*, 5-12-1935.
152. IISH, Ramón Álvarez Archive, box 443. On the summary and sentence, *Ahora*, 28-4-1936.
153. AGMA, political background, dkt. 2, folder 4. Telegrams between provincial military commanders and Ministry of War, October–November 1934.
154. AEHGC, Oviedo Civil Guard Headquarters records.
155. AEHGC. Personal file Lisardo Doval Bravo.
156. Letter from Gordón Ordás to Lerroux, 19-12-1934. IISH, archive: FAI, sig. 4.1-18. "Documentos para la historia. La represión en Asturias y León". FAI leaflet on repression in Asturias and León. Published in Cuenca, 1935.
157. AGMA, political background, dkt. 4, folder 5. Telegram Minister of State to Minister of War, 29-10-1934.
158. AGMA, political background, dkt. 4, folder 5. Telegrams Minister of State to Minister of War, 2, 4, 8-11-1934.
159. AGMA, political background, dkt. 1, folder 1. Telegrams from Ministry of War delegation in Oviedo and Central General Staff.
160. APPP, sig. BA 2160. Report Paris Police Prefecture.
161. AGMS, T- 310. Personal file Civil Guard Captain Nilo Tella Cantos.
162. AEHGC. Personal file Lisardo Doval Bravo.
163. AGMA, political background, dkt. 4, folder 2. Central General Staff. Information Service; Ballbé (1983), pp. 375–377; *La Vanguardia*, 30-3-1935; Cardona (1993), pp. 208–211.
164. Letter from Félix Gordón Ordás to Lerroux, 19-12-1934. IISH, archive: FAI, sig. 4.1-18. "Documentos para la historia. La represión en Asturias y León, Folleto FAI sobre represión en Asturias y León. Editado en Cuenca, 1935.
165. IISH, Ramón Álvarez Archive, box 444. Langreo Town Council Archive; *La Tierra*, 3-11-1934.
166. Proclamations in: IISH, Ramón Álvarez Archive, box 441; Proclamation Revolutionary Committee Grado, October 1934, in Peirats (1971), pp. 96–97.
167. AEHGC, Records Civil Guard Headquarters.
168. *La Nueva España*, 17-10-1984.
169. Bizcarrondo (2008), pp. 137–138; More figures Ruiz (2008), pp. 10–11 and 317.

5 Between Rectification and Continuity(May 1935–July 1936)

1. AGMA, Political background, dkt. 4, folders 4 and 5. Telegram Ministry of War to Ministry of Communications, 15-10-1934; Telegram Ministry of State to Ministry of War, 19-10-1934; telegram General 4ª division to the Ministry of War, 2-11-1934.
2. IISH, Ramón Álvarez Archive, box 444. Langreo Town Council Documents.
3. Juárez, Eduardo (2015), *Crónicas de un real sitio. Lucha política, guerra y represión (1934–1939)*, Madrid, HG Editores, pp. 68–69.
4. Cabrera (1983), pp. 160, 222–226; Bizcarrondo (2008), pp. 166–167.
5. Ruiz (2008), pp. 333–335; Cabrera (1983), pp. 240–242.
6. *Revolución Social*, 1-12-1934; *Solidaridad Obrera*, 13-2-1935; *Antorcha*, 16-2-1935; *En Marcha*, 27-4-1935; *Sindicalismo*, 23-5-1935; Cabrera (1983), pp. 240–242; Ruiz (2008), pp. 333–335.
7. Fontana (1987), pp. 9–22.
8. Malefakis (1987), pp. 37–48; Cabrera (1983), pp. 171-172.

9. IISH, Ramón Álvarez Archive, box 444. Town Council Archives.
10. AGMA, political background, dkt. 2, folder 6. Telegram General 4ª Division, Catalonia, to the Ministry of War, 5-12-1934.
11. AGMA, political background, dkt. 4, folder 2. Central General Staff. Information Service.
12. IISH, Ramón Álvarez Archive, box 444. CNT NC manifestos, Zaragoza October 1934, and FAI, December 1934; IISH, CNT, 68 A. Minutes of National Plenum, Zaragoza, 11-11-1934.
13. *Tiempos Nuevos*, 10-1-1935.
14. *Tiempos Nuevos*, 24-1-1935.
15. *Tiempos Nuevos*, 4-4-1935.
16. IISH, CNT, 50 A and CDMHS sig. F-1450. National Committee Report to National Plenum, April 1935; and CDMHS, sig. FA. 101. Minutes National Plenum, Zaragoza, 26-5-35.
17. IISH, CNT, 50 A; and in CDMHS, sig. F-1450. National Committee Report to National Plenum, April 1935.
18. CDMHS, sig. FA. 101. Minutes National Plenum, Zaragoza, 26-5-35.
19. *Sindicalismo*, 13-6-1935.
20. IISH, CNT, 50 A; and CDMHS, sig. F-1450. National Committee Report to National Plenum, May 1935.
21. ADF, series Z, sig. 259. Report Herbette to Pierre Laval, Foreign Minister, 27-2-1935.
22. CDMHS, sig. FA. 101. Minutes National Plenum, Zaragoza, 26-5-35.
23. IISH, CNT, 50 A; and CDMHS, sig. F-145. National Committee Report to National Plenum, April 1935; CDMHS, sig. FA. 101. Minutes National Plenum, Zaragoza, 26-5-35
24. APPP, sig. BA 2160. Ministerial Circular, 31-10-1934.
25. AFSS, Folder AHNS PS-Gijon, F, C.97. Account by José Cenitagoya Echeondia, signed in Rennes (France), 31-7-1935.
26. APPP, sig. BA 2160. Paris Police Prefecture Reports.
27. *Le Peuple*, 30-10-1934; *L'Oeuvre*, 4-11-1934; *L'Humanité*, 6-12-1934.
28. AGMA, political background, dkt. 4, folder 5. Telegram Ministry of State to Ministry of War.
29. APPP, sig: BA 2160. Paris Police Prefecture Reports.
30. Elorza and Bizcarrondo (1999), pp. 229–232; Bizcarrondo (2008), p. 163.
31. CDMHS, sig. FA 101. Minutes National Plenum, Zaragoza, 26-5-35.
32. FSS, archive; prior to Civil War, box 3. Letter from NSV of Holland, Amsterdam, to Asturian comrades, 17-1-1936. IISH, Ramón Álvarez Archive, box 432, Ramón Álvarez, *Ramonín*, said that the group of refugees was formed by: Emeterio Díaz, killed on the Levante front during the Civil War; Lino Meana, a refugee in Mexico; Harmodio Argüelles, killed in France at the end of the war; Luis Meana, executed by firing squad after the fall of Asturias; Acracio Bartolomé, died in Marseille; Avelino Martínez, shot; Manuel Sánchez, *Nelin*, sentenced to death and died in Venezuela; José Mª de Arriba, executed by firing squad after the fall of Asturias; Aurelio Pernia, refugee in France; Francisco Arias, killed on the Luarca front; Avelino G. Entrialgo, returned to Spain after 40 years in exile in France; Horacio Argüelles and Roberto Blanco, converted to communism after their stay in Russia.

33. IISH, CNT, 50 A. Report CNT national prisoners' aid committee to the Zaragoza extraordinary Congress, 31-3-1936.
34. IISH, Fondo Ramón Álvarez Archive, box 432. CNT Regional Congress, Asturias, León and Palencia, April 1936.
35. IISH, Ramón Álvarez Archive, box 443. Letter from Horacio Argüelles, Paris, to Avelino G. Entrialgo, 24-6-1935.
36. IISH, CNT, 50 A. Report CNT delegate to the SAC Congress, 23-6-1935.
37. CNT (1955), pp. 111–116; IISH, Ramón Álvarez Archive, box 443. Letter from Horacio Argüelles, Paris, to Avelino G. Entrialgo, 24-6-1935.
38. Cardona (1993), pp. 212-213; Blaney Jr. Gerald (2012), "En defensa de la democracia: políticas de orden público en la España republicana, 1931–1936", *Ayer* nº 88, pp. 99–123.
39. *Sindicalismo*, 27-6-1935.
40. CDMHS, sig: FA 101. Minutes National Plenum, Zaragoza, 26-5-35.
41. CDMHS, sig: PS Madrid, 527, 7. NC Circular nº 10, 8-8-1935.
42. Gil (2006), p. 214.
43. AEHGC, Huelva and Huesca Civil Guard HQ records, 1935.
44. *Solidaridad Obrera*, 8-3-1935; ADF, series Z, sig. 162. Report Herbette to Pierre Laval, Foreign Minister, 5-5-1935, in which he said that unemployment was higher than the 700,000 workers on official records; Unemployment statistics for December 1933 and March 1934 in official records for the period, in Gil (2006); and Bizcarrondo (2008), pp. 64–65.
45. Comín, Francisco (2011), "Política y economía: los factores determinantes de la crisis económica durante la Segunda República (1931–1936)", *Historia y Política*, nº 26, July-December, pp. 47–79.
46. Bizcarrondo (2008), p. 68.
47. *El Combate Sindicalista*, 13, 27-9-1935; 4, 11-10-1935; 8-11-1935; *Sindicalismo*, 16-6-1935; *Solidaridad Obrera*, 4-8-1935.
48. Juliá (2008), pp. 350–356; Elorza and Bizcarrondo (1999), p. 236.
49. IISH, Ramón Álvarez Archive, box 444.
50. Elorza and Bizcarrondo (1999), pp. 190–191, 219–225, 260–277; Bizcarrondo (2008), pp. 155–159.
51. Elorza and Bizcarrondo (1999), pp. 255–256.
52. Gil (2006), pp. 317–318.
53. Cardona (1993), pp. 365 and ff.; Avilés et al (2002); Ballbé (1983), pp. 383–4.
54. Gil Robles (1978), pp. 356–357.
55. Elorza and Bizcarrondo (1999), pp. 258–259.
56. Bizcarrondo (2008), pp. 174–176; Gil (2006).
57. *Solidaridad Obrera*, 8, 17-1-1936.
58. FSS, archive; prior to Civil War, box 3. Letter from Horacio Argüelles, Moscow, to Avelino G. Entrialgo, 21-1-1936; *El Combate Sindicalista*, 19-12-1935
59. *El Combate Sindicalista*, 25-10-1935.
60. IISH, Ramón Álvarez Archive, box 444. National Plenum, Madrid 26/31-1-1936.
61. IISH, CNT, 50 A. FAI National Plenum, Madrid, 31-1, 1-2-1936; *Tierra y Libertad*, 7-2-1936.
62. IISH, CNT, 68 A. Minutes Extraordinary Regional Conference Unions Catalonia, January 1936.
63. *Solidaridad Obrera*, 4, 5, 6, 8, 9, 12, 13-2-1936.
64. IISH, CNT, 50 A. CNT NC communique, 3-2-1936.

65. CNT NC manifesto, 20-1-1935, *Solidaridad Obrera*, 27-1-1935; *Tiempos Nuevos*, 24-1, 21-2, 21-3-1935.
66. IISH, CNT, 50 A. CNT agreements for AIT congress, August 1935.
67. *El Combate Sindicalista*, 6-9, 13-9, 20-9-1935.
68. *Solidaridad Obrera*, 9-1-1936.
69. FSS, archive; prior to civil War, box 3. Letter José Villaverde, Coruña, to Avelino G. Entrialgo, 29-11-1935; *Solidaridad Obrera*, 19-11-1935; *El Combate Sindicalista*, 21-11-1935.
70. IISH, CNT, 50 A. Letter from CNT NC to FL Single Unions Zaragoza, 10-12-1935, and to the Levante Regional Committee, 13-12-1935.
71. *Solidaridad Obrera*, 21 and 24-1-1936.
72. IISH, CNT, 68 A. Catalonia Unions Extraordinary Regional Conference, 25-1-1936.
73. IISH, CNT, 68 A. Catalonia Unions Extraordinary Regional Conference, 25-1-1936.
74. *Solidaridad Obrera*, 10-1-1936.
75. IISH, Ramón Álvarez Archive, box 443. Letter Horacio Argüelles, Paris, to Avelino G. Entrialgo, 6-8-1935.
76. *Sindicalismo*, 22-8-1935.
77. IISH, Ramón Álvarez Archive, box 443. Horacio Argüelles copies what he is told by "the mother of Pardo", a victim of the October repression. Letter Horacio Argüelles, Paris, to Avelino G. Entrialgo, 6-8-1935.
78. FSS, archive; prior to Civil War, box 3. Letter José Villaverde, Coruña, to Avelino G. Entrialgo, 29-11-1935.
79. IISH, Ramón Álvarez Archive, box 444. National Plenum, Madrid 26/31-1-1936.
80. IISH, CNT, 68 A. Catalonia Unions Extraordinary Regional Conference, 25-1-1936.
81. IISH, Ramón Álvare Archive, box 444. National Plenum, Madrid 26/31-1-1936.
82. IISH, CNT, 50 A. FAI National Plenum, Madrid, 31-1, 1-2-1936.
83. *Solidaridad Obrera*, 16-2-1936.
84. CNT (1955), p. 147.
85. Vega (1987), pp. 218–219.
86. *El Combate Sindicalista*, 19-12-1935.
87. *Solidaridad Obrera*, 16-2-1936.
88. *Tiempos Nuevos*, 21-3-1935.
89. IISH, Ramón Álvarez Archive, box 449. Historical notes.
90. Abad de Santillán, Diego (1974), *De Alfonso XIII a Franco*, Buenos Aires, TEA, p. 289.
91. *Tierra y Libertad*, 7-1-1936.
92. *La Libertad*, 7-3-1936.
93. *Tierra y Libertad*, 21-2-1936.
94. *Tiempos Nuevos*, May–June 1937.
95. Martínez Lorenzo (1969), p. 73.
96. Different results in: Gil (2006), pp. 323–324, Frente Popular: 278 MPs, Right: 124, Centre: 51; Martínez Lorenzo (1969), p. 72, Frente Popular: 271; on these elections, see: Álvarez Tardío, Manuel and Villa, Roberto (2017), *1936. Fraude y violencia en las elecciones del Frente Popular*, Madrid, Espasa; also see reviews by Santos Juliá, *El País*, 30-3-2017; and Ángel Luis López Villaverde, *CTXT*, nº 115, 3-5-2017; an excellent example of elections in a small city, in Herrerín, Eduardo

(2015), "Las elecciones de febrero de 1936 en Segovia. El Frente Popular", *Estudios Segovianos*, tomo LVII, nº 114, pp. 425–454.
97. Martínez Lorenzo (2006), p. 105.
98. Caro, Diego (2013), pp. 45–66; Martínez Lorenzo (1969), p. 72.
99. *Tierra y Libertad*, 13-3-1936.
100. Gil Robles (1978), pp. 506–509–450.
101. Abad de Santillán, Diego (1975), *Por qué pedimos la guerra*, Madrid, G. del Toro Editor, p. 53.
102. ADF, series Z, sig. 165 and 166. Report Herbette to E. Flandin, Foreign Minister, 19-2, 2-3-1936.
103. Ballbé (1983), pp. 385–386; Cardona (1993), pp. 227–228.
104. Azaña (1981), p. 10.
105. ADF, series Z, sig. 165. Report Lagmartres, French Consul in San Sebastian, to Herbette, 18-2-1936; and report Herbette to E. Flandin, 19-2-1936.
106. APPP, sig: BA 2160. Paris Police Prefecture Report, 7-3-1936.
107. ADF, series Z, sig. 165. Report Herbette to E. Flandin, 19-2-1936.
108. *Solidaridad Obrera*, 18-2-1936.
109. ADF, serie Z, sig. 165. Informe François Poncet, Embajador francés en Berlín, a Herbette, 18-2-1936; Fontana (1987), pp. 9–22.
110. ADF, series Z, sig. 165. Reports Herbette to E. Flandin, 19, 20-2-1936.
111. ADF, series Z, 166. Report Herbette to E. Flandin, 19-2-1936.
112. Azaña (1981), pp. 11–18.
113. ADF, series Z, sig. 165. Report Marcassin, French consul in Valencia, to Herbette, 21-2-1936; ADF, series Z, sig. 166. Report Herbette to P. E. Flandis, 2-3-1936; *Noroeste*, 21-2-1936.
114. AEHGC. Levante Civil Guard HQ records.
115. *Solidaridad Obrera*, 27-2-1936.
116. *Solidaridad Obrera*, 18, 19, 21-2-1936.
117. Azaña (1981), pp. 11-18.
118. *La Libertad*, 29-2, 13-3-1936; *Solidaridad Obrera*, 14-3-1936; *El Socialista*, 18-3-1936.
119. *Solidaridad Obrera*, 14-3-1936.
120. Malefakis (1987), pp. 37–48; Gil (2006); Cabrera (1983), pp. 292–295.
121. *Solidaridad Obrera*, 18, 27-2-1936, 3, 7, 26, 31-3-1936, 12-4-1936.
122. Sánchez, Francisco (2013b), "Las reformas de la primavera del 36 (en la Gaceta y en la calle)", in Sánchez, Francisco (Coord.), *Los mitos del 18 de julio*, Barcelona, Crítica, pp. 291–312.
123. ADF, serie Z, sig. 166. Informe Herbette a P. E. Flandin, 2-3-1936.
124. *Solidaridad Obrera*, 8-3-1936.
125. *Solidaridad Obrera*, 3, 8, 10-3-1936.
126. ADF, series Z, sig. 166. Report Herbette to P. E. Flandin, 2-3-1936.
127. ADF, series Z, sig. 259. Report Herbette to P. E. Flandin, 23-4-1936.
128. ADF, series Z, sig 165. Report Herbette to Pierre Laval, Council President, 9-1-1936.
129. Sánchez (2013b), pp. 291–312; *Solidaridad Obrera*, 7-6-1936.
130. *Sindicalismo*, 31-7-1935.
131. CDMHS, sig: PS Barcelona 383, folder 272, file 10. Letter Pestaña to Fenollar, 22-11-1934.
132. *Sindicalismo*, 13-6-1935.

133. CDMHS, sig: FA 101. Minutes National Plenum, Zaragoza, 26-5-35.
134. Communique National Committee Opposition Unions, 19-10-1935, in *El Combate Sindicalista*, 25-10-1935.
135. IISH, CNT, 50 A. NC circular to regional confederations, 16-3-1936.
136. IISH, CNT, 50 A. Circular Levante RC to regional unions, 21-12-1935, and letter to the NC, 10-1-1936.
137. IISH, CNT, 50 A. Document Levante RC to Levante Opposition Union workers, January 1936.
138. IISH, CNT, 50 A. Regional Union Plenum CNT Levante, 8/11-2-1936.
139. IISH, CNT, 68 A. Minutes Extraordinary Regional Conference Unions Catalonia, January 1936.
140. Elorza (1973), p. 466.
141. IISH, CNT, 50 A. Levante RC, from Alcoy, to the CNT NC, 1-4-1936, and letter from Opposition Unions to CNT NC, 3-4-1936, and reply, 11-4-1936; *Solidaridad Obrera*, 7-4-1936.
142. IISH, CNT, 72 D. Circular Opposition Unions NC.
143. *La Revista Blanca*, 17-4-1936; *El Luchador*, 21-10-1932.
144. IISH, Horacio Martínez Prieto Archive, sig. Utopistas, p. 156.
145. IISH, CNT, 50 A. RC Levante, from Alcoy, to CNT NC, 1-4-1936, and to the regional confederation unions, 3-4-1936.
146. Levante Regional Congress, summer 1932, *Sindicalismo* 14-7-1933, and Vega (1987), pp. 110 and 222.
147. CNT (1955), p. 25.
148. Note Opposition Unions National Committee, *Solidaridad Obrera*, 22-4-1936.
149. *Solidaridad Obrera*, 26-4-1936.
150. These same figures appear in documents from Eduardo de Guzman's personal archive (henceforth APEG), Martínez Lorenzo (1969), p. 74, Elorza (1973), p. 467; Peirats (1971), p. 117; Brademas quotes the same number of members for the congress, but differs with regard to those represented by the Opposition Unions, which he situates at 70,000, Brademas (1973), p. 169; Casanova gives the figure of 559,294, Casanova (1997), p. 148.
151. The 800,000 members in Elorza (1973), pp. 448–449; Casanova (1997), p. 84; The 200,000 in ADF, series Z, sig. 259. Report Herbette to Pierre Laval, Foreign minister, 27-2-1935.
152. CNT (1955), pp. 18–47.
153. *La Revista Blanca*, 22, 15-5-1936.
154. See, for example, the summary of the Minutes of the Barcelona local union congress, *Solidaridad Obrera*, 30-9-1931.
155. Minutes Regional Plenum, Madrid, 13/16-4-1932, *Boletín de la CNT*, May1932.
156. *Sindicalismo*, 24-2-1933.
157. *Boletín de la CNT*, April-May 1933.
158. *El Combate Sindicalista*, 18-10-1935.
159. IISH, CNT, 50 A. NC circular to regional confederations, 16-3-1936.
160. *La Revista Blanca*, 15-5-1936.
161. Everything on the Revolutionary Alliance in: CNT (1955); IISH, CNT, 50 A. Motion opinion on the Revolutionary Alliance.
162. *Solidaridad Obrera*, 13 and 14-5-1936.
163. IISH, CNT, 50 A. Letter CNT NC to the UGT Executive Commission, 18-5-1936; Reply 21-5-1936; NC circular to regional confederations, 21-5-1936.

164. Elorza (1973), p. 248; Termes (2011), p. 435.
165. CNT (1990), Interview with García Oliver, pp. 19–20.
166. CNT (1955), pp. 118–166.
167. *Sindicalismo*, 14-4-1933.
168. *Sindicalismo*, 21-4-1933.
169. *Sindicalismo*, 2-6-1933.
170. Elorza (1973), pp. 391–397.
171. Prologue by Antonio Elorza, in Abad de Santillán, Diego (1976), *El anarquismo y la revolución en España. Escritos 1930/1938*, Madrid, Ayuso, pp. 38–45.
172. The debate and the opinion on libertarian communism: CNT (1955), pp. 168–169, 191–201.
173. Prologue by Antonio Elorza, in Abad de Santillán (1976), p. 45.
174. IISH, Horacio Martínez Prieto Archive, sig. Anake, p. 155.
175. Herrerín (2004), p. 340.
176. Abad de Santillán, Diego (1978), *El organismo económico de la Revolución*, Bilbao, Zero.
177. *Tiempos Nuevos*, 3-6-1934, prologue by Elorza, in Abad de Santillán (1976), p. 34.
178. This last figure in Gil Robles (2006), p. 99; the rest are in this text with their corresponding quotes.
179. CNT (1955), pp. 162–181.
180. CNT (1955), pp. 175–178, 183–186.
181. IISH, Horacio Martínez Prieto Archive, sig. Utopistas, Mariano Rodríguez Vázquez alias *Marianet*.
182. *La Revista Blanca*, 22-5-1936.
183. Intervention by Largo Caballero at a Socialist rally in Zaragoza, *Solidaridad Obrera*, 2-6-1936.
184. Cabrera (1983), p. 291.
185. Bizcarrondo (2008), p. 72.
186. CNT (1955), p. 25; Vega (1987), pp. 110–122; Elorza (1973), p. 467.
187. FSS, archive; prior to Civil War, box 1. Plenum Manufacturing and Textile Unions Catalonia 30-5, 1-6-1936; Solidaridad Obrera, 26-2-1936.
188. ADF, series Z, sig. 167. Report Herbette to Ybon Delbos, Foreign Minister, 11-6-1936; *Solidaridad Obrera*, 9-6-1936.
189. AEHGC, archive, Jaen Civil Guard HQ records, July 1936.
190. FSS, archive, prior to Civil War, box 1. Plenum Manufacturing and Textile Unions Catalonia, 30-5, 1-6-1936; *Antorcha*, 15-5-1936; IISH, CNT, 68 B. Circular nº 21 in Regional Bulletin Andalusia and Extremadura, 9-7-1936; *Solidaridad Obrera*, 3-6, 28-6, 10-7-1936; IISH, CNT, 50 A. Local Federation of Unions Alicante, 6-6-1936.
191. *Antorcha*, 15-5-1936; IISH, CNT, 68 B. Circular nº 21 in Regional Bulletin Andalusia and Extremadura, 9-7-1936.
192. ADF, series Z, 166. Report Herbette to Ybon Delbos, Foreign Minister, 11-6-1936.
193. *Solidaridad Obrera*, 10-7-1936.
194. IISH, CNT, 68 B. Minutes Centre Plenum Local and County Committees Centre Regional Confederation, Madrid, February 1935; Elorza (1973), p. 467; CNT (1955), p. 25.
195. ADF, series Z, sig. 167. Telegram Herbette, 10-7-1936.

196. *Solidaridad Obrera*, 21-5, 2-6, 28-6, 8-7-1936; Bizcarrondo (2008). p. 190.
197. Ballbé (1983), p. 393.
198. See, among others, Viñas, Ángel (2012), *La conspiración del general Franco y otras revelaciones acerca de una guerra civil desfigurada*, Barcelona, Crítica, (extended versión of the 2011 edition); by the same author (2013), "La connivencia fascista con la sublevación y otros éxitos de la trama", in Sánchez (2013a), pp. 79–182.
199. I should like to thank Professor Eduardo González Calleja for providing me with the tables with the results of his research into violence during the Republic. See also, among others, González Calleja, Eduardo (2011b), "La necro-lógica de la violencia política en la primavera de 1936", *Mélanges de la Casa Velázquez*, nº 41; González Calleja (2011a); Cruz, Rafael (2006), *En el nombre del Pueblo. República, rebelión y guerra en la España de 1936*. Madrid, Siglo XXI; Ledesma, José Luis (2013), "La 'primavera trágica' de 1936 y la pendiente hacia la guerra civil", in Sánchez (2013a), pp. 313–339.
200. IISH, Ramón Álvarez Archive, box 397. Letter from Fidel Miró to Ramón Álvarez.
201. IISH, CNT, 50 A. CNT NC communique to regional federations, 27-6-1936.
202. AEHGC. Castellón Civil Guard HQ records, 1936.
203. AEHGC. Different versions in: Albacete HQ records, 23, 24-5-1936; *El Liberal*, 31-5-1936; *Solidaridad Obrera*, 4-6-1936; *El Debate*, 6-6-1936.
204. AEHGC. Personal files: Félix Velando Gómez.
205. AEHGC. Huelva HQ records, 17-7-1936; and Tomás Sorio personal file.
206. *Solidaridad Obrera*, 15-7-1936.
207. ADF, series Z, 167. Telegrams Herbette, 10-7-1936.
208. IISH, Ramón Álvarez Archive, box 449. Historical notes.
209. Juliá (2008), p. 388.
210. IISH, CNT 50 A. Circular n º 11 CR Aragón, Rioja and Navarra, 18-7-1936.

Bibliography

Archives

Archive Congress of Deputies (ACD).
Archive of Historical Studies of the Civil Guard (AEHGC).
Archive of the Paris Police Prefecture (APPP).
Archives Diplomatiques de France (ADF).
Ávila General Military Archives (AGMA).
Eduardo de Guzmán's personal files (APEG).
Historical Memory Documentation Centre of Salamanca (CDMHS).
Institute of Military History and Culture (AIHCM).
International Institute of Social History of Amsterdam (IISH).
José Peiró's personal files (APJP).
National Historical Archive (NHA).
Salvador Seguí Foundation in Madrid (FSS).
Segovia General Military Archives (AGMS).

Press

ABC.
Boletín de la CNT.
Boletín de la Región Galaica de CNT.
Cultura Libertaria.
El Combate Sindicalista.
El Luchador.
El Perseguido (Buenos Aires).
El Socialista.
En Marcha.
L'Humanité.
L'Oeuvre.
La Batalla.
La Libertad.
La Nueva España.
La Revista Blanca.
La Tierra.
La Vanguardia.
La Voz Obrera.
Le Peuple.
Noroeste.
Revolución Social.
Sindicalismo.
Solidaridad Obrera.

Tiempos Nuevos.
Tierra y Libertad.

Books, Collections and Journals

Abad de Santillán, Diego (1974), *De Alfonso XIII a Franco*, Buenos Aires, TEA.

—— (1975), *Por qué pedimos la guerra*, Madrid, G. del Toro Editor.

—— (1976), *El anarquismo y la revolución en España. Escritos 1930/1938* (prólogo de Antonio Elorza), Madrid, Ayuso.

—— (1978), *El organismo económico de la Revolución*, Bilbao, Zero.

Álvarez Junco, José (1976), *La ideología política del anarquismo español (1868–1910)*, Siglo XXI, Madrid

Álvarez Junco, José y Cabrera, Mercedes (eds.) (2011), *La mirada del historiador. Un viaje por la obra de Santos Juliá*, Madrid, Taurus.

Álvarez Tardío, Manuel y Villa García, Roberto (2017), *1936. Fraude y violencia en las elecciones del Frente Popular*, Madrid, Espasa.

Aróstegui, Julio (2013a), *Largo Caballero. El tesón y la quimera*, Madrid, Debate.

—— (2013b) "Una izquierda en busca de la revolución (El fracaso de la segunda revolución)", en Francisco Sánchez Pérez (Coord.), *Los mitos del 18 de julio*, Barcelona, Crítica, pp. 183–220.

Avilés, Juan et all (2002), *Historia política, 1875–1939*, Madrid, Istmo.

Avilés, Juan (2006), *La izquierda burguesa y la tragedia de la II República* (primera edición en Espasa Calpe, 1985), Madrid, CC.AA. Madrid.

—— (2008), "Los socialistas y la insurrección de octubre de 1934", *Espacio, tiempo y forma* nº 20, pp. 129–158.

—— (2016), "Una República anacrónica, una derecha reaccionaria y un fascismo incipiente: España en los informes diplomáticos italianos, 1931–1936", *Alcores*, nº 20, pp. 69–90.

Azaña, Manuel (1981), *Memorias políticas y de guerra*, I, Barcelona, Crítica.

—— (1992), *Discursos parlamentarios*, Madrid, Publicaciones del Congreso de los Diputados.

—— (1983), *Diarios, 1932–1933, "los cuadernos robados"*, Barcelona, Crítica, 1997.

Ballbé, Manuel (1983), *Orden público y militarismo en la España constitucional*, Madrid, Alianza Editorial.

Bar, Antonio (1981), *La CNT en los años rojos, del sindicalismo revolucionario al anarcosindicalismo (1910–1926)*, Madrid, AKAL.

Barrio, Ángeles (1984), "La CNT de Asturias, León y Palencia y la Alianza Obrera de 1934", *Estudios de Historia Social* nº 31, pp. 123–129.

—— (1988), *Anarquismo y anarcosindicalismo en Asturias (1890–1936)*, Madrid, Siglo XXI.

Berdah, Jean François (2000), *La démocratie assassinée. La Republique espagnole et les grandes puissances, 1931–1939*, París, Berg International Éditeurs.

Bizcarrondo, Marta (2008), *Historia de la UGT. Entre la democracia y la revolución, 1931–1936*, Madrid, Siglo XXI.

Blaney, Gerald Jr. (2012), "En defensa de la democracia: políticas de orden público en la España republicana, 1931–1936, *Ayer* nº 88, pp. 99–123.

Bonamusa, Francesc (ed.) (1991), *La Huelga General*, *Ayer*, nº 4.

Borderías, Cristina y Vilanova, Mercedes (1983), "Cronología de una insurrección: Figols en 1932", *Estudios de Historia Social*, nº 24–25, pp. 187–199.

Bosch, Aurora, Carnero, T. y Valero, S. (eds.) (2013), *Entre la reforma y la revolución. La construcción de la democracia desde la izquierda*, Granada, Comares.

Brademas, John (1973), *Anarcosindicalismo y revolución en España (1930–1937)*, Barcelona, Horas de España.

Cabrera, Mercedes (1983), *La patronal ante la II República. Organizaciones y estrategia (1931–1936)*, Madrid, Siglo XXI.

Cardona, Gabriel (1987), "Estado y poder militar en la Segunda República", en VVAA. *La II República. Una esperanza frustrada.* Actas del congreso: Valencia Capital de la República (abril 1986), Valencia, Edicions Alfons El Magnànim.

—— (1993), *El poder militar en la España contemporánea hasta la guerra civil*, Madrid, Siglo XXI.

Caro, Diego (2013), "El anarcosindicalismo y la victoria del Frente Popular en las elecciones de 1936", *Historia Social*, nº 76, pp. 45–66.

Casanova, Julián (1997), *De la calle al frente. El anarcosindicalismo en España (1931–1939)*, Madrid, Crítica.

—— (2007), *República y guerra civil*, Madrid, Crítica-Marcial Pons.

CNT (1955), *El Congreso Confederal de Zaragoza*, Toulouse, Publicaciones CNT.

CNT (1977), *Congresos Anarcosindicalistas en España, 1870–1936*, Ediciones CNT, Toulouse (Francia).

CNT (1990), *Colección de Historia oral: El movimiento libertario en España*, Madrid, Fundación Salvador Seguí.

Comín, Francisco (2011), "Política y economía: los factores determinantes de la crisis económica durante la Segunda República (1931–1936)", *Historia y Política*, nº 26, julio–diciembre, pp. 47–79.

Cruz, Rafael (2006), *En el nombre del Pueblo. República, rebelión y guerra en la España de 1936*, Madrid, Siglo XXI.

Cuadrat, Xavier (1976), *Socialismo y anarquismo en Cataluña. Los orígenes de la CNT*, Madrid, Revista del Trabajo.

De Guzmán, Eduardo (2007), *La tragedia de Casas Viejas, 1933*, Madrid, Vosa.

De los Santos, Mercedes (1996), "El devenir revolucionario de Buenaventura Durruti", pp. 13–54, en Morales, Antonio y Ortega, Javier (eds.), *El lenguaje de los hechos*, Madrid, Los libros de la Catarata.

Egido, Ángeles (1987), *La concepción de la política exterior española durante la Segunda República (1931–1936)*, Madrid, UNED.

—— (2006), *Manuel Azaña entre el mito y la leyenda*, Valladolid, Junta de Castilla y León.

Elorza, Antonio (1973), *La utopía anarquista durante la guerra civil española*, Madrid, Editorial Ayuso (la primera vez publicado en *Revista de Trabajo*, 1971, nº 32).

—— (2013), *Anarquismo y utopía. Bakunin y la revolución social en España (1868–1936)*, Madrid, Cinca.

Elorza, Antonio y Bizcarrondo, Marta (1999), *Queridos camaradas. La Internacional comunista y España (1919–1939)*, Barcelona, Planeta.

Fontana, Josep (1987), *La II República. Una esperanza frustrada.* Actas del congreso Valencia Capital de la República (abril 1986), Valencia, Edicions Alfons El Magnànim.

García Oliver, Juan (2008), *El eco de los pasos*, Barcelona, Backlist (1ª edición: París, Ruedo Ibérico, 1978).

García, Fernando (2014), *España en la Gran Guerra. Espías, diplomáticos y traficantes*, Barcelona, Galaxia Gutenberg.

Gil, Carlos (2002), *La República en la plaza: los sucesos de Arnedo de 1932*, Logroño, Gobierno de la Rioja.

Gil Robles, José María (1978), *No fue posible la paz. Memorias*, Barcelona, Planeta.

Gil, Julio (1994), *Conservadores subversivos: la derecha autoritaria alfonsina (1913–1936)*, Madrid, Eudema.

—— (2006), *Segunda República Española (1931–1936)*, Madrid, Biblioteca Nueva.

Giráldez, Jesús (2009), *Creyeron que éramos rebaño. La insurrección del Alto llobregat y la deportación de anarquistas a Canarias y África durante la II República*, Málaga, editoriales: Zambra, Libreando y Balandre.

González Calleja, Eduardo (1999), *El máuser y el sufragio. Orden público, subversión y violencia política en la crisis de la Restauración (1917–1931)*, Madrid, CSIC.

—— (2011a), *Contrarrevolucionarios: radicalización violenta de las derechas durante la Segunda República, 1931–1936*, Madrid, Alianza Editorial.

—— (2011b), "La necro-lógica de la violencia política en la primavera de 1936", *Mélanges de la Casa Velázquez*, nº 41, 1.

—— (2014), *En nombre de la Autoridad. La defensa del orden público durante la Segunda* República (1931–1936), Granada, Comares.

González Calleja, Eduardo, Cobo, Francisco, Martínez, Ana y Sánchez, Francisco (2015), *La Segunda República Española*, Barcelona, Pasado y Presente.

Hennessy, C.A.M. (2010), *La República Federal en España. Pi y Margall y el movimiento republicano Federal, 1868–1874*, Los libros de la Catarata, Madrid.

Herrerín, Ángel (2004), *La CNT durante el franquismo. Clandestinidad y exilio (1939–1975)*, Madrid, Siglo XXI.

—— (2007), *El dinero del exilio. Indalecio Prieto y las pugnas de poguerra (1939–1947)*, Madrid, Siglo XXI.

—— (2010), "De la lucha por la revolución a la defensa de los derechos. El 1º de Mayo en España a través de sus manifiestos", en Lucía Rivas (dir.), *El Primero de Mayo en España. 120 aniversario (1890–2010)*, Madrid, Fundación Primero de Mayo, pp. 69–94.

—— (2011a), *Anarquía, dinamita y revolución social. Violencia y represión en la España de entre siglos (1868–1909)*, Madrid, Los libros de la Catarata.

—— (2011b), "Mémoires libertaires de la Seconde République", Dossier: Manuel Azaña: Nation et mémoire en débat, *Arkheia revue d`Histoire* (France), pp. 115–126.

—— (2014), "República y Sindicalismo: Entre la democracia y la insurrección", Aguado, Ana y Sanfeliu, Luz (eds.), *Caminos de democracia. Ciudadanías y culturas democráticas en el siglo XX*, Granada, Comares, pp. 169–185.

—— (2015), "El insurreccionalismo anarquista durante la II República", *Bulletin d`Histoire Contemporaine de L`Espagne* (France) nº 51, pp. 101–118.

—— (2016a), "La CNT en el movimiento de octubre de 1934: entre el boicot y la participación", *Hispania*, vol. LXXVI, nº 252, enero-abril, pp. 217–244.

—— (2016b), "Los valores republicanos de la diplomacia francesa: entre el miedo a la revolución y los intereses patrios", *Alcores* nº 20, pp. 47–66.

—— (2017a), "El movimiento de enero de 1932: Insurrección cenetista o asalto anarquista al poder sindical", *Les Cahiers de Framespa* [En ligne], 25, URL: http://journals.openedition.org/framespa/4436; DOI: 10.4000/framespa.4436.

—— (2017b), "La CNT pendant la Guerre civile: pouvoir et révolution", Jean Pierre Amalric, Geneviève Dreyfus-Armand et Bruno Vargas (eds.), *Huit ans de*

République en Espagne: entre réforme, guerre et révolution, 1931–1939, Toulouse, Méridiennes/Presses Universitaires du Midi, pp. 245–260.

—— (2017c), "La CNT pendant les deux premières années de la Republique: du syndicalisme à l'insurrection", Jean Pierre Amalric, Geneviève Dreyfus-Armand et Bruno Vargas (eds.), *Huit ans de République en Espagne: entre réforme, guerre et révolution*, Toulouse, Méridiennes/Presses Universitaires du Midi, pp. 151–174.

Herrerín, Ángel y Sueiro, Susana (2017), "¿Quantité négligeable o rival terrible?: la imagen francesa de la España primorriverista», *Pasado y Memoria. Revista de Historia Contemporánea*, nº 16, pp. 17–45.

Herrerín, Eduardo (2015), "Las elecciones de febrero de 1936 en Segovia. El Frente Popular", *Estudios Segovianos*, tomo LVII, nº 114, pp. 425–454.

Juárez, Eduardo (2015), *Crónicas de un real sitio. Lucha política, guerra y represión (1934–1939)*, Madrid, HG Editores.

Juliá, Santos (1984), *Madrid, 1931–1934. De la fiesta popular a la lucha de clases*, Madrid, Siglo XXI.

—— (1997), *Los socialistas en la política española, 1879–1982*, Madrid, Taurus.

—— (2008), *Vida y tiempo de Manuel Azaña (1880–1940)*, Madrid, Taurus.

Ledesma, José Luis (2013), "La 'primavera trágica' de 1936 y la pendiente hacia la guerra civil", en Francisco Sánchez Pérez (Coord.), *Los mitos del 18 de julio*, Barcelona, Crítica pp. 313–339.

Lida, Clara (1972), *Anarquismo y revolución en la España del siglo XIX*, Madrid, Siglo XXI.

Lorenzo, Anselmo (1974), *El proletariado militante. Memorias de un internacional*, Madrid, Zero.

Macarro, José Manuel (2011), "Los socialistas en la Segunda República", en Ávarez Junco, José y Cabrera, Mercedes (eds.), *La mirada del historiador. Un viaje por la obra de Santos Juliá*, Madrid, Taurus.

Maitron, Jean (1975), *Le mouvement anarchiste en France, Vol. I : Des origines à 1914*, Gallimard editions, París.

Malefakis, Edward (1987), "El problema agrario y la República", en VVAA., *La II República. Una esperanza frustrada.* Actas del congreso Valencia Capital de la República (abril 1986), Valencia, Edicions Alfons El Magnànim, pp. 37–48.

—— (2001), *Reforma agraria y revolución campesina en la España del siglo XX*, Madrid, Espasa Calpe.

Martínez Lorenzo, César (1969), *Los anarquistas españoles y el poder*, París, Ruedo Ibérico.

—— (2006), *Le mouvement anarchiste en Espagne. Poyvoir et revolution sociale*, Toulouse, Les Éditions Libertaires.

Maura, Miguel (1995), *Así cayó Alfonso XIII*, Barcelona, Ariel, (primera edición de 1962).

Monjo, Anna (2003), *Militants. Democràcia i participación a la CNT als anys trenta*, Barcelona, Laertes.

Navarro, Francisco Javier (2002), *Ateneos y grupos ácratas. Vida y actividad cultural de las asociaciones anarquistas valencianas durante la Segunda República y la Guerra civil*, Valencia, Generalitat Valenciana.

—— (2013), "Diversidad y dualismos. La(s) cultura(s) política(s) del movimiento libertario español", en Bosch, Aurora, Carnero T. y Valero S. (eds), *Entre la reforma y la revolución. La construcción de la democracia desde la izquierda*, Granada, Comares.

Olmedo, Ángel (1997), *El anarquismo extremeño frente al poder. Estudio de un periódico libertario. El Amigo del Pueblo, 1930–1933*, Cáceres, Institución Cultural "El Brocense".

Paniagua, Javier (1982), *La sociedad libertaria*, Barcelona, Crítica.

—— (1992), *Libertarios y sindicalistas*, Madrid, Anaya.

—— (2001) (edición y estudio preliminar), *Orto (1932–1934), revista de documentación social*, 2 vols., Valencia, UNED.

—— (2008), *La larga marcha hacia la anarquía. Pensamiento y acción del movimiento libertario*, Madrid, Síntesis.

Paz, Abel (1996), *Durruti en la revolución española*, Madrid, Fundación Anselmo Lorenzo.

Peirats, José (1971), *La CNT en la revolución española*, tomo 1, Cary-Colombes, Ruedo Ibérico.

Pérez, Guadalupe (2002), "La colonia penitenciaria de Villa Cisneros. Deportaciones y fugas durante la Segunda República", *Historia y Comunicación social*, vol. 7, pp. 169–186.

Pestaña, Ángel (1970), Por qué se constituyó el Partido Sindicalista, Madrid, Zero ZYX.

—— (1973), *Lo que aprendí en la vida II*, Bilbao, Zero.

—— (1974), *Trayectoria Sindicalista*, Madrid, Tebas.

—— (1979), *Terrorismo en Barcelona. La autodestrucción del movimiento obrero por el terrorismo*, Barcelona, Planeta.

Preston, Paul (1978), *La destrucción de la democracia en España. Reacción, reforma y revolución en la Segunda República*, Madrid, Turner.

Quijada, Domingo (2015), "Los conflictos políticos sociales en Navalmoral durante la II República", *Revista de Estudios Extremeños*, tomo LXXI.

Ramos, Tano (2012), *Casas Viejas: crónica de una insidia (1933–1936)*, Barcelona, Tusquets.

Reyes, Esmeralda (2016), *Anarcosindicalismo en el norte de Extremadura durante la II República. Navalmoral-Plasencia- Peraleda de la Mata. Diciembre 1933*, Trabajo Fin de Máster, sin publicar.

Rivas, Lucía (dir.) (2010), *El Primero de Mayo en España. 120 aniversario (1890–2010)*, Madrid, Fundación Primero de Mayo.

Ruiz, David (2008), Octubre de 1934. Revolución en la República española, Madrid, Síntesis.

Sánchez, Francisco (Coord.) (2013a), *Los mitos del 18 de julio*, Barcelona, Crítica.

—— (2013b), "Las reformas de la primavera del 36 (en la Gaceta y en la calle)", en Sánchez, Francisco (Coord.), *Los mitos del 18 de julio*, Barcelona, Crítica, pp. 291–312.

Según, Manuel (2013), "El anticlericalismo de la cerilla y la gasolina: la quema de conventos de mayo de 1931 en Madrid", *Alcores*, nº 16, pp. 181–203.

Sender, Ramón J. (2004), *Casas Viejas*, Zaragoza, Larumbe.

—— (2005), *Siete domingos rojos*, Barcelona, Virus (primera edición a finales de 1932).

Souto, Sandra (2004), *Y ¿Madrid? ¿Qué hace Madrid?: movimiento revolucionario y acción colectiva (1933–1936)*, Madrid Siglo XXI.

Termes, Josep (2000), *Anarquismo y sindicalismo en España (1864–1881)*, Barcelona, Crítica, (primera publicación en 1965).

—— (2011), *Historia del anarquismo en España (1870–1980)*, Barcelona, RBA.

Townson, Nigel (2002), *La República que no pudo ser. La política de centro en España (1931–1936)*, Madrid, Taurus.

Tuñon de Lara, Manuel (1972), *El movimiento obrero en la Historia de España*, Taurus, Madrid.

Trullén, Ramiro (2015), "Castilblanco como sinécdoque. El discurso contrarrevolucionario de interpretación de la Segunda República", *Historia Social* nº 83, pp. 55–71.

Vega, Eulalia (1980), *El treintisme a Catalunya. Divergències ideològiques en la CNT (1930–1933)*, Barcelona, Curial.

—— (1987), *Anarquistas y sindicalistas durante la Segunda República. La CNT y los Sindicatos de Oposición en el País Valenciano, 1931–1936*, Valencia, Edicions Alfons el Magnànim.

Vilanova, Mercedes (1996), *Las mayorías invisibles*, Barcelona, Icaria.

Villa, Roberto (2011a), *La República en las urnas. El despertar de la democracia en España*, Madrid, Marcial Pons.

—— (2011b), "La CNT contra la república: La insurrección revolucionaria de diciembre de 1933", *Historia y Política* nº 5, enero–junio, pp. 177–205.

Viñas, Ángel (2012), *La conspiración del general Franco y otras revelaciones acerca de una guerra civil desfigurada*, Barcelona, Crítica, (edición ampliada a la de 2011).

—— (2013), "La connivencia fascista con la sublevación y otros éxitos de la trama", en Francisco Sánchez (Coord.), *Los mitos del 18 de julio*, Barcelona, Crítica, pp. 79–182.

VV.AA. (1974), *El movimiento libertario español. Pasado, presente y futuro*, Cuaderno de Ruedo Ibérico.

VV.AA. (1987), *La II República. Una esperanza frustrada*. Actas del congreso Valencia Capital de la República (abril 1986), Valencia, Edicions Alfons El Magnànim.

VV.AA. (1990), *Colección de Historia oral: El movimiento libertario en España*, Madrid, Fundación Salvador Seguí.

Index

About the Author

Ángel Herrerín is a doctor in History (Ph.D. in History) and is a Full Professor in the Department of Contemporary History of the Universidad Nacional de Educación a Distancia (UNED). He has been a Visiting Professor at the University of Minnesota (USA) in 2005 and 2010. He was the National Graduation Prize winner in 1996 and he obtained the Outstanding Doctorate Award in 2002. His academic research focuses on anarchism, francoism, the Spanish civil war and its exile, and political violence. His more than fifty publications include book chapters and papers in national and international journals. His monograph publications include *The CNT during the Franco Regime* (2004–2005), for which he was a finalist in the 2006 National History Prize; *The Money of Exile* (2007); and *Anarchy, Dynamite and Social Revolution* (2011). He has also coordinator for *The Birth of Terrorism in the West: Anarchy, Nihilism and Revolutionary Violence* (2008).

Printed and bound by CPI Group (UK) Ltd, Croydon, CR0 4YY

13/09/2026

14961101-0006